Dance in the
Hollywood Musical

Studies in
Photography and Cinematography, No. 4

Diane M. Kirkpatrick

Associate Professor, History of Art
University of Michigan

Other Titles in This Series

No. 1 Joris Ivens, Film-Maker: Facing Reality   Carlos Böker

*No. 2 Semiotics and Lighting: A Study of Six
Modern French Cameramen*   Sharon A. Russell

No. 3 The Film Narratives of Alain Resnais   Freddy Sweet

*No. 5 Comedian Comedy: A Tradition in Hollywood
Film*   Steve Seidman

No. 6 The Films of Jean Vigo   William G. Simon

Dance in the Hollywood Musical

by
Jerome Delamater

RESEARCH PRESS

A portion of Chapter 3 was originally published in slightly different form under the title "Busby Berkeley: An American Surrealist" in *Wide Angle,* Vol. I, No. 1 (Spring 1976; reprinted as Vol. I, No. 1, revised and expanded, 1979). Used by permission.

Lyrics from "I Only Have Eyes for You," words by Al Dubin and music by Harry Warren, ©1934 WARNER BROS. INC.
Copyright Renewed
All Rights Reserved
Used by Permission of WARNER BROS. MUSIC

Produced and distributed by
UMI Research Press
an imprint of
University Microfilms International
Ann Arbor, Michigan 48106

Library of Congress Cataloging in Publication Data

Delamater, Jerome.
   Dance in the Hollywood musical.

   (Studies in photography and cinematography ; no. 4)
   A revision of the author's thesis—Northwestern University, 1978.
   Bibliography: p.
   Includes index.
   1. Dancing in moving-pictures, television, etc.—History.
I. Title. II. Series.

GV1779.D44 1981   793.3'2   81-7513
ISBN 0-8357-1198-6   AACR2

To the memory of
Paddy Whannel

Contents

Acknowledgments

Many people contributed in a variety of ways during my research and writing, but I am especially indebted to Douglas Lemza of Films, Inc., for making available to me the majority of the films necessary for this study. Kerry Hubata, Juanita Lopez, and Phyllis Wills of the Evanston School of Ballet provided information, critical insight, and psychological support over an extended period. Stuart Kaminsky, Jack C. Ellis, and Paddy Whannel, all of Northwestern University, contributed immeasurably by their criticism and advice. Joseph F. Hill read the original manuscript at several stages and made valuable suggestions due to his admirable sense of language. Finally, Janet Miller, who typed several rough drafts and the final copy, was a model of patience and skill. Without them I could not have completed this project.

1

Introduction

From its invention the motion picture has incorporated all the other arts. Thomas Edison had originally envisioned "such a happy combination of photography and electricity as will enable a man to sit in his own parlour and behold depicted upon a curtain before him the forms of the players in an opera upon a distant stage, and to hear the voices of the singers."[1] Although Edison's ambition was not achieved until many years later (and then, of course, by others), nonetheless the attitude implicit in his comment that film should serve as a medium to record existing arts has been present throughout the relatively short history of film. The various *film d'art* movements—most recently manifested in the American Film Theatre series—serve as examples of this desire to use film primarily as a recording device. Implicit also in Edison's comment, however, is the idea that film can include other arts since, indeed, any prescriptive notion about film always suggests a descriptive one: that film must serve to record other arts says that film is at least able to include them within its own system. And that ability to incorporate other arts has certainly been utilized. On their way to establishing film as a relatively independent means of expression, film makers experimented—often unwittingly—with already existing arts. Initially the tendency was to present one performing art, existing pro-filmically, intact on the screen. Even Georges Méliès's films operated primarily that way. Such a presentation is, of course, one method of incorporating other media into a new medium, but as film developed its own syntax, a process of integration rather than recording emerged. To incorporate theatrical spectacle, narrative fiction (in all its forms), painting and design, dance, and ultimately music into motion pictures came to mean integrating them into the system, making each as viable a filmic code as those codes which had emerged as a result of the technological and stylistic development of the medium—photography and editing primarily.

Dance is one example of another art form becoming an essential cinematic code. Indeed, dance and film have often been considered kindred art forms. Most theories of film and dance emphasize, above all, the idea of movement. Of dance, for example, Lincoln Kirstein has written, "Choreography is a map of movement—patterns for action that ballet masters ordain by design. Its composition depends on human bodies schooled in a grammar of movement whose end is legible virtuosity."[2] Doris Humphrey comments that "movement is its essence, its keynote and its language."[3] In some respects this seems almost too obvious to belabor, yet it is movement which provides dance with its potential aesthetic appeal. Movement becomes artistic expression and communication through the organization of bodies in space for certain periods of time. "Dance never exists in its totality at any one time but, rather, develops during a segment of measurable time."[4] The changing patterns of movement, the bodies interacting with each other and with the space around them, assume visual significance depending on their organization. The movement can be representational or highly abstract; it can be expressive and it can be symbolic.

Considering its kinetic, spatial, and temporal elements, one can describe film in very similar terms. Herbert Read's definition of film as "picture and motion" and his comment that "film is the art of space-time: it is a space-time continuum"[5] seem applicable as well to dance. Film can reproduce, distort, and create movement, and it is movement which distinguishes film from painting or sculpture. Various prescriptive theorists of film have considered movement the *sine qua non* of the art. Slavko Vorkapich, for instance, has emphasized the necessity of motion in film and its relation to kinesthetic responses in the viewer,[6] and Rudolf Arnheim declared that "motion being one of its outstanding properties, the film is required by aesthetic law to use and interpret motion."[7] Film movement is different from that of dance, however. Dance movement in general is only that of the dancer, whereas there are three separate kinds of movement in film: the movement of the subject (e.g., a dancer); the movement of the camera (e.g., following a dancer); and the movement of the editing (e.g., a change in space allowing a dancer to "move" from one location to another).[8]

Dance and film, as visual media, need the viewer's constant attention and reflection. Dance is an ephemeral art; each performance is unique and cannot be recaptured. Film, on the other hand, is by its very nature preserved. Unlike print, however, which can be pondered at the audience's leisure, both film and dance continue, and what has gone before must be remembered and related without chance of review. As a result, both dance and film are equally linear and non-linear. The integration of individual movements into a whole is provided by the visual memory. The principle of *synecdoche* may work in dance and film more, perhaps, than in other art forms, for complicated visual patterns can be appreciated only when viewed as an entity. The ballet term *enchaînement* (a series of different steps danced in succession) indicates the linearity of dance. The choreographer's patterns are often contrapuntally designed, several arrangements occurring simultaneously, but, at the same time, dance movement is arranged so that certain movements follow other movements and are, in turn, followed by further movements. Since this movement cannot be recaptured once it has been accomplished, dance is thus largely a medium of temporal linearity. It is also a medium of spatial linearity dependent again on the viewer's visual memory, for as the viewer sees the movements of a particular instant, he also relates it to the preceding movement and its location and connects the two in space, creating for himself a non-linear entity. "To say that a dancer is moving in a circle means that we, as audience, are imaginatively apprehending the movement as a . . . circle, which does not in fact exist."[9] By use of his visual memory the viewer thereby supersedes the linearity of the form and sees the work as a whole. The linearity of dance, in this respect, is like the linearity of film, and George Balanchine has noted that it is not unrelated to the concept of persistence of vision.

> The dance proves that movement is important in itself, for though the other visual arts, such as painting and architecture, are stationary, dance is continually in motion and any single position of a ballet is before the audience's eye for only a fleeting moment. Perhaps the eye does not see motion, but only these stationary positions, like single frames in a cinema film, but memory combines each new image with the preceeding [*sic*] image, and the ballet is created by the relation of the positions, or movements, to those which precede and follow it.[10]

It is only because the eye "remembers" that film is able to move; it is only because the visual memory creates relationships that patterns of movement, both in film and in dance, exist as more than still shots of a particular moment.

The differences between dance and film in the use of movement in time and through space are essential to any understanding of filmed dance. Unlike the live performance of dance, which uses *real* time and *real* space, film controls and manipulates its time and space. The pro-filmic event may have occurred in real time and real space, but the finished film itself ". . . consists of a succession of fragments excerpted from a spatial and temporal continuum. It is what results when the spatial fragments, or, more accurately, the succession of spatial fragments excerpted in the shooting process, converge with the temporal fragments whose duration may be roughly determined during the shooting, but whose final duration is established only on the editing table."[11] In film, space and time are constantly changing; in dance, space and time are fixed. As a result of the reality of the live performance, dance is primarily kinesthetic,[12] although it is synesthetic for its audience. Film, however, is primarily synesthetic, for, even though the movement would actually have occurred as the film was being shot, movement of the subject is only one kind of film movement. Dance does not exist except as the kinesthesia of the performer (and can exist without the synesthesia of the audience); but film does not exist without the synesthesia of the viewer (discounting, of course, the mere physical fact of the celluloid going through the projector) and can exist without any kind of kinesthesia (albeit improbably) of the pro-filmic event.

Allegra Fuller Snyder has written extensively about the ability of film to make its viewers participate in its action, especially to share in the film space, thus synesthetically providing an almost-kinesthetic experience for the viewer.

> . . . one might say that the elements . . . are the same in both dance and film, while the instruments are different, i.e. the one is the human body, the other the camera and the film which flows through it and receives the image. It would seem, therefore, that the area of study rested chiefly in the relation of the human body, which moves and feels, to the camera. The fact is, however, that the camera is much more like the human body in its abilities, in terms of what it produces on film, than are the elements of time and space like each other when we see them through the eyes of either film or dance. The camera can be made to move and feel like the human body and can even help us to achieve a deeper sense of participation and kinesthetic understanding than the average person normally feels through his body.[13]

This participation is made possible primarily through film movement. The dolly shot or the tracking shot carries one into or through filmic space, often accompanying (or, in the case of point-of-view shots, in place of) the film's performers. Similarly, the change as a result of the editing from long shot to medium shot to close-up—or its reverse—seems to bring one closer into—or remove one from—contact with the objects in filmic space. As will be shown later in this study, many film makers and choreographers have asserted that since dance has only the movement of its subject, film may provide a heightened sense of participation in dance, for as the camera moves with the dancer or becomes part of the choreography, the viewer participates synesthetically in the movement and thus becomes a dancer himself.

To a certain extent dance and film also share seeming inherent limitations or restrictions. Selma Jeanne Cohen's "A Prolegomenon to an Aesthetics of Dance" discusses the kinds of communication dance most easily expresses:

> The medium of dance is human movement. It deals with people, not with facts or ideas. And it deals with people in motion—not exhausted. We can think very well while sitting still. We can express the distance of the moon from the earth by gesturing with our fingers, but the matter is better explained in words. We might act out a marriage ceremony to identify the mother-in-law, but it is easier said than done. And what would the poor dancers do with Kant? Neither factual relations nor ideas are promising choreographic material. The area of dance is not that of concepts, which are grasped by the mind by way of words, but of percepts, which are grasped by the eye by way of movement.[14]

Victor Perkins has similar ideas about the expressive possibilities of film:

> Too great a concentration on what a film "has to say" implies that the significance of a movie is reducible to the verbal concepts which its action suggests. But films are unlikely to

replace speech or writing as the medium for examining and conveying ideas. Moral, political, philosophical and other concepts can attain in words an (at least apparent) clarity and precision which no other medium can rival. The movie's claim to significance lies in its embodiment of tensions, complexities and ambiguities. It has a built-in tendency to favour the communication of vision and experience. . . .[15]

At the same time Perkins's statement does illustrate that there are obvious differences: post-1927 film does, after all, use speech and can verbalize concepts. Film, as Perkins emphasizes, is, however, *more* than verbalized concepts. It is those additional elements which bring it into a closer affinity with dance and make the possibilities of dance and film combined an exciting field.

Dance as movement in time and through space can, in one sense, be construed to include all human movement. Certainly this was true in the pre-history of dance; its development as an art grew out of utilitarian movement by way of religious and folk dance. Most theorists today, however, largely concerned with theatrical dancing, would insist on the necessary presence of expressiveness, communication through movement. Further on in her essay Ms. Cohen even more strictly defines the limits of dance: expression and communication are elements of all art; it is, therefore, the *stylization* of movement which makes that expression applicable to dance. "The designing of the movement of the human body is the unique property of dance as an art medium."[16] Her concern with theatrical dancing compels her to exclude parade and pantomime, for instance, as dance and implies the necessity of systems of movement: ballet, modern, and tap. Obviously, dance systems are both the most easily recognizable and most readily acceptable manifestations of movement in time and through space. With the more expansive spatial possibilities of film, though, all forms of spectacle—parade, marching, circus routines, for example—can become a means of expressive communication. Simultaneously, since film can also present more restricted space than the stage, minute movement can be similarly expressive. Movement less controlled than that of standard dance systems can become dance on the screen; for, as Shirley Clarke has said, "I understood that dance in film was not only a human being whirling in space in *pirouettes* and *tour jetés,* but also someone walking down the street or an eye looking up at you or hair waving in the breeze. All this was the material of dance, and—more importantly—the very essence of film."[17]

The problems inherent in filmed dance are, in a sense, a microcosm of the disagreements among film theorists. Film is a re-producing agent according to Siegfried Kracauer and André Bazin; film is primarily a manipulating medium according to Rudolf Arnheim, Bela Balazs, Sergei Eisenstein, and others. And, as Victor Perkins suggests, film is synthesis, embodying an almost infinite range of artistic possibilities. In the filming of dance, likewise, there are those who would insist that the integrity of the dance must be honored. Fred Astaire, for one, had such an approach in his films; Allegra Snyder even considers him "among the greatest documentary dance film makers."[18] There are also those who would insist on fragmenting the dance, selecting parts—rather than the choreographic entity—for the camera. Agnes de Mille tells, for example, of her work for George Cukor's *Romeo and Juliet:* "They shot the dance, which I had planned as a fugal arrangement of five groups of girls pivoting around the soloist . . . as a series of closeups . . . . "[19] Finally, then, there are those who insist on synthesis, the collaboration in "choreo-cinema," of the dance and the film. Gardner Compton, a dance film maker, has written, "A pas de deux on stage is a dance for two people (usually a boy and a girl), whereas a pas de deux on film is a dance for a boy, a girl, *and* camera. If cinematographic movement techniques are used successfully with dance a successful marriage can result. One must wed the movement of one art to the movement of the other in order to achieve a true choreographic end."[20]

John Martin, former dance reviewer for the *New York Times,* has elaborated on some of the problems of filmed dance as he saw them: as a recording medium film can be used to emphasize dance, but film is also its own artistic medium and dance in film must, of necessity, be subordinate to film.

> There has been a good deal of sprightly talk over the past few years about the affinity that exists between the dance and the movies and the many ways in which they can be made to supplement each other, yet except for the production of a considerable footage of dance sequences by both professional and amateur photographers, virtually nothing has been done to justify all the conversation. The reason may lie somewhat deeper than mere Hollywood indifference, which usually gets the blame; it may indeed be that the natural affinity of the two mediums [*sic*] has been exaggerated. Quite possibly insufficient distinction has been made between the motion picture camera as an instrument and the cinema as an art. The camera per se can render incalculable service to music. The cinema art, however, is, even more than the theater, an art of synthesis, and all the individual arts which contribute to it must necessarily sacrifice their own highest potentialities in the interest of the common good. This way we may expect the ultimate emergence of a great cinema art, which is eminently to be desired, but the development of the dance in its own right from this collaboration will obviously be negligible.[21]

Mr. Compton has also written extensively, and in greater detail, about filming dance. One of the major problems, as he sees it, is the lack of understanding between the choreographer and the film makers. "A choreographer sees work in his own way. A cameraman sees this same work in another way. Many times the choreographer is not aware of the creative potentials, capabilities, and sensitiveness of the camera. Similarly, the cameraman may have only a rudimentary knowledge of dance. The editor may have still another concept of the whole."[22]

Problems involving movement and space in dance film also concern Mr. Compton and are worth extensive quotation leading into more concrete examples of dance films, for he applies the theories in a practical way.

Movement is one of the main common denominators of both film and dance. Yet this common denominator is often neglected, or even ignored. The simple technique of following the dancers and keeping them within the camera frame frequently destroys the movement. Empty space is as important to film frame as silence is to music. Silence is as much a part of music as sound. In choreo-cinema, the dance subject is no more important than space, for unless both are included, one or the other can become meaningless. If a dancer moves across a film frame and the camera constantly follows him, the eye has not really witnessed an event, for there is no beginning or end to it. However, if the dancer flashes onto the left of the screen and exits the other side or stops within the frame, something happens. Time has gone by; space has been consumed.

. . . A cameraman should film a dancer so that the last object to leave the frame is that portion of the body that moves the energy from space to space. The camera itself should also move the energy from one space to another, or it is not contributing. Timing and framing are the essential tools of a dance cameraman. One must frame on space and let the dancer move into it. Space is the dancer's canvas, whether on stage or on film. Both space and movement, too, may have to be modified or distorted to make the choreo-cinema effective to an audience.

The camera is the eye of the audience, the establisher of the involvement, the point of view, the movement. Why should the joy of movement be limited to the dancers? The members of the audience, too, can enjoy it, but only if the camera works for them.[23]

Although Mr. Compton's statements in general may be too dogmatic, he does recognize the synesthetic possibilities of the film medium, that through film the dance audience's synesthetic responses can be heightened.

Practical application of theory is seldom attempted. Dance and film, in some respects, however, have received their most active combined work among experimental film makers who were also theorists and writers. Maya Deren and Shirley Clarke, particularly, both dancers and film makers, have also written about their experiences and ideas regarding the filming of dance. Shirley Clarke, as with many other dancers turned film makers, first confronted the problem of filming pre-staged dances. Her *Dance in the Sun* and *Bullfight,* both based on stage performances, moved, as a result of the filming, far beyond the world of documented dance. Ms. Clarke comments on the problems as she encountered them with *Dance in the Sun*:

I'd seen it on stage many times and thought it'd be great for a film, because it reminded me of the sun and sea. So I trotted Danny [dancer Daniel Nagrin] out to Jones Beach and filmed him dancing. I brought back the film to the city and developed and looked at it and I was absolutely horrified. It didn't work, you couldn't put this human body dancing abstractly on the beach against the glories of nature, the sun and the sky and the beach. Nature diminished the beauty of the dance. What occurred to me then was to recreate what had happened to me: I had seen the dance originally in a theatre, and it was there that I had gotten a feeling of a place and a time, so the thing to do was to go back to the theatre and do for the audience what had happened to me. So I shot the identical dance on stage and on the beach and then I intercut the two. What happened was, you kept being swung back and forth between the stage and the beach and the movements seemed enormous, in time and space.[24]

It was with *Bullfight,* her third film, that Shirley Clarke felt that she could not make completely successful dance films based on stage performances, that the dances would have to be choreographed instead specifically for the camera. *A Moment in Love* was the logical progression of her experiments, for here she and choreographer Anna Sokolow created a dance that could exist only on film. Signs leading toward this are evident in both of her earlier films, but they did have their genesis on the stage. In *A Moment in Love,* however, as in Maya Deren's *A Study in Choreography for Camera,* the dancers are able to participate in the space denied them on the stage. In the former, the dancers, Carmela Gutierez and Paul Sanasardo, leap over clouds, for example, and in the latter Talley Beatty steps from inside the Metropolitan Museum of Art in New York and almost literally sails through space amid clouds and trees to the top of a hill.

Other experimental dance films also illustrate explorations of time and space which the two media combined present. Hilary Harris's *Nine Variations on a Dance Theme* shows dancer Bettie de Jong performing the same dance nine times with the camera providing the variations as each time it selects a different aspect of her body or the dance. Gardner Compton's *Seafall* superimposes scenes of realism and fantasy and contrasts a stylized dance against the rather austere brutality of a New England coastal setting. Shown in negative, Maya Deren's *The Very Eye of Night* eliminates the floor, the horizon, and all aspects of ground to give the impression of dancers performing in space. "In choreo-cinema it is possible to do away with every limitation of the choreographic art on stage, except rhythm and pattern. Gravity, time, and space can be shaped at the will of the film maker."[25]

Perhaps because the experimental film makers were often also both writers and theorists and because they were often reacting hostilely to feature film production, the theoretical considerations have usually been ignored as they apply to feature films. Feature films—and particularly the musical— have also explored the shaping of gravity, time, and space, however. Indeed, dance in all its forms and the theoretical considerations of both film and dance are present in the Hollywood feature musical. Fred Astaire's walking on air in Charles Walters's *Belle of New York* and dancing on the walls and ceiling in Stanley Donen's *Royal Wedding* are as evident of a cinematic ability to shape—indeed, defy—gravity as is any avant-garde film. Likewise, the jump cut, which provides Talley Beatty with the ability to dance from one location to another, also provides Gene Kelly, Frank Sinatra, and Jules Munshin with the ability to see New York rapidly in the early montage sequences of *On the Town.* Similarly, the feature musical is representative, to a certain extent, of the problem of documenting dance versus the creation of "cine-dance," for one of the major concerns of Hollywood choreographers has been that of retaining the integrity of the dance numbers as a unit while at the same time using the medium for which they were creating the number. Furthermore, in seeming fulfillment of the conclusions of most theorists of filmed dance that "a dance must be planned for the camera," that "it is useless to try to film choreography intended for the stage,"[26] the history of the Hollywood musical displays a movement toward integration among the choreography, the photography, and the editing.

The dance forms actually used in the choreography, the ways in which the film makers approached choreographing the dances for the screen and in turn of filming those dances, and the attempts by the film makers to relate the dances to the totality of the films are all part of the process of integration within the musical; and all will be considered as the basis for understanding the integration of dance into film. At certain points in the history of the genre, the film makers consciously worked toward integration, for they believed it to be an outgrowth of previous trends which they were fulfilling; furthermore, they believed the integrated musical to be a goal, superior to other forms of musicals. Without judging the integrated musical as superior, one, nonetheless, can recognize it as the logical culmination of certain traditions and as the historical end toward which the genre had been moving. It is then as a critical and historical analysis of that move toward integration of all elements that this study of dance within the Hollywood musical has been arranged.

2

Dance in Film Before 1930

Dance has been part of film since the very earliest days; indeed, the first commercially projected screening in the United States, at Koster and Bial's Music Hall, New York City, on April 23, 1896, included two dance sequences. Two girls did a parasol dance in which their dresses were hand tinted pink and blue, and Annabelle the Dancer performed one of her dances in the concluding film of the group. Thomas Armat is cited as remembering "how the audience went wild and cheered when the dancer Annabelle appeared life-size on the screen."[1] Dance sequences had been filmed even earlier, however, and were, in fact, among the most common filmed events in the early years of the Kinetoscope.

Movement was, of course, the major interest in the early years of film making and, as Lewis Jacobs has put it, "nothing was too trivial to photograph: people walking, trees swaying, trains speeding, horses jumping, were esteemed as good subjects."[2] Film makers, seeking subjects with whom movement was a specialty, would almost naturally look among those performing on the various New York stages for dancers who would be willing to appear and do their acts in front of the cameras. Edward Wagenknecht has suggested that "the popularity of dancers and prize fighters in early times was not planned, nor necessarily an evidence of public taste, but primarily determined by the fact that prize fights and solo dances were action subjects which could easily be accommodated to the space which the bulky immovable camera of those days could comfortably take in."[3]

Among those whose dance-hall fame led them to be invited to perform for the camera were three whose names have become almost synonymous with early dance films: Annabelle, Carmencita, and Fatima. Annabelle, particularly, achieved ever-widening fame as a result of her film appearances and, indeed, many have had a certain limited influence on films themselves. Terry Ramsaye has written at some length about her:

Annabelle Moore, another beauty of considerable music hall fame under the name of Annabelle-the-Dancer performed a little fifty-foot version of her act on the Edison stage. Annabelle appeared in the serpentine dance, wafting and manipulating endless yards of silken draperies. On the variety theatre stage this was one of the most popular numbers. The dancer was illuminated with changing shafts of colored light thrown by tint slides in a stereopticon. The Edison pictures were led into the first screen endeavors at color in imitation of the stage effect. Many of the prints of the Annabelle picture were tinted with slide colors, by hand, a frame at a time. . . .[4]

Annabelle originally appeared before the cameras at Edison's West Orange, New Jersey, studio in 1894, and the films were used for the Kinetoscope peep show and subsequently for the early non-commercial experiments in projection. As a result, her fame as a dancer on Broadway spread throughout the country. Furthermore, she may, as Ramsaye suggests, have been the first film celebrity. A minor scandal in her personal life increased the demand for prints of her *Butterfly Dance* so that the price was raised to forty dollars a copy: "Annabelle had become the highest priced film feature in the world."[5]

A popular Spanish dancer, Carmencita also appeared before the Edison cameras in 1894. Fatima, whose *Coochee-Coochee Dance* is listed in several early film catalogues, is described as "the lady whose graceful interpretations of the poetry of motion has made this dance so popular of recent years."[6] Fatima is known to have danced for films perhaps as early as 1893, doing her *Dance du Ventre* or belly dance on the stage of the Black Maria. Dancing on what seems to be a boardwalk in front of a painted backdrop, she begins by doing eight turns, then goes into a series of movements of the upper part of her body, shaking her breasts and arms. The dance continues as she undulates the lower part of her body, particularly moving her pelvis backward and forward. All the while, she is playing the castanets and emphasizing the dangling objects which are an important part of her costume. The film ends as the dance is going on, possibly because the camera ran out of film at that moment. In some prints Fatima's dance has a fence-like superimposition blocking out her breasts and hips. Eileen Bowser suggests that the censored version, "surely intended satirically, perhaps appeared during one of the many cries for censorship that arose in the early days of the movies."[7] A popular vaudeville dancer, Eva Tanguay, performed *Her Sambo Dance,* and even Ruth St. Denis, then just Ruth Dennis, was filmed in a number entitled *Dance* at the Edison studios, probably also in 1894.

Although dance films during the silent era included ethnic, social, and theatrical dancing, certainly the most predominant in the very early period was theatrical. Nonetheless, there were a number of films which showed various kinds of folk dances as well as social dancing among different classes of people. Four Pueblo Indian dances, copyrighted on February 24, 1898, on paper prints in the Library of Congress, were shot on location and are entitled *Buck Dance, Circle Dance, Eagle Dance,* and *Wand Dance.* The Edison Company is also on record as having made films of dances done by other tribal groups performing for such organizations as Buffalo Bill's Wild West Show.

Numerous titles with references to dance appear consistently in lists of early films: *Dancing Darkey Boy, Cake Walk, Bally-Hoo Cake Walk, Comedy Cake Walk, Maypole Dance, Turkish Dance, Japanese Dance, Girls Dancing Can-Can, Ghost Dance, Highland Fling,* and *The Giddy Dancing Master* are just a few brought out by either Edison or Biograph during the first several years of film production. Other companies were involved as well. Lewis Jacobs writes about a "film-slide-lecture" show about New York, prepared in 1903 by the Kleine Optical Company, which included a film called *Dancing on the Bowery.*[8]

Dance continued to play a part in films even with the development of the narrative film. *The Great Train Robbery* has two dance sequences representative of the kind of social dance often used in fiction films. The western setting calls for the square dance and the Virginia reel, both of which are shown here. In the first cutaway from the train station, the film shows a group doing a square dance. We see four couples do a do-si-do of their partners and then go into a promenade. Before the film changes location again, we also see one man forced to do a kind of jig as the others shoot at his feet. Subsequently, the film returns to the social hall and we see the beginnings of a Virginia reel. Although the routines have little to do with the narrative line and, being shot with an immovable camera, have nothing to do with certain technical advances for which the film has some fame, they do seem to help to establish locale, to depict the types of people involved, and to provide scenes for the intercutting of parallel lines of action. Dance sequences in later and ostensibly more sophisticated films often did not have even that degree of integration with the rest of the film's material.

A number of dancers of considerable fame were filmed later in the silent era as well. In 1913 Ted Shawn appeared in *A Dance of the Ages,* which gives a survey of dance styles from Neanderthal man to current ballroom dances of the period, particularly the bunny hug and the turkey-trot, including ancient, medieval, and Spanish numbers. (Later he danced in Cecil B. DeMille's *Don't Change Your Husband,* starring Gloria Swanson.) Anna Pavlova first appeared in films in *The Dumb Girl of Portici,* 1916, an adaptation of a musical play. In 1924 she danced a selection of the solos for which she was most well known on the stage, including *The Dying Swan;* the film was called *Anna Pavlova's Solo Dances.* In 1914 and 1915 Vernon and Irene Castle danced in two films, *Mr. and Mrs. Vernon Castle Before the Camera* and *The Whirl of Life;* in the latter film they demonstrated the Castle walk, the maxixe, and the tango, all of which they had made popular as ballroom dances.

Many stars of the silent era either came from dance backgrounds or studied dancing to improve their ability to move with grace and ease. In 1915 Ted Shawn and Ruth St. Denis opened the Denishawn School in Los Angeles and among the stars who studied there were Lillian and Dorothy Gish, Mabel

Normand, Colleen Moore, and Myrna Loy. Among the stars who had begun their careers as dancers were Bessie Love, Gilda Gray, and Mae Murray who, starting as a chorus dancer, became featured with Ziegfeld, which led in turn to films. Although she appeared in many films which called for her to dance— *On with the Dance, Broadway Rose, The Gilded Lilly, Jazzmania*—perhaps Mae Murray's most famous dancing sequence on the screen was in Erich Von Stroheim's *The Merry Widow,* in which she and John Gilbert dance "The Merry Widow Waltz," a seductive courtship, complete with backbends; love-making rituals, always an important part of screen dancing in musicals, began even before the musical era itself. Rudolph Valentino also began his career as a dancer, originally performing in vaudeville and cabarets. Richard Griffith has said of Valentino that "the graceful gestures, the sense of poise and rhythm he had acquired as an exhibition dancer, gave to his movements on the screen a singularly impressive quality. . . ."[9] His dancing the tango with Beatrice Dominguez in *The Four Horsemen of the Apocalypse* and the minuet with Doris Kenyon in *Monsieur Beaucaire,* particularly, were part of his overall screen image. "Not only were they models of suave dancing technique, but they combined dancing with dramatic content in a way that has rarely been excelled since."[10] Gilda Gray did the shimmy in *The Devil Dancer;* Wallace Reid and Bebe Daniels do several dance routines in *Dancin' Fool,* where, interestingly enough, the dances become almost metaphorical: Reid's abilities as a dancer seem equated with his financial wizardry and expertise. D.W. Griffith often favored social dance sequences in his films as examples of the life and styles of the times he was depicting. There is a square dance sequence in *Way Down East,* for example, and in *Orphans of the Storm* he contrasts the uninhibited dancing of the revolutionaries in the streets with the reserved elegance and stateliness of the minuet at the French court.

Although strictly speaking Charlie Chaplin is not a dancer, certainly he made a contribution to dance in films. W.C. Fields allegedly remarked that Chaplin was the greatest ballet dancer who ever lived and even Martha Graham has said that "in a deep sense Chaplin is a dancer because he has always danced his roles. He also has a complete awareness of movement."[11]

> . . . Chaplin has contributed many notable and unforgettable dance sequences to his films over the years. One of his earliest . . . was his dream ballet in the three-reel *Sunnyside,* made in 1919. Here piping Pan-like on a daisy, he joined a flock of girls, dressed in diaphanous Greek tunics, in a pastoral dance. Bursts of Bacchanalian frenzy overtook him as he stepped into a cactus patch. His disdainful removal of the cactus from his feet while still trying to keep his place in the dance was, perhaps, the high spot of this number, which concluded in a bed of flowers with Chaplin surrounded by a bevy of handmaidens.[12]

His use of dance-pantomime is evident throughout his entire work as he generally uses movement to express his feelings at any particular moment. The joy and/or sadness evident in such numbers as the roller skating sequence in *Modern Times* or the dance with the rolls in *The Gold Rush* are indicative of later use of dance as well, for the expression of interior feeling is perhaps the prime motivation for dance in many films. Furthermore, Chaplin's walk, which seems based on the turn-out necessary in ballet, certainly looks like someone walking around in first position; curiously enough, a black dancer, Rufus Greenlee, who worked with Chaplin on his first American vaudeville engagement, said of him: "He wasn't doing that walk then, he saw some colored fellow later and copied him."[13]

A recurrent image of the 1920s is the dancer doing the Charleston. Perhaps the quintessential image of the "jazz age," the Charleston was both an exhibition, theatrical dance and a social dance, presented by performers for audiences to see and, in turn, performed on the regular dance floor by the average person. Marshall and Jean Stearns have suggested that "the Charleston . . . first destroyed the distinction in the United States between a dance to watch and a dance to perform—everybody seemed to be doing it around 1925."[14] Several films made in the late twenties have displays of the Charleston, the most famous, perhaps, being Joan Crawford in *Our Dancing Daughters*. Shot as a silent film, it had an added synchronized score when it was finally released in 1928 after *The Jazz Singer*'s success.

Although dance has been part of film since the 1890s and, furthermore, a part of several different kinds of films, it was not until the advent of sound that dancing could become a really vital part of films, for just as singing could not be an aspect of the silent film, neither could dancing that was truly accompanied by music; the orchestras and pianos which did accompany silent films were generally able to play anything they wished, and although they may have been quite clever and capable at matching sound and movement, any true affinity between what may be called choreography and music needed the sound which was actually part of the choreographic process during the filming of the dances themselves. Moreover, since the late 1920s dance has been most evident in musical films, for the musical is a genre that was a direct result of the coming of sound.

The 1920s was a period of considerable change in dance. Among other things there was a sign of elimination of distinction between certain kinds of theatrical dancing and social dance as was already mentioned regarding the Charleston. Styles of dance moved in the other direction as well: social dances were adopted by performers and elaborated into show-piece presentations. Similarly there was a gradual blurring of the distinctions between the various forms of theatrical dancing on the stage (a blurring that would become more and more evident during the entire period of the musical film); ballet, relatively new to American popular audiences, was being adopted into musical comedy just as European clog dancing had been integrated into black and jazz movements like the shuffle to form tap dancing. The strong influence of black dance, though certainly felt in vaudeville and through white imitators of black styles, received a particular boost with the presentation on Broadway of the all-black musical *Shuffle Along* in 1921. "Negro musicals were in demand thereafter, and dancing in musical comedy finally took wing."[15] As a result of the several black shows appearing in New York in the twenties, " 'steps became more intricate, daring, perilous.' Dancing became more rhythmic, and jazz drummers were getting ideas from tap dancers."[16] Also present on the stage were the revues, best known for their spectacular displays of chorus girls going through fundamental dance movements in elaborate arrangements using extraordinary technical stage facilities. Musical comedies had developed to a sophisticated point where dance was being used as an integral part of the entire show. The quality of dancing was improving, too, as more and more Broadway dancers were getting serious dance training. Nevertheless, all of these were in states of transition and experimentation when the advent of sound in films made these theatrical sources contributors to the film musical.

There is a general distinction in the film musical between those films that emphasize singing, often thereby totally excluding dance, and those that emphasize dancing. (Of the three major theatrical sources contributing to the film musical—the operetta, the musical comedy, and the musical revue—the one that contributed the least to dance in the musical film was the operetta, for dance was never an important part of the form on the stage. With its emphasis on singing of an almost operatic nature, the operetta has never fared as well nor as enduringly as the musical comedy itself in film.) "Dancers' musicals are more likely, like the majority of the Astaire-Rogers vehicles, to be light, fast and modern in their setting; singers' musicals are more likely, like the majority of the MacDonald-Eddy vehicles, to look back nostalgically to glamorous and romantic periods and to the more expansive world of the operetta as opposed to the slick and jazzy musical comedy."[17] Nonetheless, there are certain unifying characteristics that inform the genre. Musicals seem to dwell in a world of the fantastic, for one assumes that people dance and sing their way through life as a basis of the form. Indeed, as John Russell Taylor says, it is a "momentary lift into another world of fantasy [which] characterizes the true musical."[18] A thematic and narrative consistency is that of a boy-girl relationship. Such love stories play at least an adjunct role in most musicals; in many—and perhaps most—instances they provide the major plot situations, and in all but a very few films the situations are resolved satisfactorily, as well. Related to both of these characteristics is a stylized quality in which relationships are acted out through song and dance. In a sense the musical numbers become rituals: "celebrations of friendship, marriage, work, take the form of dance or song rather than a literal enactment of the event."[19]

In one sense, though, these characteristics imply a Platonic ideal for the genre. This ideal suggests, in turn, that the songs and dances be integrated with and advance the action of the plot; that the non-musical scenes be directed in a manner consistent with the musical scenes; that the rhythms govern and shape the film as a whole. This ideal, furthermore, would become a conscious goal for later film makers who believed that they were developing a new form of the genre (though one growing out of certain traditions on the stage and the screen): the integrated musical. Certainly one of the bases for this study is that this move toward integration is part of the evolution of dance as a cinematic code, yet such an ideal can be too restrictive for many of the early films, for integration was not one of the conventions of the early musical. Many of the more popular films—especially those of the "backstage" variety—used a different set of conventions, and integration was in many respects alien to the accepted norms of those films. Considering the early musicals, therefore, it may be more helpful to work from the simpler definition that a musical is a film in which songs and, for these purposes, dances play an important part.

It has become a cliché of film history that musicals inundated the screen after 1927 but that the public grew tired of them shortly and by 1930 they were box-office poison. Like most clichés this one has some basis in fact, though, also like most clichés, it is too simplistic. The exigencies of production being what they are, 1929 was the first year in which many real musicals were released, and *The Blue Book of Hollywood Musicals* lists fifty-two musicals in release that year. In 1930 there were sixty-seven, but in 1931 there were only seventeen. Obviously some effect had been caused by the overabundance of musicals in the first years of sound. The question should be raised, therefore, as to what kinds of musicals were being produced, why did they become tiresome to the public, and to what extent was dance in those films a contributing factor.

Hollywood film makers, not accustomed to the novelty of sound, called upon the services of New York stage people to move to California and share their expertise. Naturally the established and recognized Broadway creators were the first to be invited to the West Coast, and dancers were no exception. As with most other films of the period, the early musicals adhered to the successes of the Broadway stage. The most well-established form of the time was the revue; hence the Ziegfeld production number would carry over into film. Similarly, the dance of the black performers of the period, influential on white performers but restricted in actual performing situations to a few all-black shows, would carry over to all-black films such as *Hearts in Dixie* and *Hallelujah* or to isolated sequences in white films (Stepin Fetchit's dance in *Fox Movietone Follies of 1929* is an example). Likewise, the problem of having a camera encased in a sound-proof box restricted the possibilities of the equipment to participate in the dance. As a result, most early dance sequences were filmed as if from front row center, and the dances performed literally on stages. Choreographers, trained to create for the proscenium arch stage, seldom tried expanding beyond that limitation. Even with the discovery, allegedly during the filming of *Broadway Melody,* of the method of recording and then filming during playback, few dance directors moved beyond the limitations they brought with them from the theater. Nevertheless, there were many hesitant attempts to use this new medium to its advantage.

Several reactions to the advent of sound occurred on the part of the various studios in relationship to musicals. First, with the problems of recording sound the use of music became important. Songs were easy to record; New York performers could just stand and sing as they did on the stage. As a result, early films stressed songs and imported singers like Al Jolson and operettas like *The Desert Song.* "The obvious convenience of music as a means of conveying sound led to the selection of stories in which songs could be used dramatically. The Warners had run to night-club stories. Thalberg was one of the first to sense the possibilities of a musical comedy film."[20] Studios bought out song-writing firms in order to ensure a steady supply of songs; Warners, for example, purchased three publishing houses, Harms, Witmark, and Remick, thus securing a ten million dollar backlog of music. Broadway stars were brought to Hollywood for their singing and dancing abilities often in the very vehicles in which they had made their names or, at least, were appearing at that time. Marilyn Miller was one of the most important performers to exemplify this; she appeared, reputedly for one thousand dollars an hour, in both *Sally,* 1929, and *Sunny,* 1930, both musicals shot as stage shows with cast, props, and sets almost literally intact from Broadway. Broadway dance directors were also among the many imported for their talents: Albertina Rasch, Sammy Lee, Seymour Felix, and Larry Ceballos arrived in Hollywood early in the sound era and stayed to play a major role if not in creating dance, per se, then at least in creating production numbers. Similarly, several important New York-based song writing figures were also induced to go west; DeSylva, Brown, and Henderson; Irving Berlin; Jerome Kern; Sigmund Romberg; George Gershwin; and Rodgers and Hart all went to California between 1929 and 1931. Their contributions would vary; some would stay and play an active part in the creation of the Hollywood musical whereas others would give only minimal time to films and return to make their contribution in New York. They were years of change, but years in which the influence of New York would be strongly felt in the making of films in general and in the creation of dance for films in particular.

Richard Griffith has described those early years of musicals:

The first musicals featured Broadway and vaudeville singers, dancers, and comedians who simply repeated their stage routines for a fixed camera. Soon, established Hollywood favorites sought to prove that they had passed the talkie test by indulging in songs and dances for which most of them had neither training nor aptitude. Whether they featured newcomers or familiar faces, the early musicals rigidly followed the conventions of their stage ancestors. The public tired of these tin-pot substitutes for the musical theater so abruptly that several reached the screen with their musical numbers excised at the last moment.[21]

Paul Rotha has said that early musicals "suffer from their lack of camera movement and other filmic properties, being successful because of their musical numbers and chorus work."[22] These early musicals were of several types, but perhaps the most pervasive was the revue, a carry-over from the revue on the stage which was itself a higher class version of the vaudeville show that incorporated many different kinds of acts into a variety show. Films like *Show of Shows, Fox Movietone Follies, King of Jazz,* and *Paramount on Parade* reflected the revue's vaudeville and burlesque backgrounds as well as the more sophisticated and respectable influence of the Ziegfeld *Follies,* George White's *Scandals,* and similar revues. These films were spectacular exhibition pieces for each studio's major stars and served as means of experimentation for various technical innovations. Color, particularly, was part of these films as each usually had at least one two-color technicolor sequence; Warner's feature *On with the Show* was billed as the first all-color talkie when it was released in 1929.

One example of the revue films of the period was MGM's *Hollywood Revue of 1929* which featured most of that studio's major contract players. Photographed as if it were being presented on a stage, each number began and ended with a curtain. Similarly, a master of ceremonies, Jack Benny, introduced each routine and connected them with his stand-up comic's banter. Although there was an occasional attempt to use high-angle shots of dancing ensembles or trick photography to make Bessie Love and Marion Davies into midgets, nonetheless most of the numbers were shot in one take from one theatrically-seated camera position. The film's rewards, therefore, depended upon the contributions of its performers: Buster Keaton's "underwater" dance is probably a result of his being accustomed to working in a similar cinematic style and, therefore, using his physicality for comic effect.

The dance directors on the film were Sammy Lee and Albertina Rasch. Both were among those who went to Hollywood in the late twenties from New York; yet they represent completely different backgrounds, and their work in this film displays some of the disparateness of the revue films in general. Sammy Lee, a typical Broadway dance director, had worked for the Ziegfeld *Follies* and Earl Carroll's *Vanities* and had even been the dance director on the musical comedy *Lady, Be Good!* which had starred Fred and Adele Astaire. Albertina Rasch, on the other hand, had been a ballerina trained in Vienna and gave an air of "quality" to the films she worked on, choreographing the ballet and "serious" dance numbers in the films just as she had during her years in vaudeville: a group of dancers, trained by her as a *corps de ballet*, provided a "concession to mass notions of education and uplift," the high art contrast to the low art of the rest of the performance.[23] This notion carried over to *Hollywood Revue*, for the film was basically a vaudeville show.

One of the purposes of the film was to get all the MGM stars to perform in ways they had never performed before. As Bessie Love tells it:

> In *Hollywood Revue*, we all just did sketches and bits. They wanted everybody at MGM to do something they had never done before. They asked me if I had ever done an acrobatic dance. I told them I hadn't; so they said, "OK you're doing an acrobatic dance!" And it was fun! Charles Reisner directed it all, to the best of my knowledge, and Sammy Lee staged the musical numbers, as he had for *Broadway Melody.*[24]

The dance numbers themselves were generally derived from revues on the New York stage. The two ballet numbers by the Albertina Rasch Ballet Company showed very little in the way of innovation. In the first there is an overhead shot while the dancers perform in flower patterns suggestive of later Berkeley routines. In the second they are part of the elaborate finale which leads into the singing of "Singin' in the Rain" by the entire company:

> The large finale, in two-tone colour, begins with Miss Rasch's girls, partially invisible, in green tutus against a green orchard. The orchard is dotted with brilliant oranges. The ballet over, the scene shifts to a shot of Noah's Ark on Mount Ararat . . . and as the storm clouds clear and the sun emerges, the MGM parade of stars, dressed in clear plastic raincoats and hats, troupes on for the grand finale, led by Ukelele Ike in the song "Singin' in the Rain". It was the great hit of its day.[25]

There is a compulsory, for the time, toe-tap number, and Joan Crawford also sings and does a short dance (not the Charleston). The film's influence was tremendous and, the first of its kind, it started a trend that was copied by all the other studios.

The dance routines in the other revue films were similarly derived from the Broadway stage. Nonetheless, there were some attempts to explore the possibilities of the new medium. Larry Ceballos's work in Warner Brothers' *Show of Shows* displays a certain creativity, credit for which is generally reserved for Berkeley. In one scene, for example, he has a group of approximately two hundred girls all in rhythm climbing ladders arranged in a criss-cross pattern; in another number, suggestive, too, of the "Continental" in *The Gay Divorcee*, half the girls are dressed in black and half in white, performing movements which exploit their costumes for the number's effects. In general Ceballos's work is not well remembered; he began his career at Warner Brothers with Jolson's second film, *The Singing Fool*, and continued working in Hollywood off and on until the mid-forties, yet he rarely worked on major films that have endured. Mary Jane Hungerford has suggested that "he was far ahead of his contemporaries in a grasp of the artistic possibilities of dance in the film. He believed in cutting a dance before shooting it. That is, he planned dances for the camera angles, rather than shooting a stage number from three angles simultaneously and letting the cutter assemble the choreography. He insisted upon simplicity and logic." "As a rule, Ceballos used buck, rhythm tap, and soft-shoe work in his dances. But he also used more ballet and character dancing than most of his colleagues."[26] Most of Ceballos's work was created as if for the stage, however (since most of the films had backstage plots or were revue musicals), and his innovations were copied by other dance directors and given even fancier and more elaborate treatment in other films.

The revue films were naturally limited in their means of using the medium simply because they were attempting to be nothing more than copies of a stage tradition. The musical comedies, however, could have tried moving beyond their ancestors' limitations. Such was not yet the case, primarily because most of the shows were themselves transferred almost intact from the theater. In addition to the aforementioned *Sunny* and *Sally, Rio Rita, Gold Diggers of Broadway, Showboat,* and a number of operettas such as *The Vagabond King, The Desert Song,* and *New Moon* were filmed by 1930. It was Metro-Goldwyn-Mayer, however, in a move perhaps prophetic of its subsequent role involving musical production, which first created the original movie musical. *Broadway Melody,* limited and stagebound as it is, was nonetheless an attempt to create something for films which had not been seen previously on the stage. Even the musical score, created for the film (or at least using material not previously used on the stage), was composed by two men who were not well known as writers of musicals in New York: Nacio Herb Brown and Arthur Freed.

    Broadway Melody was a story of backstage intrigues involving two girls trying to make good on Broadway; most of its numbers were performed as part of the Zanfield revue for which they had been hired as performers, and the film has many holdovers from silent film technique. There are, for example, a number of inserted titles, usually used to identify locations (almost as if the film makers did not trust the audience's ability to identify the changes wrought by a cut or as if they did not have the ability somehow to work an identification into the dialogue.) Similarly, the film is often cut like a silent film; reaction shots to underscore some emotional point or to emphasize a statement are used throughout. In one sense, such cutting simply does not adhere to the standard long take and immobile camera "required" by the equipment of the period; nevertheless, the shots are frequently repetitive of points made through the dialogue.

There are moments in the early sequences of the film, however, which seem particularly to be attempts to work away from the limitations of the enclosed camera. The film opens with aerial shots of New York City and continues with a montage of buildings, places, and activities somewhat similar to the opening of *West Side Story* in 1961. Although each shot is itself filmed with a static camera, there seems to be a sense of overcoming that limitation with rather short takes. In the Gleason Music Company scenes, for instance, each shot has an action-filled frame, and there is a great deal of motivated sound. During the singing of "Broadway Melody" ten people are in the frame, several singing, one playing the banjo, another the saxophone. Occasionally, the camera does move as well, but it is done rather hesitantly and then simply to keep people in the frame. (In order not to move too much, however, there are times when rather awkward framing results from performers positioning themselves too far to the left or right.)

There are also moments that make the film at least contributory to the development of the musical genre. One song, for example, "You Were Meant for Me," is integrated into the plot when Charles King sings it for Anita Page. (It is given an excuse for being, however, inasmuch as King's character is a songwriter, who says that he has written the song for her.) Later the same song plays a more significant role when Page and her gigolo boyfriend start to dance to the number and she asks that the band play something else when she realizes what it is they are playing. The dance numbers themselves, however, are all part of the show with the exception of a short exhibition solo which Bessie Love does in their apartment when King first introduces her and Anita Page to the song "Broadway Melody." The obligatory rehearsal scene, always part of later backstage musicals as well, introduces a row of chorus girls doing a precision tap routine. As usual, the dance director is annoyed that the girls are not getting the rhythm exactly as he wants.

There are four production numbers in the film, two as part of the dress rehearsal and two as part of the actual production. In the first, the "Broadway Melody" number itself, Charles King sings in front of painted backdrops of the New York skyline. As the number begins, Bessie Love and Anita Page come on stage to back him up, doing the same routine with which they auditioned for the show, an attempt to be "twins" by precisely matching each other's movements. (The plot intrudes into the number as Zanfield, realizing that the number will be too long, eliminates the girls from the number and then calls for it to continue.) A group of chorus girls comes on to the stage behind King, making their entrance in a line, taking two steps to the left and then doing a control kick with their right legs. When all the girls are on the stage, they move around each other in a do-si-do fashion and then begin a precision tap routine, the one for which we had previously seen them rehearsing. Their portion of the number ends as they all kick in succession, moving from screen left to screen right, and, reversing, moving from screen right to screen left, they all bend forward one after the other. Subsequently one of the girls does a toe-tap solo. The chorus routine had been shot in several takes but always in long shot; the solo, on the other hand, was shot with an intermingling of close-ups, medium shots, and long shots. As soon as the soloist starts to dance, there is a cut to a close-up of her feet, then a cut back to a medium long shot of her body with the feet immediately out of the bottom of the frame; most of the number is shot from this position. Toward the end there is another cut to her feet and she performs a combination of taps with her right foot in several different rhythmic patterns (bearing no relationship to the musical rhythms of the song) while her left foot moves back and forth in counterpoint to the right foot. It ends with a long shot of her entire body, as she does a series of cartwheels, so that one can see the arms and legs moving simultaneously.

   Broadway Melody exemplifies the combinations of dance that were popular on the stage at the time and which were evident in the other films of the period as well. Toe-tapping, for example, was a short-lived musical comedy form which provided almost-compulsory exhibition pieces; it was an outgrowth of tap itself, a combination of forms resulting from the mixing of black dance steps of the minstrel era with European clog dancing, and of the ballet-inspired pointe dancing. The musical revue routines of girls doing control kicks and precision taps were also evident in the "Broadway Melody" number, but perhaps the best example of the combination of elements was in "The Wedding of the Painted Doll," for here there is a mixture of ballet and acrobatics which almost seems to point to the work of Michael Kidd three decades later; cartwheels and somersaults are choreographed into patterns with *jetés en tournant, chaîné* turns, and *fouetté* pirouettes. Although at first one assumes that the number Bessie Love and Anita Page do for their audition ("We're the Harmony Sisters from Melody Lane") is intentionally bad, subsequently the ineptness of all the dancers makes one wonder. According to traditional standards of dance ability, chorus lines of the period were notoriously inadequate; few girls had genuine dance training and standards were low. *Broadway Melody* was reflective of its era.

   In other respects *Broadway Melody* is also indicative of its era and of its position as the first of a long line of original film musicals. There are sequences in which the sound is used for its own sake or for a means of underscoring other moments. During the first romantic scene between Charles King and Anita Page, for example, there is a sound-over of tapping and of the piano playing from the girls' rehearsal which we had just seen. The presence of the sound lends an element to the scene which would have been otherwise unavailable; the sense of the theater as a controlling force in their lives becomes evident from the off-screen space. Sound as creative force, as a controlling factor in the filming process of the time is important in the film, too, and color in one sequence was similarly reflective of the fashion of the era. Bosley Crowther tells about some aspects of the technical problems and alleged innovations of the production:

> It took all of thirty days to shoot it, and its total cost was $350,000, including the use of color for the big chorus production number to *The Wedding of the Painted Dolls* [sic].

> The decision to use color on that number was a bold one for Thalberg to make, but he topped it when he later ordered the completed sequence to be reshot. He had been in New York when they first filmed it and looked at the footage on his return. He thought it smacked too much of a stage number that had been photographed literally from one spot. He was right. The task of shooting from the "greenhouse" had inhibited the camera work. Thalberg got a dance director to lay out new routines that would be interesting when viewed from different angles.

> They made a discovery while redoing the *Painted Dolls* number that was to be of invaluable convenience and economy in the future making of musical films. When Thalberg ordered the original footage tossed into the trash can, it occurred to Douglas Shearer that it would be a shame and a waste to abandon the musical recording that had been made along with it. Not only was it a good recording, but it would cost a lot of money to call back a full orchestra to play the music while they were shooting the scene again.

> Shearer told Thalberg he had an idea: why not shoot the scene to an amplified playback of the recording and then match the footage and the recording in the cutting room? Thalberg was persuaded they could do it, and the experiment was successfully tried. Thus the technique of "pre-scoring" was devised on the first musical film. Later they discovered it was practical even to record vocal numbers in advance and then have the performer synchronize his (or her) lip movements to the play-back while the scene was being photographed.[27]

Broadway Melody is a seminal film, for it not only displayed the primary musical elements of its day but also it introduced ideas which other film makers and other films would use more fully.

Nineteen twenty-nine was a full year for musicals at MGM, and one of its contributions was *Hallelujah,* directed by King Vidor. *Hallelujah* was the second all-black musical of the sound era (the first had been Fox's *Hearts in Dixie*) and seemed to be a direct result of an awareness of the contribution blacks could make to film. "From the start, Hollywood was aware that talking movies needed sounds—music, rhythm, pizzazz, singing, dancing, clowning. And who, according to American myth, were more rhythmic or more musical than Negroes?"[28] Such a project had long been among Vidor's ideas and, by investing his own money into it, he was able to persuade MGM to produce it. Filming many scenes on location, using Negro spirituals and other folk songs as well as some Stephen Foster numbers (with Irving Berlin songs included in the final film), Vidor presented an impression of the difficulty of life among rural blacks of the South. In film terms, *Hallelujah* makes several advances. First, Vidor felt no compulsion to record everything synchronously. As a result there are many sequences, principally those shot in the fields, which contrast noticeably with those shot synchronously: in the latter the camera never moves, whereas in the former there is fluidity and inventiveness to the camera work.

There is, moreover, a choreographic quality to the entire film which, in spite of its generally somber tone, makes it related to the integrated dance musicals of the future. Although perhaps a result of the stereotype that blacks will with the slightest provocation burst into song and dance, the musical numbers become integrated into the essence of the film. There are, indeed, several numbers in which the performers seem just to be inspired and therefore start to dance. In one moment, for example, two little boys, hearing a banjo, jump onto the table and start to tap out a few variations on the time step. There is no attempt to explain why they do it or where they might have learned the routines; it is presented as accepted fact that they are naturally capable of such a thing. Dance is used also as the means of suggesting the character traits of Nina Mae McKinney's role. The dances in the cafe, which are presented with both a moving camera and an intercutting of long shots to present the full figure and close-ups of the feet to give detail of the steps, become rituals of seduction as well as revelations of the girl's inner state. It is implicit in her number that only a girl of great sexual fervor could dance with such abandon. Donald Bogle has suggested that there is an affinity between sex and religion in this film.[29] And that affinity achieves its high point perhaps during the sermon-dance in which McKinney is converted from her evil ways. Daniel Hayes's sermon about the train to Hell becomes a dance as he enacts the movements of the train beginning to move and increasing speed as it carries sinners closer and closer to perdition. Performing with his entire body in religious fervor, he suggests the sexual fervor which her dance earlier had done. Significantly it is during this dance that she feels the religious call to abandon one fervor for another. In two manifestations the dance has become the means of presenting character and of advancing the narrative.

Isolated moments of dance in otherwise non-dance musicals become significant means of presenting information about characters or are simply *divertissements* within the structure of the film itself. In Ernst Lubitsch's *Love Parade,* for example, the opening shot of chorines doing high kicks in the background while the frame is emphasized by two champagne bottles in the foreground, presents the character of Maurice Chevalier as a playboy with one succinct image. Subsequently Lupino Lane and Lillian Roth, the second leads, servants respectively to Chevalier and Jeanette MacDonald, act out their love affair in a song and dance number, "Let's Be Common." Presented with an emphasis on Lane's athletic skill, the dance contrasts with the singing courtship of MacDonald and Chevalier; the servants, less inhibited than their masters, can express themselves through dance whereas the leads, inhibited aristocrats, must satisfy themselves through song alone. (Although it is implicit in the film, this contrast, of course, is the result of the fact that the two leads were singers with little, if any, ability to dance whereas the supporting players were capable and, therefore, used for that purpose. The limitations of performers either as dancers or as singers would follow as an important motivation for the type of musical being made at any particular time.)

In general, the musicals of the pre-Berkeley era have not survived except as curiosities of the history of film. Certainly tied to the limitations of the new equipment of the sound era, they were, nevertheless, hesitantly experimental, and in some instances they show characteristics which would be important in later musicals. As with most of the dramatic films of the period, the musical had difficulty getting away from its stage ancestors. This was true of the dance, too. The dance directors, almost all from New York stage backgrounds, seemed to have very little interest in developing dance for film. The forms were primarily stage forms, tap, softshoe, chorus-girl ensembles, some ballet, and a touch of athletic tricks, or the social-cum-performance forms popular at the time, such as the Charleston. There were attempts to go beyond the limits of the stage, however, and in this respect the films were considerably more innovative than they have subsequently been given credit for. The overhead shot, cuts to close-ups of the performers, tracking cameras, and designed patterns of movement were evident in the first musical films. The films themselves, however, were generally derived from the stage and alike to such an extent that production decreased in 1930 and 1931. It was just at that point, though, that Busby Berkeley arrived in Hollywood to make *Whoopee;* within three years he would help revive the form.

3

Busby Berkeley at Warner Brothers

Although Busby Berkeley has been given credit by many people, and probably most notably by Gene Kelly, for having eliminated the proscenium arch from dance film, nevertheless, he used very little dance as such in his films. Instead, he substituted enormous lines of girls, elaborate geometric patterns, and trick effects to create a world of fantasy within the more natural world of the rest of the film. What little dance there is, generally limited to chorus girls going through a routine during the rehearsal sequences of the films or as an exhibition number for a particular performer as part of a larger number, uses very standard steps of the period: tap and soft-shoe particularly, or dance-related movements such as running in rhythm or marching. Berkeley's work is more an outgrowth of the revue traditions present on the New York stage in the twenties—girls in rows and lines going through very simplified motions but serving as attractions in themselves. He used almost none of the current dance styles of the thirties, particularly since he didn't use social dance situations in his films; nor is there much evidence of jazz dance, which was of increasing importance in most other dance forms of the period.

This is not to say that Berkeley's contribution is insignificant. It is, in fact, most significant; however, it is not a contribution to *dance;* it is a contribution to the use of movement, a contribution to the musical (though one which would not be followed by film makers who succeeded him in the forties and fifties), and, finally, a contribution to film in general. First, it is generally acknowledged that *Forty-second Street* did help restore the musical to a position of popularity among film genres. Second, often copied by other studios and other dance directors during the thirties, Berkeley has been given credit for being a spectacular innovator and creative genius. This may well be true; however, it is simplistic, for earlier dance directors had used material in ways that have always been associated with Berkeley. Larry Ceballos, particularly, had used certain of those effects: his use of some two hundred girls in one number of *The Show of Shows* is just one example. *The Hollywood Revue* had an overhead shot of some fairly elaborate dance movement of the Albertina Rasch dancers as well. Berkeley seemed to do the job better than anyone else, but he also had the fortune to work with collaborators with particular skills and on a group of films that were clever, fast-paced, and witty. When Berkeley directed the entire film himself, even the clever and witty plots seem to be missing, and in those instances only his elaborate routines stand out as imaginative.

Berkeley had no dance training whatsoever, a point which he was almost proud of in later years. Although he came from a theatrical family, he had very little theatrical experience until he was an adult. What experience he did have (which seems to have left its mark on his work) was military regimentation. In France during World War I, among his other duties Berkeley had to conduct parade drill. He says of the experience:

> I got tired of the old routine, and to make things more interesting, I asked the Colonel to let me try something different. I had worked out a trick drill for the twelve hundred men. I explained the movements by numbers and gave the section leaders instructions for their companies and had them do the whole thing without any audible orders. Since the routines were numbered the men could count out their measures once they had learned them. It was quite something to see a parade square full of squads and companies of men marching in patterns in total silence.[1]

In stock theater during the twenties, Bekeley gained a largely undeserved reputation as a dance director. He had first obtained dance director jobs through sheer nerve and the realization that the dancers at that time did little more than kick their feet in the air.

> Busby Berkeley operated very largely on nerve. He had acquired a reputation as a choreographer, yet he had never studied the art and had never taken a dancing lesson. His bluff had never been called, and so far the game was successful, but on *A Connecticut Yankee* he had reason to worry. "The second act opened with Queen Guinevere's dancing class in the castle. I thought it would be a good ploy to start the scene with the Queen teaching the class the first five positions of dance. The trouble was I didn't even know the first position, let alone the others. So I walked around the stage rubbing my head and pretending I was thinking up something. I said to one of the girls, 'I think I'll have the Queen start off by showing the first position.' She said, 'Oh, you mean this,' and pointed her feet in a certain way. I looked out of the corner of my eye to see what she was doing and then pointed to another girl. 'Second position,' and so on. In this way and without their knowing it I learned the five positions of dance."[2]

The ludicrousness of this to anyone who knows dance is emphasized by the way he tells the story in other interviews: " I hen I suggested they try the second position, and watched them do the steps. It took me all morning, watching them work out the first five positions. . . ."[3] First, the positions are not steps; they are positions that are set, danced into and out of. No dancer would have to spend a morning working them out. And second, because they are not steps, they would be almost useless to someone who didn't know what to do with them. It is, therefore, more believable that he became known as the "One-Two-Three-Kick! Kid" for his work in New York.[4]

Busby Berkeley had twenty-one Broadway musicals to his credit by the time he went to Hollywood at Eddie Cantor's request to be the dance director for the Samuel Goldwyn production of *Whoopee*. Although he had not actually worked for the Ziegfeld *Follies* in New York, Berkeley had been the dance director for one of Earl Carroll's *Vanities,* revues similar to those of Ziegfeld. And Ziegfeld was, in fact, a co-producer of the film of *Whoopee*. Berkeley was, furthermore, one of the "Big Four" Broadway dance directors of the twenties, all of whom had worked in the Ziegfeld revue tradition if not actually for Ziegfeld himself, and all of whom were among the leading Hollywood dance directors of the thirties; the other three were Seymour Felix, who would become the leading dance director at Fox; Sammy Lee, who first made his mark at MGM; and Bobby Connolly, who worked for most of the major studios and who was probably Berkeley's chief competitor as a Hollywood dance director. The Ziegfeld tradition is strong in all their work, but it seems particularly so in Berkeley's.

Robert Banayoun has pointed out that the *Follies,* the *Vanities,* and George White's *Scandals,* the leading Broadway revues of the twenties, had imposed certain rituals on dance production numbers,[5] rituals which would receive their major manifestations in Berkeley's work at Warner Brothers during the thirties. The stairway, the revolving platform, and the stage thrust into the audience, all full of beautiful girls, were the trademarks of the revues. In a sense, all of these were attempts to move beyond the limitations of the theater. The thrust stage, particularly, seemed to be an attempt to do away with the proscenium arch; Berkeley would, then, simply follow these early leads to their logical conclusions when he had the superior resources of film studios available to him.

When he arrived in Hollywood, Berkeley knew nothing about filming dance, yet he was dissatisfied with the kinds of dance that had been evident in the early musicals, particularly the lack of respect for the unity and integrity of the number. He made it his business to become acquainted with the equipment and to learn all he could about the use of the camera. The attitude which had helped him overcome his lack of training on the stage ("I took suggestions. I watched the girls rehearse, and I picked up most of my knowledge from them. It's really amazing how much you can really acquire if you are inquisitive and want to learn."[6]) also prevailed in his film work. Spending time watching others at work on various films, Berkeley came to a major conclusion about film:

> I soon realized that in the theater your eyes can go any place you want, but in pictures the only way I could entertain an audience was through the single eye of the camera. But with

that single eye I could go anywhere *I* wanted to. You couldn't get any of my sets onto a legit stage, but I didn't care about that. To be entertaining and spectacular, that's what I cared about.[7]

Berkeley credits Richard Day, the art director for *Whoopee,* for making this evident to him,[8] and, he claims, it has been the motivation for all his work since and for his working method as well.

In spite of his great ability to adapt and his willingness to learn from observation, it seems particularly bold of him to have approached the actual shooting with the confidence he has since expressed.

It was then customary for the film's director to take over when it came to the actual shooting of the numbers, and I was supposed to step aside. I had never worked that way on Broadway and I wasn't going to work like that now. I went to Goldwyn and told him that I wanted to film my own numbers. He hedged and asked me if I thought I could handle it. I replied, "Mr. Goldwyn, I don't think I can, I *know* I can." This kind of confidence seemed to impress him and I got his permission. When I walked on the set to start shooting, I saw four cameras and four crews. This was something else I didn't know about, and I asked my assistant for an explanation. He told me that standard technique was for a routine to be filmed from four directions and that the cutter would assemble the shots, make a selection, and put the scene together. With another show of confidence I announced, "Oh? Well, it's not my technique. I use only one camera, so let the others go." I finally got my way, and during my entire career in films I have never used more than one camera on anything. My idea was to plan every shot and edit in the camera.[9]

It seems largely through inexperience, therefore, that Berkeley acquired a technique that became almost a fetish with him. He claims, moreover, never to have reshot anything and never to have eliminated more than six feet of film in the editing rooms. ("I have never had, in all my experience in pictures, a retake in my life. I've had an added scene or a whole scene rewritten, and shot the rewrite of the scene; but I've never had a retake in my life. The secret of my work is preparation, which is nine-tenths of the battle."[10])

In order to achieve his results Berkeley did prepare his numbers and rehearse them with exacting demands. His major asset as a dance director was his ability to move great masses of people, usually girls, around the stages in strict time to the music; "as for the dance routines themselves, Berkeley left the teaching of the actual steps to underlings."[11] Instead, Berkeley planned his elaborate routines with thorough detail, envisioning how they would look on the screen and then illustrating them for the dancers.

Before rehearsing the big musical routines, I would gather the girls around a blackboard, and as in a classroom, have them sit and watch me explain the movements with diagrams. This always captured their interest—explaining the purpose of the routine, where the camera would be, where they would be. I would also draw a sketch of the final shot. This procedure was especially helpful in doing the overhead shots of the complicated patterns.[12]

The concepts Berkeley employed in creating his production numbers actually favored his method of preparing in such a way as to shoot with one camera, edit in the camera, and not shoot retakes. One of his complaints about early musicals was that they cut away to other bits of action during the numbers. For him this was unforgivable.

> You see, I claimed that a number is no good unless you watch it from beginning to end; and my numbers have always carried continuity. If, at one angle I showed all the girls running over here, the next angle would pick them up over here, but it would be a different effect with the camera; and it would all carry continuity.[13]

The impression one gets, furthermore, from watching the films that there is often no relationship between the numbers and the rest of the film is borne out by the attitude he had during the creation of the numbers. He never bothered particularly with the story line, using it primarily as the slight motivation for his fantastic sequences. " 'I did my numbers and the director did the story,' Berkeley recalls. 'Sometimes I'd even forget who was directing.' No one ever knew exactly what would finally emerge from such a collaboration until the day of the first screening."[14] For him there was no need for integration of the numbers into the plot of the film; in fact, there was an almost conscious effort to avoid it, and when such integration does occur, as, for instance, in "I'm Going Shopping with You" in *Gold Diggers of 1935,* it stands out as an anomaly among the general impression of his work.

Berkeley's underlying concern was to have beautiful girls performing arranged patterns, displaying themselves in the most alluring ways he could imagine. Choreographer Jack Cole puts it very strongly:

> Busby Berkeley had no involvement with dancing. I don't know why one would want to talk about *dancing* when talking about his films. He was interested only in photographing designs and doing long traveling shots, which he did very well. He had the patience to build up a long crane shot forever and then really rehearse it and keep rehearsing it until he got it exactly the way it was supposed to be. He never looked at what the girls were *doing.* He was just watching for marks of the camera in relationship to musical bars. He was just creating wallpaper.[15]

Berkeley admitted as well that he hired his girls for their looks, not for their ability to dance. "I never cared whether a girl knew her right from her left, so long as she was beautiful. I'd get her to move or dance or something."[16] All she needed, he felt, was a good sense of rhythm and he could then manipulate her into the arranged movements so characteristic of his style.

These characteristic geometric designs are evident from his earliest work—even that prior to Hollywood. There is a picture in *The Busby Berkeley Book* (p. 22) of one of his arrangements for Earl Carroll's *Vanities of 1928,* which, although taken, naturally, from a frontal position, seems a definite preliminary to his later screen work. The girls form a triangle; at the apex is a girl in a bathing suit standing as the statue of a fountain. Approximately twenty other girls are arranged to lead up to her with their arms outstretched to form the sides of the triangle. At the base of the fountain are about a half dozen other girls looking straight forward and elaborately costumed to fill the space and provide a balanced composition. Although it is generally considered that his first films did not permit him the opportunities to indulge his fantasies which the later ones did (indeed, Samuel Goldwyn denied him the permission to have a revolving turntable in *The Kid from Spain,* telling him, "Do it the way it is now, and if you must revolve them, do that at some other studio."[17]), there is still evidence of his imagination at work in the familiar Berkeley routines. In *Whoopee,* for example, he was first able to use the famous Berkeley top-shot; in one number a group of scantily-clad girls wearing Indian headdresses are arranged in a typical pattern: about fourteen girls form the outer rim of a circle, bending forward toward the outer edge of the circle, arms intertwined behind their backs; ten girls form the inner circle, bending forward into the center, arms also intertwined; all are standing on a floor patterned with a sixteen-pointed star, itself inside a dark circle. The movements of the girls inside the patterns on the floor provide the kaleidoscopic display of the number itself.

Berkeley's work is generally considered in terms of crowds or groups, not individuals, yet Berkeley himself feels that one of his contributions was in the introduction of the close-up into production numbers as a means of giving identity to the girls. In the Stetson hat routine of *Whoopee,* for example, he opened with the camera on Betty Grable twirling a rope and then moved the camera back to include the others.

> He says he was the first director to use close-ups of chorus girls in production numbers . . . , and Berkeley took great pains to cut to those faces in most of his future numbers. His art of cutting from the great to the small has been cited as one of the best reasons for calling him a genius. "I worked with human beings," he told a British interviewer. "It's from that you get the exhilaration. I'd always splash in a close-up to show that those lines of girls, those designs, were really human beings."[18]

Another frequent motif in his numbers is a tracking shot in close-up past the faces of his dancers, but these are certainly examples of the paradoxical nature both of Berkeley's attitude toward his work and of the numbers themselves. Having expressed his preference for girls he could manipulate into his colossal patterns—rather than dancers who might be able to express an individuality he would be unable to control—he also seemed to try to overcome that by availing himself of the close-ups to provide the performers with an otherwise denied individuality. In spite of what he says, the close-ups seem isolated instances and just as impersonal as the chorus routines; the general impression of his work is one of massed figures moving like automatons, and usually the girl whose face stands out at all is a girl who was important in the rest of the film as well.

The other films he did for Goldwyn with Eddie Cantor, *Palmy Days, The Kid from Spain,* and *Roman Scandals,* all suggest his subsequent work at Warners but without the degree of elaborateness provided by Warners's facilities. (Strictly speaking, *Roman Scandals* was something of a reversion since it was made after *Forty-second Street, Gold Diggers of 1933,* and *Footlight Parade* in order to fulfill the obligations of his Goldwyn contract. He also had meanwhile directed the numbers for *Flying High* for MGM, *Night World* for Universal, and *Bird of Paradise* for RKO.) Denied those resources for *Roman Scandals,* for instance, he turned instead to an emphasis of the eroticism and suggestiveness which was always underlying his work. *Roman Scandals* is perhaps best known as the film in which the girls actually appeared nude—albeit covered with blonde wigs.

> ... we had one number sung by Ruth Etting called "No More Love." It was supposed to be set in a slave market where they auction off beautiful girls as slaves. We had a large circular-like elevation in the center of an arena. It looked like a pedestal. Girls were draped around each level of the pedestal which graduated in tiers. This is where they auctioned off to the buyers.
>
> It made a very striking thing with all of them chained to this block, way up high, with the appearance that they were nude, with nothing but long, blonde hair. I realized that if I wanted to do close-ups, that fleshlings on them would show up as being obvious; so I asked the girls if they would mind being photographed nude, provided that it was done in a beautiful and artistic manner by dressing their hair over their breasts, etc. They said they would do it if I would close the set and film it only at night to avoid unnecessary visitors. Nothing was objectionable, and I shot it, and very few people realize today that the sequence was done with the girls completely nude, except for their long, blonde wigs .... It was the only time in any musical that this has been done.[19]

(Designing a special bathing-cap and suit which looked like hair covering parts of the body, Berkeley also gave a semi-nude appearance to the girls in the "By a Waterfall" number of *Footlight Parade*.) In spite of the general restrictions of the films not done for Warners, Berkeley was still able to indulge his penchant for some of his more recognizable techniques and motifs: overhead camera angles and girls performing a routine in a locker room and gym *(Palmy Days);* men in uniform *(Flying High);* girls swimming in formation and undressing in silhouette behind screens and an elaborate night club number *(The Kid from Spain).* All would be carried over into his later and more popular films. The overhead camera angle—the Berkeley top-shot—became ubiquitous. Girls caught in bathrooms or other places where they could be seen in stages of undress, often silhouetted "nude," appeared in *Gold Diggers of 1933* and *Dames,* for example. The military motif is highlighted at the end of the "Shanghai Lil" sequence of *Footlight Parade,* and, in addition to "By a Waterfall" from the same film, Berkeley designed several ostentatious water ballets for Esther Williams in *Million Dollar Mermaid* and *Easy to Love* while working at MGM in the early fifties. And the world of night clubs, particularly in *In Caliente* and *Wonder Bar,* provided Berkeley with almost as many opportunities for his macrocosmic fantasies as the world of the theater did in his better known films.

The world of the theater, the back-stage story, so to speak, has provided consistent interest in the film musical, but this particular sub-genre reached its apex with the Berkeley films. These films differed from the other musicals of the period—the operettas—in that they were modern stories, often related to the Depression era. Similarly, they were tough and brash, not sentimental and romantic, like the operettas. Most important, they were known for their extravagant, mechanically precise dance numbers and musical routines, the climactic moments of the film toward which the plot of "putting on the show" had been moving from the beginning. The *Gold Diggers* series, as well as *Forty-second Street, Footlight Parade, Dames,* and others, were the product of Berkeley's collaboration with a number of directors, principally Lloyd Bacon, and stars, notably Dick Powell and Ruby Keeler. The films all bear the stamp of Berkeley's particular brand of cinematic inventiveness and are appreciated today primarily for his routines.

In most of the films, the financial problems of putting on a show must be overcome. In *Forty-second Street* the show is in jeopardy because the star is planning to end her affair with the principal backer. With that crisis solved, the show again is threatened when she is injured and cannot perform. Ruby Keeler, however, is whipped into shape in time for the premiere, and the film presents the show *Pretty Lady* as its highlight. The *Gold Diggers of 1933* opens with a typical Berkeley number, "We're in the Money," which is cut short when an announcement is made that the show for which the girls are rehearsing has run out of funds. The rest of the film shows the gold-digging chorus girls hunting for a show to appear in and for men to finance them. Inevitably, the film ends with the production of a show written by Dick Powell, the rich boy in disguise. James Cagney, as a producer of musical numbers to be presented during intermissions in movie theaters, has his business threatened by both outside competition and inside betrayal in *Footlight Parade.* The elaborate production numbers that end the film are the result of the cast's hard work and sacrifices as they pull together to triumph over the forces of the Depression. The plots, though often witty and clever, serve primarily as an excuse for Berkeley's grand-scale spectacles.

Although they were ostensibly performed in theaters, the dances in Berkeley's films never could have been limited to a theater stage; the enormous numbers of people, the complicated visual patterns, and the overwhelming production values were reserved for the film-studio stage. "On the whole, however, the routines of Berkeley's choruses were really more drill than dance; and increasingly the traditional idea of dancing as a physical expression was being abandoned for dance as a visual experience, camera inventiveness taking the place of invention within the dance form."[20] Dance as expression of love and joy or of sadness and depression, the exteriorizing of interior feelings, as it were, or as rituals of courtship, all means of using dance as textually integral with the totality of the film, were irrelevant here. The production numbers became purely visual—never textual; at times they were almost examples of pure—that is, non-narrative—cinema, whereas at other times they provided a completely self-contained narrative, their own discourse, separate from and unrelated to the film. Berkeley's inventiveness, further-more, was somewhat less that *of* the camera, than of what he staged *for* the camera—often from its overhead point of view. The geometric patterns of his performers often were the result of mechanical set-ups and stage devices such as turntables, but built on a scale beyond that of any theater stage. Likewise, the camera saw the production numbers from positions no member of a theater audience ever could.

A typical Berkeley number begins with the awareness that the number is being staged in a theater. In "I'm Young and Healthy" from *Forty-second Street,* for example, the frame encompasses the stage, and Dick Powell enters from off screen. For the first part of the number the camera concentrates on Powell and Toby Wing. First, the camera starts to dolly in to Powell; then after a cut to a different angle dollies in to a medium shot, followed by a cut to Toby Wing sitting alone on a platform on the stage. Powell enters the frame and sits next to her. Their seat sinks into the floor and starts to turn and the film cuts to an overhead shot of the two, making the transition into the elaborate staging. The camera moves into the world of the number and reveals an unlimited potential for the use of space, cinematic illusion, mechanical devices, and human bodies. The girls—and men, too, in this number—form circles on rotating platforms and run in place as the turntable moves, forming patterns for the overhead camera. Strips of cloth held by the dancers and moved back and forth in rhythm give a machine-like effect to the pattern as well. The number finishes with the camera dollying through the dancers' wide-spread legs to a close-up of Powell and Wing lying at the end of the tunnel formed by the girls' legs. Typically, also, at the end of the sequence, having fully exploited the potential for the moment, the camera re-establishes the number in the world of the theater. Berkeley uses any number of effects to make the transition from the stage to the unlimited world within the routine itself. A dissolve from a detail of the stage routine to a similar detail of the inner world becomes the means in *Gold Diggers of 1935* for revealing the choreographed pianos of "The Words Are in My Heart." Similarly, in other numbers the camera will dolly in or cut to a close-up and upon dollying back will reveal the patterned extravaganza.

In many respects Berkeley seems the consummate surrealist of the American screen. The numbers which Berkeley did for his many films seem manifestations of his own inner fantasies more than signs of the inner feelings of the characters in the films. Working as they most often do with their own diegesis, separate from and only tangentially related to the diegesis of the rest of the film, the numbers provided Berkeley with one opportunity to express himself in a manner which gives a stylistic and thematic unity to the films—regardless of who directed the regular narrative elements—and assuredly makes him seem the auteur. Strictly speaking, Berkeley was probably unaware of the Surrealist movement, per se; nor is there any direct connection between him and the Surrealists, but that does not negate the surrealistic qualities and overtones which imbue his films and provide them with that unity and consistency which can only be inferred but, indeed, are evident throughout his entire career. Other writers have occasionally called Berkeley's numbers surrealistic, but little serious analysis of that catch-all term has been applied to his work. Yet it seems that the most fruitful and comprehensive analysis of his material can be achieved working with the assumption that he was an unwitting surrealist, for it explains the nature of his dance creations, their relationship to the totality of the films, and the relationship of his contribution to the development of cinematic dance in a way that no other approach can.

Dance has often provided an outlet for surrealistic experimentation; indeed, the word *surrealism* was coined by Guillaume Apollinaire for the ballet *Parade* in 1917.[21] Experimental dance films of the 1920s—*Ballet Mécanique* and *Entr'Acte,* for example—were associated with, if not direct results of, the French Surrealist movement. Berkeley's work includes most of the major forces implicit in surrealism, though it lacks the force and power which drove the Surrealist movement itself; the revolutionary spirit, the desire to *"épater le bourgeois,"* seems totally absent from his films, yet the worlds of fantasy, irrationality, and eroticism so important to the Surrealists are the controlling factors in Berkeley's work. In his introduction to the English-language translation of Maurice Nadeau's *History of Surrealism,* Roger Shattuck defines *surrealism* in its "current accepted usage" as "something crazy, dreamlike, and funny . . . ."[22] This definition, rather too amorphous, perhaps, nonetheless provides a basis for exploration. More specifically, major elements of surrealism also evident in Berkeley's films are the idolization of female eroticism; the concretization of dream experience and its corollary, the absurdity and illogicality of reality; the relativity of time and space; the mechanization of life; the freedom of imagination. Ultimately, an expansion of real experience—super-realism as Herbert Read prefers to call it—is the driving force behind surrealistic manifestations. In spite of those areas where Berkeley seems unrelated to the movement itself, his dance routines are, undoubtedly, manifestations of an attempt to expand reality, that is, to move beyond the limits of real experience into worlds where the laws of nature no longer apply.

Perhaps the most evident surrealistic aspect of Berkeley's work is his use of the female form as object; Nahma Sandrow has noted that "for some surrealists, woman took on an almost mystical sexual power 'to mediate between man and the marvelous.' "[23] Anna Balakian has written that the Surrealists explored eroticism "with scientific relentlessness and meticulous observations as an avenue of physio-mystical experience and revelation. . . ."[24] And, of course, "mad love" was one of the basic surrealist concepts (*L'Amour Fou* being the title of one of André Breton's works). In Berkeley's work the erotic element is most obvious in his choice of scantily-clad chorus girls in almost all routines. At times, however, he moves beyond a simple appreciation of female beauty and into a realm of voyeurism and sexual symbolism. The seemingly innocuous camera dollying through the chorus girls' legs in "I'm Young and Healthy" suggests a less innocent interpretation in light of subsequent routines.

Two outstanding voyeuristic scenes are in *The Kid from Spain* and *Gold Diggers of 1933*, in both of which girls, seemingly nude, are silhouetted behind screens. In *The Kid from Spain* the camera dollies past the screen and around behind it in what seems an attempt to catch the girls without their clothes, and, as the camera does move behind the screen, the girls—wrapped in towels by this time—scream as if the camera were indeed a character catching them unaware. Similarly the girls in "Pettin' in the Park," *Gold Diggers of 1933*, having been caught in the rain, run behind a screen to change their clothes. The midget, playing a voyeuristic child (as he does in "Honeymoon Hotel" from *Footlight Parade*), coyly looks at the camera to apprise the audience of his intentions, and raises the screen—only to reveal the girls in metal bathing suits which, in turn, their fellows will try to get through by using can openers. The previously mentioned hair-covered nudity in *Roman Scandals* and nude-appearing bathing suits in *Footlight Parade* as well as scenes in bathrooms and boudoirs in *Dames* (where again the camera is treated as an intruder), the "Honeymoon Hotel" sequence in *Footlight Parade,* and the attempt to reveal the honeymooning couple in the Pullman coach of "Shuffle off to Buffalo," *Forty-second Street,* all support a voyeuristic interpretation.

Berkeley admits that he was more interested in the girls as objects to be admired than as dancers to be appreciated. One of his first jobs in the theater had taught him the value of girls as entertainment. Working on a show in Baltimore, he defeated competition which had a girl appear with one breast showing by hiring eight girls who were willing to appear almost nude and having the leading lady's breasts bared at one moment in the production. Jack Cole has also spoken of Berkeley in this regard.

> But he was interesting as a cultural object reflecting the erotic attitudes of the middle class. He was like a really old theatrical agent in New York who liked girls alot. He got lots of blonde girls and photographed them in as many ways as were acceptable to the middle class. He couldn't get them completely nude, but he would get them with their legs open and their breasts hanging. It was all about looking at gorgeous women erotically with the camera as a penis substitute.[25]

Other sexual imagery prevails as well, either overtly or by innuendo. The bananas of "The Lady in the Tutti Frutti Hat" from *The Gang's All Here* become obviously phallic as they are raised into erection in a recurrent Berkeley motif: a group of girls holding them lowered in front, raise them in succession one after the other and, reversing the process, lower them in succession. In "All's Fair in Love and War," *Gold Diggers of 1937,* the pieces of an exploding cannon come together to form couples sitting in a rocking chair while another cannon fires shots which form pictures of three girls; later at MGM the "I Got Rhythm" number from *Girl Crazy* ends with an enormous cannon exploding its charge directly at the camera. Often the geometric patterns of his big production numbers resemble the vaginal opening, the symbolism emphasized—and supporting Jack Cole's contention—when the camera or some object begins to move toward the center of the pattern before the film cuts or the pattern itself breaks up to form another one. Working in eras both before and after Hollywood's self-imposed censorship, Berkeley managed to create a form of erotic dance which, while it used dance only to a limited extent, did display a world in which dance elements could suggest something not usually associated with dance.

One reason that film fascinated certain Surrealists was its ability to make visible the creations of the imagination. Dream images can be made concrete on film, and implicit in those dream images are the surrealistic notions of absurdity and illogicality, the juxtapositions of unrelated elements, and the eliciting of Freudian sublimations. "For the surrealists dreams became a full cult of revelation. They were obsessed by dreams as glimpses of, gateways to, and metaphors for the marvelous irrational essence of the universe...."[26] The film maker then with his ability to "create a universe which is all his own, unhampered by laws of gravity, time, logic"[27] can be, in certain respects, the ultimate surrealist; and Berkeley with his erotic, Freudian evocations as well as his non-erotic irrational images presented a truly illogical and surrealistic dream world. Berkeley's numbers, unlike certain surrealistic dances in some Vincente Minnelli films, for example, were rarely dream outgrowths of the films' narratives; they were more his own dreams, for the "narrative existed as a means to explore his fantasies," as Peter Cowie suggests.[28] The eroticism of

Berkeley's work seems a Freudian evocation of those fantasies, but other—non-erotic—images reminiscent of Méliès are manifold: disembodied heads and limbs; people turning into objects; objects brought together to form images of people; seemingly self-propelled inanimate objects; multiple heads—indeed, everything presented in multiples; characters emerging from eyes or other startling places; and people becoming parts of mechanical objects such as harps or typewriters. Most important overall, however, seems to be the creation of self-contained diegetic worlds which contain all of these surrealistic dream images yet which are unrelated to the rest of the film.

Creating self-contained worlds separate from the films, Berkeley ignored—if not defied—the limits of time and space implicit in the narrative of the individual films. The limitless quality of filmic time and space is of necessity controlled by the limits of the film's narrative world. As it has developed apart from Berkeley, the backstage musical, in general, provides that its numbers be limited to the stage, that the points of view presented by the camera be possibly those of the audience, the performers, the stage hands, or, at most, someone who is part of the world of the film. Cinematic convention does, of course, permit leeway to those points of view: the camera can become a "performer" as it were; close-ups can be inserted to emphasize detail; overhead shots can present patterns otherwise unappreciated; and production values can be—perhaps should be—more elaborate than possible on a real stage. The conventions of the quintessential Berkeley films, however, demanded a time and space completely removed from the more restricted time and space of the film's own narrative. Implicit in the "camp" appreciation of Berkeley's material is the awareness that Berkeley's numbers could never be presented on a theater stage without the awareness that his numbers employed the surrealistic concepts that time and space were only relative; camp enthusiasts impose the conventions of other backstage musicals without realizing that Berkeley's were different. Time and space *are* limitless for Berkeley and, therefore, provide him with one opportunity to present worlds within the film that have their own conventions and possibilities; indeed, Berkeley's hundreds of performers, the surrealistic dream images already mentioned, and the opening up of the real-stage space and time to a cinematic space and time require an expansion of spatial and temporal realms beyond those normally associated with the backstage musical.

Berkeley's use of space and time works primarily in two ways. In some numbers he is concerned exclusively with the visual possibilities resulting from expanded space and creates abstract numbers with geometric patterns and formations—the "typical" Berkeley routine. In other numbers, however, he creates actual narratives which not only expand the space of the theatrical presentation which gives the number its *raison d'être* but also create another time within the film's world. It is the second variety which is particularly surreal, for it incorporates so many of those elements of non-rationality, illogicality, and unexpected juxtaposition evident both of the Surrealist movement and of surrealism in general. "Lullaby of Broadway" from *Gold Diggers of 1935* is such a number and serves as a good example if only because Berkeley has repeatedly cited it as his favorite. In this sequence, which begins with a black frame, singer Wini Shaw's head appears very small in the distance; as the camera, on a specially-built monorail, dollies very slowly in to a large close-up, her head turns upside down and becomes an image of Manhattan, the setting for the number's diegesis. This is followed by a "city symphony" of Manhattan waking up, the surreal quality emphasized by tilting the camera at certain moments in the montage. The Broadway Babe, Wini Shaw, arrives home from her all-night revels and sleeps during the day— presented through the turning hands of a clock—only to awaken for another night on the town. She and Dick Powell attend a night club performance for which they are the only members of the audience (and here is the only genuine dancing in the number, done to variations of the "Lullaby of Broadway" song, including a couple doing a Spanish dance and a hundred-plus male and female dancers performing a musically unaccompanied tap dance for thirty-two bars). The elaborate routines are shot from every possible angle: front, back, top, side, and bottom and in long shot and close-up. Present, too, is the Berkeley motif of dancers doing action in succession as a line of girls fall back one after the other into their partner's arms and, reversing the process, the guys throw them back again into an upright position. Powell and Shaw, observers throughout most of the number, participate briefly in the dancing, but Shaw, running inexplicably from the action after its climax, falls to her death from the heights of the building. The circularity of the number is completed as the sequence returns to her apartment (with her cat pointedly awaiting her return) and the awakening New York montage—accompanied by a softly-sung reprise of the song itself. It concludes with the reverse of the opening shot; Wini Shaw's head becomes smaller and smaller as the camera dollies back and the screen fades to black. Similarly morbid episodes occur in at least two other Berkeley routines: a shooting and a stabbing are part of the "Forty-second Street" number and Dolores Del Rio stabs Ricardo Cortez during their "Tango del Rio" in *Wonder Bar*. For Berkeley this morbidity seems a surrealistic element of surprise, juxtaposing the unexpected shock with the dance routine's normal gaiety.

Other self-contained narrative dance numbers include "Honeymoon Hotel" and "Shanghai Lil" from *Footlight Parade*, "Muchacha" from *In Caliente*, "Going to Heaven on a Mule" from *Wonder Bar*, "I Only Have Eyes for You" from *Dames*, and the "Forty-second Street" number itself. Each contains major surrealistic elements. At the end of "Shanghai Lil," for example, one of Berkeley's elaborate military drill routines becomes a chauvinistic *tour de force* with marching placards forming the flag and the face of Franklin D. Roosevelt while earlier in the routine bodies seem to appear and disappear in the smoke-filled haze of an opium den. A black-faced Al Jolson goes to a surrealistic Hollywood heaven on a mule in his night club routine in *Wonder Bar*. Starting in an elaborate Southern rural setting, he goes to church on a mule, the church becoming a black-face heaven where a portrait of Abraham Lincoln is on the wall behind Saint Peter's desk, where Jolson reads a Yiddish newspaper, and where a real black man (the only one in the number) tap dances out of a watermelon. Taking a ride on what appears to be a real train in "I Only Have Eyes for You" in *Dames*, Dick Powell and Ruby Keeler fall asleep and Powell dreams a routine in which people appear and disappear as he sings, "I don't know if we're in a garden, / Or on a crowded avenue. / You are here, so am I, / Maybe millions of people go by, / But they all disappear from view, / And I only have eyes for you." Multiple disembodied heads of Ruby Keeler dance around the frame; the female dancers, all with placards on their backs, move together to form a frame-filling jigsaw puzzle picture of Keeler's face; and Keeler herself emerges from the iris of a large eye at another point. *In Caliente*'s "Muchacha" is a night club routine which opens into a vast mountain setting with real horses and a gambling parlor. The *trompe l'oeil* opening of "Forty-second Street" (Nahma Sandrow points out that the Surrealists "did not discover but adopted enthusiastically . . . (the) visual pun" aspects of *trompe l'oeil*[29]) has Ruby Keeler tap dancing on what appears to be the stage of the theater, but the camera dollies back to reveal her tapping on the roof of a taxicab on Forty-second Street. Subsequently the female dancers hold cards which form an image of the New York skyline, and the buildings appear to dance; toward the end of the number a stairway seems to become a very tall skyscraper.

Interpolated within Berkeley's non-narrative numbers, furthermore, there are often incidental moments and sequences of a surrealistic nature, many of which appear as motifs or are, at least, reminiscent of similar sequences throughout his work. In the title song of *Dames,* for instance, the female dancers, as if self-levitating, fly into close-up; in *The Kid from Spain* the dancers, carrying placards, come together to form the head of a bull; violins, rimmed in neon, appear to move without visible support and all come together to form an enormous neon violin in "Shadow Waltz" from *Gold Diggers of 1933;* similarly, the choreographed pianos of "The Words Are in My Heart," *Gold Diggers of 1935,* seem self-animated as they move together and apart to form various patterns, disappear as the players perform a dance alone, and reappear to form a jigsaw pattern, coming together to form a dance floor for a single female dancer. (A Berkeley *trompe l'oeil* introduces the pianos as well: once inside the unlimited space of the number, the film shows a group of girls singing, then cuts to a close-up of fingers on a keyboard; the camera then moves around, revealing the entire piano and, finally, pulls back to display the entire group of choreographed pianos.) Girls form the front piece of harps in *Fashions of 1934;* surrounding the black-faced Eddie Cantor in *The Kid from Spain,* a group of girls wear hats which are painted to resemble black-face masks; and, though considerably later in Berkeley's career but showing his continuing interest in surreal subjects, Ann Miller dances among disembodied arms playing musical instruments in *Small Town Girl.*

Moving into the limitless space and time of his production numbers, Berkeley was able to present a dream world akin to both Susanne Langer's aesthetic of film as dream and the surrealists' aesthetic while giving fulfillment to and indulging in his own dream-like fantasies. He could set free his imagination in these spaces in a way that more conventionally limited spatial realms would never have permitted. Robert Benayoun has written an article entitled "Berkeley le Centupleur" (Berkeley the multiplier by a hundred) which points out the essence of this increased spatialization in his films.

> Why slave to film ten people when a hundred would suffice? Berkeley himself has recounted how at the sight of four pianos on a stage, he imagined as many as a hundred of them, how at the sight of a single violinist doing a "control kick" on the stage of a music hall in 1920, he conceived what would be the "Shadow Waltz" of *Gold Diggers of 1933.* His megaloscopic spirit doesn't count less than a hundred. A hundred girls, a hundred violins, a hundred pianos, a hundred mules on a hundred clouds, a hundred beds. A hundred harps marched past on these small screens with which the era would have to be content. In Todd-A-O or in Cinerama a thousand would have been the key number.[30]

Employing his enormous resources, Berkeley developed recurring motifs which, while seldom using true dance, nonetheless make his numbers extraordinarily identifiable and in the broadest sense a special kind of cinematic dance; for movement in the most controlled patterns ever put on the screen does give a surrealistic dance life to his hundreds of performers.

Dance in the traditional sense of the term is limited in all of Berkeley's work, and the reasons can easily be inferred from information cited previously. Not being a dancer, he could in no way choreograph dance steps; working out of a tradition which was interested only in beautiful bodies, he simply did not care if his performers could dance. His interests lay with expanding the possibilities of stage space, glorifying the patterns and movements which he had developed in Broadway revues via the less limited resources of the film medium, and exploring his own imaginative narratives in production numbers which used song and dance as a means toward an unintentional surrealistic end rather than as a means toward furthering the film's own narrative or as ends in themselves. Yet there *is* dance in Berkeley's films, and, although it has had little influence on the development of dance in the musical film, it is worth exploring if only to realize his attitude toward true dance in film. Berkeley had to rely on whatever dance ability his individual performers had and that was usually small. As a result, the dances are usually restricted to basic time-step precision tap routines in the rehearsal sequences of the films' own narratives. Preparing for the show within the films, the dancers audition or rehearse by doing a tap dance in *Forty-second Street, Dames,* and *Stage Struck,* for example. Only occasionally, as in *Gold Diggers of 1933,* is there a carry-over from the rehearsal dance into a dance in the show itself. By contrast, this is particularly evident in *Gold Diggers of 1935* where Adolph Menjou's dagger number, shown almost complete in rehearsal, is never seen in the show. Short dance routines do occur in several numbers within the various shows, however. A rather simple walking movement leads into a soft-shoe routine in "You're Getting to be a Habit with Me" in *Forty-second Street.* Often a soft-shoe or a tap will open a number which when the number's space opens up will be subordinated to the multiple performers' patterned, massed movements or to the number's internal diegesis. This is true of "Shuffle off to Buffalo" (the song, in fact, taking its name from the standard combination cross-over, wing traveling tap step) and "Forty-second Street." Similarly, individual short tap sequences form part of larger numbers. James Cagney and Ruby Keeler tap briefly on top of a bar in "Shanghai Lil," for example, and there are isolated tap routines in "Going to Heaven on a Mule" in *Wonder Bar* and "Let's Put Our Heads Together" in *Gold Diggers of 1937.* "Don't Say Goodnight" from *Wonder Bar* actually contains waltzing—first by Dolores Del Rio and Ricardo Cortez and subsequently by a large group— but the waltzing as a dance element becomes unimportant as the dancers begin dancing with movable columns and on a rotating platform inside an octagon of mirrors used to multiply the numbers even further. In later years working with Eleanor Powell in *Lady Be Good* and Ann Miller in *Small Town Girl,* Berkeley would give full dance routines as befitted their tap-dancing specialties, but this only emphasized the absence of such routines in his earlier films and pointed up his interest in the spectacle of numbers rather than the dance talent of individuals.

As in later films the few intimate dance routines of Berkeley's Warner Brothers' films were often of an established performer or couple doing their specialty acts. The DeMarcos, for example, perform their Latin routine as a unit within the larger "Lady in Red" of *In Caliente,* and here Berkeley maintained a camera/dancer relationship befitting the integrity of their number. Beginning and ending with a high angle shot, Berkeley cuts to a closer shot for the greater part of their dance but maintains them in full figure. Seldom cutting into their material, the camera instead moves with them— Astaire fashion—as they circle around the night club floor. Similarly, Lee Dixon has two numbers in *Gold Diggers of 1937* which display his somewhat unique—perhaps eccentric—tap style, and Berkeley allows his camera to dwell on Dixon almost without interruption. Dancing to variations of the song "Speaking of the Weather," Dixon moves through basic tap steps embellished by undulating hips and by movements in which his lower legs extend outward from the knees. At one point he dances in a straight line across the set, camera tracking with him, which looks like a simple walking movement but which is highlighted by an intricate heel/toe tap rhythm. At the end of the line he swings athletically around a pole, dances up steps to a platform, stands on his hands, and then walks on his hands across the outstretched intertwined arms of a line of girls. Usually kept in full figure throughout the number—with one close-up of his feet—Dixon is allowed to do his routine uninterrupted by the numbers of people kept in the background for most of the number. Later in the film, during "All's Fair in Love and War," he does a similar dance as a tiny figure on an enormous rocking chair, this dance embellished by his clicking his heels into "bells." The number is short, however, and is only part of the larger Berkeley extravaganza; as he leaps off the chair, he discovers a bomb under it which blows the chair up and reforms it into a cannon. More typically, groups of girls doing running steps in formation or going through military routines, photographed in every possible way and from every possible angle, constitute Berkeleyan dance.

Military drill and military motifs are so much a part of Berkeley's work that it is difficult to separate them from his attitude toward dance. Precision is important in all dance. Precision tap routines, groups of girls doing exactly the same steps in perfect synchronization, were present in most early musical films and are evident in many rehearsal numbers in Berkeley's. The precision of any group in dance—a line of girls in arabesque in ballet, for example— adds to the effect desired, and, by contrast, when the precision is not present, when one dancer is out of step or is not matched exactly with the others, the effect is diminished if not destroyed. But precision is only one element in most dance; for Berkeley, however, it was the primary element. In film precision is possible in a way that it is difficult to achieve on the stage simply because of numerous rehearsals and the ability to retake shots. Berkeley's massed dancers had to perform in unison, and he rehearsed them strictly and with great discipline in their routines in order to achieve the military preciseness he had cultivated as a soldier in World War I. (His phobia for reshooting, however, did result in occasional mistakes; one girl starts to swim in the wrong direction in "By a Waterfall," for example.) Precision routines become more obviously military with Berkeley, though, as he dressed his dancers in military uniforms and put them in military situations. The three most directly military routines are "The Forgotten Man," "Shanghai Lil," and "All's Fair in Love and War." The latter number includes girls in military review, marching in various frame-filling patterns, but also has a line of girls and a line of guys firing guns at each other in the "war of love"; the girls exchange their rifles for perfume bottles as the two lines, both on a mechanical device, move toward each other; it ends as the guys surrender and the two lines come together and the couples kiss. Precision flag waving results in heart-shaped patterns at one point as well. The number differs from earlier Berkeley routines in that it has few high angle shots or mechanical contraptions to implement his designs. Except for the rocking chairs and cannons, the set is basically a plain backdrop, and the large groups performing their marches and patterns provide the parade effect without benefit of further elaboration.

Social dance, always a vital contributor to the development of dance and significant in musical films throughout the period, has no function in Berkeley's dance scheme and plays almost no role in the films. Party sequences, ballroom ensembles—particularly in the operettas where great waltzes usually became the courtship rituals or the displays of codes of class, for example—or folk-cum-social numbers—again serving as codes of characterization or representations of a period or of a group's homogeneity—were important in most other musicals. Even the Astaire-Rogers films with their displacement in context of any social period used social dance as the basis if not the framework for their more elaborate material. Yet Berkeley's films, in spite of their constant references to the Depression and its problems, showed no relevant social dance of the thirties. The few instances of social dance served simply as an introduction to other material. A ballroom dance in *In Caliente* serves as an introduction to Dolores Del Rio as a professional dancer within the context of the film as everyone else stops dancing in order to watch her, and, similarly, at the poolside party in *Gold Diggers of 1937* everyone, singing "Let's Put Our Heads Together," dances some kind of social dance which is difficult to ascertain since it is shot only in medium shot and close-up but which serves principally as a lead-in to Lee Dixon's tap dance to "Speaking of the Weather." Even in his later non-Warner Brothers' films, such as the Rooney-Garland ones at MGM, it became a means of elaboration and extravaganza—albeit limited by the resources available to him.

Even though dance as such did not interest Berkeley, the means of presenting it on film did impress him, and his film making career is a constant manifestation of the gimmickry, technical resources, and special effects which made possible an expansion of all that he found restrictive about vaudeville and revue on the stage. When denied the resources he wanted, as he was with Goldwyn, later in his term at Warners, and occasionally at MGM, he still invented ways to overcome the limitations and present his hordes of dancers in impressive ways. When he did have the resources, his imagination seemed almost as boundless as the inner space of his screen realms. Berkeley's most characteristic shot—the top-shot—was generally achieved by shooting with a wide-angle lens at a height of about sixty feet, though he has said that on several occasions he had holes cut in the ceilings of sound stages in order to get higher than the building would otherwise allow. Berkeley also takes credit for developing a monorail which could improve the possibilities of shots which formerly used a boom.

> . . . when we used a boom, we had five or six men on the stage floor pushing the boom; then we had two or three operators to lower the boom; and it moved slowly and all that; so I had them build a monorail to speed up everything. It was actually two rails, way up high in the rafters. Then they put a rigging that went straight down, just like a frame rigging, and the camera car went up and down the side of that rigging. But to operate that, I only needed two operators up above in a little coupe.
>
> I shot many numbers using this method of transporting the camera for greater flexibility.
>
> In those days, they didn't have a boom that could move that fast. It was the first time in any studio that this was done; and I pioneered it.[31]

At the height of his period at Warners, Berkeley was able to spend as much as $125,000 on a production number,[32] and design elaborate and intricate mechanical sets. The "By a Waterfall" set was one of his most lavish and expensive. Designed so that he could shoot from every possible angle, including underneath the girls, the set was constructed as a huge tank with thick glass plates for shooting up through the water. The falls pumped twenty thousand gallons of water a minute, and the set as a whole was underlaid with hydraulic lifts.

Four years later, however, "by 1937, the tide had turned; *Varsity Show* and *Hollywood Hotel* were the last of the gigantic Warner spectacular song-and-dance numbers. Afterwards they produced only occasional musicals, and these stressed romance and comedy."[33] As a result, required to be more restrained in his use of mechanical devices, the numbers for *Gold Diggers of 1937* are constructed differently from his earlier routines. Using a plain black floor and a black cyclorama, Berkeley achieved the effects of "All's Fair in Love and War" through his enormous numbers of performers and through special effects.

> This shows what can happen when you have to become completely resourceful and make use of a handful of essentials without a big set. I used a rocking chair in the number, as high as a house; then I exploded the chair, and the pieces all came down through the air and went into a cannon. . . . The chair was exploded in miniature by the trick department.[34]

Shooting a number in regular action but showing it in reverse (the girls flying into the camera in *Dames*), dressing stagehands in black to blend in with the floors to create seemingly self-propelled movement (the pianos in *Gold Diggers of 1935*), as well as turntables, specially designed sets, and the monorail helped Berkeley to achieve through mechanical and cinematic means his particular brand of dance movement.

The conventions of a spatially infinite theater within the world of the film; of abstract dance movement forming patterns of circles, flowers, snowflakes, and kaleidoscopic abstractions; of self-contained diegetic worlds unrelated to the external diegesis of the rest of the film—all achieved through mechanical devices and stage sets supplemented by a camera which seemed to allow "movement in any plane, at any angle, or at any speed"[35]—were the bases for Berkeley's dance.

> ... Berkeley was producing the purest combination of visual and sound that had yet come from the American studios. His dance sequences were abstract, complete in themselves and, ultimately self-defeating, an artistic cul-de-sac without links to the more common narrative forms. But, like the avant-garde of the twenties, they were both stimulating and provocative, suggesting to others new ways of using the freedom that Berkeley had found for himself.[36]

Other films would attempt to copy his style and flair though never completely employing the resources. Military motifs, massed numbers of dancers, and, occasionally, separate diegetic routines would all appear in the thirties, but most of the other films would maintain a basis in dance within the numbers as befitted their more accomplished dance stars; for, unlike the Warners-Berkeley films, other thirties musicals usually served as vehicles for dancers rather than as outlets for an auteurist dance director's imagination.

Richard Griffith has summarized Berkeley's role in both a social and cinematic context:

> The convention tried to serve two contradictory purposes at once. For more than a generation Florenz Ziegfeld had dazzled tired businessmen with stage extravaganzas that combined sensuality and a splendor that, however vulgar, was nevertheless undeniably beauty of a sort. The enjoyment of these spectacles was one of the rewards of business achievement. Musicals of the thirties sought to offer the same enchantments to a Depression-struck family audience at bargain prices, but on a more lavish and magical scale than Ziegfeld could manage. Yet at the same time these movies sought to preserve the feeling that the spectator was being introduced to privileges which only Privilege could enjoy, hence the preservation of the Broadway theater or nightclub as their nominal locale. Contemporary urban criticism was neither deceived nor impressed: it tagged these films as *ersatz*, characterized the "production numbers," so staggering when seen today, as tired and imitative, and lumped Busby Berkeley . . . with his numerous competitors as third-rate routinists all. Thirty years passed before this kind of musical could be sufficiently detached from the circumstances that produced it to become a mystique.[37]

Working out of the Ziegfeld tradition, Berkeley produced a more elaborate revue than was possible on the stage, but he remained principally a stage dance director. In spite of his innovative use of certain aspects of film, he was never concerned with filming dance and, as a result, did little to influence the development of the form. His approach remained unique of the period, for he was seldom able to carry his ideas over to his later work, nor was any other dance director able or willing further to develop his material. As the revue form died with Ziegfeld, so, in a sense, did the Berkeley extravaganza die with his departure from Warner Brothers. Although isolated instances would appear—notably *The Gang's All Here* at Fox and *Million Dollar Mermaid* and *Easy to Love* at MGM—they only seemed to emphasize the demise of his approach to dance. Instead, it would be trained dancers and genuine choreographers who would try to make cinematic dance an important element in the musical film, an element that would become as essential a cinematic code as music, lighting, and camerawork, rather than an isolated display of a particular skill or an intrusion into the combined codes otherwise working to make a unified cinematic experience.

4

Astaire and Rogers at RKO

Concurrent with Busby Berkeley's work at Warner Brothers, Fred Astaire was making films at RKO which were interesting principally for their use of dance and, moreover, which would contribute significantly to the development of dance as a cinematic code of the musical genre. The nine films which Astaire made with Ginger Rogers between 1933 and 1939 display an approach which, unlike Berkeley's, would be of continuing influence on the musical. The seriousness of purpose, the attempts to discover a form of cinematic dance, and the diversity and eclecticism of Astaire's style contributed to the development of the musical as a genre and, more importantly, to the acceptance of dance as one of its necessary elements. Trained in dance, Astaire was a performer who experimented in choreographing solos and duets rather than chorus numbers; coming from the musical comedy (rather than the revue) tradition on the the stage, Astaire was interested in the attraction of dance—not in the attraction of huge numbers of performers. Combining elements of ballroom, exotic, tap, jazz, and, to a certain extent, ballet dancing, Astaire developed what he has called an "outlaw" style. Concerned with how best to photograph his dance numbers, Astaire, as Gary Carey has suggested, "emphasized the intimacy that the camera could bring to dance, rather than the grandeur of wide open spaces. The camera stays close to Astaire, moving out only when the dancer needs more space for a larger movement."[1] The Astaire-Rogers series, as well as—though to a lesser extent—the films he made with other partners (Joan Fontaine, Eleanor Powell, Joan Leslie) were a 1930s and early 1940s alternative to the Berkeleyan extravaganzas and as such have served as the major forerunners of the dance-musical tradition.

Fred Astaire started working in film after a long and successful career on the stage, beginning, in fact, with appearances in vaudeville as a child. In almost exclusive partnership with his sister Adele, Astaire performed on vaudeville circuits until he and his sister were adopted into musicals for the revue *Over the Top* in 1917. Their pattern of success continued both on Broadway and in London, but it was a pattern of partnership. Referring to his work in 1917, Astaire wrote, "I didn't do any solo numbers in those days.

Everything was with my sister. I subsequently did several dances leading a large chorus but didn't tackle any real solo spots until years later."[2] It was in approximately 1921-22 while working on the show *For Goodness Sake* that Astaire first began choreographing their material,[3] and in 1925 he went one step further and embellished "The Half of It Dearie Blues" into a solo number in *Lady, Be Good!* The influence of this work with his sister persisted throughout his career. His dancing style was formed largely on the basis of that partnership, and it carried over into his films.

Perhaps the earliest and most important influence on that style was the work of Vernon and Irene Castle. Slightly older than the Astaires, the Castles became popular around 1912 and had their biggest success during the teens, the years that Fred and Adele were touring in vaudeville. Astaire admits to this influence, as well: "They were a tremendous influence in our careers, not that we copied them completely, but we did appropriate some of their ballroom steps and style for our vaudeville act."[4] Exactly to what extent the Castles' work reappears in Astaire's films can be inferred from only meager material, yet the persistence of ballroom dances, albeit more intricate and complex than what must have been the Castles' socially-oriented variety, suggests a grounding in the Castles' style if not in the purpose for which they prepared their dances. Ballroom dance for Astaire became another form of spectacle, a performance with which to entertain a passive public, not a form to have the public adopt as its own. As Marshall and Jean Stearns have suggested, by the time the Astaires were performing on Broadway—and surely by the time Fred was appearing in films—ballroom dancing in the musical had developed beyond the capabilities of the average theatergoer.

> On Broadway a dance might be linked to a new tune—especially in musicals—and the lyrics might attempt some description of the dance, but the over-all message was merely a feverish recommendation. The listener is no longer urged to participate—he is merely a spectator whose fantasies are perhaps nudged. In the film *Flying Down to Rio* (1933), the "Carioca" tells the audience that it is "a new rhythm, a blue rhythm that sighs." As directions for performing the dance, the lyrics are meaningless, and besides, Ginger Rogers and Fred Astaire are already executing steps that the audience would never dream of attempting.[5]

"Ballroom dancing was the basic ingredient of Astaire's style," the Stearns continue, ". . . and Astaire created an almost endless variety within that style."[6] The duet ballroom numbers, developed in a non-romantic way with his sister, continued into his films—one or more such numbers were present in every film, where they usually became the means of courting between Astaire and Rogers—and culminated in their final RKO film together as an homage to the Castles in *The Story of Vernon and Irene Castle.*

Astaire went to Hollywood after his sister had retired from active performing. It was an auspicious moment for such a move; not attracted to films with the discovery of sound, Astaire had managed to bypass the era of encumbered equipment and early sound musicals with all their problems. Instead he arrived in 1933 at a time of peak revival of the musical and would help sustain that revival throughout the thirties. Always popular on the stage, he became even more popular on the screen, and, once established in films, he never returned to stage performing. Astaire claims that he found film work more interesting than theatre,[7] and he worked almost from the beginning on developing a way of choreographing his numbers and subsequently of filming them which would best illustrate what he wanted to say—combining his style as a dancer with his style as an actor within the narrative of the film. And the Astaire-Rogers films are important for these several reasons. An attempt was made to work with dance and dancers, including experiments in how best to film dance sequences (showing the dancer's full body and shooting in long takes were the usual result, thus maintaining a pervasive theatricality throughout). A further attempt was made to fit the songs and dances into the action of the film, generally by presenting them in non-theatrical settings. There was a unity and consistency between the numbers and the narratives and an intimate dance style to the Astaire-Rogers films that made them different from the other musicals of their era.

Astaire made one film prior to actually beginning the series at RKO: he appeared with Joan Crawford in *Dancing Lady* for MGM. Continuing, in a sense, to test himself in films, he appeared for the first time with Rogers as second lead in *Flying Down to Rio*. Neither film has much of the Astaire style, both ending with rather elaborate Berkeleyan routines (they are production numbers within shows), yet each provided him with the opportunity to observe film making and to make the decision to persist. "Knowing absolutely nothing about photographing a dance for the screen, I did a great deal of listening and studying. I was pleased with lots of things but kept thinking of what I would like to try if I ever got in a position to make my own decisions."[8] Sammy Lee and Dave Gould were respectively the dance directors on his first two films and, though he credits them for teaching him about filming dance, it was largely his dissatisfaction with the results that caused him to persist. "The numbers in *Rio* were put together rather hurriedly, I thought, and I was not at all pleased with my work."[9] The success with the audience, however, caused him to react, "if they think that's good, surely I can do something better...."[10] And it was with the series films themselves that he was able to overcome his dissatisfaction with the fragmentation of most cinematic dance and, in turn, to assert his role as a dancer, thus having, as Gordon Gow suggests, "... the performer taking precedence over the medium...."[11]

The Astaire-Rogers series is an example of a possible theory of *performer* as auteur, for each of the films is dominated by the style of its stars. The narratives, the songs, and the visual rhythms seem to be a direct result of their foot-loose and easy-going personae. Each of the series films is consequently similar, being a variation on the formulas of each preceding one. Astaire always felt the necessity to explain his ability to dance within the narrative; he establishes early in the films that he is a professional dancer, thus providing his "right" to dance his way through his private life as well. In *The Gay Divorcee* he has to dance for his supper in a Paris club when it seems that both he and sidekick Edward Everett Horton have forgotten their wallets. (This role, in fact, was changed from that of a writer in the original show, *The Gay Divorce,* to that of a professional dancer for the film; Astaire thought that was better because it made the numbers drop "into place more naturally."[12]) In *Top Hat* he shocks the members of a staid British men's club as he does a tap routine while leaving their reading lounge; in *Shall We Dance* he is a ballet dancer who, tired of that role, wants to master popular dance. Even when Astaire is not a professional dancer during his role in the film's diegesis, motivation is provided by allusion to some dance background: a sailor in *Follow the Fleet,* he and Rogers were, nonetheless, dancing partners prior to his enlistment, and in *Carefree,* his furthest remove from professional performing, he is a psychiatrist—but one who had wanted to be a dancer in his youth. And, of course, the role is epitomized in his casting as Vernon Castle in *The Story of Vernon and Irene Castle.*

The plot lines of the films are also similar. Astaire usually meets Ginger Rogers through a series of minor accidents which antagonize her, but for Astaire it is always love at first sight. In *The Gay Divorcee* they meet when Rogers gets her dress caught in a trunk and Astaire cuts it off to set her free. In *Top Hat* he awakens her when he dances in the hotel room above hers; that situation becomes complicated when she mistakes him for her best friend's husband and is infuriated that he is making a pass at her. In *Shall We Dance* he falls in love with her picture before he ever meets her and consequently insinuates himself into her life as they return to the States on the same ship. Although he has known and worked with her in *Follow the Fleet,* he, nonetheless, alienates her in his attempts to win her, causing her to lose her job, for example, and to fail an audition when he puts bicarbonate in her glass of water, mistakenly thinking it is meant for someone else. The song and dance routines become the rituals through which the two work out their animosities, leading ultimately, of course, to love. Astaire usually manages to get Rogers alone, away from the public, in a park or summer house somewhere, and there almost convinces her of his sincerity. She joins in the song and dance ("Night and Day," "Isn't It a Lovely Day to be Caught in the Rain?"), almost convincing herself of his love; at the end of the ritual, however, her illusions shattered, she demands that they return to her friends. Naturally, the films end happily; with the help of the standard group of supporting players, Edward Everett Horton, Eric Blore, and Helen Broderick (or Alice Brady, Victor

Moore, Luella Gear, and second leads like Randolph Scott, Jack Carson, Harriet Hilliard, and others, depending on the individual films), Astaire and Rogers do get together. Rogers does not marry the foreign gigolo (Erik Rhodes, Georges Metaxa) or the unstylish American—Ralph Bellamy in *Carefree*—and the films often end with an elaborate climactic dance routine ("The Continental," "The Piccolino").

The nature of the dance routines as rituals of courtship and lovemaking, as exhibition pieces, or as solo expressions of a character's moods and the relationship of those routines to the film's diegesis make the Astaire-Rogers series transitional films in the development of dance in the musical. The non-diegetic quality of most of the Berkeley routines and their lack of formal dance elements generally keep the Berkeley films from contributing to the development of dance. The Astaire-Rogers films, however, combine aspects of the integrated musical with the backstage musical; as a result, the dances function in multiple ways: they flow more or less naturally from the film's narrative; they serve as routines of a show within the film; they are dreams; they are both diegetically motivated and non-diegetically inserted into the narrative. The characters in the films are comfortable performing the numbers both on a stage and simply for each other; indeed, there is a quality of performance to the numbers at all times ("My numbers were built for applause reactions...," Astaire has said[13]) in the nature of both the choreography and the camera work. The films seem transitional because they echo Berkeley's work in the ensemble dance numbers (though without the extent of Berkeley's elaboration) while at the same time forecasting the interpolation of more intimate dance in the musicals of the late forties and fifties.

Those numbers which serve as routines from the shows within the film in a sense tie the Astaire-Rogers films most closely to their period, particularly inasmuch as they contribute to the requisite explanation that the Astaire character is a professional performer. Jerry Travers, a professional dancer in *Top Hat,* must be seen in his current London show and the "Top Hat" number itself is from that show, a number which, incidentally, was carried over from an Astaire stage show, *Smiles,* where it was called "Young Man of Manhattan." Astaire often had ideas which he wanted to incorporate into routines yet could not easily fit them into numbers which grew directly out of the film. Such numbers, more suited to the stage routines within the show, often used tricks or gimmicks for their appeal. In "Top Hat" he uses his cane as a shotgun to kill the men in the dancing chorus, finishing them all off at the end while tapping out sounds like machine gun fire. "Bojangles of Harlem" from *Swing Time* is another example. In an homage to Bill Robinson, a black-face Astaire uses trick photography in which silhouette shadows accompany him on a screen; paradoxically, of course, this "stage" number could be presented only on film.

Follow the Fleet presents a particularly interesting situation in that most of the numbers, while presented as part of a show—either in rehearsal or in actual performance—still retain the quality of identifying the Astaire-Rogers relationship. Their first number together, "Let Yourself Go," presented as the dance contest in the Paradise Ballroom where Astaire has discovered Rogers working, denotes the competitiveness of their relationship as they try to outdo each other with their dancing ability. Similarly, the humor of "I'm Putting All My Eggs in One Basket," a number in rehearsal for their show, reflects the state of their love affair at that point. Rogers, still annoyed that Astaire has lost her a job and ruined her audition, seems to be upsetting his plans for the dance even though it is obvious that her actions are built into the choreography. As she continues performing certain steps when he has gone on to others and when she bumps him off the stage and almost out of frame, she seems to be acting out her hostility for his interference with her life; she purposely does not cooperate in order to show that he doesn't have the control over her that he thinks he has. Finally, in "Let's Face the Music and Dance" (the courtship number reflective of "Night and Day" and "Cheek to Cheek"), their love stabilized and secure, they display their off-stage feelings in the on-stage performance. As they leave the stage together with the simultaneous deep back-bend, right leg raised to take them beyond the curtain, there is little doubt that they will remain together. Their relationship has developed into unity through the medium of dance.

These codes of courtship and love, however, are most often expressed in the dances which are integrated into the diegesis, and it is these routines which foreshadow the use of dance in later musicals. Astaire has spoken repeatedly about the necessity for integrated dance routines:

> It is extremely important for a dance cue to flow naturally in and out of the story. I think the audience always slumps—even more in the movies than on the stage—when they hear an obvious dance cue, and both the picture *and the dance* seem to lose some of their continuity. Each dance ought to spring somehow out of character or situation, otherwise it is simply a vaudeville act.[14]

Motivated by character or situation, the dances serve various purposes and spring from the narratives in many different ways, yet they still fit easily into the overall formula controlling the individual films. Solos in which Astaire acts out his exuberance, his depression, his joy; duets in which Astaire and Rogers explore their romantic involvement; and ensemble numbers in which a large group—usually led by the two stars—reflects the period's craze for dance all serve in specific films at one point or another to further the narrative thrust. This kind of relationship between the numbers and the film's plot line links the Astaire-Rogers series directly with both the MGM musicals of the forties and fifties—particularly the Kelly-Donen tetralogy—and with the more dogmatic experiments with the integrated musical which were taking place in the New

York theater. In spite of Astaire's comments, each dance did not get its motivation from the plot line; those which did, however, can serve as examples of both Astaire's style and the contributions which the films make to cinematic dance.

The solos which Astaire created for himself, though sometimes having only tenuous relationships with the diegesis, at other times do serve to characterize him as a dancer within the film as well as to suggest his feelings at the moment. In *The Gay Divorcee,* for example, he plans to hunt for Ginger Rogers in London, comparing the chore to hunting for "A Needle in a Haystack." Singing and dancing as he dresses for the search, he experiments with dance steps—particularly as he stands at the fireplace—almost as if he were experimenting with how to find her. As Arlene Croce has suggested, "here he demonstrates that screen choreography could consist of a man dancing alone in his living room."[15] After the number fades out, the film fades in to a montage of Astaire looking for Rogers among the women of London; the particularized problem presented through song and dance then becomes broadened in scope and made to appear as difficult as he imagined it would be. "No Strings (I'm Fancy Free)" serves a dual function in *Top Hat;* not only does it characterize the Astaire character Jerry Travers but also it brings him together for the first time with Ginger Rogers. Explaining himself to Edward Everett Horton while fixing drinks, he begins talking in almost-rhymed dialogue: "In me you see a youth who's completely on the loose. No yens, no yearning, [and then without a break sings] no strings, and no connections. . . ." The song leads naturally into a dance expression of that same footloose characterization, and in a single shot as he taps, the camera booms down to reveal Rogers trying to sleep in the room below. Here, too, the number takes on greater implications, for the dance gets interrupted when Rogers storms upstairs; Astaire resumes the particular number as a sand dance to lull her back to sleep, but in a sense the dance is really completed only when the two of them finally get together later in the film.

The solo dances present only one aspect of his interests, and, further-more, the solos often exist primarily to display that interest. "Slap that Bass" from *Shall We Dance,* for example, gives him the opportunity to dance with sets, props, and tricks since the motivation comes from the percussive rhythm of the ship's engines rather than from any plot device. Similarly, in *Carefree* he does a golf-dance with "Since They Turned 'Loch Lomond' into Swing." Ostensibly, he is showing off for Ginger Rogers who has him especially rattled at that point; actually, he is displaying an adroitness for multiple actions incorporated into dance. He plays the harmonica while dancing, does a jazzed up Highland Fling over crossed golf clubs, and taps between each stroke of his golf club. "Top Hat," "Bojangles of Harlem," and other numbers he does as a performer only reinforce the tenuous relationship of certain solo numbers to

the narrative. The duets with Rogers, however, seem more fully to complement the film. It is in this sense, then, that the interrupted solo of *Top Hat*
becomes complete when they dance together later in the film: theirs is a dance
relationship—expressed through dance, fulfilled through dance; when she
interrupts his solo in the beginning of the film, she becomes obliged to
"complete" it with him in order to fulfill the expectations their relationship has
established in all the films.

Each film contains at least one ballroom dance duet for Astaire and
Rogers, a number in which he tries to convince her of his love. Often, as in
"Night and Day" and "Cheek to Cheek," she is submitting to him only
momentarily and, in fact, doesn't really like him very much at the time.
Through those numbers, however, she is persuaded—even if only for the
duration of the dance—of his good intentions. (It is almost as if she believed
that someone who dances as he does cannot be all bad.) "I Used to Be Color
Blind" from *Carefree* presents their exhibition ballroom number as a dream.
A psychiatrist, Astaire has alienated Rogers by his attitude about her before
meeting her (she accidentally overhears his comments on a recording), but she
does agree, at his behest, to undergo a dream-inducing meal. The resultant
dream-dance makes her realize that she is in love with him. These numbers
usually occur within the narrative at a moment of exploration in the couple's
relationship, and the choreography itself reflects that exploration. Often
beginning tentatively, the dancing continues through a series of attractions
and repulsions—Astaire first pulling Rogers toward him, then her pulling
away—leading to precision duplication of movement—sometimes tap, sometimes circling the floor arm in arm, sometimes simply matching each other
step for step. The climactic moment of the choreography as well as of the
inherent drama of the routine comes with a series of fast circles ending in some
form of a lift (in *Carefree* the dream-dance reaches its high point when Astaire
and Rogers meet for their first screen kiss). Each number also ends with a
denouement of movement as they prepare to return to the world of their fellow
characters. The movements of the dance show the initial tenuousness of their
relationship, the development of her appreciation of his style, a fulfillment of
that relationship, and a diminishing of their contact as they separate to end the
number. Growing out of a narrative context, the numbers initiate the
relationship which will be fulfilled with the outcome of the film.

The Astaire-Rogers relationship, the character of their dance partnership,
and, indeed, the quality of the films themselves seem particularly explainable
in terms of the influence and control which Astaire has over Rogers both as
characters within the films and as dancer and mentor during the preparation
of those films. Theirs was not a true partnership of equals; it was, instead, a
Pygmalion-Galatea/Svengali-Trilby relationship. Although Ginger Rogers

was a performer with a considerable reputation prior to being paired with Fred Astaire, nonetheless it was a result of his influence and teaching that she came to be known as a dancer. Speaking some years later, Astaire acknowledged a refusal to work further with non-dancers.

> It's been quite a collection . . ., Joan Crawford, Ginger Rogers, Joan Fontaine. They dance with me, then go on to win Academy awards for their acting.
> . . . Why, they've even suggested I dance with Hedy Lamarr. Somehow, I'm supposed to be able to make a dancer out of any girl. If she's so much as danced in the chorus I can make her great. Well, it's not true.[16]

In spite of that disclaimer, Astaire did mold Ginger Rogers into a partner to suit his purposes. In general Arlene Croce contends in *The Fred Astaire and Ginger Rogers Book* that Rogers improved as the series progressed because Astaire had made her a better dancer; she "had turned from brass to gold under his touch. . . ."[17] Although that may be too judgmental a statement of Rogers's abilities, it is evident from looking at the films that she does perform trickier material and more complicated steps and patterns and that she follows Astaire more closely in the later films. Preparing to choreograph *Yolanda and the Thief* with Astaire in the 1940s, Eugene Loring looked at all the Astaire numbers edited together, and he remarked: "We sat for about six hours, and it was marvelous to see Ginger Rogers when she could hardly walk and then later really develop."[18] In *Carefree,* their next-to-last film together at RKO, "the partnership seems more solid than ever," according to Croce. "Astaire and Rogers never stopped proving themselves. In this film they even seem to have reached a new understanding of each other, a new intimacy and confidence in their dancing and in their scenes together. . . ."[19]

In an interesting parallel to the way Astaire brought Rogers to life as a dancer, the roles they play in the films reflect a similar situation. The Astaire character frequently molds the Rogers character into some vision he has of her—usually as his wife—"rescuing" her from her own vision of herself or from some other man's grasp. The dance duets become manifestations of this Pygmalion-Galatea relationship, as well. In almost all the films the first way he must change her is to get her to like him. Although at first he blunders in many of his attempts, ultimately he does change her. In *The Gay Divorcee* he rescues her from a predicament by cutting her dress, which, of course, antagonizes her. He spends most of the rest of the film attempting to make up for that mistake. By clearing up her impression that he is the hired co-respondent in her divorce suit, he convinces her of his affection. He also rescues the two of them from "imprisonment" in her room in order for them to go to the esplanade to dance "The Continental." Similarly, mistaken impressions in *Top Hat, Swing Time,* and *Shall We Dance* must be cleared up before they can get together. In *Shall We Dance,* as well, he even creates multiple images of Linda Keene, the Rogers character. Not being able to dance with Keene, he has the entire chorus wear "Ginger Masks" in the title number, only to discover Keene herself behind one of the masks during the routine. As part of the number, therefore, he reveals the true character behind the masked one, and together they display their love in the final, brief duet. Perhaps the strongest support of Astaire's mesmerizing control over Rogers occurs in *Carefree* where, as a psychiatrist, he literally controls her feelings by hypnotizing her. Although she loves him, he hypnotizes her and tells her to forget him—only winning her back by re-hypnotizing her to release her from the control of the previous instruction. Related to screwball comedies of the same era, *Carefree* also presents Rogers in a series of whacky, uninhibited actions, the result of being anesthetized by Astaire in an attempt to free her inner self. Considerably later in their careers, Astaire and Rogers were reunited by MGM in *The Barkleys of Broadway,* a film in which the suggestions of Astaire as a Svengali, implicit in the earlier films, are made manifest. The problems within the narrative spring from Dinah Barkley's dependence on her husband. Rogers, as Dinah, rebels when Hans Conried, as a painter, conceives of their relationship in terms of a pancake (Dinah) molded by the frying pan (Josh Barkley-Astaire) and, when asked for his reasons, explains that theirs is an association like Pygmalion and Galatea or Svengali and Trilby. Ironically for the Rogers character, when she leaves her husband in order to become a dramatic actress, he—unknown to her—shapes her performance and creates her success. *The Barkleys of Broadway* was, in fact, a not too subtle parody of the Astaire-Rogers partnership, growing out of the on-screen myth of her submitting to him through dance as well as referring to their off-screen association: Astaire as teacher, leader, trainer; Rogers as pupil and follower.

The dances themselves also reflect the recurrence of the Pygmalion-Galatea myth within the Astaire-Rogers films. Describing those dance duets, John Russell Taylor says:

> Again and again the movements play out a small drama of difficult courtship: Astaire beckons and enchants with mesmeric hand-movements, Rogers almost against her will drifts into concerted movement with him, a close rapport is established and grows in romantic abandon to a point where everything stops, a pause, a decisive moment after which Rogers breaks away, or tries to, and has to be summoned back. A constant hallmark of Astaire-Rogers routines is this magical pause, a hesitation seemingly on the brink of something attractive yet frightening—of really deep emotion perhaps.[20]

Taylor's emphasis on the mesmerism and magic of their numbers also suggests the qualities mentioned above. In the reprise of "Change Partners" from *Carefree,* Astaire incorporates hypnosis into the dance. His gestures replicate the gestures he used earlier in the film to put her under his spell. In "Let's Face

the Music and Dance," part of the show within the film of *Follow the Fleet,*
Astaire saves Rogers from jumping to her death (as he is on the way to shoot
himself); when he begins to dance, his gestures are identical to those in which
he attempts to dance-hypnotize her during *Carefree.* The only variation in this
image of mesmerism between the two films is a difference in camera position.
The sense of control which Astaire holds over Rogers is not so evident as in
Carefree but is certainly present in their romantic dance duets throughout all
the films. Their synchronous movements—always dictated by him—lead into
supported lifts during which she is completely dependent on him. The
relationship between male and female dancers is often one of support and
dependence, yet compared to similar situations in other films, the Astaire-
Rogers dances take on unique significance. Lifts are relatively rare with Gene
Kelly, for example, except when he is being consciously balletic as with Leslie
Caron at the end of *An American in Paris* or with Cyd Charisse in "The
Heather on the Hill" from *Brigadoon.* And even Astaire himself when dancing
with certain other partners often eschews the image created with Rogers. With
Eleanor Powell in *Broadway Melody of 1940,* for example, Astaire is in no
way able to control her performance; their duets are clearly those of equals—
indeed, competitors. When paired with Rogers, however, Astaire—in his
roles—seemed to cast her under a spell during which she became subject to his
whims and desires. The Rogers character lost her sense of disdain for him and
no longer objected to his attention. Away from the world in "Night and Day,"
"Cheek to Cheek," and "Isn't It a Lovely Day . . .," she willingly submitted to
him and thus "came to life" while falling in love. Her return to her former
attitudes at the end of each dance—when the spell was broken, so to speak—
only reinforce the "magical" power which the Astaire character seemed to
have during those dances.

The big dance routines which frequently serve to climax the films can be
perceived as links to the other musicals of the period, particularly the
Berkeley-choreographed films, and to the large ballroom dance crazes of the
thirties such as the Lindy. Within the individual films they often serve as well
to bring together all the personnel into one number which Astaire and Rogers
lead. Astaire and Rogers were first paired in such a number, "The Carioca," in
Flying Down to Rio, and in the subsequent films the large production routine
seemed to be the climactic point—a celebration—of their resolved relationship as well as of the film itself. As the series progressed, however, and they
established themselves as dancers of more intimate routines, the big number
became less important; similarly, in the later films, the big number became
more influenced by *their* style. "The Continental" from *The Gay Divorcee,*
therefore, is flamboyant with many performers and lasting more than fifteen
minutes. "The Yam" from *Carefree,* on the other hand, is an elaborated

Astaire-Rogers routine, led by them and characterized by a dancing style recognized by that time to be their own.

The ensemble numbers are usually presented as night club routines, yet they relate to the diegesis as expressions of fulfillment of the Astaire-Rogers relationship. "The Carioca" is a production number in a club where the band to which they belong is playing. The audience joins in after Astaire and Rogers introduce the song. "The Continental" is also a night club number, but one which Astaire and Rogers (and seemingly everyone else staying at the hotel in Brightbourne) join. This number also serves as a further elaboration of their screen relationship, though, for having finally come to an understanding of Astaire's role, Rogers wants to dance with him, and he concocts a scheme for them to get away from her hired co-respondent. Once on the dance floor, they are able to express their joy with each other, visually "echoed" by the black and white-costumed chorus members. Furthermore, a slight sense of mystery and suspense is built up when Erik Rhodes as the co-respondent comes on to the balcony to join in the singing. "The Piccolino" also climaxes their on-screen relationship in *Top Hat.* Having been marooned together aboard a gondola as a result of Eric Blore's machinations, they again come to an understanding of their feelings for each other and, joined by the cast—and again in a night club setting—dance "The Piccolino" as the expression of their finally fruitful romance. "The Yam," the last of such production numbers in their films, is both smaller in scale and different in diegetic function. It comes in the middle of the film, rather than at the end, is the result of Rogers's role as a well-known singer, and does not serve as an expression of their fulfilled relationship. Only in *The Story of Vernon and Irene Castle,* where Astaire and Rogers (through their role as the inventors or introducers of the Castle walk, the maxixe, the tango, and others) would somewhat naturally lead larger ensemble numbers, did the series return to a dance style which—though present in other thirties films—Astaire and Rogers had together replaced with an intimate, self-expressive kind of popular dancing.

Although Astaire is only occasionally listed as being in charge of the dances on his films (*Roberta* is the only series film which credits him for the dances), in general the evidence shows that he designed the dances (especially his solos and the duets), controlled the camera work during shooting, and supervised the editing. The credited dance director, serving as an assistant to Astaire or responsible for the large routines, usually made little contribution to the dances themselves. Dave Gould was credited for the dances in *Flying Down to Rio* and *The Gay Divorcee,* Hermes Pan for the other films; by their wording, though, the credits do often imply the dance director's limited role: "Dance ensembles staged by Dave Gould" *(The Gay Divorcee);* "Ensembles staged by Hermes Pan" (*Top Hat* and *Follow the Fleet*) are examples. Writing about

Dave Gould (whom she characterizes as being of the "Berkeley school") and Hermes Pan in her chapter on *The Gay Divorcee,* Arlene Croce says, "Pan . . . did the bulk of the group choreography for the film, while Gould 'staged' it, i.e. devised the ideas and planned the camera angles. Gould's star fell as Pan's rose. Astaire wasn't interested in competing with Busby Berkeley; he was Berkeley's opposite."[21] Morton Eustis, writing in 1937 about the Astaire films to that date, comments, "Astaire works out his own steps and those of his partner. In pictures, he usually leaves the chorus routines to the supervision of the dance director, unless the dancing of the chorus has an important bearing on his own work, in which case he will outline routines for the girls and tell the dance director what he wants."[22] Astaire's intimate and eclectic "outlaw style," his concern for photographing dance in the most viable way for the enhancement of both the dance and the film, and his desire for continued variety ("I have always tried to carry out my steadfast rule of not repeating anything in dance that I've done before," Astaire said in his autobiography[23]) have all contributed to the distinctiveness of Astaire's films.

Marshall and Jean Stearns in their book *Jazz Dance* describe Astaire's eclecticism.

> The nature of Astaire's "outlaw style" is formed by the fusion of ballet, tap, and ballroom dancing, under the constant pressure of choreographing new dances. The process consists of arranging whatever styles and steps seem right—anything is right if it *works*—into an artistic whole according to Astaire's standards; the purpose, which shapes the standards, being simply to entertain by dancing some sort of story.[24]

It is difficult to compartmentalize Astaire's work because he does fuse the elements ("He used balletic turns . . . , but came out of them with a jazz kick and slide," observed dancer Cholly Atkins[25]), yet in general the routines follow certain patterns. He uses tap dancing usually in his solo routines, often emphasizing the beat with some external sound. "Slap that Bass" from *Shall We Dance*—supported by the beat of the ship's engines—and "I'd Rather Lead a Band" from *Follow the Fleet*—counterpointed by the sailors' marching feet—are two examples. Although he does tap occasionally in duets with Ginger Rogers, such dancing is used primarily for humorous effect as in the roller-skate tap, "Let's Call the Whole Thing Off," in *Shall We Dance,* "I'll Be Hard to Handle" in *Roberta,* or "I'm Putting All My Eggs in One Basket" in *Follow the Fleet.* More usually, social dancing, that is the exhibition ballroom numbers, characterizes his duets with Ginger Rogers where the languid style of couples arm in arm becomes a code of courtship and seduction. "Night and Day," "Cheek to Cheek," "Let's Face the Music and Dance," "Waltz in Swing Time," and "I Used to Be Color Blind" are the principal Astaire-Rogers ballroom dances. Ballet is less obvious in its influence because Astaire eschews routines that are completely balletic. "They

Can't Take That Away from Me" in *Shall We Dance* is the closest to a full ballet-oriented number in the series films. Astaire's role, however, is limited, and the piece becomes primarily a vehicle for Harriet Hoctor's *bourrées* while bent double backwards in the shape of a horseshoe. (Furthermore, the film's credits list "Ballet staged by Hermes Pan and Harry Losee.") Nonetheless, Astaire did use ballet turns, jumps, and steps incorporated into his other dance material and his use of ballet—limited though it was—did contribute to his overall attempt, as he stated in *Steps in Time,* "to cover ground and also get off the floor and up in the air a lot."[26]

The eclecticism seems to be a result of the variety in Astaire's dance training as well as the necessity to perform in many different situations during his years of partnership on the stage with his sister Adele. His early training was in ballet, but it was limited, and, indeed, he rebelled against its restrictions to a certain extent.

> Sometimes my work is referred to in terms of ballet, but I am not, of course, a ballet dancer. Ballet is the finest training a dancer can get and I had some of it, as a child. But I never cared for it as applied to me. I wanted to do all my dancing my own way . . . . I always resented being told that I couldn't point my toe *in,* or some other such rule.[27]

Astaire also retained a certain disdain for ballet as arty, a disdain which carried over into certain films. The good-humored anti-ballet/pro-popular dance attitude represented by the Astaire character in *Shall We Dance* (and in *The Band Wagon* later in his career) seems to reflect Astaire's own position: "But I do nothing that I don't like, such as inventing 'up' to the arty or 'down' to the corny. I happen to relish a certain type of corn. What I think is the really dangerous approach is the 'let's be artistic' attitude."[28] And choreographer Eugene Loring, who worked with Astaire some years later, has said: "If you say arabesque, then he doesn't want to do it. Ballet to him is sissy. I'd always have to say, 'When you stick your leg out in back.' I had to be very careful not to use ballet terms with him."[29] Nevertheless, he did use ballet. In addition to the previously mentioned turns—and, significantly, he almost always has Rogers doing balletic turns, as well—he frequently jumps in ballet fashion. At the end of "We Joined the Navy" at the beginning of *Follow the Fleet,* for example, he jumps into the air and beats his legs in *entrechats* on the way down; and during "Let's Face the Music and Dance" he jumps with his legs together out to the side and similarly does beats before landing. In *Shall We Dance* Pete Peters, the Astaire character, trying to convince Edward Everett Horton of the value of integrating tap and ballet, does an *entrechat trois* plain and then taps into and out of that same ballet movement, thus illustrating Peters's character as well as Astaire's own ability to combine disparate dance elements.

Astaire's training as a tap dancer also began early, but it continued throughout his pre-film career. He studied it seriously and revised and developed his tap style to suit his needs. His most important training seems to have been at Ned Wayburn's school in New York where he learned what was called musical comedy dancing—the simplest of tap steps and routines. He also received training indirectly from certain well-known black dancers. Adele Astaire studied with both Buddy Bradley and Herbie Harper; Harper is quoted as saying, "I'd teach her first, and he'd get it from her."[30] And Bradley said that "Fred based his tap on the clog dancing he learned with [Ned] Wayburn . . . which helps explain his highly selective use of tap."[31] Perhaps a more plausible explanation of his selectivity in using tap is that Astaire simply did not want to be tied to any one style and preferred instead to use his varied dance training to suit the goals of a particular routine. Tapping by itself did not suit Astaire, for as the Stearns wrote, "To be successful, each dance must revolve around an 'idea'—straight hoofing is not enough."[32]

> Fred Astaire developed a style of dancing, which although it did not employ the best tapping in the world, made good use of it in combination with other movements. "He uses a lot of old soft-shoe steps," says Charles "Cholly" Atkins, "like the scissors." He likes to write of himself as a "hoofer," which he decidedly is *not*, for the word usually designates the one-spot tapping of an old-timer who works only with his feet. "Fred dances beautiful," says James Barton, "but he's no hoofer."[33]

The Stearns go on to say that Astaire's "consistent use of tap reinforced the acute sense of rhythm on which all of his dancing is based." This sense of rhythm is particularly noticeable in certain of the solo tap routines, through the emphasis Astaire gives to the taps in "Top Hat," for example, or, later in his career, by the firecrackers used to "explode" the taps in the Fourth of July routine from *Holiday Inn*.

Astaire credits Aurelia Coccia as "the most influential, as far as dancing goes, of any man in my career"[34]; it was Coccia who taught him and Adele the tango, waltz, and other ballroom dances which they had seen the Castles perform and which would become the staple of their performances and subsequently the most identifiable type of dancing for Astaire on the screen. Mary Jane Hungerford has suggested that "the popularity of Astaire films is due as much to the exhibition ballroom numbers as to his solos. These duets apparently satisfy a fundamental human wish. All of us would like to be able to glide over a floor with grace and skill that never interfere with our faultless grooming . . . and in the arms of a partner whose face radiates undiluted bliss."[35] Combining the ballroom numbers with tap and ballet, Astaire was able to create an almost infinite variety in those numbers. A particular way he turns and lifts Rogers in their different numbers can serve as an example. In "Let's Face the Music and Dance" from *Follow the Fleet* the number begins as Astaire, saving her from jumping to her death, pulls her off the ledge and releases her into a three-turn spin; later in the number she turns into a *retiré* (one leg up, stork-fashion, against the other) and leans on him as they pause for a beat before continuing. By contrast, "Pick Yourself Up" from *Swing Time*—the lyrics of which seem to be giving the same advice as "Let's Face the Music"—is a humorous number, yet he uses turns and lifts which have a similar appearance but which stand out by their difference. The turns here are the last part of a double three-step combination (once to the left, once to the right); and the lifts are the ones back and forth over the rail around the dance studio. Finally, in "The Yam" from *Carefree* Astaire designed lifts quite similar in effect to the ones in "Pick Yourself Up," yet, here too, they are strikingly different, for instead of a railing which they alternately jump over, he extends his leg in front of him, foot supported by a table, and twirls her over the leg.

Dancer Charles "Honi" Coles has said of Astaire that "he's a *descriptive* dancer who works painstakingly with his musical accompaniment; he was the first to dance to programme music, describing every note in the dance."[36] Although Coles's statement is correct about only some of the dances, it does seem correct to a great extent about the tap routines where Astaire emphasizes the beat with his taps. The aforementioned "Top Hat" number is an example. Similarly, Astaire often moves or gestures in a way that seems a visual correlative to the sound. He will go up when the music goes up the scale and down when the music goes down, or he will slide as the music "slides" up or down the scale. As Arlene Croce has pointed out,[37] the tap routines often began with a simple rhythm but built up to a faster one. Astaire would frequently have the rhythm and timing of a song changed during a number in order to accommodate his desires. In "I'm Putting All My Eggs in One Basket" the changes are particularly pronounced to add to the comic effect as the band alternates between playing it as a languid waltz—with Astaire and Rogers dancing arm in arm—and as a fast, jazzy bit—with the two of them trying to keep up with both the music and each other. Having established expectations for a certain kind of choreographic interpretation of the music, Astaire would change his approach and purposely work against the music. Choreographing to the accompaniment rather than the melody; speeding up where the music seems to call for slowing down—and the opposite; doing simple movements where the drama of the number, as well as the orchestration, seems to call for complexity; and, in general, building his routines without the customary repetition of movement to accompany musical repetition all serve as approaches to Astaire's choreographic style. That style, determined by his training, his eclecticism, and the situation within the film, is characterized, therefore, by these several features: an illustrating of the music, every movement a natural outgrowth of the rhythm; a seeming contradiction, the use of dance against the music, thus defying the expectations built up by the first aspect of his style; sharp juxtapositions "from flowing movements to sudden stops, posing for a moment before proceeding to the next step—stop and go, freeze and melt"[38]; utilizing tricks, props, and gimmicks to underscore the dance movement; and, finally, a cinematic obeisance to the dance itself resulting in single-shot takes with the full-figured performer always centered in the frame.

The American popular song traditionally has been written in thirty-two measures with the form AABA and in 4/4 time. (The reason for this, as Alec Wilder points out in his book *American Popular Song,* is that "the dancing public demanded strict-time music in 4/4 in order to fox-trot properly."[39]) Astaire, though working very much out of that popular song tradition in creating his dances, had great variety in his material while still retaining a strong grounding in the four-beat rhythm. Choreographer Jack Cole in my interview with him pointed out that there are few waltzes in Astaire's films because of his preference for the four rather than the three-beat rhythm, thus supporting the observations of Stearns, Croce, and others about Astaire's dances. (Stearns: "Astaire always danced with some sort of a beat"; Croce: "Astaire used a strong beat in a ballad."[40]) Alec Wilder discusses the great variety in structure in songs written for Fred Astaire:

> . . . [Irving Berling] certainly tossed all his writing habits aside with *Cheek to Cheek.* For it is a highly extended song having the structure A (16 measures)-A(16)-B(8)-B(8)-C(8)-A(16). It's the added C element which amazes me. With Astaire, however, anything could happen, and maybe he had a need for this extra phrase.

> . . . every song written for Fred Astaire seems to bear his mark. Every writer, in my opinion, was vitalized by Astaire and wrote in a manner they had never quite written in before: he brought out in them something a little better than their best—a little more subtlety, flair, sophistication, wit, and style, qualities he himself possesses in generous measure.[41]

And Arlene Croce has pointed out that

> Except for the writing of the songs, Astaire controlled every phase of the development of a number, and there are probably numerous instances in which he even affected the actual composing. The songs did not pass through an arranger before they came to him. They came to him directly, and the arrangement was laid out, after weeks of rehearsal, at Hal Borne's piano. Astaire is himself a trained musician and he knew how to manipulate a composition for maximum theatrical effect without distortion. Composers trusted him. Berlin has said that he would rather have Astaire introduce his songs than any other performer.[42]

In addition to controlling the arranging of the songs, Astaire often directly controls the music by adapting it to his own ends. An article in *Photoplay* for April 1935 notes how Astaire started creating the dances even before he had the music and subsequently changed the music to adapt to his steps.[43] The

Astaire style seems, in a sense, to be a direct result of the music to which he had to dance, yet he also seems to have developed that music so that it could provide the variety and experimentation that he desired.

Visual symmetry would suggest that the general pattern of choreography would follow the aural pattern of the song, that a song which was structured AABA would have a visual equivalent in the dancing and, indeed, that is often true with choreography. A repeated musical motif is frequently the source of a repeated dancing motif. That is almost never true of Astaire's work, however. The general structure of Astaire's numbers is one of a constant building with new material. The repeats within the song and the reprises of the entire song—always with different orchestrations each time and often too with different accompaniments and harmonization as well—never are cause for repeat of dance patterns. They are, instead, cause for different patterns within the total. Once they start dancing to "Night and Day," the song is reprised four times, yet they never repeat a pattern once they have moved on to another. The second time the song is played a descant-like accompaniment in the strings becomes the musical grounds for their steps, for example. Toward the end the music slows down for dramatic effect, yet in defiance Astaire does a series of fast turns with Rogers in double time to the music. And the cadence of the song is completely rewritten to accommodate the ending he wants to give to the dance itself. Astaire works against the music in numerous ways in other songs, ways similar to and different from "Night and Day." He turns Rogers in double time to the music at one point toward the end of "Let's Face the Music and Dance," yet the very end of the number with its big orchestral sound shows them moving slowly and languorously against the normal expectation of that sound. The song itself ends with a four-measure tag which, during the dance, becomes the vehicle for the kick and bend with which Astaire and Rogers leave the frame. Astaire seems fond also of dancing unaccompanied by sound—often considered a "new" idea by recent choreographers— and will frequently tap during sixteen or thirty-two bar tacits. They tap four times unaccompanied during "Isn't It a Lovely Day . . . ," and after one of these tacits, they stop dancing when the music picks up . Breaks or sudden stops are something of an Astaire trademark and appear constantly in the ballroom duets; furthermore, they serve as examples of other aspects of his style, as he uses breaks both with and against the music. In "Let's Face the Music . . . " the first several breaks occur with the breaks in the music, and the poses are holds during silence. As the number progresses, however, the breaks occur at moments when least expected   not even on musical high points—and the poses are held while the music continues. The C or release section of "Cheek to Cheek" ("Dance with me. I want my arms about you. . . .") is not only musically striking, as Alec Wilder has noted, but also provides sharp choreographic contrasts. Tapping synchronously in the preceding B section, as the music suddenly increases in volume—the orchestra led by the brass section—Astaire and Rogers change pace immediately and together do *sissonnes* (ballet scissors jumps) across the floor; it is the only strictly balletic step in the dance and lasts only long enough to make a transition to the A section and a return to their more customary ballroom style.

Astaire's use of props and devices as elements of his dances would become considerably stronger later in his career when he would slide down a piano top in *Let's Dance,* break the glassware in a bar in *The Sky's the Limit,* dance in a toy store in *Easter Parade,* and choreograph gymnastic equipment in *Royal Wedding;* yet he displayed this penchant from his first films. In *The Gay Divorcee* he dances with his clothes and the furniture, tapping out rhythms with his hands on the mantelpiece and jumping over a sofa in "A Needle in a Haystack"; at the end when everything has been resolved in their relationship, he and Ginger Rogers reprise "The Continental"—now rewritten as a waltz—and he lifts her over a sofa, and together they dance up a chair to a table and down again. In *Top Hat* he accompanies himself as he dances by beating out the rhythm on the enclosed shelves along the wall during "Fancy Free"; he kicks the end tables as part of his tap routines and ends the number dancing with a statue he has almost knocked off its pedestal. Shortly thereafter he does the soft-shoe sand dance in order to lull Rogers back to sleep. His cane as a machinegun in "Top Hat," the roller skates in "Let's Call the Whole Thing Off" in *Shall We Dance,* the moving sidewalk, distorting mirrors, and other amusement park gadgets from "Stiff Upper Lip" in *Damsel in Distress,* the golf club in *Carefree,* the firecrackers in *Holiday Inn* all are further examples of his desire for innovation through devices and gimmicks both in his films with Rogers and in his films with others.

Astaire's dissatisfaction with the ways dance was filmed in the early thirties was echoed by almost all choreographers and dancers moving from New York to Hollywood at that time, yet Astaire was one of the few who did anything substantive about it. He subsequently gained complete control over the preparation, shooting, and editing of his numbers, but the first films still reflect someone else's presence, and, indeed, the contrast between his own numbers and those under another person's control in his later films is quite evident. In an interview-article in *Theatre Arts,* May 1937, Astaire expressed strong feelings about the nature of filming dance.

> In the old days . . ., they used to cut up all the dances on the screen. In the middle of a sequence, they would show you a close-up of the actor's face, or of his feet, insert trick angles taken from the floor, the ceiling, through lattice work or a maze of fancy shadows. The result was that the dance had no continuity. The audience was far more conscious of the camera than of the dance. And no matter how effective the trick angles and cockeyed shots might have been in themselves, they destroyed the flow of the dance—a factor which is just as important on the screen as on the stage.

I have always tried to run a dance straight in the movies, keeping the full figure of the dancer, or dancers, in view and retaining the flow of the movement intact. In every kind of dancing, even tap, the movement of the upper part of the body is as important as that of the legs. Keeping the whole body always in action before the camera, there are certain obvious advantages that the screen has over the stage. You can concentrate your action on the dancer; the audience can follow intricate steps that were all but lost behind the footlights, and each person in the audience sees the dance from the same perspective. In consequence, I think that the audience can get a bigger reaction watching a dance on the screen than behind a fixed proscenium arch—probably because they get a larger, clearer and better-focused view, and so derive a larger emotional response.[44]

The numbers in *The Gay Divorcee* look like Astaire's description of early dance on the screen. There are several changes in camera position in "Night and Day," including a shot through lattice work, and "The Continental" with its numerous changes in personnel and dancing style and its numerous cutaways to details of plot is almost a model of the style Astaire would reject.

General observation suggests a fairly strict ordering of the camera during the routines. The song itself is usually in medium shot, sometimes in one take but also frequently in several shots from different angles; as soon as the dance starts, though, there is a cut to a full-figured long shot, and the camera keeps the dancers centered in the frame. Many of the numbers—particularly the ballroom duets—are thus shot in one take: "Cheek to Cheek," "Waltz in Swingtime," "Let's Face the Music and Dance," for example. Astaire usually worked with three cameras, each filming at approximately eye-level, one in the center, one to the right, and one to the left, with the best of the three being chosen for the final film.

"The 'B' rush, taken a little from one side," says Astaire, "sometimes has a more interesting composition than the direct shot. One shot may be more alive than the next. It is almost impossible to be sure which recording will be the most satisfactory; the eye of the camera is so entirely different from the human eye. It can look at you from different angles, follow without altering the perspective. If possible, one 'take' will be used for the whole dance. If, however, the 'B' take is much better in one sequence while the 'A' is better in another, the best sequences are pieced together, but the sequence of the dance itself is never broken. The audience may be conscious of a change of angle, but it will never be conscious that the flow of the dance has been interrupted."[45]

Those moments in which the dance continuity is interrupted stand out markedly, yet they do tie the number closely to the film's narrative. In *Shall We Dance* the Astaire-Rogers duet to "They All Laughed" contains a number of cutaways to Ginger Rogers in close-up during the breaks in the dance (breaks which consistently correspond, incidentally, to breaks in the music), yet they work because the competitiveness of the number as well as the inherent dialectic between the nature of ballet (European, high art) and tap dancing (American, popular art) needs her reactions to give it force: she is surprised that Pete Peters, alias Petrov the Russian ballet star, can do the intricate tap numbers she has set for him. And "Let Yourself Go" from *Follow the Fleet* is not really a unified dance so that the cuts between the two competing couples and the cutaways to the sailors cheering for their buddy Astaire do not interrupt the *pastiche* nature of the routine.

A special "Astaire dolly" (which Astaire wrote to me that he had no knowledge of)[46] was used to maintain the camera/dancer relationship. According to H.C. Potter, the director of *The Story of Vernon and Irene Castle,* they used a forty millimeter lens with the lens about two feet above the ground (which seems low and not verified by the films), and "every time Fred and Ginger moved toward us, the camera had to go back, and every time they moved back, the camera went in. The head grip who was in charge of pushing this thing was a joy to watch. He would maintain a consistent distance, and when they were in the midst of a hectic dance that's quite a stunt."[47]

Astaire has a reputation as a diligent worker—indeed, taskmaster—in preparation of numbers. He would start preparing the dancers eight or nine months before production with actual rehearsals about six weeks on the routines. Eugene Loring has said, "He is an absolutely exhaustive, tireless worker. He would come into that studio at nine o'clock in the morning and rehearse until six. He is a meticulous worker, like a watch maker."[48] Barbara Jamison has written that ". . . rehearsals go on until every turn, every flip, every hop is letter perfect. Through it all Astaire is tight, unsmiling, and worried. He's the first one in the hall in the morning, the last to leave at night. He brings his lunch in a sack, eats in contemplative silence in his dressing room, and maintains a strict quarantine."[49] Together with his assistant Hermes Pan, they prepared the dances before Ginger Rogers saw them, and, in fact, Pan taught them to her. With Astaire he would dance Rogers's roles and with Rogers he would be Fred Astaire.

Opinion about Astaire's dancing varies. In an article in *Dance,* January 1947, Ann Miller said that Astaire's ballet technique was "just about the world's worst."[50] Fayard Nicholas does an imitation of Astaire which he describes: "I flap my legs out in a jerky figure-eight pattern and alternate between using my elbows with dangling hands and throwing my arms out like a windmill," and "Bill Robinson has been quoted describing Astaire as an 'eccentric dancer'—a rather unenthusiastic way of saying Astaire is no tap dancer but has a style of his own."[51] Some of the criticism is beside the point. His ballet technique may not be outstanding, but he makes no pretense to be a ballet dancer; indeed, he may use his defiance of ballet rules as part of his own style, for instead of using the turn-out necessary to ballet, he intentionally turns his legs in and rotates them and does ballet-inspired jumps and beats, all with legs turned in, thus creating a style out of his own physicality. Ballet did help him "release the upper part of his body before elevation, and showed that a dancer could use much more than his feet."[52] There are times, too, when Astaire's arms seem uncontrolled, particularly when he taps, yet he did use his arms and hands as part of the routines (Astaire and Rogers raising them in unison during "Waltz in Swing Time," for example) in contrast to most hoofers of the day who kept their arms and hands close to their body or simply extended them straight out during "trench" slides or similar big movements. Marshall and Jean Stearns feel that "Astaire's use of his arms and hands, and indeed his entire body, was one of his greatest contributions to American vernacular dance."[53] Calling Astaire an eccentric dancer seems a misapplication of the term because he is not an eccentric like his contemporaries Lee Dixon and Buddy Ebsen who were dancing in films of the thirties with styles based on moves which only their individual bodies seemed capable of making. Yet there are individual dances and individual movements which bring him close to eccentric dancing at times. He likes isolating leg movements, for example, so that one foot is tapping while the other is still or he taps one rhythm—an accompanying straight beat—with one foot while the other is tapping out a fancier, more involved and complex rhythm as he does in "Fancy Free" from *Top Hat*. Perhaps the most eccentric looking of the numbers in the Astaire-Rogers films is "Let Yourself Go," the contest dance at the Paradise Ballroom in *Follow the Fleet;* while competing with each other as well as with another couple, they perform some of their most intricate maneuvers. Basing the choreography on a solid tap ground, he nonetheless has them move quickly into and out of a two-step ballroom dance at one point and incorporates more free-form movements (at one moment doing a rotation of the hip and leg that looks like Bob Fosse's choreography) than is his wont. Stiff-legged turns in profile, jumps over one extended leg, and undulating bodies all suggest a side to Astaire that is seldom unleashed. Arlene Croce noted their "crazy legs" in this number, and that does suggest the eccentric dance quality. Ballet, tap, ballroom dancing in the fashion of the Castles, and even, perhaps, eccentric dancing contribute to the Astaire image, an image which most dancers agree is one with class: "poise, charm, nonchalance, grace, sophistication, elegance, and so on."[54]

Concern for dancing space as it is presented on the screen, an eclectic choreographic style which reflected his roots in musical comedy on the stage, and an interest in dances that were motivated in and of themselves while still serving as an integral part of the whole film make the Astaire-Rogers films important in the development of dance in the musical film. Existing apart from the social milieu in which they were made, the films make little reference to the Depression, and the dances reflect an attitude of escape: grounded in certain popular dance forms of the thirties, the Astaire numbers nonetheless display an ability and competence available only to the trained performer.

Astaire's contribution to film has been recognized since his debut. Writing in 1936, C.A. Lejeune said, "For Mr. Astaire, along with Chaplin and Disney, is one of the only really significant trio that the cinema has yet evolved."[55] Though the assumptions of her statement would be considerably challenged today, Astaire's reputation has not diminished. Working later in his career, particularly at MGM, Astaire would be influenced by some of his successors and, therefore, would modify some of his positions on filming dance, but Astaire's work with Ginger Rogers in the thirties did lead the way for further exploration of dance in the musical. Attempting to integrate the dances into the diegesis; having the dances serve as expressions of joy and sadness, as codes of courtship and love; exploring the relationship between camera and dancer, film and dance; and understanding the spatial concepts of both, Astaire created new possibilites for the use of dance in film. As Freda Bruce Lockhart has suggested, "Without Astaire we might never have seen musicals take wing, without him directors like Vincent Minelli [*sic*] and Stanley Donen might never have been inspired to reveal the reality of the dancing musical."[56]

5

Dance in Film (1930–1945)

During the thirties and early forties there were a great many musicals produced in addition to those associated with Busby Berkeley and Fred Astaire. Those other musicals were strongly influenced both by the Astaire-Rogers presence and by the Berkeley extravaganzas, yet they had qualities of their own, and the dance in those films was often important as representative of general trends in dance and occasionally as an influence on dance in later musicals. There were several major characteristics of dance in the period and these were represented by particular films, performers, and choreographers. It was an age of considerable virtuoso tap dancing, and dancers like Bill Robinson and Eleanor Powell, whose styles were primarily tap oriented, became leading figures in musicals because of their tap virtuosity. It was also an age of ballet; in an attempt to give status and respectability to a popular medium, producers—both on Broadway and in Hollywood—appealed to dancers and choreographers—notably Vera Zorina and George Balanchine— to attempt to incorporate ballet into musicals. But it was primarily an age of borrowing, an age of trying to duplicate the distinctiveness and success of Berkeley and Astaire. Other studios tried pairing their stars into musical teams as an Astaire-Rogers equivalent: George Raft and Carole Lombard were teamed in *Bolero,* 1934, and *Rumba,* 1935; and MGM seemed to be trying to find a steady—though non-dancing—partner for Eleanor Powell with James Stewart in *Born to Dance,* 1936, and Robert Taylor in *Broadway Melody of 1936* and . . . *1938.* Dance directors like Seymour Felix, Bobby Connolly and LeRoy Prinz had a similarity of style that made it seem as if they felt the necessity of incorporating each other's styles and motifs into their work. As a result, a large chorus routine (the dancers often in military costumes) was part of every major musical, even those musicals otherwise characterized by a different kind of dancing. The climactic routines in Shirley Temple's films, for example, were often extravagant with many special effects, huge sets, and numerous extras. Finally, the musicals were primarily back-stage stories, outgrowths of the revue tradition of the early years of sound, and the dances also tended to be conventional within that tradition: dance as spectacle rather than as an expression of some aspect of the narrative. They seldom attempted to integrate the dance into the diegesis, for integration was not one of their conventions. The use of dance primarily as an embellishment to the film would persist in musicals into the fifties; many dance directors didn't feel the need to adapt to the changes occurring elsewhere in dance, nor to the explorations into the dance musical occurring in film. What one might call the "thirties musical" lasted long after the thirties, side by side with a new and different musical form.

Almost every studio was producing musicals during the thirties, many of which had very little dancing. The Jeanette MacDonald operettas at Paramount and MGM did use social dance as codes of class (the grand ballroom dancing established the aristocratic nature of the people involved in Ernst Lubitsch's *The Merry Widow,* for example), but dance as integral to the plot would have been extraneous in these predominantly vocal musicals. More common, though, was the musical in which the numbers, including the dances, were almost exclusively a part of a show.[1] At Twentieth Century-Fox the films with Alice Faye in the thirties and with Betty Grable in the forties all followed the same formula, and the studio produced musicals through the early fifties which seldom reflected the changes in the genre being attempted elsewhere—particularly at MGM. With few exceptions (the characters expressing their happiness by dancing in their hotel rooms in *Moon Over Miami,* for example) the formula called for the dances to be performed in a show, and dance directors Seymour Felix in the thirties and Hermes Pan in the forties served as overseers of the dance as spectacle, which was the all-important motivation. John Kobal notes how much the use of color and sets played in this sense of spectacle, as well.

> The Fox colour processing was strikingly bold and gay, the tones vivid, the images razor-sharp. The fiery-furnace reds, pigeon-blues and peppermint greens, the yellows and oranges that seemingly burst from the screen, belonged to a deliberately hallucinatory colour scheme that heightened the fantastic effect of their big musical numbers—with girls as artichokes, girls as snowflakes, girls as the opening leaves of a water lily, and Carmen Miranda as a veritable one-woman citrus grove.

> The plot locations were exotic . . . , with boats cruising along tropic shores, horses racing over South American pampas, planes flying over Miami, disclosing vistas of breathtaking landscapes . . . .[2]

Primarily a singer, Alice Faye rarely danced in her films. The opening number of *Hello, Frisco, Hello* (directed by H. Bruce Humberstone, 1943, with dance director credit to Hermes Pan) is on a stage with the four principals kicking their legs simultaneously and the girls shaking their skirts. Usually, however, as when she sings "You'll Never Know," her face is kept in close-up, and the camera doesn't move. The regular dance numbers in the film, performed without the principals, serve as exhibition numbers for dancing that is reminiscent of circus tricks. A social dance being introduced at one of the clubs is called the grizzly bear; the dance itself is akin to a fox trot but with the added attraction of the girl being flipped over the guy's head. Another specialty number is "danced" on roller skates, recalling both Chaplin's *Modern Times* and the Astaire-Rogers "Let's Call the Whole Thing Off" from *Shall We Dance,* but the similarity stops there, for the self-imposed limits of those films give way here to another kind of spectacle. At one point, the male skater, holding the girl straight out in front of him with her feet around his neck, twirls her around in circles. Later he repeats the number holding her by a bit between his teeth, the bit attached to her feet. Unlike Alice Faye, Betty Grable did dance. Having begun her career in films working for Berkeley in *Whoopee* and having continued it in, among other films, *The Gay Divorcee* (where she "K-nocks K-nees" with Edward Everett Horton), Grable performed a variety of dances, all suggested by the exotic setting of the films: a hula in *Song of the Islands,* a Latin American heel tap in *Down Argentine Way,* an Irish jig in *Sweet Rosie O'Grady.* These dances are only ethnic by suggestion, however; the clothes indicate the type of dance it is supposed to be more than the dance itself does. There is no evidence, either internal or external—as there is, for example, with Eleanor Powell—that Grable was responsible in any way for her dances. Befitting the conventions of these films, dance had only a tangential relationship to the narrative. The star was usually a performer who was trying to gain her way to stardom (*Hello, Frisco, Hello; Tin-Pan Alley; Footlight Serenade; Mother Wore Tights*) or, alternatively, if she was not aiming for a show-business career, she was fortune-hunting someone who would take her to places where shows could be seen (*Moon Over Miami; Down Argentine Way*). In either case the dances were part of the shows produced, were entertainment at the night clubs visited, or were performances at parties attended by the principals.

Individual performers, successful as tap dancers, as eccentric dancers, or as specialty dancers, were common in films at the time and, indeed, continued into the fifties. Sometimes in major roles, (Eleanor Powell, Bill Robinson), sometimes serving as featured players (Lee Dixon, Buddy Ebsen), and sometimes present for just one or two numbers (the De Marcos, the Nicholas Brothers), these dancers are perhaps best characterized by their own particular styles. Their numbers are usually quite different from the other dances in the films and are in marked contrast with those of other dancers who appeared with them.

In a series of films at MGM from the mid-thirties to the mid-forties, Eleanor Powell danced with a number of different men, yet retained a style so unique that it seemed incidental that it was being performed in any special film. Each number could have been transferred among the various, films without destroying the sense of the film's plot nor of what the dance was attempting to do. (In fact, such a transfer did occur. The footage for the climactic on-stage performance of "Swingin' the Jinx Away" in Vincente Minnelli's *I Dood It*, 1943, was taken directly from Roy Del Ruth's *Born to Dance*, 1936. The only attempt to ground the number in the diegesis of *I Dood It* is an occasional cutaway to Red Skelton in close-up, supposedly watching the performance on the stage.) There is considerable evidence that Powell did her own choreography, for the routines are similar from film to film and her particular abilities and idiosyncracies are repeated in each number. Powell's style could perhaps even be called eccentric; it is a combination of gymnastics and acrobatics, ballet, and tap—with an emphasis on the latter. (Such a combination was unusual at the time because the training in several dance disciplines which would characterize work in the later forties and fifties had not yet begun to manifest itself on the screen; in addition, even when acrobatics became an important part of dance with Gene Kelly, Michael Kidd, and others, it remained exclusively male territory.) Acrobatics strongly flavored all of Powell's dancing, giving it a flamboyance which would otherwise have been missing. Her entrances during a number were often dynamic (running down staircases, sliding down poles—usually in glittering or sequined costumes) and the number built on that intensity to a rousing finale incorporating all of her specialties: high kicks, which made her at times look like a contortionist, moving directly into splits; a series of very fast *grandes pirouettes,* her leg extended in ballet's second position—a movement usually reserved for men; tapping into and out of cartwheels, butterflies, and back flips. Her entrance to the "Anchors Aweigh" number in *Broadway Melody of 1940* is made sliding down the mast of a ship, and the finale is a series of cartwheels. The sailor motif, used in several of her films, also occurs in "Swingin' the Jinx Away" where she performs on a ramp under, over, and among a series of crossed trombones. She used only certain aspects of ballet technique, those which showed her off to advantage. She dances on pointe, for example, in "I Concentrate on You" in *Broadway Melody of 1940* and ends the number with a series of very rapid *chaîné* turns; *chaîné* turns were, in fact, incorporated into many of her routines, in one of which—in *Rosalie*—she "bursts" through several paper-covered hoops while doing the turns. Tap dancing was her forte, though, and she often made other dancers in the films seem like amateurs when she came on. In *Broadway Melody of 1936* the "Broadway Rhythm" finale actually used that idea as its basis when she is the last of several dancers to perform at a producer's party, thus securing the recognition she has been striving for throughout the film.

In general, Powell's male leads were non-dancers: James Stewart in *Born to Dance,* Robert Taylor in *Broadway Melody of 1936* and . . . *1938,* Robert Young in *Honolulu,* Red Skelton in *Lady Be Good* and *I Dood It.* In *Broadway Melody of 1940,* however, she was paired with Fred Astaire, and the film presents an interesting view of different styles. Dance director credit on her prior films had gone to Dave Gould (shared in *Broadway Melody of 1936* with Albertina Rasch) who was principally a so-called idea man, and the conception of Powell's numbers does seem akin to that of the "flying" finale of *Flying Down to Rio,* which Gould had also done. Although Bobby Connolly had dance director credit on *Broadway Melody of 1940,* it is evident that his work is little different from Gould's: the similarity between "Anchors Aweigh" and "Swingin' the Jinx Away," each number ending with a chorus singing "Anchors Aweigh," is just one example. With both men it seems safe to say that Eleanor Powell designed her own steps, placing them within the setting arranged by a dance director who at that time was responsible for the total impression, including the camera set-ups, rather than the individual dances. With Astaire, however, there would be noticeable changes, for, although she prepared her solo material, they collaborated on the numbers they danced together.[3] In contrast to the other numbers in which she appears, the finale to "Begin the Beguine" has many of Astaire's trademarks. Her double number with George Murphy earlier in the film, "Between You and Me," has merely been to exhibit her; the number ends, for example, as he tosses her into the air and she lands in a one-kneed kneeling position. Although "Begin the Beguine" does start with Powell and a chorus line, the attention is transferred to Astaire and Powell and in a typically Astaire/atypically Powell long take with frontal camera, they tap together as Powell never did with her usual partners. Intricate syncopation to the already rather irregular beguine rhythm, emphasizing the regular musical breaks by dance breaks, and tapping to silence—all previously noted as elements of Astaire's style—predominate. Unlike his work with Rogers—where dancing in unison or precision tapping was the norm—here they compete with each other, their dancing often in counterpoint. The number ends with them matching each other movement for movement as they dance faster and faster, climaxing with a series of rapid tap turns around each other.

"We rather specialized in tap dancing for that film," Astaire wrote in his autobiography. "Eleanor . . . certainly rates as one of the all-time great dancing girls. Her tap work was individual. She 'put 'em down' like a man, no ricky-ticky sissy stuff with Ellie. She really knocked out a tap dance in a class by herself."[4] Powell's work with Astaire was curiously separated from any sense of partnership, however: ". . . the numbers with Eleanor Powell were not as successful as previous tap numbers with Ginger Rogers, because Eleanor had her own style, which she did not change, while Ginger copied Astaire exactly and fitted in more harmoniously."[5] Few attempts were made to integrate her dances into the narrative, for the dances represented an aggressive individuality which *was* the Powell persona. The stylistic consistency of her work manifested that persona in all her roles. Conventional costuming concealed neither the persona nor the style. In *I Dood It,* for example, Red Skelton dreams of Powell doing a Hawaiian dance, but it is Hawaiian only in costume, for she does her usual tap-augmented turns and spectacular kicks. Many of the films, furthermore, had a revue quality (each of the *Broadway Melody* series has sequences as parts of auditions, of shows being rehearsed, or of chance encounters interpolated into the plots in which some unusual act is displayed: a little girl who juggles, a group of trained dogs, or a man who sneezes, yawns, or coughs in a variety of ways) which suggested that she was one of a group of specialty performers brought together in front of one camera. Nevertheless, she stood out as the main performer of that group and as the character who achieved success because of her talent. Eleanor Powell was a dancer of ability, "perhaps the best," according to Marshall and Jean Stearns, of the white female tap dancers who achieved considerable fame on Broadway or in Hollywood. There were no other dancers quite like her at the time; only Ann Miller has been a possible successor to her style and the persona it suggests.

Other individual performers appearing in films of the thirties and early forties were often known as eccentric dancers, that is "dancers who have their own non-standard movements and sell themselves on their individual styles."[6] Eccentric dancers in general have often been black, but with the prevailing fear in Hollywood that black performers might hurt a film's chances of success, few got the opportunity to establish themselves. Those who did, however, left a strong mark, for their performances not only displayed their own individual talents but also represented the enormous influence—direct and indirect—which black dancers had on all other contemporary popular dancers. Blacks had invented tap dancing as we know it, and they had, in turn, taught it to whites who, in their turn, became famous exploiting what they had learned; teachers like Buddy Bradley and Herbie Harper made an indirect contribution to the development of dance in film even though they never appeared on the screen nor behind the scenes. But Bill Robinson, John Bubbles, the Nicholas Brothers, and a few others did make a direct contribution, appearing in a number of films, dancing in an uninhibited, spontaneous manner which contrasted sharply with the more refined adaptations which whites had made of their steps. Bill Robinson and the Nicholas Brothers were perhaps the most significant of these black dancers. They appeared in more films with a greater variety of roles than did other blacks (John Bubbles, for example, appeared in only three films, one being the all-black *Cabin in the Sky*), and they were widely admired. More important, however, were their appearances with white dancers. Although it is unfortunate that more of the great black dancers of the first half of the twentieth century did not appear in film, it is a fact that dance in film has been almost exclusively a white dancer's field. Robinson and the Nicholas Brothers, therefore, serve to represent the black dancer's contribution to the development of dance in the musical.

Bill "Bojangles" Robinson was perhaps the best known of the black dancers in film; he appeared in fourteen films (four with Shirley Temple), and choreographed one, *Dimples*, in 1936. Although Robinson was really a hoofer and not an eccentric dancer (" . . . Robinson did not make much use of his hands, nor did he employ body motion to any great extent—most of the action was from the waist down.["])[7], he did make it possible—by his very presence— for other blacks to appear in films. He went to Hollywood in 1932 having had a successful career in vaudeville and in the Negro musicals of the 1920's on Broadway, and it was in the films with Shirley Temple, *The Littlest Rebel, The Little Colonel, Just Around the Corner*, and *Rebecca of Sunnybrook Farm*, that he "led the way in breaking down a variety of economic and social barriers while creating a new and much larger public for vernacular dance."[8] Robinson actually coached Shirley Temple, and in the four films they become partners in using dance as a means of overcoming the Depression or of achieving their other various goals. In *The Little Colonel*, the film which gives him the greatest opportunity to dance, he plays Walker, the old colonel's butler and, as such, is the "little colonel's" confidant. Particularly known for his stair dance, Robinson uses it here to persuade Shirley Temple to go upstairs to go to sleep. Singing and humming his own accompaniment, he teaches her how to use the steps and the risers to provide the percussive sound, telling her, "All you got to do is listen with your feet." His dances were an expression of his control of a situation, of his calm, rational approaches to a problem, and of his ability to overcome seeming defeat. He uses his dances as a way of earning money for them to get up North in *The Littlest Rebel* and as part of the show to help people overcome the Depression in *Just Around the Corner*. As Donald Bogle has suggested,

> Robinson's greatest gift as a dancer in the movies was that his sense of rhythm, his physical dexterity, and his easy-going naturalness all combined to convey an optimistic—a copasetic—air. As he tapped across the room his sheer joy made audiences think that life after all was what you made of it. The real significance of a Bill Robinson performance was therefore never as much in what he had to say as in what he came to represent.[9]

Robinson actually had a very limited range in spite of the kudos he has received over the years. Writer Langston Hughes, for example, has described Robinson's dancing as " . . . *human percussion*. No dancer ever developed the art of tap dancing to a more delicate perfection, creating little running trills of rippling softness or terrific syncopated rolls of mounting sound, rollicking little nuances of tap-tap-toe, or staccato runs like a series of gun-shots."[10] More to the point, perhaps, was Ethel Waters's remark: "I wasn't knocked over [by Robinson's dancing] because I had seen other great Negro dancers who could challenge Bill Robinson or any other hoofer, including Fred Astaire . . . two of these men were King Rastus [Brown] and Jack Ginger Wiggins. . . . White people never saw them, but that's the white folks' loss."[11] His arms rarely moving from his sides, Robinson uses only several basic tap steps (The Buck and Wing, the Time Step, a few cross-over steps), though he does combine them rather intricately. The stair tap in *The Little Colonel* is primarily a toe followed by a double heel tap, also using a soft-shoe shuffle. The "Oh, Susanna" competition number with Shirley Temple in that same film has the same basic steps but does expand into somewhat showier material. He slides, for example, to the side with the supporting leg while the other leg wings out in the air from the knee down. On the whole, though, he avoided the somewhat acrobatic steps and routines which came to be referred to as "flash" (and even ordinary steps like Falling off a Log, Over the Top, Through the Trenches, and Shuffle off to Buffalo), for they simply were not to his taste. The limitations of his material on film may have been due to his age—he was in his sixties—but he did purposely restrict his range: "Robinson's career is proof that a tap dancer with technique and personality can make relatively simple tap dancing an exciting art."[12]

Bill Robinson appeared in his last film in 1943; *Stormy Weather* was an all-black revue tribute to Robinson with a suggestion of a plot stringing together the various numbers by such performers as Lena Horne, Fats Waller, Cab Calloway, the Nicholas Brothers, and Robinson himself (called Bill Williamson in the film). His dancing is even more limited in *Stormy Weather* than in his earlier films, though he does have one number during which he jumps from drum to drum, beating out the rhythms with his feet (Robinson didn't use standard soft-soled shoes with toe and heel metal plates; instead, he wore wooden-soled shoes[13] which would have given him the possibility of a full-shoe sound but which would have been more difficult to dance in because of their lack of flexibility). Yet he does come across as a person with "educated feet," as someone says in the film. In fact, within the film he just cannot keep his feet still; like Astaire in *Follow the Fleet*, where he starts to dance every time he hears the "Bugle Call Rag" fanfare, Robinson's feet start moving every time he hears a musical cue. Robinson's numbers are usually shot to accentuate his feet, as well, for they alternate between full-figured medium long shots and close-ups which show the intricate foot work. (This is true of his numbers with Shirley Temple, too. In those films the contrast between the filming of the intimate partnership and the filming of the full-blown production numbers—staged by Seymour Felix or Nick Castle—is particularly evident.) According to Marshall and Jean Stearns, Robinson's contribution to tap dancing in general was that he brought it up on its toes, giving a light and airy quality previously unknown. That quality is not especially noticeable in any of the films, nor is it suggested in the "survey" of his life in *Stormy Weather*. Rather, using his "superb sense of rhythm" and "easy nonchalance"[14] and in spite of his Uncle Tom reputation, Robinson paved the way for black dancers to appear in films—thus giving direct evidence of their indirect influence—and helped to overcome some of the barriers against black talent.

Among the other black performers who appeared to give evidence of the inventiveness and vigor of contemporary black dance were the Nicholas Brothers, a specialty team who excelled in "flash" dancing. First appearing in films with Eddie Cantor in *Kid Millions* in 1934 (when Harold was only ten and Fayard sixteen), they danced in clubs and on Broadway while alternately performing in about ten films through the late forties. Their style is agile and acrobatic, combining tap and even ballet with gymnastics. Perhaps best known for their splits, the Nicholas Brothers nonetheless sing as well as dance. Each film seems to contain one or two of their idiosyncratic routines and illustrates their background and training. They worked with people as disparate as Buddy Bradley, George Balanchine, and Nick Castle, and graciously give all of them credit for influencing their style. Although they never had any ballet training, they were impressed by ballet splits—with legs straight out in both front and back—as opposed to the usual splits of people like the Berry Brothers who folded the back leg under. They worked with George Balanchine in *Babes in Arms* on Broadway and credit him with giving them the idea for their most distinctive routine: the split-slide beneath each other's legs with the snap back onto both feet as soon as each comes through. (They repeated this particular movement in the "Be a Clown" number in *The Pirate* with Gene Kelly.) Another of their split specialties was the ten-foot leap into splits, used in *Down Argentine Way* and repeated in *Stormy Weather*, where they varied it by alternately jump-splitting over each other down an over-sized staircase, ending the number with simultaneous split-slides down ramps next to the stairs and a snap back into an erect position at the end. "It was Nick Castle who thought up their most difficult stunt . . . . 'He had us take a long run,' says Fayard, 'climb up a wall for two full steps, and backflip, no hands, into a split, bouncing up from the split on the beat. We're the only ones who could do it . . . .' "[15] To the song "Alabamy Bound" in *The Great American Broadcast*, they danced on suitcases and jumped through the window of a moving train; to the song "Chattanooga Choo Choo" in *Sun Valley Serenade* they danced on and off the platform of a train car.

What did the flash acts contribute to vernacular dance? In ballet the movements are entirely choreographed; among straight acrobatic teams, the routines are set . . . . The flash acts blow these customs sky high. They spice their routines with *ad lib* acrobatics. Without any warning or apparent preparation, they insert a variety of floor and air steps—a spin or flip or knee-drop or split—in the midst of a regular routine, and then, without a moment's hesitation, go back to the routine.

Flash dancers *compress* acrobatic and jazz dance together, creating a shock effect.[16]

Although it is doubtful that they would have ad libbed any of their routines during the shooting of a film, nonetheless, the Nicholas Brothers did use the "*ad lib* acrobatics" referred to by the Stearns. Furthermore, their influence—or at least the influence they represent—can be seen in other performers in other films: Donald O'Connor's backflips off the wall in "Make 'em Laugh" in *Singin' in the Rain;* Gene Kelly's bounces sideways on his hands and toes—body extended in push-up position—in *DuBarry Was a Lady, The Pirate* (where he does the bounces with the Nicholas Brothers), and *Invitation to the Dance;* Russ Tamblyn's toe-touching splits off a raised board in *Seven Brides for Seven Brothers* are just a few examples. The flash stunts of the Nicholas Brothers represent an extension of the meaning of the word *dance*, and their appearances in films make that extension a valuable and influential contribution to the medium.

Among the white dancers who appeared contemporaneously with these blacks were some who could also be called eccentric dancers. Although some—like Lee Dixon—would have only limited exposure, others—particularly Buddy Ebsen and Ray Bolger—would have successful careers as dancers and continue into other areas of show business. Both Ebsen and Bolger, limber-legged and agile, had distinct styles. In addition, their roles suggest something about the nature of dance styles as identifying character type. Always slightly comic second leads, they used dance in a completely unromantic way. Ebsen, particularly, played a boy-next-door type, someone to cheer up Eleanor Powell in *Born to Dance* and *Broadway Melody of 1936* and . . . *1938,* and his dances, accordingly, were witty and jovial. "Sing Before Breakfast," from *Broadway Melody of 1938,* is a trio (with Powell and Ebsen's sister Vilma) in which they encourage each other in their at-that-point unsuccessful attempts to make it on Broadway. Unusually tall for a dancer, Ebsen used his height to advantage. Towering over the other dancers, his legs moving in opposite directions from an undulating pelvis, Ebsen simply looked funny, thus causing the other characters within the film, as well as the audience, to laugh. Although Ebsen did use tap, it was his ability to use his gangly physicality in particular ways which gave him his special quality. Bolger, on the other hand, used his eccentric dance for multiple purposes. Having been trained in ballet as well as tap, Bolger was able to combine elements unavailable to less well-trained eccentric dancers. Before going to Hollywood, he had acquired a reputation as a satiric dancer on Broadway, imitating and parodying other dancers.[17] His first film appearance was in *The*

Great Ziegfeld, and he followed that with the role of the Scarecrow in *The Wizard of Oz,* continuing in *Sunny, The Harvey Girls, Look for the Silver Lining,* and others into the mid-sixties. Although the satiric dance for which Bolger first became famous was not particularly evident in his films, he nonetheless contributed specific movements which represent his humorous eccentricity. In *The Harvey Girls,* for example, he leads the group dancers in an imitation of the train moving in "The Atcheson, Topeka, and the Santa Fe," jumping into high strut steps as he undulates his body in a rhythm akin to the turning wheels of the train.

Perhaps the eccentric dancers' major contribution to film dance is that of humor. The nature of dance seems not to be humorous, in general. When a routine or number is funny it is usually a result of situation, costuming, setting, or some external source; rarely is the dance itself that source. Eccentric dancers, however, broadened the range of dance expression by making dance itself be a possible code of humor, although that was certainly not the only aspect of eccentric dance. The eccentric dancer's wont was to re-interpret traditional dance steps according to his own body—that body often disproportioned in some way—and, with a knowledge of traditional dance steps, one could delight in the variations. In addition, the dancer would often exaggerate movements or so grossly defy the musical and dramatic "require-ments" of the number that it would become a parody. In Minnelli's *Cabin in the Sky* both Bill Bailey and John W. Bubbles perform eccentric dances which illustrate these points. Bailey, on the scene because he has just delivered a new washer to Joe and Petunia, "interprets" the song "Takin' a Chance on Love" which Ethel Waters (Petunia) is singing to Eddie Anderson (Joe). Bailey's dance is exaggeratedly slow, his body seeming to ooze through the move-ments. All the steps and turns are performed at half-time to the music; at one point, however, in sharp contrast to the rest of the number, he does an alternating toe-heel tap with his right foot in triple time to the music: forty-eight taps to four measures. Bubbles, as Domino, the card sharp who is Joe's nemesis, performs a number called "Shine" which characterizes him as both humorous and sinister. Single-movement profile turns, with his head always back looking over his shoulder, his hat down over his eyes, and stylized struts up the stairs to the gambling room provide him with the means to express an exaggerated character through exaggerated movement. Although eccentric dance—like so much of vernacular dance—began to diminish in the forties, nonetheless it had influence which persists today. Much of Bob Fosse's choreography uses certain principles of eccentric dance but applied to non-eccentric dancers, and particular performers—because of their special physical attributes—continue to make dance into a representation of what only they can do. Most recently, Tommy Tune has been the exemplar of eccentric dancing in *Hello, Dolly!* and *The Boy Friend.*

Although there are many individual dancers worth considering during this period, certain ones seem to stand out as particularly representative of styles and movements within the musical. One such person is James Cagney who, although appearing in relatively few musicals (nine films out of sixty), danced in several important films which bear his particular mark but also conveyed a dancer's style to his many non-musical roles. Like many other dancers of the period, he had no formal dance training; unlike those others, however, he developed into a dancer of singular ability and became a star. Although he could be called an eccentric dancer in one sense (he simply looks different from other dancers), in no film does he display the usual eccentric dancer's ability to create inventive movement out of his own physicality. Always using standard tap steps and musical comedy routines, he molds them into something different with his body thrust forward at a slight angle, his chin jutting out, and his feet splayed. He got his first job as a dancer when, as a young adult in need of money, he went to an audition and copied the dance director's steps (asking him to repeat them once).[18] Busby Berkeley, who worked with Cagney on *Footlight Parade*, supports his abilities as a fast learner: "Cagney could learn whatever you gave him very quickly. You could count on him to be prepared. And expert mimic that he is, he could pick up the most subtle inflections of movement. It made his work very exciting."[19] Most closely identified with his role as George M. Cohan in *Yankee Doodle Dandy* (a role which he repeated in a guest spot in *The Seven Little Foys*), Cagney, nonetheless, energized all his roles as if they were being danced.

> There is a great deal of rhythm, for example, in the cockiness, the forcefulness, the dynamism of the star personality who is famous for his underworld or action-plot roles. Notice the way Cagney *climbs* a staircase, *whirls* around when confronted by a known or unseen enemy, *struts* down a street, or actually *bounds* into a scene. These rhythmic movements have personified hardness and fearlessness; the style being a compound of the dancer's agile grace and the hustler's electric energy.[20]

Cagney taps briefly with Ruby Keeler in *Footlight Parade* and dances again in *Something to Sing About;* however, his quintessential dancing role is that of Cohan, for he not only imitated Cohan's style and certain Cohan-associated steps but turned them into his own material, thus making one think of what Cagney does in *Yankee Doodle Dandy* as being what Cohan did on the stage. Certain steps and movements had always been associated with Cohan on the stage: a forceful swagger and strut accompanied by jabbing arm movements, indicative of the egotistical personality Cohan allegedly presented both on and off stage; the kangaroo step, a stiff-legged prancing strut on the toes; and the run up the wall of the proscenium arch.[21] Although LeRoy Prinz and Seymour Felix have dance direction credit on *Yankee Doodle Dandy*, it was Johnny Boyle who taught Cagney the Cohan routines. Cagney made them peculiarly his own. Befitting the musical biography of a theater person, all the numbers in *Yankee Doodle Dandy* are presented as if on the stage of a theater. Cagney's shortness is heightened by a slightly low angle shot for most dances, and he performs almost all the dance sequences sideways to the camera, moving from stage right to stage left and back, parallel to the apron. This presentation accentuates the forward tilt of his body, the stiff-leggedness, and the strutting quality of his walk. Furthermore, it emphasizes the feeling of Cohan always being in a hurry, a feeling carried over into the narrative itself because Cagney maintains the same rushed quality to his movements and gestures even in off-stage scenes. Helping to put on a show at West Point in *West Point Story*, 1950, Cagney taps and even interpolates some acrobatic movements in "The Brooklyn Number." And he does a short tap with Bob Hope in *The Seven Little Foys*, 1955. Although Cagney's fame does lie with non-dancing roles, he is often thought of as a hoofer because of the influence his dancing had on his career. He has not made the contribution to film dance of Astaire or Kelly, but he does represent the Hollywood dance man of the period: someone coming from a career in vaudeville or on Broadway who had a certain expertise in dance and turned that into a broader performing ability. George Raft and Pat O'Brien are two others who, though never quite so identified as dancers, did follow Cagney's route. Through performers like them dance as a force in the musical has, perhaps, influenced more than just musicals.

Perhaps the most pervasive and continuing influence on film dance which began in the thirties was the introduction of ballet. True, ballet had been present throughout; ballet dancers had been recorded on celluloid almost from the advent of film, and various Hollywood dance directors—notably Albertina Rasch—had introduced balletic elements into film; Fred Astaire and other dancers incorporated elements of ballet into their dancing styles. But as an element in its own right, ballet was not considered a proper dance medium for film. A number of factors would change that attitude, however. Ballet had been an increasing presence in America for almost twenty years. Following the Russian Revolution many dancers and others associated with Russian ballet—particularly the St. Petersburg Maryinsky troupe—emigrated to the West. Gradually, many of these people came to the United States where they became associated with already existing dance groups, often at opera houses, or started dance schools in the hope of someday preparing people for a troupe of their own. One major result was the increased excellence of dance training; another was the increased interest on the part of show business entrepreneurs, for ballet was becoming a commodity to be exploited as tap and organized extravaganza had been before it. "Ballet was in the air," Arlene Croce has written,[22] and it was only natural that Hollywood would try to make use of it in films.

Among Hollywood's first attempts to capitalize on this new interest in ballet were two non-musical films. Bronislava Nijinska was hired to stage the dances for *A Midsummer Night's Dream*, the Max Reinhardt production for Warner Brothers in 1935, and Agnes de Mille designed the dances for MGM's *Romeo and Juliet*, directed by George Cukor, in 1936. Excluding incidental moments of ballet such as Harriet Hoctor's dance in *Shall We Dance*, the first film musical to wholly import a ballet troupe was *The Goldwyn Follies*, which used two numbers choreographed by George Balanchine and danced by his American Ballet Company. Balanchine, an *émigré* from the Maryinsky company, had been a dancer and then choreographer for Serge Diaghilev's *Ballets Russes*, but after Diaghilev's death and several unsuccessful attempts to involve himself with other projects in Europe, he traveled to New York where in 1934 he co-founded the School of American Ballet, the base of all his operations since. In 1936 Balanchine provided the dances for the stage version of Rodgers's and Hart's *On Your Toes*. (It was with this production, according to Bernard Taper, Balanchine's biographer, that he first instituted the use of the term *choreography by* as part of a Broadway production's billing.[23]) Samuel Goldwyn became interested in Balanchine's work as a result of the success of *On Your Toes*, and commissioned him to create the dances for his revue *The Goldwyn Follies*, the last project for which Gershwin contributed material prior to his death.

> It had occurred to Balanchine even before Gershwin's death that Gershwin's *American in Paris* suite might be suitable for ballet, and now together with Ira Gershwin he worked out a libretto. In this project Balanchine intended to put into effect his ideas about ballet in movies. The possibilities of the medium intrigued him, and the opportunity to try out some of his conceptions had been one of the temptations that had lured him to Hollywood. A movie ballet, he felt, ought not to be merely a stage ballet on film. It need not be a continuous dance observed from a fixed angle, as the stage required, but could be a montage of dance shots, photographed from whatever angle or distance one wished. And it could employ effects the stage could never achieve, especially in the realm of fantasy, which seemed to Balanchine a quality particularly suited to the film medium.

> The *American in Paris* ballet was conceived of as a fantasy quest. The milieu was to suggest the Paris Exposition, through which an American, portrayed by the tap dancer, George King, would search for Zorina, the girl of his dreams. Seductive, tantalizing, ever elusive, she would manifest herself now here, now there—at one moment in a Spanish pavilion, another time in a Ferris wheel, yet again high overhead among the stars of the zodiac in a planetarium—always just beyond reach, and vanishing each time just as the American was about to take her in his arms. It would be the first ballet that had been expressly designed to take advantage of the motion picture camera's resources.[24]

Goldwyn rejected Balanchine's idea for the ballet. (It may be a sign of how film dance had progressed by the early fifties that Gene Kelly's *An American in Paris* ballet could be so similar in conception to Balanchine's imagined one.) He asked Balanchine ". . . to make for me a ballet I can put a chair in front of and enjoy, without having to worry about how it's going to work out and how much it will cost if it doesn't."[25]

Balanchine "conceived and staged" (credit as a "choreographer" was not yet to be given on the screen) two ballets for *The Goldwyn Follies*. The first was a Romeo and Juliet dance, done as an on-stage production within the film, in which two different dance styles become means of characterization: the Capulets are ballet dancers, the Montagues jazz dancers. The two families compete with each other through dance with the Capulets coming across as somewhat effete, elegant, and reserved, whereas the Montagues are vibrant, earthy, and energetic. At the end of the number, each has learned from the other, and part of their lesson in tolerance means not only understanding the other's style but adopting part of it as well. The second ballet was a more traditional ballet of an ethereal creature emerging from the water during a pool-side party, dancing with one of the guests for whom she represents some idealized vision, and returning to the water, leaving him with only memories of the experience. "In ballet," as Taper says, "people are always falling in love with nymphs or birds, and having to suffer for it. The art form is better suited than any other for expressing the unconsummatable. So at the end the nymph returns to her watery element, and the human lover is left forlorn beside the pool."[26] Taper's comment also suggests something about the range of dance expression in film made possible by the introduction of these two full-scale ballets. Ballet itself could become a code of characterization or even representative of a broad spectrum of interpretation: it would, very shortly, become consistently a symbol of high culture (as it had been with Astaire in *Shall We Dance*) and more popular, vernacular dance would symbolize popular culture, and the dichotomy between the two—a recurrent theme in movies from *Dance, Girl, Dance* to *The Band Wagon* and beyond—would usually be played out through dance. Dances of ethereality, imagination, and dream would more likely be presented through ballet than through the other dance forms.

Balanchine did not get to experiment quite as much as he wanted on *The Goldwyn Follies*, nor was he in any way the first person who had "expressly designed [a ballet] to take advantage of the motion picture camera's resources." *The Goldwyn Follies'* dances are shot full figure with relatively few shots, each shot being of an isolated section of the dance. In an interview with Louis Marcorelles in 1957 Balanchine said,

> In close collaboration with Gregg Toland, I shot only one take per section of the ballet, and always with a single camera. I had myself established a very detailed shooting script, from which I didn't vary a single second; even before shooting my editing was already fixed in my head. In fact I didn't reject a single meter of film in my final editing.[27]

Balanchine was also given "dance direction" credit to recreate his material for *On Your Toes*, but there is considerable difference in shooting style compared to his previous film. "Slaughter on Tenth Avenue" (again a number presented as a stage show within the film), particularly, has camera movement which participates to a certain degree in the choreography. The camera frequently dollies into close-up when no actual dancing is going on; there are shots made with a tilted and upside down camera and speeded up motion, all used to express particular emotional states. One necessary change was used to cover the fact that Eddie Albert had a stand-in for the intricate tap dancing: a medium close shot of the stand-in holds on his hoofing feet for one long take during his special part of the whole number. David Vaughan has written that the dances in On Your Toes "compare unfavorably with the stage originals: inevitably, subtle comic and dramatic effects were broadened."[28] (In "The Princess Zenobia" parody of Scheherazade, for example, much of the humor derives from the almost farcical mistakes Eddie Albert keeps making.) But Vaughan's criticism may miss the point, for Balanchine was probably trying to achieve something different on the screen. "It is possible," Balanchine has said, "to transpose any ballet, classical or modern, to the screen, on condition that it be reconceived entirely in terms of film, that is to say, taking into account the fundamental optical difference between the stage and the screen. In the theatre each spectator has a different view of the spectacle; in the cinema each one sees the same thing, exactly from the same angle."[29]

Balanchine's influence on dance in film is not limited to his film work itself; rather, as one of the leading dance figures in the world he has trained or indirectly motivated almost every dancer appearing from the forties on. The actual film work is simply a representation of the increased use of ballet on the musical stage and subsequently on film. Although he has shown himself to be concerned with ways of photographing dance, he has never expressed an interest in the musical itself nor in the general function of dance as part of the musical. The Goldwyn Follies is a revue in which the numbers are strung together by a plot of a producer looking for talent as he is putting together a film. "Slaughter on Tenth Avenue" is linked to the plot of On Your Toes in that at the end of the number the lead dancer is shot by one of the gangsters hunting for him throughout the film, but it is still an isolated stage performance. And his Swan Lake recreation was simply tacked on to the end of I Was an Adventuress with no attempt made to explain it. But ballet had come into film as it had onto the Broadway stage, and its performance by particular performers—more than its use by particular choreographers, in fact—would persist through the sixties.

The eclecticism which has characterized particular dancers' styles, particular films, and, indeed, the ability of Hollywood in general to adapt for its own purposes the resources of all the other arts has characterized dance in general in the musical film. This eclecticism would, in fact, keep the Hollywood musical vibrant and energetic, allowing it to combine vernacular dance and ballet at a time when the Broadway musical seemed beset by a self-conscious artiness and pretense which would ultimately lead to its becoming moribund; this moribund quality would be delayed in Hollywood for twenty years perhaps because of the movies' ability to see popular dance as a viable entity where Broadway no longer could. "Following the Depression and into the forties, eccentric dancers and even comedians ran into trouble on Broadway . . . . Bert Lahr remarked sadly: 'In the thirties . . . suddenly the funny man was out. Everyone wanted ballet and dream sequences' . . . ."[30] Similarly, Cecil Smith has written that "an undue worship of ballet threatened to rob the American musical theatre of its traditions of popular dance."[31] The Hollywood musical never seemed to have that problem; it may be that Hollywood musicals took over the role previously played by Broadway musicals, for many of the popular dancers turned to film after their careers on the stage and thus continued to perform their specialties well into the fifties. Nor did ballet get entrenched as *the* dance form. It was used to lend status to certain productions, true, but more often it became just another mode of dance expression, used where convenient, ignored where not. Its introduction into film would lend a more serious approach to dance and would provide better dancers than had previously been available, but its strongest characteristics as represented by particular dancers and choreographers would not be felt until the next decade when the striving for integrated musicals had become a conscious effort on the part of film makers, particularly those at MGM.

The role of the dance director throughout the thirties and early forties was a peculiar one. Many of them were like Berkeley and had no dance training; instead, they were idea men who designed the routines and planned how they were to be shot rather than actually designing the choreography itself. They often relied on already-trained dancers doing their own numbers rather than creating their own dances and training dancers to do them. There were, in fact, two different types of dance directors, one in charge of the dances themselves and one who was able to direct the photographing of the dances.[32] There has never been a dance directors' or choreographers' union in Hollywood so that the first group had little power, and members of the second group had to belong to the Screen Directors Guild. It was indeed unusual when someone like Fred Astaire had permission to design and control the camera work of the dances as well as to design the steps themselves. Although the screen credits for dance direction seldom delineate their various roles (as with most other studio departments the head received sole or major credit even if he had not been involved in the work), often several dance directors would share responsibility for a film, one preparing ballet-oriented routines, another the popular dances, and perhaps even a third the Latin or exotic material.

Albertina Rasch and Dave Gould, for example, shared direction credit on several films at MGM during the late thirties. *Broadway Melody of 1936* and *Rosalie* may serve as good examples, for, in addition to Rasch's ballet routines and Gould's grand designs for other numbers, Eleanor Powell evidently imposed her own material on to both of theirs. This kind of diversity was characteristic of many of the period musicals and, of course, would be one of the things which Gene Kelly and others would shortly attempt to overcome.

Because of their numerous screen credits throughout the thirties and early forties, because of their positions of authority, and because of their similarities in style and approach—an entrenchment within the Hollywood studio system to which others would react in the next era—Dave Gould, Seymour Felix, Bobby Connolly, LeRoy Prinz, and Hermes Pan can serve to represent some of the general trends of dance within the musical at this time. Although working under contract to specific studios for certain periods of time, many dance directors moved easily from one studio to the next, thus giving manifestation to their concepts of large-scale productions in many different films. After his tenure at Warner Brothers, Busby Berkeley moved to MGM and there both directed and arranged the numbers for many films; on loan-out to Twentieth Century-Fox in 1943 he did *The Gang's All Here* as well. After his stint at RKO, Dave Gould also went to MGM and worked there through the thirties. Although working principally at Fox during the thirties, Seymour Felix also contributed to several films at other studios. Bobby Connolly was at Warner Brothers from 1934 to 1938 and at MGM from 1939 to 1943; LeRoy Prinz worked at Paramount throughout the thirties but became head of the dance department at Warner Brothers in 1942. The work of all these men is surprisingly similar. Sharing backgrounds in vaudeville and Broadway revues, they moved to Hollywood in the early thirties. There they designed large-scale revue numbers which had no necessary relation to the films. In general allowing their performers to provide their own steps, they were interested more in the overall effect produced by the sight of the number. Probably inspired principally by Berkeley's success, they borrowed from each other, thus providing the recurrent trends of military motifs, beautiful blondes lined up for drill work, and bizarre camera angles accentuating the non-dance aspects of the production numbers.

Seymour Felix, unlike most of the thirties dance directors, had some dance training and performing experience early in his career. First at Twentieth Century-Fox, Felix provided the routines for two Shirley Temple vehicles, *Just Around the Corner* and *The Little Colonel*. In *Just Around the Corner* Felix presents an elaborate show at the end of the film, a show which the Shirley Temple character has devised to earn money to help people hurt by the Depression. Although Bill Robinson dances briefly as part of the show, his role is not as big as in *The Little Colonel* where he quite obviously had a greater say about the nature of his material. "A Pretty Girl Is Like a Melody" from *The Great Ziegfeld* is perhaps the high point of Felix's career not only because it won him an Academy Award but also because it combines almost every element of spectacle with which he and the other thirties dance directors were identified. Taking place on one enormous turning set with an elaborately costumed cast of over a hundred, the number combines several varieties of music and dance. Beginning in a tight long shot which restricts the field of vision throughout the number, the camera gradually moves up the stairs identifying different singers and dancers until it reaches the ultimate "pretty girl" at the top. Although the integrity of the number is maintained throughout, the filmic space is changed by a moving camera, by the moving turntable of the set, and by cuts from one area of pro-filmic space to another. Not until the very end when the camera moves back into extreme long shot can one see that the set is of a piece and that the combined elements are arranged in layers of black and white to give an overall impression of the ultimate Ziegfeld spectacle. Beginning with the "Pretty Girl" song, the number continues into an operatic *aria*, "Un Bel Di" from *Madame Butterfly*, as the camera reveals the lower part of the set populated by elaborately dressed girls sitting or standing in arranged patterns. Higher up the set costumed couples waltz to "The Blue Danube" which leads in turn to a man singing "Vesti La Giuba" from *I Pagliacci*. Moving to the top, accompanied by *Rhapsody in Blue*, the camera reveals the Ziegfeld queen and then begins its descent as girls dressed in black dance four to a step down the stairs, arms linked, doing high kicks and deep back bends. The music of the title song returns, and the entire colossal ensemble joins in as the spatial unity of the piece becomes evident. Although Felix continued working up through the early fifties, as with most of the important thirties dance directors, he continued to stage dances as if for the proscenium arch stage or numbers which emphasized spectacle rather than individual performers. It is significant that Gene Kelly had Seymour Felix replaced on *DuBarry Was a Lady* because he felt that Felix's ideas were simply not in keeping with his own; when Kelly took over the male lead in *Cover Girl*, he also took over Felix's choreographic chores, although some of Felix's numbers, shot before Kelly was hired, do remain in the film. The age of spectacle, a holdover from the revue tradition, was giving way to an age of dance.

Bobby Connolly worked at Warner Brothers and at MGM at much the same time as Busby Berkeley, and, although he also generally prepared large-scale production numbers, his work was overshadowed by Berkeley's. Connolly, nonetheless, did work with dancers and stars with considerable reputations. As was the custom, though, those performers surely prepared their own material and set them into his designs. Like Berkeley, Connolly was fascinated with military motifs and they recur periodically throughout his work in films as different as *Flirtation Walk, Broadway Melody of 1940, For Me and My Gal, Ship Ahoy,* and *I Dood It.* The latter three, all filmed during the war, present a reasonable excuse for military numbers, but his most explicitly military film was Frank Borzage's *Flirtation Walk,* 1934, in which he makes a constant association between the military parade drill at West Point and the dances on-stage during the cadets' show.[33] Even the military maneuvers of the ships and planes in the beginning of the film look like production numbers. Overhead shots of cadets marching in circular and rectangular patterns suggest Berkeley's influence, and the camera moving into the separate diegesis of the hundredth-night show, giving a second narrative level as well as an entirely new world of screen space, makes the film rather distinctively a product of Warner Brothers in the thirties. The Spanish cafe dance and the black-face routine in Archie Mayo's *Go Into Your Dance,* 1935, and "The Playboy of Paris" from *Broadway Hostess,* 1935, (in which girls dance inside champagne glasses) all tie Connolly's work to the period and to the studio. Two particular things seem evident about Connolly's work: one is that while at Warners, especially, he simply worked within the mode already established at that studio; the second is that at MGM he was completely subservient to the specialties of the performers who starred in the pictures. There is little evidence of any individuality in his material. The black-face routines of *Go Into Your Dance* were surely as much the result of Al Jolson's presence as of Connolly's own inventiveness. The structural affinities among the Fred Astaire and Eleanor Powell films are more evident in *Broadway Melody of 1940* than they are between Connolly's other films and that one, and although the on-stage vaudeville routines of *For Me and My Gal* do suggest Connolly's (and Busby Berkeley's—who was the director) influence, the intimate "For Me and My Gal" between Gene Kelly and Judy Garland in a coffee shop harks to the future rather than the past. Similarly, the dance routines of *The Wizard of Oz* reveal less of Connolly than they do, say, of Ray Bolger as the Scarecrow. After his contract ran out at MGM, Connolly did not continue directing dance material in films; he, too, was a victim of an increased interest in a different approach to dance material.

Another leading dance director whose work seems representative of the period was Dave Gould, mentioned earlier in relation to Astaire's first films at RKO. Working at MGM (with some films at Fox) after the mid-thirties, Gould, too, would be shunted aside by the new ideas overtaking musicals at MGM in the mid-forties. Responsible for the girls dancing on the airplane wings at the end of *Flying Down to Rio,* the black and white costumed chorus dancers in "The Continental" from *The Gay Divorcee,* the "Straw Hat" from *Folies Bergère,* and the "Great Guns" revue at the end of *Born to Dance,* Gould's preferences definitely seemed to lie with the large production number rather than with more intimate partner or solo dancing. As with other dance directors at the time, he would incorporate smaller routines into his films, but it would be specialty acts of established dancers doing the material for which they were best known; as Berkeley used the De Marcos, for example, Gould used Georges and Jalna to do "I've Got You Under My Skin" in *Born to Dance*. The revolving turntable of the "Straw Hat" number and the acrobatic show complete with trampoline as part of "Great Guns" stand out in marked contrast to genuine dance, even to Eleanor Powell's gymnastic style, for Powell incorporated her acrobatics into dance whereas Gould made no pretense that the material was dance. His choruses presented organized exhibitions which often used dance but just as often eschewed dance which might interfere with the spectacle for its own sake.

Two final dance directors to be considered are LeRoy Prinz and Hermes Pan. Both men began their work in the thirties, but both also continued into the fifties (and sixties for Pan), contributing material to well over fifty films each. Prinz worked at Paramount during the thirties and did the numbers for the *Big Broadcast* films; in 1942 he became the head of the dance department at Warner Brothers. Although Prinz did adapt his style somewhat to the changing times, he nonetheless remained primarily responsible for numbers which took place on stages for shows within the film.[34] An idea man—rather than a choreographer, per se—like most of his contemporaries, Prinz's own routines were also large, extravagant production numbers which combined numerous dance elements like the "Ballet in Jive" from *Hollywood Canteen,* 1944. But he also incorporated more specialty acts into his films, and, aware of the increasing trend toward ballet, he hired ballet dancers to represent that particular trend. Ray Bolger does his eccentric tapping in *Look for the Silver Lining,* 1949 (the number is shot with Bolger full figure, the camera following him to keep him more or less center frame throughout, as well); George Zoritch and Mlada Mladova present "I've Got You under My Skin" as a ballet in *Night and Day,* 1945. Prinz's material was often as extravagant as his colleagues', yet he rarely opened up the number into different areas of filmic space. The numbers were rarely shot integrally (the aforementioned Bolger number perhaps reflecting either Bolger's own influence or Prinz's awareness of changes in filming dance by that late date); the frequent cutaways to "back stage" business in *Yankee Doodle Dandy* and the returning to Cole Porter listening to his music over the telephone during the ballet in *Night and Day,* for example, indicate a preference for grounding the on-stage numbers in the narrative even though the numbers do not advance the narrative. Nor does he seem concerned that any unity within the numbers and any innate drama of the number is violated by such an approach.

Hermes Pan has one of the most extensive careers—extending from 1933 to the present—of any Hollywood dance director. Pan had had no dance training of significance but had worked for LeRoy Prinz and Dave Gould and was working as Gould's assistant on "The Carioca" in *Flying Down to Rio* when Fred Astaire tapped him to become his assistant. He has remained closely associated with Astaire, working with him on nineteen films, but the evidence from his own choreography—the ensemble numbers in the Astaire-Rogers series, dances in many films at Twentieth Century-Fox where he worked principally in the forties, and choreography in numerous other films as recently as the musical remake of *Lost Horizon*—shows little of Astaire's influence. Overhead shots to incorporate patterns in the floor are an important part of "The Piccolino" from *Top Hat;* revolving doors and interchanging figures in black and white suggest Gould and Prinz—and perhaps even Berkeley—more than Astaire. Steps in strict time to the music (with little syncopation à la Astaire), lifts on musical high points (cymbals clash at each lift in "The Continental"), and cutting during the dances to different areas of the pro-filmic space suggest that on his own Pan had different interests from Astaire in filming dance. Pan, nonetheless, does seem more a choreographer than his contemporaries of the thirties and forties; he even dances in *Moon Over Miami, My Gal Sal, Sweet Rosie O'Grady,* and *Pin-Up Girl.* Although his preferences seem to be for large production numbers, within those numbers his performers always dance. And—unlike his thirties colleagues who worked into the fifties—Pan would also contribute to the integrated musical of the forties and fifties, for in spite of his background, his interest always seemed to be in *dance* rather than spectacle.

The thirties tradition in dance in the musical extends into the forties and fifties because certain dance directors and studios continued making financially successful films that exploited that tradition. At the same time, however, different ideas were being introduced—ideas which would become more important as dance, per se, became a more important part of the totality of the films. The dance directors of the thirties were often untrained dancers and just idea men; they also staged all musical numbers and not just the dance routines, frequently contributing more to the efficiency of a production than to the use of dance: with a separate dance director the various parts of a film could be prepared simultaneously, thus freeing the assigned director for the narrative elements or even for other projects. It was an era of extraordinary diversity of dance styles that were largely dependent on the characteristics of individual performers whose work was often unrelated to the background material provided by the dance director. Most of the dance directors, furthermore, were not concerned with presenting dance as an uninterrupted unit; frequent cutting to varied areas of space and fragmentation both of the pro-filmic subject and of the editing suggested that whatever worked to emphasize the spectacle determined the shooting and editing styles. Different trends were appearing, however. In addition to Astaire's striving for integration of dance and narrative and his concern for respect of the wholeness of dance routines, there was an interest in new forms of dance. In addition to the introduction of ballet, there was a new emphasis on the breaking down of all dance barriers; distinctions among ballet, modern, tap, ethnic, and gymnastic varieties were disappearing. Dancers trained in several traditions were blending their styles into something homogeneous. And this homogeneity would make dance the prime element in the integrated musical of the forties and fifties. New figures arriving in Hollywood in the early forties would accept certain elements of earlier musicals, reject others, and, most importantly, contribute their own material to films which would become a wholly new tradition—the dance musical.

6

The Integrated Dance Musical

The idea of integration in the musical is an old one, and although it did not really flourish in the film musical until the forties, nonetheless, those films came from a long tradition of attempts to unify songs, plot, and characters into a meaningful whole. The operetta in general with its roots in grand opera would somewhat naturally adhere to a policy of integration: musical numbers as expressions of character and outgrowths of plot developments. Gilbert and Sullivan's *H.M.S. Pinafore,* the first of their operettas to be imported to the United States, opened in Boston in 1878, and its influence spread to subsequent American productions like Willard Spencer's *The Tycoon,* 1886, and John Philip Sousa's *El Capitan,* 1896. The musical comedy, however, with no such tradition behind it would have to find its own way, and the characteristics often associated with the integrated musical film developed through a series of trials and errors on both stage and—after 1927—screen. One of the first shows to be called a musical comedy was *Evangeline* in 1847; unlike earlier shows of its type which culled music from various sources and always used current popular songs as well, *Evangeline* had a score written specifically for that production. The exotic elements of plot and setting, so often associated with operetta, were also present in nineteenth-century musical comedy, but probably starting with George M. Cohan's *Little Johnny Jones* in 1904, musical comedies began to use contemporary American subjects. (The tensions between exotic—indeed, fantastic—elements and down-to-earth, contemporary subjects would operate in musicals from that point on, and, in fact, would become the source of certain recurrent themes of the film musical.) Furthermore, the Princess Theater shows of Jerome Kern, P.G. Wodehouse, and Guy Bolton, presented between 1915 and 1918, *consciously* worked toward an integration of material. It was not until *Show Boat,* 1927, and its successors, however, that the integrated musical achieved status; subsequently what John Russell Taylor calls the "dogmatic" approach to integration became dominant on the stage. By this time, though, sound had come to the screen and film musicals would be providing their own forms of experimentation with unifying plot and musical numbers.

Although the traditions for the integrated musical come from the stage, the idea of integration presents certain theoretical issues which are especially applicable to the nature of the film medium. Furthermore, the nature of integration of the film musical lies not simply with the idea that the musical numbers and the dances, in particular, should advance the plot but also suggests an integration of the entire cinematic process. The way in which the dances in a particular film are photographed, for example, suggests a kind of integration of the film making process with the dance process and that *together* they contribute to the integrity of the film. The integrated film musical of the forties and fifties emphasized dance—dance in all its variety. In a sense, integration is also the key word for the dance itself; for Gene Kelly, Bob Fosse, Eugene Loring, Jack Cole, and Michael Kidd, among others, combined many kinds of dance into their individual styles. Fred Astaire, too, doing some of his most significant work at this same time, and, always open to change, used more varied dance forms than he had earlier at RKO; continuing to explore the relationship between the camera and the performer, he also modified somewhat his full-figured, single-take shooting style. It is not farfetched, perhaps, to speak of the integrated film musical as the dance musical; although not all integrated musicals emphasized dance, nor were all musicals with dance integrated, nonetheless, a good percentage were dance musicals.[1] Consciously choosing to work within the musical genre and to explore the possibilities of all avenues of integration, choreographers, producers, directors, performers, and even certain studios pooled their resources to make dance musicals. The genre itself had always been dependent on studio resources, and the dance musical continued that dependence. In fact, the studio system was the *sine qua non* of the dance musical, for without the cooperation engendered by that system, the "repertory company" associations of contract musicians, dancers, designers, and technicians, the dance musical could not have been made with such consistency. The reasons that musicals were phased out of production in Hollywood after the mid-fifties except in isolated, specific instances are probably many, but surely one major factor was the disintegration of the contract system through which studios employed the personnel necessary to make musicals. (In the forties Columbia sponsored a trained dance troupe; MGM and others employed a full symphony orchestra.) When it was no longer economically feasible to maintain such resources, the musical as a staple genre was doomed.

Every studio made musicals regularly until the mid-fifties, and each had its unique qualities, usually based on a particular star or group of performers. Deanna Durbin was Universal's musical star, for example, and provided Universal with a teenage formula for its films, *100 Men and a Girl,* 1936; *That Certain Age,* 1938; *First Love,* 1939; *Nice Girl,* 1941; *Christmas Holiday,* 1944; *Can't Help Singing,* 1945; *Up in Central Park,* 1948; and others. Numerous other stars had films tailored to their particular talent as well. Bing

Crosby, working principally at Paramount, together with Bob Hope and Dorothy Lamour, made the *Road* series, among other films, between 1940 (*The Road to Singapore*) and 1952 (*The Road to Bali; The Road to Hong Kong*, 1962, was a revival of the series—much like *The Barkleys of Broadway* was for Astaire and Rogers—and was released through United Artists). Danny Kaye worked for Samuel Goldwyn in such films as *Up in Arms*, 1944; *The Kid from Brooklyn*, 1946; *A Song is Born*, 1948; and *Hans Christian Andersen*, 1952. Most of these films included dance, yet none could be called dance musicals in the sense that dance was the controlling factor in the film. In the *Road* films Hope and Crosby often joined in some native dance sequence but usually for comic effect, seldom attempting actually to dance. The "Karigoon" dance in *The Road to Singapore* (credited to LeRoy Prinz, at that time head of Paramount's dance department) contains "native" costumes and the standard movements and gestures which had become codes to represent the South Seas: grass skirts and leis; the hula; bare feet; swaying hips; and arm and hand movements supposedly narrating a story. Its significance, however, lies with Bob Hope, who pretends to be a native at that point, almost getting married as a result of his involvement in the dance, and with his attempts to free himself from the problem. Danny Kaye did dance, but his roles were geared to his clowning, and the dance numbers usually reflected his buffoonery. The "Manic-Depression Presents" number from *Up in Arms*, more a production number than a dance, in any case, spoofs movie credit sequences; the Siamese dance he does with Vera-Ellen in *Wonder Man* is a stage performance, as he is trying to present himself in place of his more accomplished twin brother. *Hans Christian Andersen* has an extended ballet sequence in Roland Petit's choreography for the "Little Mermaid Ballet," but the dance in that film exists apart from Kaye's performance; indeed, in the film's diegesis his character envisions the ballet as it is being performed to his libretto, since he has been prevented from seeing the actual performance on stage. (*Merry Andrew*, 1958, may be the exception to prove the rule; it seems a dance musical by virtue of Michael Kidd's choreography and direction, for Kaye dances only limitedly in the film and then in routines controlled by Kidd's established style.) The dance musical was also dependent on the talents of individual stars like Gene Kelly, yet there was also a commingling of talents which gave a pre-eminence not just to the performers but also to the choreographer and, at times, to the directors. Of all the studios making musicals Metro-Goldwyn-Mayer was the one most consistently producing dance musicals. Indeed, the MGM musical seems to contain every element which characterizes the musical as a genre; the concepts of the star vehicle, studio style, the producer's touch, and the Platonic ideal of the integrated musical come together at MGM and become manifest in many of that studio's films from the late-thirties to the mid-fifties.

The major period of MGM musicals probably began in 1939 with Arthur

Freed's productions of *Babes in Arms* and *The Wizard of Oz*. Although there had been many earlier MGM musicals, especially the MacDonald-Eddy operettas and the Eleanor Powell vehicles, these films brought together two of the most important contributors, Freed and Judy Garland. Together, separately, and, even more importantly, in combination with other leading figures, they are significant of the direction the studio would take with the genre. Judy Garland and Mickey Rooney starred together in several teenage success story musicals such as *Babes in Arms, Babes on Broadway,* and *Strike Up the Band*. Vincente Minnelli, working under Freed's aegis, directed many of the films. He, Garland, and Freed came together for *Meet Me in St. Louis* in 1944. Gene Kelly made his debut with Judy Garland in the Freed-produced *For Me and My Gal* in 1942. And the four—Minnelli, Freed, Garland and Kelly—collaborated on *The Pirate* in 1948. Committed to the idea of the integrated musical, yet wanting material that would display the singing and dancing of his stars, Freed took chances on relatively untried talents and attracted established ones. Kelly was, from the first, permitted to do his own choreography; later, in conjunction with his assistant Stanley Donen, he was permitted to direct. Freed brought Fred Astaire to MGM to continue his explorations of dance in the musical, and other major contributors to dance in film, people like Bob Fosse, Michael Kidd, Robert Alton, Eugene Loring, and Jack Cole, all at some point in their careers participated in the dance musical at Metro. Most important, perhaps, Freed encouraged "original" film musicals—not just pre-tested Broadway adaptations—that had relatively small casts of equal ability. The "original" musicals resulted not in extravaganzas, but in more intimate production numbers, limited in size, which grew out of the narratives and governed the visual style of the entire film. Such "original" musicals were not the exclusive product of MGM, of course; other studios made films with the same commitment to integration and the predominance of dance. Not surprisingly, though, many of the non-Metro musicals, films as different as Columbia's *Cover Girl,* 1944, and Paramount's *Funny Face,* 1956, reflected the contributions of numerous people normally associated with MGM: Kelly, Donen, Astaire, Loring, Roger Edens, and Adolph Deutsch on just those two films, for example. The integrated musical was the result of a number of people working together—primarily at MGM but also elsewhere—all committed to a concept of film making which took the musical seriously and which considered it a proper vehicle for their expressions of popular culture. Dance was only one aspect of that expression, but it was often the most important aspect.

A major characteristic of the dance musicals of this period is the considerable overlapping of the personnel involved. Perhaps indicative of the integration of material in the dance musical, *several* personalities prevail in many of the films, and each film can—in some respects—fit in with analysis from different perspectives. Performers, choreographers, and directors worked together and in many instances one cannot discern the auteur, as it were, or—more accurately—there seem to be several auteurs. Vincente Minnelli directed films in which Astaire appeared (*Ziegfeld Follies, Yolanda and the Thief, The Band Wagon*) and in which Kelly appeared (*The Pirate, An American in Paris, Brigadoon*). All those films have qualities related to Minnelli's work, and, in particular films, qualities of Astaire and Kelly. Astaire worked with choreographer Eugene Loring (*Yolanda and the Thief, Funny Face, Silk Stockings*) and with Michael Kidd (*The Band Wagon*). Kelly worked with Kidd (*It's Always Fair Weather, Hello, Dolly!*). Kidd worked with Stanley Donen (*Seven Brides for Seven Brothers, It's Always Fair Weather*). Astaire worked with Donen (*Royal Wedding, Funny Face*). Donen worked with Bob Fosse (*Give a Girl a Break, Damn Yankees, The Pajama Game*). The list goes on. Many of the major figures operate in several capacities as well: performer, choreographer, and director. Astaire rarely took choreographer credit—giving it almost exclusively to his assistant Hermes Pan—though he did devise most of his own material, and he never directed a film. But he was the exception because other figures of the musical tended to expand their involvement in the film making process. Dancers (often appearing at least in minor roles) became choreographers, then directors. Kelly, of course, is the prime example. Others are Donen, Fosse, Charles Walters, Richard Quine, and Herbert Ross. And none of this takes into account other major contributors: Judy Garland; writers Betty Comden and Adolph Green; choreographers Robert Alton and Jack Cole; art directors Jack Martin Smith, Preston Ames, Randall Duell—all of whom contributed substantially to the musical (particularly at MGM) in conjunction with different people for different films. One problem this presents to the author is that of satisfactorily organizing material and avoiding needless repetition while at the same time giving proper credit to and understanding all the possible factors which influence a particular film. Since the focus of this study is the use of dance, it seems wise, therefore, to organize a section on the dance musical around the dance itself, realizing that this too presents problems because of the conglomerate nature of dance as used in the film musical during this period.

In his study of entertainment and show business values as represented in the musical film, Richard Dyer correctly observes " . . . that musical numbers frequently draw on a great variety of styles of dancing, which are combined and changed about with great fluidity and inventiveness. Often styles set one another off, provide contrasts or comments to one predominant style and so on."[2] Dyer, however, shuns talking about any examples that display this combination, choosing instead to illustrate his points through the "pure" examples of ballet (which for him is a very loose term encompassing so-called "high art" forms, including modern dance), social dance (including folk and Latin-American types as well as ballroom), and show business styles (tap, musical comedy, vaudeville, and others), all of which he admits are—in that pure form—a minority of the dancing in musical films. Each of these types does have a certain role, usually signifying certain conventional attitudes (e.g., the minuet conventionally signifies eighteenth-century aristocracy), irrespective of the accuracy of those attitudes. It is important to analyze the repetitive types of dance as they are individually manifested in the films, but it is probably more important to understand how the different types interact and how the various personnel used the dances for their particular purposes. (One comment seems necessary here: since chapter 7 will detail Kelly's work as the major example of this eclecticism, in this chapter most references to his films and dances will serve only to support general points or to give further examples; the major focus here will be on other figures in films they made independently of Kelly.)

In motion pictures traditional or classical ballet, when existing by itself and not in combination with other dance forms, has assumed certain conventional associations, particularly as a designation of the high art/popular art dichotomy which later comes to the fore in musicals. Dyer has suggested that "in films, the classical ballet—the ballerina on pointe in tutu—has above all had the useful iconographic function of placing the performer as an 'Artist'."[3] The differences between the Cyd Charisse and Fred Astaire characters in *The Band Wagon* are differences in their roles as dancers, and the rest of the film exploits these differences in its preference for popular entertainment. Charisse as a ballet dancer reacts negatively to working with Astaire, a "mere hoofer." Astaire responds similarly to her but is more intimidated by her, for he knows his limitations. Ultimately, the ballet is linked with the pretentiousness of Jack Buchanan as Cordova, for it isn't until Charisse joins with Astaire—on Astaire's terms and in his dancing style—that their love blossoms, and it isn't until Buchanan agrees to subordinate his ideas about a "class" show to Astaire's ideas for an entertaining one that the show succeeds. Cyd Charisse plays a similar role in *Meet Me in Las Vegas*. As a ballerina "slumming," as it were, in a Las Vegas show, she doesn't become really involved with Dan Dailey until she recognizes the merits of a different kind of dance and can dance with him at his ranch. A frequent alternative use of ballet is the dream sequence, for the somewhat ethereal quality of ballet movement, often spoken of in terms of weightlessness and height, lends itself to the nature of dreams (ballet in general being designed to use the floor primarily as a means to get up into the air in jumps and the ballerina's pointe work supposedly making her seem suspended in air). Not all dream sequences, of course, are balletic, but even in those films with emphasis on different kinds of dance, dreams will have more ballet movements. Vera-Ellen in *On the*

Town and Leslie Caron in *An American in Paris*, for example, dance on pointe in the dream sequences but do not in the other dances. The dream dances which Roland Petit choreographed for *Daddy Long Legs* and *Hans Christian Andersen* are both ballets, though Leslie Caron does change her style of dancing in the *Daddy Long Legs* ballet when she dreams of going to the Hong Kong Cafe and the carnival in Rio. A third association with ballet in the musical is that of the on-stage performance; most of the ballet numbers are performed on stages within the diegesis of the film or, as is the case with most of the dream ballets, are photographed as if on a stage. In *The Band Wagon* Astaire goes to see Cyd Charisse perform as the star of a ballet company, and the camera work emphasizes the theatrical nature of the dance; it is shot in frontal long takes with only an occasional dolly-in or cut-to-medium shot of Cyd Charisse. The "Sleeping Beauty" ballet from *Meet Me in Las Vegas* is performed on a stage as part of Charisse's night club act; likewise, Barbara Streisand's parody of "Swan Lake" in *Funny Girl* is part of Fanny Brice's stage show. The dream ballets of both *On the Town* and *Hans Christian Andersen* are dreamed as if they were performances as well: in *On the Town* because Kelly has seen a poster of a show, "A Day in New York," which motivates his dream; and in *Hans Christian Andersen* because Danny Kaye, not being able to attend the show, must imagine what it looks like. In *Daddy Long Legs* Leslie Caron does not perform on a stage, but the number is shot as if on a stage with a generally immobile camera photographing in long shot. (Interestingly, though, the number does use the cinematic trick, harking back to Méliès, but also reminiscent of "Miss Turnstiles" in *On the Town,* of having Leslie Caron change costumes as she goes through doors.) Even "A Day in New York" with its generally participatory camera work is shot all from the front in order to take advantage of (or because it is restricted by) the stage-set quality of the movie set.

Pure ballet, while relatively limited in most musicals, has been influential, however, because almost all the major choreographers after approximately 1940 use ballet in their work even if their emphasis lies elsewhere. In his article "Prélude à la Danse," Louis Marcorelles notes that though Gene Kelly, Jerome Robbins, Michael Kidd, and Bob Fosse received classical training, they chose to experiment with all types of dance both on stage and on screen.[4] The term *ballet* has, in fact, become almost synonymous with any kind of dance except pure hoofing, simply because the distinctions among various dance forms which began to break down after the 1920s have now become almost completely blurred. (In film the term *ballet* is often applied to those rather longer dance numbers—irrespective of the type of dance used in them—not usually introduced by or associated with a specific song. "A Day in New York" and "Miss Turnstiles" from *On the Town;* "An American in Paris" from that film; the barnraising ballet from *Seven Brides for Seven Brothers* are examples. Certain of these longer numbers or ballets do use songs—e.g., the Broadway ballet from *Singin' in the Rain*—but an off-screen chorus rather than the on-screen dancer provides the music. Kelly's singing within the Broadway ballet—"Gotta Dance"—and his joining the chorus at the end only emphasize that he has danced—not sung—during the number itself.) The principles of turning as developed in ballet have become standard in all dance. Marshall and Jean Stearns' descriptions of early tap dancing in *Jazz Dance* rarely mention turning, yet as a result of the interaction among dance types, various kinds of turns have become important in recent tap. Conversely tap has made its way into ballet; Balanchine combined the two for "Slaughter on Tenth Avenue" in *On Your Toes* (stage and film) and Agnes de Mille used tap and ballet together in her ballet *Rodeo,* which served as a forerunner of her choreography for *Oklahoma!* (stage and film here, too). These are among the earliest and most obvious examples; others seem too numerous to mention. Richard Dyer, referring to Agnes de Mille and others, calls this combination form *American* ballet. And choreographer "[Eugene Loring] maintains that there certainly is a distinctive American ballet, the spirit and form of which are the principles of his own choreographic work";[5] Loring, generally credited with being one of the initiators of an eclectic American ballet, calls it "freestyle," a combination form, the basics of which are modern dance, jazz, and traditional ballet.[6]

The modern dance aspect of this freestyle American ballet is less evident in its overall influence on and commingling with other dance forms because by its very nature it does not have the same kind of recognizable movements and steps. Represented initially by people like Mary Wigman, Martha Graham, Doris Humphrey, and Charles Weidman, modern dance, also frequently called free dance, was often intended as a reaction against the restrictions and structures—the formalism—of ballet. Dancers were supposed to be free to express themselves through body movements which were constantly being invented and reinvented rather than being arranged and rearranged into new patterns as in ballet.

> Theoretically modern dance covers the complete range of aesthetic possibilities for the dance, but in practice it has developed a distinctive range of movements and meanings. In shape, opposition and asymmetry are favoured, expressing strength and excitement. It uses sharp dynamics, percussive and collapsing, insistent rhythms piling up emotional energy, and has developed emotional gesture above all others. It is thus most apt for expressing extreme, violent, passionate and neurotic feelings.[7]

Modern dance does not have a vocabulary for its movements as ballet and tap do, for example; it is significant that in his comment above Dyer talks about the "range of movements" in modern dance and cannot be more precise in his descriptions than to talk about rhythm and energy. Modern dance tends to be the opposite of ballet: ground oriented rather than air oriented; heavy rather than light; cerebral rather than physical. Whereas in ballet the ability to make difficult movements seem easy is a goal, in modern dance to make obvious the effort expended in expressing one's emotions is part of the system. In ballet the lightness and *ballon*—a term used to describe the ability to go high in the air and to hang there momentarily—give it certain characteristics; in modern dance the heaviness is the result of no *ballon*—height and apparent weightlessness not being necessarily a desirable end. The influence of modern dance on other dance forms seems to be twofold: first, it has helped other dance forms move away from a rigid, prescriptive vocabulary of movements. The turnout in ballet, while still essential to ballet technique, can be modified; turning the legs in can be an alternative. Secondly, ethnic, oriental, and folk dance (among the strong influences on modern dancers Katherine Dunham, Martha Graham, Ted Shawn, and Ruth St. Denis) in their original religious and ritual manifestations were introduced into dance for performance, though usually in the form of movements and poses rather than truly ethnic recreations.

Modern dance in a so-called pure state is used even less than ballet in the film musical. Its influence can be seen in the work of particular choreographers and particular dance routines, however. Conventionally modern dance has assumed certain of the same connotations of high art that ballet has, but it has also assumed the role of being the dance form that expresses anguish, mental torment, and ennui. The more characteristic joy of the musical therefore suggests reasons for its limited use. When used in its pure form or as an influential part of a different dance style, it is usually a stage performance within the film or an exteriorizing of a character's serious problem (or both). An early instance of modern dance in the musical was the number Katherine Dunham's dance troupe did to the title song of *Stormy Weather*. A modern routine with a strong ethnic element reflecting Dunham's anthropological research into native dances in Haiti, "Stormy Weather" features black dancers performing primarily to the beat of drums. The dance is a dream within the mind of the Lena Horne character as she is singing in a stage show, reflecting some of her depression over the state of her relationship with the Bill Robinson character in their off-stage life. Audrey Hepburn's dance in the Cave, the Empathicalist club, in *Funny Face* begins as a modern dance with the character even saying that she is going to dance as a way of expressing herself. The dance reflects her intellectual involvement with the movement, her self-doubts about getting caught up in the glamorous world of high fashion, and her confusion about her involvement with Fred Astaire. Moreover, the somberness is enhanced by the way the number was shot.

In this dark, smoke-filled Left Bank hang-out for Existentialists, to the accompaniment of an atonal and all but arhythmic trio, Audrey Hepburn slithers through an uninhibited routine wholly appropriate to the locale. Equally appropriate is Avedon's lighting scheme for the sequence—harsh blues and naked reds that blaze into the camera or slash across the screen to provide color rather than illumination. Miss Hepburn's slender figure clad in tight black sweater and pants, is barely visible against the haze, now merging with it as she writhes momentarily with the orchestra, now leaping clear for a frantic, acrobatic tap with two energetic young men. The murkiness of the cellar, the mounting fever of the dance are both augmented by a lighting style that knowingly breaks all the rules . . . .[8]

It is clear from this description, though, that the dance does not remain pure modern dance. The dance even seems to reflect the pattern of Hepburn's emotions throughout the film, for the modern dance beginning of the number, danced to somewhat atonal music, changes to a lighter, faster-paced, jazz-oriented style in which she taps and even does a pirouette at one point as the music becomes that of the song "Funny Face." As Richard Dyer has put it, "Her intellectualism is really a passing aberration: she will fall for solid Fred Astaire in the end. But at this point she is still deceived by the empathicalist establishment: in her dancing she adopts their style, but her Americanness shines through rendering the neurotic exhilarating, the morbid life-asser-tive."[9] Parodies of modern dance, like those of ballet in *Funny Girl* and *Bye, Bye Birdie*, emphasize the conventions and associations generally attributed to it. "Choreography" from *White Christmas*, presented by Danny Kaye, contrasts modern dance as high art with a vaudeville or musical comedy routine, danced by Vera-Ellen and a male dancer, as popular art. "Where Kaye is heavy, insistent, asymmetrical, Vera-Ellen is light, throw-away, symmetrical. The two styles are a deliberate comment on one another, but there is no doubt which side the film is on. The modern dance is seen as decadent, pretentious, morbid and generally all that is distrustful in 'Art', as opposed to the glittering high-spirits and optimism of show business."[10]

The major choreographers of the period were all people who had trained in more than one dance discipline, who combined those dance forms into a new form which did not follow predisposed rules, and who were concerned with ways of preparing dance for the camera. All worked at MGM, though, as was the case with Jack Cole who did most of his work at Columbia, they also worked at other studios. Eugene Loring, Jack Cole, Michael Kidd, and Bob Fosse (and, of course, Gene Kelly) all went to Hollywood after 1940, all with established reputations in the New York dance and theater worlds. All were prolific as well, working in some capacity on many musicals: Loring—thirteen; Cole—nineteen; Kidd—eight; Fosse—nine; Kelly—twenty-three. There were, of course, other choreographers, and, prolific though they were, most of them were holdovers from an earlier period and few of them had the dance training which characterized the work of the newcomers. In most instances when they worked with real dancers, as most of them did, the dancer's style prevails or dance director credit is shared. Whereas the four major choreographers named above seem to have distinctive styles rooted in their particular backgrounds (Loring's in ballet, Cole's in modern dance, Kidd's in ballet and gymnastics, and Fosse's in gymnastics and jazz), Robert Alton and Hermes Pan seldom show such distinctiveness.

Hermes Pan, identified so closely with Fred Astaire during the early part of his career, moved into independent work after 1940. Of the thirty-eight films he did between 1940 and 1973, only six were with Astaire. In most instances he seems to have staged the musical numbers—often literally on a stage—rather than choreographing dance, for many of the films use dance only minimally. In *Pal Joey,* for example, Frank Sinatra participates briefly in only one dance routine, his dream number, "What Do I Care for a Dame." Neither of the other principals, Rita Hayworth and Kim Novak, does much more. Hayworth's solo, "Zip," is a stylized strip tease in which she simulates removing her clothes while doing the traditional bump and grind. Novak does "That Terrific Rainbow" with the chorus dancers as part of her night club act, but they simply move around the stage in patterns, occasionally kicking their legs. Her big number, "My Funny Valentine," has her singing in the heart-shaped frame of a stage set (initially seen in close-up), but she does not dance. The routines are similar in *Darling Lili.* All the numbers are on the stage of English music halls rather than part of night club acts, but there is still not much dancing; what there is usually is subordinated to the singing. The film begins with a can-can, shot in full figure, but when Julie Andrews makes her entrance, the dance is relegated to the background. Not principally a dancer, Andrews is given different kinds of stage material in which to perform. In one number she sings while moving back and forth on an elaborately designed, flower-bedecked swing. In some of the films adapted from stage shows Pan kept the ideas and, in some cases, even the movements from the original. "Grant Avenue" from *Flower Drum Song* is quite clearly adapted from Gene Kelly's choreography for the stage version and the stylized walking of "The Ascot Gavotte" from *My Fair Lady* is adapted from Onna White's original. The contrasting styles of "From This Moment On" from *Kiss Me Kate* also seem to be the result of the individual dancers involved—Tommy Rall and Bob Fosse, Fosse, at least, having done some of his own choreography for the film.[11] Similarly, the dance Marge and Gower Champion do to "Smoke Gets in Your Eyes" from *Lovely to Look At* is very similar to the one they do on the rooftop of *Give a Girl a Break,* for which Gower Champion is co-credited with choreography. John Green, who worked closely with Pan on several films, said, "Hermes Pan often served as Fred Astaire's number-one assistant. He was indispensable, the perfect choreographic amenuensis for Fred Astaire."[12] Green's implication is that Pan's contribution was little more than that, however. Indeed, Pan's association with Fred Astaire strongly defines his career, and his work in the integrated musical remains close to that in thirties and forties backstage and revue films. He prepared the material within which dancers could do their own routines, designing the number, seeing that it related to the rest of the film, but not actually choreographing. His was an important function, but it was seldom one in which the dance material itself would become a major part of the film.

Speaking of her work with Robert Alton, Betty Garrett has said, "Bob Alton staged the numbers I did in *Words and Music* and those were done the day before we shot. Bob came in and said, 'Now, dear, do this . . . ,' and they sort of look it. There's nothing terribly exciting about them. It was almost as if it were an afterthought: oh, we'd better do something about staging this."[13] Alton, too, primarily staged musical numbers and provided the setting in which others would operate. Gene Kelly's comments on collaborating with Alton support this.

> We shared credit on *The Pirate*, but I would have given Bob Alton credit just out of gratefulness for what he had done for me in the Broadway theater, because he had told producers and directors on Broadway (I worked under him in three shows) that I was working on a new style of dance and to let me do it. So, for example, in *Pal Joey* where Robert Alton was the choreographer . . . , whatever things I did, he'd say, "Go ahead, Kelly. Just let me see what you've got in mind and what you do." He encouraged me greatly and did more than encourage me. He let me have my head, and I give him a lot of credit. In *The Pirate* he had so much work and so little time he'd say, "Well, you take this over there and see what happens, and I'll take the group around you, and then we'll see if we can put it together."[14]

Alton apparently was responsible for the overall design—including the patterns of the chorus dancers—while Kelly tended to his own dances and those closely linked with him. As with Pan's work the idea of "staging" numbers is appropriate because many of Alton's routines were done as if on a stage. The numbers in *Till the Clouds Roll By* and *Words and Music*, both musical biographies of song writers, Jerome Kern and Rodgers and Hart respectively, are almost all done as stage numbers for shows they may have been composed for. Likewise, many of the numbers in *The Barkleys of Broadway, Easter Parade, Annie Get Your Gun, Show Boat, The Belle of New York, There's No Business Like Show Business* and *White Christmas* are stage numbers, suiting the backstage aspects generally present in those films. Robert Alton's reputation had been established on the stage. Walter Terry has written of his stage work, "Alton decided that since dancers could dance they should be given an opportunity to do so. Using popular dance forms, jazz and Latin-American rhythms, Alton did something about the old-style line patterns. He did away with most of them—except where they were pertinent—and substituted imaginative designs, intricate movements and actions which had meaning as well as rhythm."[15] Although Alton had done only one film prior to 1940 (*Strike Me Pink*, 1935), much of his film work seems influenced more by earlier dance directors than by his contemporary choreographers. "Ol' Man River" from *Till the Clouds Roll By* and the finale singing of "There's No Business like Show Business" from *Annie Get Your Gun* are examples. In the first Frank Sinatra stands on a platform of boxes surrounded by the orchestra and chorus while a roving camera explores the massive set; in the second a camera on a boom gradually pulls back into an extreme high angle shot revealing the enormous number of horses and riders all moving in alternate directions in a circle. As with Berkeley the pattern and design created by the set, the placement of the performers, and the relationship of the camera to them have a significance which individual dance movement could not.

Fred Astaire, of course, is another holdover from earlier musicals, yet he is considerably different from both the other dancers and the other choreographers who cross the arbitrary line of 1940. In one sense the integrated dance musical of the forties and fifties is a descendant of the Astaire-Rogers vehicles at RKO, for Astaire not only consciously worked toward integrating dance in those films but also after 1940 continued to explore the subject, always remaining open to new ideas and new suggestions. Astaire worked almost exclusively with Hermes Pan prior to 1940. After that date they collaborated less frequently: of the eighteen musicals Astaire made after 1940, the six with Pan were *Blue Skies, Let's Dance, The Barkleys of Broadway, Three Little Words, Silk Stockings,* and *Finian's Rainbow.* Astaire worked with numerous directors and choreographers in his attempt to develop new ideas and to present a viable form of cinematic dance. There is considerable evidence of his modifying the photographic pattern and style he had established at RKO while nonetheless retaining a distinctive dancing and choreographic style.

Although Astaire's basic dancing style did not change, he continued to refine it and develop it, but the relationship among the dances in his many films is clear. A dance strongly rooted in tap prevails in his solos; a dance strongly rooted in exhibition ballroom prevails in the duets, irrespective of his partners. After he left RKO, Astaire worked with several different partners, Rita Hayworth, Joan Leslie, Judy Garland, Cyd Charisse, Leslie Caron, and, of course, Ginger Rogers again in *The Barkleys of Broadway.* The relationship established between Rogers and Astaire is occasionally the same— though never so strong—when he danced with other women. In the narratives of the films and in the dance numbers themselves, the Astaire persona is sometimes that of a mentor to a woman who needs to be trained—to dance (Garland in *Easter Parade*), to dance in a new way (Charisse in *The Band Wagon*), to grow up (Caron in *Daddy Long Legs*), or to accept her proper show business role (Rogers in *The Barkleys of Broadway*). And in each case that training coincides with her falling in love with him, the dances being stages in and metaphorical for their love making.

"Dancing in the Dark" from *The Band Wagon* is the number perhaps most reminiscent of the ballroom numbers Astaire did in the RKO series films. Walking together in Central Park, Astaire and Charisse come upon a group dancing. They walk among them then find a small courtyard isolated from the rest of the world, a place to be alone. Like so many of his duets, it is a stylized ballroom number with a four-beat—rather than a three-beat waltz— rhythm. The music for the song (which, incidentally, is never sung), though written in C major, is somewhat somber and pensive (probably the result of the accidentals which take the music out of its natural progressions in C major. The words *Why, by,* and *and* in the following quotation from the lyrics are on the notes B flat, A flat, and E flat respectively: " . . . the wonder of *why* we're here. Time passes *by,* we're here *and* gone"). Astaire follows the lead of the song in his choreography. The dancing is slow and hesitant with deep bends corresponding to drops in the notes of the music. The ending of the song is a five-note repeat ("Dancing in the Dark") of C with the accompaniment modulating to a C major resolution over four measures. Each time that is repeated, the dance itself comes to a climactic point (e.g., he lifts Cyd Charisse). The ending of the dance is most unusual, however, and atypical. They do *chaîné* turns up the stairs out of the enclosure and simply walk away to a waiting carriage as the music fades out.

One recurring aspect of Astaire's dances is the obvious enjoyment of props and tricks and his incorporating them into particular routines. Present in his films with Rogers, they reach something of an apex with his later films, for almost every film has at least one number in which he dances with an object or which requires special effects. In *The Belle of New York* he does a sand dance (similar to the one in *Top Hat*) to the song "I Wanna Be a Dancin' Man." In *Easter Parade* and *Daddy Long Legs* he does dances in which he also plays the drums—he had done this also in *Damsel in Distress*—perhaps fulfilling Marshall and Jean Stearns's comment that " . . . most tappers thought of themselves as drummers . . . ."[16] "Shine on Your Shoes" from *The Band Wagon* has him dancing among the various items of an amusement arcade while "Let's Kiss and Make Up" from *Funny Face* has him dancing with an umbrella and then his raincoat as he pantomimes being a bullfighter. The use of special effects became particularly important in Astaire's later films, in two of which he did dance routines that always amaze people. He dances on the walls and ceiling of his hotel room in *Royal Wedding* and in the air and on tops of buildings in *The Belle of New York*.[17] In "Steppin' Out with My Baby" from *Easter Parade* he dances in slow motion in the foreground while the rest of the cast dances at regular speed in the background, and he dances with seemingly animated shoes during the song "Shoes with Wings On" from *The Barkleys of Broadway*. These dances are not just gimmicks, however, for in each one a specific diegetic point relates the number to the whole film and provides Astaire with the motivation for that dance idea.

Most specifically, the various trick numbers serve to characterize Astaire in his role in the particular films, usually in terms of the established Astaire persona. Choreographer and film director Herbert Ross, who worked with Astaire on television specials in the sixties, said that Astaire's image is "A witty, intelligent image, civilized and urbane. Many dancers are merely physical or exotic. Astaire manages to project intelligence."[18] This image seems present in each character he plays, and the dances reinforce that image. The special effects numbers from *Royal Wedding* and *The Belle of New York* are both motivated by his love for a woman; being able to defy gravity in each instance—though in different ways—seems the logical—indeed, natural—result of wanting to express one's love for another person. Dancing in the arcade in *The Band Wagon* shows his puzzlement at the changes wrought in New York since his last visit but also suggests his willingness to adapt to those changes. Several of the numbers are on-stage numbers ("I Wanna Be a Dancin' Man," "Steppin' Out with My Baby," "Shoes with Wings On") reflecting the professional dancer role which he has in most of those films and which he has generally had in all films—providing that "excuse" for his ability to dance. Nonetheless, the on-stage dances usually serve two functions: they are numbers as part of a show but they also reflect the feelings of the character at that point. The Astaire and Garland characters have just come to a realization about their relationship when he sings "Steppin' Out with My Baby" in *Easter Parade*, and, though Rogers and Astaire do "They Can't Take that Away from Me" on the stage in *The Barkleys of Broadway*, their on-stage performance is reflective of their off-stage relationship.

In general Astaire's work after he left RKO does not seem very different from his work there. In some instances he elaborated on ideas from the earlier films or allowed things to develop more fully, but the style remains the same, the Astaire persona remains the same, though older. There is one fundamental change, however. The conscious choice to have his dances photographed in full-figure and in long takes (often single takes) with multiple camera set-ups gave way to a more noticeable integration of camera and dance, with match cutting on action, and a general equality of relationship between camera and dance rather than the subordinating of camera to dance which prevailed in his earlier work. There seem to be two possible reasons for this. One may be that working with directors, other stars, and other choreographers of importance, Astaire was not the "boss" that he had been at RKO. The other may be that the growing interest in film on the part of new choreographers, the experiments which they were making with filming dance, had influenced Astaire to experiment similarly. The use of special effects, while still an outgrowth of his obvious interest in tricks and props, is nonetheless a decided change toward allowing cinema to intrude on the dance or at least to be incorporated into the dance. Of course, there are still many instances of long and single take dance sequences. Part of the effect of his dancing on the ceiling and walls in *Royal Wedding* comes from the number's being shot in one take, thus allowing one to absorb it as whole, respecting the dramatic space, as it were, according to André Bazin's realist aesthetic. In other instances (e.g., the dance after he plays the drums in *Daddy Long Legs*), long takes allow him to develop a dance idea and to "play it out," so to speak, without stopping in order to change camera angle. But the general tendency of his earlier films—to allow nothing but long takes—gives way to an accommodation to the particular dance and to the space it inhabits. "Let's Kiss and Make Up" from *Funny Face* takes place in the courtyard outside Audrey Hepburn's room. Several match cuts on action provide the opportunity to move in different directions, creating, in a sense, new areas of space in which Astaire can dance. A cutaway to Hepburn's face at one point also provides an appropriate grounding in the narrative: she is willing to kiss and make up *because* of the dance he is doing. (The cuts in some of the numbers are prompted by non-dance considerations; in "Shoes with Wings On," for example, the technical considerations of having the shoes seem self-propelled make certain cuts necessary.) A roving, seemingly choreographed camera—not just one which follows the dancers to keep them center frame and full figure—participating in the dances and combining with cutting to allow for changes in camera angle, location, and lens is the rule in "Will You Marry Me," the dream ballet of *Yolanda and the Thief*, the "Girl Hunt" ballet and "Dancing in the Dark" from *The Band Wagon*, "He Loves and She Loves" from *Funny Face*, "All of You" from *Silk Stockings*, and "This Heart of Mine" and "Limehouse Blues" from *Ziegfeld Follies*. Vincente Minnelli has said that a technical matter like the choice of camera angle " . . . doesn't mean . . . much to Fred as long as his dances come off on the screen, are literally beautiful. . . . "[19] The implications of Minnelli's statement and the inferences drawn from the films are that Astaire simply was not dogmatic, was open to new ideas on photographing his dances, and allowed others with whom he worked to show him different possibilities.

Choreographer and dancer Jack Cole prefers to call much of contemporary dance *urban dance;* "it's a kind of urban folklore, an expression of the way people act."[20] Cole's dance style is strongly rooted in modern dance, yet he rejected modern dance as an end in itself and, during the thirties, sought to learn more about black popular dance as displayed at places like the Savoy Ballroom in Harlem and about dances as representative of numerous world cultures. Cole began his career as a dancer with Ruth St. Denis and Ted Shawn and was a member of the Denishawn Company.

> It took me a very short time—even though I was in the company and had gone on tour for two seasons—to know that that really wasn't *my* kind of thing. It was such a romantic, sentimental approach, not very real. I used to go at that time to the Savoy and had to do a

lot of jazzing and talking to get in. I was very young looking, very blond and blue-eyed, and it was rough for a kid to get into the Savoy. But they were amused with me because I seemed nice; I wasn't like a nut or a freak. Sometimes I'd go with girls and we'd dance, or I'd go by myself and eventually I got comfortable enough.

The Savoy was where all the good bands were and so everybody wanted to go there. Every once in a while I'd go over to a table if I saw a couple who could dance absolutely marvelously. The only way you can learn that kind of dancing is to dance with somebody who is very good.

I was interested in many things. I was interested in the Oriental theater, Japanese and Indian particularly. I was always interested in the culture of people and how they expressed themselves. I never wanted to *be*—people are always confusing why you are teaching them; they think you want to teach them to *be* an Indian dancer—but I was trying to expose them to a different attitude, to give them the excitement and the discovery of the thousand ways there are to move that are peculiar and different, totally different, that would never enter your head here. It opens up a new vocabulary of movement, different ways to approach the problem, rather than a balletic way. When I am going to do a certain kind of conflict, male conflict, I always think of Japanese theater because they do that particular kind of thing in a highly successful, very formal, stylized way.

Cole's first work in film was with the film *Moon Over Miami,* for which he had originally been hired as choreographer.

When they wanted me to start the picture, I couldn't get rid of my night club obligations and so they got Hermes Pan to do it. I came out later and did one number which was mostly removed from the picture because of censorship, which was very interesting at that point. They had the most elaborate kind of censorship. One was that my navel showed and you couldn't show signs of physical birth, which was truly idiotic. You were supposed to cover it with transparent tape, put body makeup over it so that you had some strange kind of abdomen. Another was that the man could be on the floor and the woman could stand or the man could stand and the woman could be on the floor, but you both couldn't be on the floor together. That was the most perverse sexual attitude that I had heard in a long time: both people couldn't be prone on the stage at the same time. You couldn't strike a woman. I was doing some kind of betrothal Indian thing where the girl got a crack on the face. It was a very serious distortion of a real Indian ritual.

Cole first went to Metro two years later.

Metro brought me out and paid me an enormous amount of money—unbelievable—which they did everybody. They had the most incredible crafts people at Metro at the point when I first came out, which was 1943; they could do the most miraculous things. They had heard that I was an expert, and I was hired and rushed out here, but they didn't know what I really did.

But he was not very happy during his stay there.

For a long time they just get you to run around the studio and watch people at work, which I did. After a while I got curious because I got tired of watching and wanted to do it. Then they called up and asked if I would teach Ingrid Bergman to waltz for *Gaslight,* and I said, "No." I didn't want them to get the idea that I went around doing cleanup jobs, that I was a dancing teacher. That was necessary. You had to do that at places like Metro, particularly. You had to set it up right away that you didn't do certain things.

After only a brief period at MGM, Cole went to Columbia where he worked for several years. One of his major contributions while at Columbia was his founding of a permanent dance company, the first at a film studio. In February 1944 twelve dancers under contract to Columbia began regular rehearsals, six hours a day on Stage 10 and by mid-April " . . . the Cole group, trained to a fine pitch, could handle any step from ballet to boogie."[21] The troupe was used in such Columbia musicals as *Tonight and Every Night, The Jolson Story,* and *Down to Earth,* all of which he choreographed. Cole credits much of his success to the rapport he had with Harry Cohn and to the freedom Cohn allowed him.

I enjoyed working at Columbia rather than at Metro because Harry Cohn let me do everything. I really could get into the cutting room; I could get down on the sets. I got to know the whole bloody thing upside down. I was always in the middle of everything. At Metro it was always very difficult because you had all the queen bees telling you how to do it. When I did the musical numbers there was no director on the stage. Harry told everybody to leave me alone. I could do what I wanted; I designed the clothes and the sets and did the number. He used to tell the producers pretty much not to tell me how to do it. Which is a good way. Good executives give you an enormous amount of freedom and then when you flop, they don't get sore. They just don't want you to do that thing again. Harry was also pretty good about most things when it came to spending money with me because I was very good at demonstrating how I could save him money, which was how I got to develop a dance group. (Gwen Verdon and Carol Haney and all those people came out of this group.) I used to get involved with doing a lot of musicals, and I kept telling Harry that it was much better to have an expert group always ready to work.

As with most choreographers who went to Hollywood in the forties, Cole was very much interested in choreographing for the camera, and he gave serious consideration to the problems presented by filming dance.

The camera offers enormous latitude to the choreographer if he learns its powers, its whims and its evils. Like all mechanical devices, if exploited for its own sake it becomes tasteless and violently intrudes itself on an imaginative performance. The difficulty of obtaining presence on the screen is enormous. Movement always seems to be under glass, the strange paradox of seeming not real in a medium that is real above all else. The camera obliterates stress and strain and all kinetic drama is lost. Dynamics are lost and movement outline in space is emphasized. It has the power to make mediocre dances seem brilliant and strong, and brilliant stylists seem weird and distorted.[22]

Perhaps one of the reasons for Cole's dissatisfaction at Metro was a lack of rehearsal time with camera crew. Cinematographer Joseph Ruttenberg who worked with Cole on *Kismet* in 1955 said that camera rehearsals took place only after the dance was set, that he was generally not involved with preparations for filming dance sequences.[23] Yet Cole insisted on the importance of camera rehearsal.

> The thing you need most is rehearsal time with the camera because the camera is the most important object and the rehearsal of the camera and its movement requires a great deal of time. I always wanted to say, "Get away. I'll do it," but you couldn't say that even if the work somebody was doing bothered you. Lighting is quite a craft to learn for film, and you couldn't do it. You had to depend on the cameraman . . . .

Cole's own preparations included a conscious planning of the camera work and the editing.

> I used to elaborately choreograph for long crane shots, which didn't mean long shots. They were in and out with varying angles which would go in and sink and hold and then move slowly. I had the camera in mind while I was choreographing.

> I also cut the picture as I'm doing it, and I absolutely know what it's going to be like. When somebody says that we should take protection shots, I say I don't want any protection; if it doesn't come out, we do the shot over again. I know exactly what I'm doing, and it's been designed that way. I'm not going to let a cutter who doesn't know anything about it put the first cut together. I never gave them anything. All they could do is put the stuff together. If the sequence was made up of six shots, then they had six pieces to fasten together, that's all.

In general it is acknowledged that Cole's choreographic style is a combination of modern dance, oriental movement and Negro jazz.[24] There is very little ballet in Cole's dances on film, except those ballet movements like turns which have become absorbed into all dance forms. Cole has been a dance innovator, though, and has been given credit for a great deal of the development of "jazz" movement subsequently influencing Bob Fosse and others. Barrie Chase who worked as an assistant to Cole and as a stand-in for Dolores Gray in *Kismet* and Kay Kendall in *Les Girls,* both Cole-choreographed shows, has said, "I think he's the innovator of the way we move now. His combining of modern, Oriental and jazz movement, his way of digging into the ground, of breaking down dance steps and body movement, of exact counting of every part of every step—these are the things I got from Jack Cole."[25] The modern dance aspect of Cole's work comes across strongly in two routines from *Les Girls:* the parody of *The Wild One* in which Gene Kelly—in the Brando role— dances the neuroses, social and psychological, which cause the motorcycle gang members to act as they do; and the rehearsal number with Taina Elg in which she and Kelly perform a sensuous number in which he controls her with a rope like an umbilical cord. "Heat Wave" from *There's No Business like Show Business* shows a strong Latin influence, and several of the numbers from

Kismet, particularly the "Dance of Fate," reflect his interest in Oriental dance. All of these numbers are ones in which the costumes are important, showing to an extent Cole's interest in making the entire number visually and stylistically unified.

Although most of the films on which Cole worked were so-called backstage musicals or had their major dance routines presented as part of a show (*Tonight and Every Night, The Jolson Story, Down to Earth, Meet Me After the Show, Gentlemen Prefer Blondes, There's No Business like Show Business, Les Girls,* and *Let's Make Love* are all show business oriented), Cole was concerned with integrating the numbers into the film, particularly in creating some kind of stylistic relationship with the rest of the film: ". . . often . . . the dance sequences are simply inserted without either preparation or logic or, worst of all, consistency of style."[26] He was distressed at the haphazard way in which numbers are inserted into a film after the script has been finished.

> If they have confidence in you . . . , you might be called in when the script is only two-thirds done. Then you still have some chance of influencing the character development, or creating an integration between your dance sequences and the story line. My own feeling is that the dance director should work with the film director on the three or four minutes that immediately precede and follow the dances to create a smooth transition from one to the other.[27]

Cole's influence ultimately seems to have little to do with his films but is more the result of the training he gave to dancers, and the assistance he provided to people like Marilyn Monroe and Kay Kendall. Along with Matt Mattox and others he was responsible for developing the principle of isolation in modern jazz dance, a principle which receives its most significant manifestation in Bob Fosse's choreography. One can infer from Cole's interviews (mine, with Arthur Knight, and with Hugh Fordin for *The World of Entertainment!*) that he was never very happy working in Hollywood, that he found it very difficult to be innovative there. He told Knight, "In Hollywood, you're always running up against the attitude, 'We've done it this way for over twenty years, and we're not going to change things.' It's almost hopeless to try to fight against that sort of thing."[28] His plans for *Kismet* (to do something "very unrealistic in style, low-keyed color, inviting the imagination all the way"[29]) were thwarted during production, though, interestingly enough, the numbers for *Kismet* were perhaps more integrated than those of his other films. The "Dance of Fate," for example, provides a cover, so to speak, during which Howard Keel as the Emir can make his escape, and during the dance in which the prospective wives for the Caliph present themselves, each woman tries to attract the Caliph's attention by her dance movements. Cole spoke disparagingly of most directors with whom he worked, and, although he seems to have had considerable freedom in developing his own routines, he never directed a film nor, apparently, did he have much input beyond the dance sequences. During a question and answer session with the audience of the Athens, Ohio, Film Festival in May 1976, Howard Hawks said that he (Hawks) had nothing to do with the filming of the musical sequences of *Gentlemen Prefer Blondes,* that he was not even on the set. That can be inferred from the film as well, for Hawks's rigorously understated camera work and refined image composition give way in "Diamonds Are a Girl's Best Friend" to Cole's roving camera and lush costuming. The stylistic unity usually associated with the integrated dance musical is, by Cole's own admission, seldom present in his films. Dance as the controlling feature of the musical—the choreographer as auteur, as it were—is not present in those even to the extent it was for Astaire at RKO and certainly not to the extent it was when the choreographer was, in fact, the director.

Eugene Loring, who has had an extensive career as both dancer and choreographer on stage and in films and television, began his career as a ballet dancer, and although he has been a principal in the development of the style which incorporates jazz and modern as well as ballet, he remains essentially a ballet choreographer, for his dances are strongly rooted in ballet technique. (He is the only choreographer, of the four being considered here, who regularly has his female dancers on pointe, for example.) Loring worked on thirteen musicals between 1944 and 1960, collaborating with several of the important stars and directors whose names are linked with the integrated musical, Fred Astaire, Vincente Minnelli, Stanley Donen, Rouben Mamoulian, Audrey Hepburn, Cyd·Charisse, and others. Always interested in the use of the camera in regard to dance, Loring consciously choreographed for the camera, worked closely with his colleagues in unifying the whole film, and contributed significantly to several important films of the period.

Having always been interested in film, Loring, like so many others, purposely familiarized himself with the equipment of the film making process and decided early that it was necessary to prepare dance routines *for* the camera.

> Since I was not busy right away when Metro-Goldwyn-Mayer brought me out here, I made it my business to get around and watch all the shooting that I could, to learn as much as I could about lenses and the whole business of the use of the camera, the booms and all that. Then when I started to choreograph, I would choreograph with the camera movements in mind. I don't understand the other way of working, where you choreograph and then a director comes in and photographs it and there has been no idea beforehand in the composition of where the camera would be. As a matter of fact, I can't choreograph with that kind of director. I have to know where the camera is going to go in order to make an interesting composition. The other way the directors are always getting off on an oblique angle which has nothing to do with the original composition.[30]

He also learned "that it was very important who your director was," but, on the whole, he spoke highly of the rapport he established with most of the directors with whom he worked, particularly Roy Rowland (*5000 Fingers of Dr. T., Meet Me in Las Vegas*), Stanley Donen (*Deep in My Heart, Funny Face*), and Rouben Mamoulian (*Silk Stockings*).

> The way I worked with a director was to talk it all over with him first. Then I always consulted with the editors whether or not I was doing something that was wrong editingwise. My method of shooting is editing at the same time—instead of taking long shot, medium shot, close shot and letting the editor sew it together, paste it together in some manner. (They don't know what is important, really.) After talking it over with the director and the editor and when I had the work rehearsed, I asked the director and the editor to come in to see whether they were happy with what I had done. That way we could make changes before we got on the sound stage to rehearse it for the camera.

> In both *5000 Fingers* and *Yolanda and the Thief* I was in on the writing. I didn't write any of the script, but I was in on the story conferences so that I could make the scene take the plot along instead of just having a number. That generally was not the case, though.

> Some directors gave you more freedom than others. Some directors don't like to have you do all that, and they will suddenly change their mind on the sound stage and ask you to make changes. Then it's a matter of whether you agree; sometimes it's very hard to convince a director that he's wrong. They *are* in charge of the picture; they'll do what they want and that's their prerogative.

> Vincente Minnelli kept changing his mind and that was the most disconcerting thing. There were times when Fred Astaire had to put his foot down about changes on the set. Vince would get an idea about something pictorial—interesting—but Fred, being such a careful and meticulous worker, it isn't easy for him to change quickly and be comfortable and sure of himself. It wasn't always the happiest situation.

> The marvelous thing about Stanley Donen is that he understood where the camera should be. Having been a dancer, he immediately would grasp where the camera should be, and he had a memory for what the dancers were doing, which other directors don't always have. They don't know movement and it's hard for them to know when to direct the cameramen to move the camera at a certain point, but Stanley would know because he had been a dancer.

> I laid out [the dungeon ballet from *5000 Fingers*] and then Roy Rowland and I went on to the sound stage, on the set itself, and I started telling him that the people come from here and that this kind of lens will do this, etc. When we got about halfway through, he said, "Oh, you know what you're doing. Why don't you direct it? I'll stand by in case you need any advice." So I did. I did the *actual* shooting. He was marvelous to work with.

Loring's first assignment in Hollywood was to choreograph the excerpt from Verdi's opera *La Traviata* for *The Ziegfeld Follies*. The dancing is limited in that excerpt and is essentially ballroom dancing, seen largely in overhead high angle shot, which serves as the background for the lovers' first meeting. His next assignment, though, required significantly more responsibility, for it was to work with Fred Astaire and Vincente Minnelli on *Yolanda and the Thief.* The patterns present in the film's two major dance sequences (the dream ballet "Will You Marry Me?" and the carnival ballet "Coffee Time") seem much more the product of Vincente Minnelli than of either Astaire or Loring. Although dream sequences do exist in Astaire's films (e.g., *Carefree*), they are rare and his appearances brief (e.g., *Daddy Long Legs*). The surrealistic qualities of both "Will You Marry Me?" and "Coffee Time" (the man with six arms needing lights for his cigarettes; the entangling sheets; the black and white serpentine floor patterns which seem to undulate) carry over into such Minnelli dream sequences as those in *Father of the Bride, The Pirate*, and *An American in Paris*, the Halloween sequence in *Meet Me in St. Louis,* or the horsemen riding through the clouds in *The Four Horsemen of the Apocalypse.* According to Loring, he had considerable input for the numbers, not only in the writing, as mentioned above, but also in planning and approval when on the set, and Loring's own visual sense is similar to Minnelli's. The multiple levels and the bizarre instruments of the dungeon ballet in *5000 Fingers* and the use of hazy, smoky interiors and colors of the dance in the Cave from *Funny Face* are worthy of Minnelli, as well. Determining the exact responsibility for all the facets of the numbers is difficult—perhaps impossible—to determine, for there is evidence of all three men in the numbers.

"Will You Marry Me?" is a dream which the Fred Astaire character has reflecting the conflict within him: his growing love for Lucille Bremer versus the determination not to marry and to bilk her of her money. The relationship between what a sequence like this means and how that meaning is expressed through dance is a concern about which Loring has often spoken.

> He emphasized that "meaning" and "emotion" in dance were achieved neither through dramatization of movement, as in mime, nor even acting in dancing. For Loring, there is no separation between the drama of a dance and the movement of a dance, since he sees one within the other, not infusing or coloring it, but within it and integral to it.[31]

The dance is comprised of several discrete sections, each representing aspects of the Astaire character's past, present, and, possibly, future, though a future which at that point he wants to avoid. Vincente Minnelli has described the sequence in his autobiography.

> His background haunts him—we see suggestions of the sporting set, the grafters, the jockeys, the fast women in his past; the newspaperboys and Latin people of his present.
>   The main setting of the ballet is an abstraction. I wanted to suggest South American baroque without actual architectural forms, and used a series of rock formations in fantastic shapes. These were on rollers and could be grouped in different compositions for each shot. Irene Sharaff's stylized costumes complemented the action. South American touches are used in the ballet, combined with the surreal. Peruvian llamas walk by, South

American women are washing their laundry at the edge of a pond, the sidewalks of Rio de Janeiro are suggested by curving black and white stripes on the ground. The laundry women trap Astaire in between white sheets, a gauze-wrapped figure comes walking out of a smaller dark pond, totally dry, and as each veil is undone, we gradually are aware that it's Lucille Bremer as Yolanda.

The ballet ended with a bitter laugh. At the wedding, Astaire attempts to steal away with a box filled with gold coins. But he gets hopelessly enmeshed in the train of Yolanda's wedding veil. The dream ends. He wakens, all tied up in his bed sheets . . . .[32]

The dance movement itself reflects the moods as well as the specific incidents Astaire passes through. At several points his movements are less dance steps than a physical reaction to what the character is feeling: a sudden stop, a look around him, a quick turn, a slow glide in some direction. The music provides impetus for movement and support for the visual effects. His dance with the eight washer women is a calypso, for example. The dancing jockeys section of the number (in which Astaire does not dance) is a particular manifestation of Loring's attempt to dramatize through movement. It starts as four women, perhaps showgirls from his playboy past, attract him away from Lucille Bremer to a horse race where two jockeys dance the race itself. Starting in a representational fashion in which they mime riding horses, the dance becomes increasingly abstract as the competition between the two jockeys becomes a dance—indeed, ballet—competition, highlighted as they do great turning leaps around the stage. The highly mobile camera of the entire routine is used more than as a complement to the stars' dancing; it takes in objects, other dancers and people watching. The camera swoops in and out on a crane and there are startling changes from low angle close shots to extreme high angle overhead shots. In other words, the camera becomes a participant in the dance and the selection of usually nondancing aspects of the *mise-en-scène* makes them participants as well.

Perhaps the most distinctive aspect of Loring's style is his juxtapositions of unusual rhythms and the movement among various dance styles within the same routine. Unlike many choreographers, who incorporate several styles within a particular *enchaînement* (tapping into and out of ballet turns, for example), Loring is more likely to present his styles discretely. The aforementioned multiple styles in the Cave dance from *Funny Face* and the calypso plus ballet of "Will You Marry Me?" serve as examples. Another important example is the "Coffee Time" carnival dance—or, more appropriately, dances—also from *Yolanda and the Thief.* Loring has spoken of the origins of "Coffee Time," showing his interest in unusual rhythms.

One number prepared for Yolanda was a rhythm number called "Bananas." Both Fred and I hated it, and we wondered what in the world we were going to do with it. I have to sidetrack for a minute. Sometimes when you are doing a film, you have extra time, a number is not ready to go into production or whatever. I had nothing specific to do. I had always wanted to do a number that was jazz in 5, where every step had 5 counts but the music is in 4 so your accents create a secondary syncopation. So what I did was work out three different dances, no idea where I'd use them or whether I ever would. I did a moderate one, a slow one, and a fast one—a suite, and my assistant and I learned them. Harry Warren, who wrote the music for *Yolanda,* came by one day, saw what we were doing, and said, "You know, I have a hell of a tune for that sort of thing," and he sat down and played it. We called Arthur Freed down, and my assistant and I did the dances, and Harry Warren sat at the piano and played. Arthur loved it, wrote the lyrics, and called it "Coffee Time."

And "Coffee Time" in the film indeed does incorporate the three dances Loring mentioned as well as a couple of others, for the number serves not only as the manifestation of the festival spirit of the people but also as the climax of the Astaire-Bremer courtship. The townspeople begin the number in a social dance style; Astaire and Bremer join in, and the people, yielding to their superior talents, stand aside for them and clap to the beat of the music. At one point only the clapping persists, yet the two dancers continue as if dancing to castanets. Individual instruments—including cymbals—provide the accompaniment. Moving into the slow dance of the "suite," Astaire and Bremer dance their courtship, during which Astaire's final acquiescence to Bremer takes place. The people rejoin the lovers as the music becomes that of the 1940s big band era, the dancing being a somewhat more elaborate version thereof as well. This use of unusual rhythms and of discrete choreographic units within a single number is also true of "Red Blues" in *Silk Stockings,* "Let's Kiss and Make Up" in *Funny Face,* and "One Alone" in *Deep in My Heart.*

In an article in *Films and Filming* in January 1956, Michael Kidd wrote "... it was not until '45 that I tried my hand at creating a ballet, *On Stage.* This had an earthiness, a clarity and wry humour which appealed to all audiences, classic dance devotees as well as Saturday night movie goers. This was the kind of response for which I prayed."[33] This universality of appeal has carried over from Kidd's work in ballet on the stage to his choreography for the Broadway theater and to films. Kidd is the choreographer who probably more than any other has most overtly employed gymnastics within his choreographic style. With the exception of his second Hollywood assignment, *The Band Wagon* (on which his work may well have been so affected by Minnelli and Astaire as to have moderated that facet of his style), each Kidd-choreographed film is characterized by at least one dance number in which the dancers perform spectacular feats of dancing, directly or indirectly adapted from gymnastics. The most obvious example is the barn-raising competition from *Seven Brides for Seven Brothers,* but that gymnastic quality is also present in *Guys and Dolls, Merry Andrew, Li'l Abner* and *Hello, Dolly!.* The relationship between dance and gymnastics is a close one, and Kidd exploits that relationship to enhance each one, crossing the arbitrary line between the two and making dance gymnastics and gymnastics dance. Furthermore, he was conscious of the necessity to accommodate the camera to dance and dance to the camera, choreographing for film differently from the stage, and his interest also included integrating the dance into the totality of the film. Since 1952 he has choreographed eight films, appeared in two, and directed one.

In *Seven Brides for Seven Brothers* the gymnastic dancing style becomes a means of characterizing the six younger brothers. Their exuberance, their competitiveness, their general restlessness are manifested in dance. Dance in general assumes multiple functions in *Seven Brides.* In "Goin' Courtin' " it becomes a means of domesticating the brothers; in the barn-raising competition it proves the brothers' superiority over the townsmen (at the same time suggesting that the brothers haven't yet been completely domesticated, though); and "Lonesome Pole Cat" suggests the repressed sexual energy of the brothers. Kidd has written about his involvement with making the dance material essential to the point of the film.

> During preliminary talks with Jack Cummings, the film's producer, and with Stanley Donen, the director, it was emphasized that story, song and dance would all be integral parts of the musical. Each dance would tell a story, at the same time advancing the film's story.
>
> The songs were composed by Johnny Mercer and Gene de Paul as "story points" and this was the logical way of developing a musical.
>
> The hardy barn-raising number . . . expressed honest, robust pioneer men who believed in brawny competition for winning village belles. To show their characters, they were made to dance gymnastically with large strong movements that stood out clearly regardless of pace. With backs upright, chests fully expanded and feet firmly planted on the ground, the story line is told more cogently than by words.[34]

From the first entrance of the younger brothers (one jumps over a fence, one onto the porch), their robustness dominates the film and is shown in contrast to the non-dancing leads, Howard Keel and Jane Powell. Even during "Goin' Courtin' " with its attempt at a more sedate dancing style, Russ Tamblyn "lets go" and the others join by clapping their hands to his involved gyrations. The barn-raising begins with a square dance, a traditional cinematic code of the West, but the dance serves more than a simple identifying purpose. Presented with several variations, including three brothers jumping over the three others standing, it becomes a means for the six brothers to attract girls away from the townsmen who, in turn, challenge the brothers to the dancing duel to prove which group is superior. Performing primarily on two planks between sawhorses, a natural part of the construction set but resembling a gymnastic balance beam, each of the brothers does a series of gymnastic feats (somersaults, jumps into the air while touching the toes, etc.) made more difficult by doing them on the plank. The townsmen compete but are no match for the brothers. The competition ultimately turns into a real battle between the groups as they start to fight while actually putting up the barn. The fight becomes a dance—both stylized and choreographed—as the movements of putting together the barn are mixed with the movements of the fight itself. "Lonesome Polecat" is the most stylized number; the men dance their daily chores, chopping and sawing while singing about their need for companionship. The sounds of the work punctuate the dance material, and the number ends in a tableau, each man standing still in an image which later would probably have been presented as a freeze frame. As in the other dances, the men present themselves through physical exertion and do dances which incorporate that exertion into the material.

There are a number of similarities between Kidd's work for *Seven Brides* and that for his other films. In *Merry Andrew* Danny Kaye does a stylized walk in "Chin Up, Stout Fellow"; there is a choreographed fight at one point; and the exuberant folk dance quality of "Salud" suggests an uninhibitedness like that of the seven brothers. Michael Crawford's and Tommy Tune's athletic leaping and bounding in "Dancing" from *Hello, Dolly!* are also very much in the same vein as are the chorus numbers from *Li'l Abner* and *Guys and Dolls*.

> Rolling a pair of dice is the basic exercise involved in the game played in *Guys and Dolls*, and it is a simple thing to accomplish. . . . many crapshooters make the roll an elaborately gymnastic ritual. Strenuous body and powerful arm movements, suggesting a baseball pitcher's warm-up, accompany the many seemingly unrelated words which are shrieked out at the same time.
>
> I tried to make the dancers leap and whirl at dizzy speeds, giving the impression that they were men possessed of the worst form of gambling fever.[35]

Kidd's awareness of the camera as a choreographic tool (and his consciousness of the CinemaScope width in which he worked on most of his films) is important. "I have found that the camera's ability to see more than the human eye allows an emphasis on close-up shots at important moments and at the same time gives varying angles to the dance which stage audiences could not catch from their static position." And speaking of his preparations for the crap game number in *Guys and Dolls*, "I tried to visualize how the ballet would appear as seen through the roving eye of a CinemaScope lens rather than from a fixed audience viewpoint."[36] One aspect of Kidd's style is a highly mobile CinemaScope camera. Although he probably had little personal choice in terms of the aspect ratio of his films (particularly since several of his important ones were made in the mid-fifties at the beginning of widespread use of the new format), Kidd consciously used CinemaScope for effect. In *Merry Andrew,* the only film he both directed and choreographed, the camera seems always on the prowl, following Danny Kaye riding his bike or swooping in and out to achieve different perspectives during the circus acts. In "Salud" from that same film he spreads a background chorus across the frame to fill in the space while three men dance in the foreground. In "Lonesome Polecat" as well as the barn-raising sequence from *Seven Brides,* he provides multiple dance action at certain points in order to occupy the expanded space of the wider screen.

Although Kidd's eight films were relatively few, working with Astaire, Kelly, Donen, Minnelli, and others gave him the opportunity to participate in several significant films. Though perhaps restrained at times by those with whom he worked, Kidd did seem to have control over his material. Of the "Girl Hunt" ballet in *The Band Wagon,* Minnelli wrote, "The satire couldn't have come off without . . . Michael Kidd's inspired choreography." And of the Astaire-Kidd relationship he added:

> Betty Comden observed that Fred seemed wary around Michael who, despite his youth, brought a more classical approach to dancing than Fred was accustomed to. "It reminded me of the lack of common ground between the movie hoofer and the ballerina, which we had in our script," she says.
>
> But they wound up being firmly in tune, if the relatively short period of three days—in which the ballet was shot—was any indication.[37]

Performing in—but not choreographing—*It's Always Fair Weather,* Kidd did prepare a solo number, "Jack and the Space Giants."

> It was recorded and shot but not previewed. In his ballet Kidd was the solo dancer with a group of children, and André Previn speculates that it might have been deleted for what he calls "intramovie jealousy," or possibly there was simply no room for a ten-minute ballet. Kelly throws some light on this: "We also did one to order for Michael Kidd, really out of courtesy, because the public didn't know Michael, and he was the third of the trilogy which seemed to look lopsided. But that number was cut; it didn't come across—it didn't work out. And I think it was cut rightly so." On the other hand, Donen says, "It was good enough to stay in the picture. It wasn't terrible. It could have been in."[38]

If animosity between Kidd and Kelly developed as a result of *Fair Weather,* it had diminished by the time they collaborated again on *Hello, Dolly!,* for Kidd had sole choreographer credit, and Kelly apparently gave him complete freedom. In his book *The Studio* John Gregory Dunne[39] tells how Kidd worked with costume designer Irene Sharaff and production designer John DeCuir on making necessary changes to accommodate the choreography for the title number, and Kelly has written about his work with Kidd on the choreography in general.

> Except for reaching a broad agreement with Michael on where a number should take us, often I didn't become involved until he had it pretty well blocked out and said "What do you think of this?" I think that at times I provided some constructive suggestions, but the physical work belonged to him.[40]

Kidd was fortunate to be working at a time in which dance was assumed to be essential in the musical and in which the choreographer's role was as important as any other; he was unfortunate to be working when musicals in general became the victim of an increasingly moribund studio system and musicals began to be phased out of standard studio production. As a result, he contributed significantly to the dance musical but not to the degree he probably would have if he had begun his work in Hollywood a few years earlier.

Dancer, choreographer, and director Bob Fosse has, like Michael Kidd, a limited number of film credits and for many of the same reasons as Michael Kidd. Fosse first arrived in Hollywood in the early fifties, and, though appearing in several films immediately, really established his reputation after he went to Broadway when it became clear that production of film musicals was suffering a major decline. First appearing as dancer and second lead in *Give a Girl a Break, The Affairs of Dobie Gillis,* and *Kiss Me Kate,* he has gone on to choreograph and direct *Sweet Charity, Cabaret,* and *All That Jazz.*

Although he does not have credit (nor does he claim credit) in his earliest films, many of the dances have a strong affinity with his later ones. Fosse himself claims that one reason was the peculiarity of his own dancing style.

> As a dancer, I was no choreographer's dream. I just couldn't pick up anyone else's style. I was very limited as a dancer. I had to adjust everyone's work to fit my own body. I didn't work with many choreographers, but those with whom I did work soon realized that a step would look better if I could adjust it for myself. I just couldn't do some things their way. Oh, I might very much like the way it looked, but I couldn't cut it![41]

The distinctive "look" of a Fosse dance is present in his earliest solo dancing/choreography. There is, for instance, a marked difference between Fosse's movements and Tommy Rall's strongly balletic style in "From This Moment On" in *Kiss Me Kate.* One particular example is in the way they jump. Rall's leaps are usually horizontal with legs extended; Fosse's, on the other hand, are usually vertical with knees tucked under him. Fosse tends to exaggerate all movements. A stylized walk, for example, is often used in a Fosse routine, but the walk is done on the ball of the foot with the legs raised very high (in a fashion that is often called cat-like) with each step. Shoulders hunched with the head pushed forward and the torso at a slight angle to the hips are frequent basic stances for Fosse. Almost all dance "requires" a basic stance (often referred to as being on center) which suggests all parts of the body together in a perfect vertical position, a center from which all movement then proceeds. For Fosse, though, one might more accurately say his basic stance is off center—parts of the body isolated from other parts even before movement begins. There, is moreover, an athletic and somewhat gymnastic quality to Fosse's work, but it is different from Michael Kidd's and could perhaps be considered uniquely Fosse. Whereas Kidd tends to have gymnastics dominate a routine, turning gymnastics into dance, so to speak, Fosse abruptly inserts a specific gymnastic movement into an otherwise totally dance-oriented series of movements. His back flips in "Our United State" from *Give a Girl a Break* and "From This Moment On" illustrate this. The movements which one associates with Fosse as a performer one also associates with Fosse as choreographer. The cat-like walk, for example, is evident in "Steam Heat" from *Pajama Game* and that off-center basic stance is a primary sight in Shirley MacLaine's solo "If My Friends Could See Me Now" from *Sweet Charity*. Similarly, he has Tommy Rall interpolate air splits into the competition number from *My Sister Eileen*.

A more general analysis of these aspects of Fosse's dance style reveals certain major characteristics: eccentricity, isolation, repetition, and fragmentation. His work has qualities of uniqueness, growing out of his own physicality, which relates it to the eccentric dancers of the thirties and forties. The isolation of physical movement—using only parts of the body rather than the entire body at times—connects his work to other jazz dancers of the period. He tends to fragment his choreography, that is, to prepare dances in small units rather than in a continuous flow of movement throughout an entire number. And, finally, within a number he uses repetition for effect: two or three dancers often work in unison and repeat some dance step previously employed, though with the possible variations of facing another direction or of a different dancer doing the repeat, for example.

Fosse recognizes the unique quality of much of his work, his involvement with numerous dance styles, and his desire to move in new directions.

> . . . I did watch a lot of dancers when I was young, and when I was very little I was involved in something . . . called Eccentric dancing. . . . And I guess from all of these sources and from whatever I had naturally or instinctively some sort of style has evolved. I'm not terribly fond of hanging onto that style I might add; I wish I could broaden it some.[42]

He also recognizes his idiosyncratic development within that style: " . . . there are . . . certainly not names for the variations of the standard old steps that I do. . . ." The eccentricity, as it were, of Fosse's style is linked with his use of isolation in so-called jazz dance. Isolation, per se, is not unique to Fosse, as Betty Garrett has said in her interview with the author.

Matt Mattox is credited with originating and defining the isolation in jazz movement. Isolation is exactly what it says: you move one part of the body without moving anything else. If you watch really good jazz dancers like Gwen Verdon or Peter Gennaro, every section of their body seems to be self-controlled. They can literally pat their heads and rub their stomachs because they can do things separately. It's not all in one piece. That seems to be very important to jazz because, in order to get the kind of distortion that jazz has, you have to be able to isolate parts of your body and do just what you want with them.

Arlene Croce more specifically describes how Fosse makes that isolation uniquely his own: "Fosse's method is one of closing down and hugging the figure so that the only way it can move is by isolating and . . . featuring anatomical parts. . . ."[43]

Fosse's fragmentation, which in some respects will become the most important aspect of his *film* choreography, seems to take two forms: one, the somewhat disconnected aspect of the dances, each one consisting of a variety of seemingly unrelated sequences in which a back flip or a polka or a hat trick "intrudes" itself among a series of other "intrusions"; and two, a fragmentation in group choreography whereby Fosse frequently breaks the dancers down into small units operating separately, each doing a different dance in counterpoint to the other, as in "Once a Year Day" from *Pajama Game*.

Fosse's use of repetition is similarly unusual, though it is perhaps the most traditional aspect of his style. Repetition usually takes two forms in dance, one, the simultaneous repetition of movement of more than one dancer (the only kind of repetition which Astaire uses, for instance), and, two, repetition of preceding movements usually matching the customary repetition of a section of the music.[44] Fosse uses both kinds. His "entertainment" numbers are generally characterized by several dancers performing in unison. This is true in "Give Me a Band and My Baby" from *My Sister Eileen*, "Who's Got the Pain" from *Damn Yankees*, and "Steam Heat" from *Pajama Game*, for example. Fosse's tendency to have his performers often not face the audience—or the camera—directly provides a certain variety to the second kind of repetition. Since the dancers perform in profile, the repetition is often done with various alternations to the profile stance: dancers facing each other, their backs to each other, all in one direction, or all in the other direction. In "Give Me a Band and My Baby," they not only perform in profile, but each performer has his or her own variation of the repetition as they mime playing individual instruments. Repetition also frequently serves to emphasize the eccentricity of movement, the isolation effect, and the fragmentation of Fosse's style. Again in "Give Me a Band and My Baby" there is an unusual combination of movements to illustrate this. Moving the arms and legs back and forth in an "eccentric" fashion, with the arms moving in one direction and the legs in the other (isolation), Fosse, Tommy Rall, Betty Garrett, and Janet Leigh dance in unison, but also dance separately, fragmenting the unified quality while repeating the movement.

One can assume from a variety of evidence that Fosse was involved from his first films in devising at least part of his own choreography. In his interview with Joseph Hill, Fosse said that much of the work for *Give a Girl a Break* was a collaboration between him and Stanley Donen. (The credits for the film list Donen and Gower Champion as responsible for the dances. The contrast in styles within the film is striking, and the inference is that Champion did the numbers for him and his wife whereas Donen—and Fosse—were responsible for the others.) Fosse's comments suggest that the general idea for the "Balloon Dance" and "Our United State" were Donen's, but that he prepared the steps. Donen "had good ideas," Fosse said, "but he was not very good at steps."[45] Another example of Fosse's early experimentation was in "From This Moment On" from *Kiss Me Kate.*

> The one I guess I did my best work on was something like a forty-five second thing in *Kiss Me Kate* with Carol Haney, which was part of a sextet with Ann Miller, Bobby Van, Tommy Rall, and Jeanne Coyne. We each had a section, and I just went to Hermes Pan and said could I please do my section and if he didn't like it he could throw it out but could he please give me a chance. And he said, "By all means, go ahead." So I did this little forty-five second dance with Carol, and he liked it a lot and he said, "Let's keep it all in, I love it."[46]

With *My Sister Eileen* in 1955 he achieved full choreography responsibilities, thus establishing the style which had been implied in his first films and which would continue in his later ones.

All the characteristics of Fosse's choreographic style are interrelated. His eccentricity—the uniqueness of his work—applies also to his use of the isolation effect; he quite simply does it differently from everybody else. And the fragmentation within the total choreographic pattern seems the perfect corollary to the fragmentation, so to speak, of the body which isolation causes. Fosse has spoken of the change which experience has brought in his attitude about choreograpic patterns.

> Now, when I work in the studio, I go through each number and try to get a combination—or just a general feeling of what I want. Just eight bars of movement and I can build from that, with variations. And patterns . . . Patterns were difficult for me to do in the beginning because they are so strange. I mean, sometimes a simple straight line is the most effective thing you can have.
>
> Yet, I used to go the ballet and watch Balanchine's work. He has the most complicated patterns one can imagine. That used to give me a tremendous inferiority complex. You know: "I must learn and *learn.*" But now I'm more attracted to patterns. They are easier for me. I'm intrigued by the mathematics of patterns.[47]

The sustained flow of Balanchine's choreography, patterns evolving out of preceding ones, is quite different from the individuated pattern process of Fosse, though. Fosse must certainly be aware of this, too; one reason he has

refused invitations to choreograph for a ballet company has been his fear that
" . . . my work wouldn't sustain itself over four or five minutes. . . ."[48] There is
an implicit self-criticism in that fear which assumes the superiority of one style
over another. But Fosse's fragmentation simply has motivations and results
that are different from Balanchine's sequential unity. Balanchine's move
toward greater and greater abstraction of dance is not the same as attempting
integration of dance material into the overall narrative of a play or film, and
that sense of integration seems the prime motivation of Fosse's work.

    In John Kobal's *Gotta Sing Gotta Dance* Fosse enumerates the reasons
dances exist in musicals.

    1. Set the environment or atmosphere or character behaviour. . . .
    2. Move the story or character along.
    3. Express a particular emotion.
    4. The last group . . . are really what could be called just "entertainment."[49]

As with the other major choreographers of the period, he has a conscious
purpose behind his choreography: "I'm trying to get to something about what
people feel in their heads somehow. . . ."[50] His purposeful elimination of all the
so-called "book" numbers from *Cabaret* illustrated the intention behind his
work; the numbers are all provided with an "excuse" for existence, yet they
continue the roles which musical numbers have developed in films over the
years. Each one comments directly on the action in some way. Furthermore,
the restless energy which imbues the characters and situations in most Fosse
films often finds its outlet in his choreography. Shirley MacLaine's exuberance in "If My Friends Could See Me Now" is heightened by the fragmented
dance—each section generally unrelated by steps and pattern to each other
section—which in turn is augmented by the fragmented editing.

    Any film choreographer's style is a combination of dance steps and film,
i.e., camera work, editing, use of the pro-filmic space. This is, of course, no less
true for Fosse than for others. One advantage of studying Fosse's work,
however, is that comparisons can be easily made between his film choreography and his stage choreography. Unlike Astaire and Kelly, for example,
who have done little stage work recently (Astaire, in fact, has done none since
1932; Kelly has done it only limitedly), Fosse has regularly prepared
Broadway musicals, and there is little real difference between the dance
material, per se, which he designs for the stage and that which he designs for
film. There is, however, considerable difference between what he does *with*
that material in the two media. An increased fragmentation of the dance
material by means of editing, particularly, which perhaps reflects the
fragmentation suggested by the dance style itself, has become a significant
part of Fosse's film choreography. On stage that fragmentation can only be
suggested; on film it has become manifest.

The jump cut, which effectively eliminates spatial and temporal transitions in film, is an equivalent to some of Fosse's dance fragmentation, and three numbers in *Sweet Charity* are controlled by the jump cut: "My Personal Property," "If My Friends Could See Me Now," and "I'm a Brass Band." Each one has Shirley MacLaine as Charity displaying her joy and energy through a variety of dance routines in various unrelated areas of space—either different areas of New York City or just different areas of Vittorio's apartment. Liza Minnelli's Sally Bowles in *Cabaret* is an almost frenetic character in a society which is similarly frenetic in its behavior. Obviously the cabaret—which is the location of all the film's numbers except one—is meant to be both microcosmic of that society and a comment on that society. As a result, the cabaret numbers in general and Minnelli's in particular become even more disjointed than the ones in *Sweet Charity*. In fact, it is difficult to call many of them dance; for, while dance exists within them, almost no routine is a completed dance. The isolation of the Fosse dance style is taken to its extreme as he shoots legs or arms or faces in close-up. In "Maybe This Time" he even intercuts Minnelli's singing in the Kit-Kat Club with Minnelli and Michael York in her room after their affair has first begun, thus providing a direct expression of Minnelli's feelings, but "destroying," as it were, the integrity of the number. In fact, the integrity of dance routines has become non-essential in *Cabaret*, subordinated as they are to a more complex system of integration-cum-commentary.

The fragmentation of choreographic patterns, the disorienting juxtaposition of boldly contrasting movements, and the attempt to have all these elements reflect some aspect of the characters are certainly present very early in Fosse's work, but the real fruition of Fosse's camera-dance relationship comes with *Sweet Charity* and *Cabaret*, two of the films which he directed *and* choreographed. In "Our United State" from *Give a Girl a Break* he and Debbie Reynolds briefly polka in the midst of the other facets of the number, yet the camera does not observe that change within the number any differently from the rest. Similarly, "Once a Year Day" from *Pajama Game* is a choreographically rich and fragmented number which looks like organized confusion since so many different groups are dancing different routines simultaneously (e.g., people doing a leapfrog in foreground while couples twirl in background), yet the camera presents the number whole, not singling out any particular group as Fosse would probably have done later. One gets the impression in the later films, however, "that the camera . . . is always restlessly searching for a better vantage point from which to see the movements of the numbers."[51] The generally long-take style of the earlier films gives way when he has greater control to a short-take, fragmented style, but the choreography suggests Fosse trying "short takes" and "fragmentation" just within the dances themselves. There are a few signs in the earlier films, however, of camera work to come. In "Racing with the Clock" from *Pajama Game,* the camera participates, literally racing among the rows of seamstresses, not stopping to observe any one thing but still attempting to gather everything together from simultaneously multiple viewpoints. And the lateral tracking shot, so fundamental a part of Fosse's later shooting style (particularly noticeable in "Big Spender" from *Sweet Charity*), is used in "Steam Heat," also from *Pajama Game.* The extreme stylization both in dance and camera work of "The Aloof" in *Sweet Charity* seems foreshadowed by a similar stylization in the reprise of *Pajama Game's* "Racing with the Clock."

There seems a definite progression in Fosse's work which culminates in *Cabaret.* In one sense it is a movement away from dance, however, and toward exploitation of the film medium itself. The balloon number from *Give a Girl a Break* uses reverse motion; "Racing with the Clock" uses both fast and slow motion; the use of dissolves in "Big Spender" can be achieved only through film; and even the forty-five seconds of "From This Moment On" seem designed for the 3-D process in which *Kiss Me Kate* was originally shot. Although dance has been at the core of all his work, by the time he did *Cabaret* the dance had become subordinated to film. Multiple camera set ups were used to provide that desired fragmentation, taking his work full circle from Fred Astaire's, where multiple camera set ups were used to provide the ultimate in fluidity and to avoid fragmentation. Betty Garrett has said that "Bob Fosse . . . was the first to really make use of film technique in dancing, where the camera angle and what the camera caught was almost as important choreographically as the dancing." One must disagree with her considering him the "first," but there is an accuracy in her remarks. Fosse's concern seems to be one in which dancing, often controlled by the camera, becomes increasingly dependent on it until finally in *Cabaret* "the camera angle and what the camera caught" is *more* important choreographically than the dancing.

Many of those involved with making musicals in Hollywood during the forties and fifties consciously strived for integration of all the elements. Exactly why dance prevailed as the major element is difficult to determine, yet the roles played by individual people must have been one reason. Specifically interested in the musical, choreographers and performers experimented within the studio system to incorporate their ideas into an established film genre. Recognizing the conventions of the form, they worked both to use accepted forms of dance and to expand the conventions to include new material. Although all the forces of the film making team contributed to the musical during this period, Eugene Loring, Jack Cole, Michael Kidd, and Bob Fosse deserve special attention because they represent several different dance styles, different approaches to filming dance, and different phases of the genre. Fosse, particularly, seems the heir of established traditions; seemingly undeterred by others' reticence, he has contined to find the musical an outlet for his expression. Drawing on his background at MGM and on Broadway, Fosse has extended the era of the musical beyond what seemed its studio-bound limits.

Nevertheless, the musical did have a culminating period. The studio system was ideal for musical production, and the combined efforts of those at MGM gave that studio a strong claim to be *the* producer of musicals. Furthermore, in the person of Gene Kelly, MGM had a performer-choreographer-director who conscientiously worked to bring together all aspects of film and dance and to make the musical as important a form of film expression as any other genre. Interacting with those people whose work has just been considered, Kelly came to represent the integrated dance musical.

7

Gene Kelly

Film director Billy Wilder is reported to have said that Gene Kelly is perhaps the world's greatest performer because he is the most complete performer.[1] Although it does not make him the greatest—nor, indeed, superior to any other performer—it is, nonetheless, his complete involvement with film which distinguishes Kelly from almost every other person involved in the making of musical films. He and Fred Astaire are certainly the only two male dancers who ever became major stars in Hollywood, yet Astaire seemed content to remain just a star. Although he quite evidently became involved in the choreographic process—when the dances involved him—Astaire seems not to have been interested in the other aspects of film making. Kelly, on the other hand, almost from the very beginning of his film career, expressed concern about how films were made and how he could contribute on every level. Not just a singer, dancer, and actor in front of the camera, he has been a choreographer, director and—in at least one instance—writer behind the camera. The degree of control which Kelly had over his material may have changed from film to film, but there seems little doubt that in those films he did not direct, as well as those he did direct, there are manifestations of Kelly as auteur—even if multiple auteurs must be assumed. The Kelly persona is a significant factor in all his musicals; that persona is manifested in the characters he plays, in the plots of the films, in the songs he sings—and in the way he sings them—and, perhaps most importantly, in the dances he performs. His dance routines—rarely under the supervision of another choreographer—not only epitomize the characters within the context of the films but also incorporate a dancing style which is both eclectic and unique, which is constantly inventive and resourceful, and which demonstrates Kelly's strong feelings about the necessity of integrating dance and film—within the narrative as well as between the performer and the camera.

The integrated musical was an ideal—indeed, a goal—which Kelly and almost all who worked with him at MGM strived for. They believed themselves to be the heirs of a tradition within the genre which harked back to Astaire and Rogers at RKO and, in spite of Busby Berkeley's presence at the studio during the forties, not to Berkeley at Warner Brothers. Vincente Minnelli has written:

> I knew from my experience at Paramount that I wasn't going to be the Great Savior of the musical film. But I had the temerity to think I still might have something different to offer.
>
> The field seemed wide open. There weren't any musical talents before or behind cameras which impressed me . . . except one. The Fred Astaire dance numbers were the only bright spots in musicals of the late 1930's, though I found the stories inane.
>
> I wasn't impressed by Busby Berkeley's spectacular effects while at Warner Brothers. . . . His devices were ingenious, but they bore little relation to the story or to the "reality" of the piece. Like most musicals of the period, his were crudely made "backstage" stories. The songs weren't integral to the plot.[2]

And when asked directly about his approach to the integration of dance in the musical, Minnelli replied, "The dance has to progress the story. You cannot let the story stop and have a number and then go on."[3] For those at MGM there was, of course, a definite judgment involved; they believed that the integrated musical was qualitatively better. One does not need to accept that judgment, however, to recognize several things about the integrated musical at MGM: that the film makers specifically attempted to have a unity among all facets of the films; that the songs and dances generally did have a direct connection to the diegesis of the film even if they didn't necessarily advance the plot; that those films one could call dance musicals were imbued with a dance spirit which was reflected in the camera work and the general movement of the film; and that those films in which Gene Kelly was a major participant were integrated on several levels because of his considered efforts to make them so.

Understandably, Kelly's primary concern was dance, and his approach was strongly intellectual. Arriving in Hollywood at a transition point in the early forties, Kelly saw immediately that only Astaire was even approaching a style appropriate for the screen but that Astaire's style was too individual to suit anyone but Astaire, and that most other choreographers, like Busby Berkeley, preferred armies of dancers.[4] Simplistic though that analysis may be, nonetheless, it did serve as the impetus for most of Kelly's initial inquiries into the filming of dance. Although Kelly admits that his ideas about film dance first came to fruition during the filming of *Cover Girl,* he also says that those ideas started to develop very early in his film career.

> They began to crystalize during my first film, because I found out that what I would do on the stage just didn't work in films. This was in *For Me and My Gal.* Also, I found out that I was woefully ignorant about the use of the camera. Of course, the director of that first film was Busby Berkeley, and he was a master with the camera. Busby wasn't interested in dancing, per se. He was interested in doing things with the camera, and he taught everybody in Hollywood many things about camera movement. But I soon learned that a five-minute number on the stage would last only a minute in the films, and I began to ask questions, and

I found out that no one in Hollywood seemed to care. There was one dancer, Fred Astaire, with whom (as Orson Welles often put it the camera loves some people) you could set up a camera like Chaplin used to do, and as long as he was in full figure everything would be fine. But for the kind of big sweeping [movement] that I wanted to do and the stronger, kinetically speaking, physically speaking, kind of dancing that I had developed on my own, I had to pretty much start from scratch in working out what I wanted to do with the camera. That began very early . . . . in the making of *Dubarry Was a Lady* . . . Roy Del Ruth . . . wasn't really interested in having dance numbers coming off at all. So I began to set up camera angles, and I'd explain the reasons. The studio was impressed enough to let me go on. . . .[5]

Kelly's intellectualizing about dance and film was concerned with what he felt to be their innate differences.

There seems to be a common misapprehension that dancing and the motion picture are well-suited to each other . . . they are not. The dance is a three-dimensional art form, while the motion picture is two-dimensional; I would compare dancing basically to sculpture and the motion picture to painting. So the difficulties we have in transferring a dance on to film are simply those of putting a three-dimensional art form into a two-dimensional panel.[6]

The problem then, as Kelly saw it, was how to reconcile these different dimension-related art forms into a single entity.

Kelly has often written and spoken of the ways in which he tried to solve that problem. In addition to his comments, there is considerable evidence to be inferred from the films themselves of the ways in which Kelly worked to combine film and dance. Experimenting with the camera in ways specifically aimed at capturing some cinematic equivalent to the sense of kinetic energy inherent in live dance performance; utilizing the increased space made possible both by the larger sets available on studio sound stages and back lots and by the film making processes of changing camera angle, camera movement, and editing; creating a film musical personality—a cinematic persona, so to speak—which would be equally strong in the dance numbers and in the regular narrative portions of the film; developing an eclectic dance style which not only drew on previous and contemporary dance styles but also became adaptable to movements unique to the camera and to the screen in general; and, finally, integrating all elements into a cinematic whole—these were the intellectual considerations which Gene Kelly consciously used during the making of his films and are also the intuitive and inferential manifestations that are, furthermore, present in those films.

Certain choreographers have used cameras in a variety of expedient ways. For Berkeley, using a single camera became a fetish, initially to overcome his own ignorance of how films were made. For Astaire multiple camera set ups provided the fluidity he wanted to maintain his full-figured dance movements. For Kelly, however, using a single camera was part of his thinking while preparing the dances. "I used only one camera so I could have control." Though he did admit to using more than one camera in some instances, particularly during the parade sequence in *Hello, Dolly!*, in general he approached the camera work as he did other aspects of the cinematic process; greater control of lighting, color, and movement were all possible with only one camera.

The camera, to a certain extent, functions as a surrogate for the viewer, an intermediary between the dancer and the audience member. Kelly felt, therefore, that the camera's movements and/or the dancer's movements must provide some of that same kinetic force which the viewer would appreciate seeing dance on a stage.

> ... the more you can go into the camera the more force you'll get, the more impression of a third dimension. . . . You won't get three-dimension, but you'll get force. The more the dancer moves into the camera, he'll build up a force. As he goes away from the camera, he decreases that force. So he should go away from the camera as little as possible, but he should construct a dance so that if he doesn't move, the camera is making a move.

> If the camera is too high, you'll foreshorten the dancer. A dancer works all his life for a long line. If you use the camera high, you'll . . . get a stunted line.

Similarly, in his biography of Kelly, Clive Hirschhorn notes:

> ... when a camera follows a dancer from left to right—in other words, when they're moving parallel with each other—the effect is rather like two trains travelling together at sixty miles an hour, and . . . the impression given is that the trains are standing still. And so it is with dancing on film. If the camera moves at the same speed as the dancer, there's hardly any movement at all.
>
> This was one of the first things he noticed about putting a dance on film. . . . What he did in his panning shots, was to place vertical props in the background or even the foreground—the equivalent of, say, telegraph poles to further the train analogy. So, as the camera panned, and the props shot past, one did at least get some feeling of speed and movement.

> ... he realized that the eye of the camera wasn't in any way like the eye of a human being. The eye of the camera will only enclose a certain area of the "environment." So if a dancer is standing in the middle of a room, all that is seen of the room is the portion behind the dancer. On the stage this did not apply. With . . . peripheral vision, one is able to see the dancer in his complete environment in the theatre . . . which, Gene said, is as it should be . . . because the environment and the dance are inextricably linked. The one enhances the other. . . .

> With photographed dance most of the environment is eliminated—unless, of course, the camera is kept as far back as possible. But what happens then is that while the whole environment is seen, the dancer is . . . small. . . . And in a close shot of him, the background goes out of focus. . . .

He realized that unless he invented a whole new way of filming a musical number, these problems would never be satisfactorily overcome, and would put a ceiling on his impact as a dancer in pictures.[7]

Other film choreographers and dancers, of course, have made similar observations about the relationship between the camera and the performer; Kelly, however, seems to have done more self-conscious experimenting to determine exactly how that intermediary role played by the camera can serve to enhance the impression the dance has on a viewer.

Among his experiments Kelly has attempted dance in contexts available only on the screen, particularly those involving special effects cinematography of various kinds—double exposure, animation, and split screen, for example. One of his first such attempts was the so-called "Alter Ego" number from *Cover Girl,* which Kelly did on loan-out to Columbia.

The conception of this dance came from the desire to do a pure cine dance. In other words, doing something that would be impossible to do in any other medium. The "Alter Ego" number answered that description perfectly, and yet was not represented just as a cinematic "trick." There had been other "trick" numbers in movies before. I didn't want to do a "trick" number, but I did want to use the visual medium in a way so as to express an emotional struggle.[8]

As with many of Kelly's more experimental numbers and larger projects, he had to battle considerable opposition even to begin. Columbia's special effects department was convinced that the double exposure synchronized movement could not be achieved with the panning and dollying camera which Kelly had envisioned for the routine. Rudolph Mate, the film's director of photography, was convinced, however, that it could be done and felt that Kelly should be given the requisite assistance.[9] The success of that number—and of the film— made it somewhat easier for Kelly to persuade colleagues to work with him on material which had not previously been tried on film. Such experiments included the cartoon sequence with Jerry the mouse in *Anchors Aweigh* (and the later similar combination of live action and animation in *Invitation to the Dance*), the "New York, New York" montage of *On the Town,* and the threeway split screen of "Once I had a Dream" from *It's Always Fair Weather.*

These more obvious experiments are, in a sense, however, "tricks," despite Kelly's comments to the contrary, and they do illustrate certain theoretical concepts about the nature of film and dance. Richard Griffith, for example, suggests a "problem" in regard to the animation experiments.

However high or beautifully a dancer leaps, he is pulled back to earth. But in film, with its complete control of space and time, he may float at will above us all. A dream come true? It proved the opposite. For when the pull of gravity is no longer felt by the audience, felt almost kinesthetically, the achievement of the dancer too is no longer felt and the drama of the dance goes flat.[10]

There seem to be two factors which Griffith did not consider in his judgment and which are important in understanding the nature of Kelly's experiment. One is the nature of the animation itself. Griffith—and, indeed, everyone else who has written about Kelly's animation sequences—referred to the sequences from *Anchors Aweigh* and *Invitation to the Dance* as if they were the same, yet there is a fundamental difference between the two. In *Anchors Aweigh* Kelly is performing almost completely amidst real objects (i.e. the objects in the pro-filmic space are three-dimensional ones on a set) and the mouse has been drawn in, whereas in *Invitation to the Dance* Kelly—and Carol Haney and David Kasday—perform as part of a two-dimensional, painted cartoon background. The difference is substantial, for, to take note of Griffith's criticism, in *Anchors Aweigh* it is only the mouse who is weightless, who "may float at will above us all," as indeed he does: at one moment playing on the very nature of that defiance of gravity, Kelly has the mouse, tired of the workout Kelly has been giving him, lie on his side in mid-air. By contrast the three real characters of "Sinbad the Sailor," having originally been photographed against a plain backdrop, seem to walk where there is no ground and seem to leap higher and cover more space than would otherwise be the case. The second factor which Griffith failed to consider is the nature of each sequence as an integral unit, and dance, though the most important, is only one part of the sequence. Each sequence is a tale, *une fable,* in which the defiance of gravity as part of the dance is incorporated into the whole. The sequence with the mouse is one example of the self-consciously humorous way in which the film makers were commenting directly on what they were doing. And in "Sinbad the Sailor" the animation contributes in other ways to the routine. As the characters dance within the painted background, doors appear and disappear, characters get larger or smaller and, in one instance, "come to life": Scheherezade, initially a cartoon figure, changes into a "real" figure during the routine. There is no need for the audience to feel "almost kinesthetically," for one aspect of Kelly's experimentation with animation was to play on that very feeling, both to use and to defy the expectation of it within an obviously artificial setting.

The montage from *On the Town* and split screen from *It's Always Fair Weather* exemplify different aspects of dance experiment but similar aspects of film—the manipulation of time and space. In both instances the material is determined by its relationship to the whole film. "New York, New York" is not really a dance at all, but its use of the jump cut to take the three sailors around New York City, thus compressing both time and space (four hours of diegetic time become only a few minutes of screen time), makes the sequence part of the general dance patterns of the whole film. "Once I Had a Dream" is a dance, but one in which the characters, in three distinct diegetic locations, are brought together in the same screen space. Though separated within the story, they are together on the screen, each commenting, as it were, on the others' private musings—through dance—about the failures of their lives. In both these instances, as well as in the animation sequences and in the "Alter Ego" number, certain technical resources of the medium had to be considered, and—except for "New York, New York"—complicated and repetitive procedures had to be carried out in order for the movements of the various performers to match. Certain "tricks," in other words, made possible the integration of these numbers into the films.

The obviousness of these "trick" numbers makes them easy to discuss, but Kelly's experimentations were often far more subtle, concerned, as they were, with the more basic—and therefore probably more mundane and less noticeable—aspects of putting steps together into a meaningful dance sequence and of photographing that sequence. Since Kelly's numbers were rarely restricted to an on-stage performance, he was able to use space in a broader, more spread-out fashion. Not tied in, furthermore, to an aesthetic of full-figured, single-take dances, he could choreograph with a sense of *using* the space rather than simply performing within it. In this regard Kelly has said, "What I did in 'Singin' in the Rain'. . . was to take the whole street and keep the dance moving down the street . . . ." It is indeed customary for a Kelly number to use "the whole street," so to speak, to use the full spatial resources of his set. Rather than restricting the dance movement within a confined area—an invisible proscenium arch—he generally allows it to move freely over a seemingly undefined area. Changes in camera angle (either through camera movement or editing) combine with dance movement to reveal new space for the dancer; areas of off-sceen space are constantly being revealed on screen and thus become potential dance space. This is most apparent in those numbers which move from room to room; for example, in "Prehistoric Man" from *On the Town* the five dancers move into several areas of the museum, and in "Good Morning" from *Singin' in the Rain* the three dancers move through several rooms of Don Lockwood's home. But the principle is also important—though less evident, perhaps—in other numbers. Dancing along the wharf to "The Hat My Dear Old Father Wore" in *Take Me Out to the Ball Game,* Kelly's movements, accompanied by changes in camera angle, take him away from the crowd, to whom he first began singing, into another area of the set where he can be alone and perform the number more or less as a soliloquy. One essential of this style is editing with match cuts on action, for match cutting allows the dancer to go in different directions. "I Like Myself" from *It's Always Fair Weather* provides Kelly with several areas in which to roller skate/dance. At one particular moment he glides in arabesque around a corner. The camera change during the filming to capture the movement—the two shots linked with a match cut—as he rounds the corner also provides another space—in this case another street—in which Kelly can dance. Examples of this expansion into different space by moving in different directions and into different locations begin early. The dance with the broom in *Thousands Cheer,* though occurring on one set, moves from floor to soda fountain and back by means of both match cutting and camera movement. And in "Make Way for Tomorrow" from *Cover Girl* Kelly, Phil Silvers, and Rita Hayworth dance out of the bar and through the streets in a way that prefigures similar broadly-spaced movements in later films, particularly *On the Town, Singin' in the Rain,* and *It's Always Fair Weather.*

This greater involvement with the pro-filmic space required both a choreographing *of* the camera and a conscious choreographing *for* the camera. Furthermore, it made possible, as Kelly saw it, the expression of greater kinetic force which he had found missing in much dance film. With dances moving laterally across the frame within an invisible proscenium arch, there was no opportunity for that movement into the camera which he felt to be necessary to overcome the two-dimensional limitations imposed by film. Involving the camera more readily in the movement, however, giving the dancer multiple directions in which to move with a constantly changing performing front, Kelly made available both the force of the dancer moving toward the camera and also its opposite, the force of the camera moving toward the dancer—even into close-up, if necessary, with the resultant sense of a part of the body being choreographed individually. Dancing through the streets of New York (moving from one discontinuous space to another via the match cut, much as the three sailors did in *On the Town*), the three soldiers of *It's Always Fair Weather* make movements toward the camera an essential of their routine. They leap exuberantly up the street, directly toward the camera, and, at one point, using trash can lids for "shoes," they hop on the rims of the lids—again toward the camera. Kelly, O'Connor, and Reynolds strut forward at the end of "Good Morning," turning over the sofa in the process; Kelly and Sinatra bounce from bed to bed toward the camera during "I Begged Her" in *Anchors Aweigh.* Other examples abound. Interestingly enough, Kelly's dictum about movement away from the camera is manifest in the films, too; for when he wants a number to end more or less unobtrusively, to have the dancer or dancers move easily back into the narrative of the film, he ends with movement away from the camera or with the camera pulling back from the action. The three couples of *On the Town,* having left the top of the Empire State Building during the title song, walk into the camera when they get to the street, but then there is a change in camera position, and the number ends with their walking away from the camera, mingling with the crowds on the street. At the end of "Singin' in the Rain" Kelly walks away from the camera *and* the camera booms up into a high angle long shot as the image fades out. Withholding that kinetic force could serve as advantageously as emphasizing it.

Another important part of Kelly's dance/camera preparation was his organization of movement and arrangement of the pro-filmic material (people and objects) within the pro-filmic space to create the illusion of depth, so often denied to dance on the screen, and to give a heightened sense of the cinematic, even to those numbers which retain a certain quality of being performed within a proscenium arch. Indeed many Kelly numbers are danced as if for an audience—with varying degrees of involvement between the performers and the camera and, of course, there are those numbers actually performed on a stage as part of the narrative. "A Day in New York" from *On the Town* displays several aspects of both organization and photographic principles. Since it is danced on a stage (with Kelly imagining that he is seeing it performed), there is only one basic frontal camera position with each section of the piece shot in one take. The camera generally follows action, as it does when Kelly slides on his knees to the Miss Turnstiles poster, for instance, or remains still as when Kelly and Vera-Ellen dance in the ballet studio. This particular scene also uses lights and shadows to create a balanced frame and the illusion of depth. Kelly and Vera-Ellen are always slightly to the left in the frame and their shadows to the right. Performing against a bright red backdrop makes their dark shadows stand out like silhouettes and become "another couple" performing the dance behind them. The set of "A Day in New York" is built on two levels with a raised platform halfway back. This platform fulfills a couple of functions as it is made part of the choreography. Dancers in front do not block dancers behind, and, furthermore, Kelly, particularly, uses it to advantage as he moves easily between the levels; in fact, it serves to show him off at his most dancingly athletic.

Kelly's eclecticism always prevails, however; one can never infer set rules to his cinematographic style. "Slaughter on Tenth Avenue" is performed on a stage in *Words and Music,* yet the camera becomes much more closely involved with the dance, joining the dancers on the stage, so to speak. And in "Be a Clown" with the Nicholas Brothers in *The Pirate,* Kelly leaves the stage on which they are performing and takes the dance into the audience. Though not performed on a diegetic stage, certain other dances have been choreographed with a very conscious awareness of the audience-camera. On top of the Empire State Building in the "Shore Leave Blues" sequence *(On the Town)* the three women, performing lined up as if on a stage, kneel at the feet of the three guys and turn their heads at one point to look directly into the camera. Yet always aware of the need to organize for the film image and to create the sense of depth, Kelly has the guys twice jump up on benches so that they can be seen above the women.

One of the most self-consciously audience-oriented aspects of Kelly's work was his designing material for applause—a creation of dance which took into account the sense of spectacle innate in much dance, though without the multitudes generally associated with spectacle in film. Astaire allegedly always designed the endings of his numbers to elicit applause, but the endings of Kelly's numbers follow two patterns, each reflecting a conscious manipulation of space and the camera. One ending was to diminish the sense of the number *as* a number and have the dancers simply return to their "real" lives in the narrative (often associated with a pull-back of the camera or the performer moving away from the camera, as previously mentioned). At the end of the squeaky board/torn newspaper dance in *Summer Stock,* for example, Kelly simply picks up part of the paper and, reading, casually walks off stage. Many numbers, on the other hand, emphasize the number as a number by a climactic final display (often associated again, though in contrast to the other endings, with movement—dancers toward the camera or camera toward the dancers, including dollying in to close-up of Kelly's smiling face at times). A tableau arrangement of several dancers holding a final position, all facing the camera-audience, ends "O'Brien to Ryan to Goldberg" *(Take Me Out to the Ball Game),* "You Can Count on Me" *(On the Town),* "Dig for Your Dinner" *(Summer Stock),* and "Moses Supposes" *(Singin' in the Rain);* each number has that punctuating final movement, as well—a slide down the table in "Dig for Your Dinner," a camera movement into medium shot in "Moses Supposes." (Occasionally the "applause" for such an ending is diegetically grounded. At the end of "I Like Myself" in *It's Always Fair Weather* Kelly has attracted a crowd who spontaneously compliment him for his skating/dancing. And naturally those numbers which are performed on a stage usually have similar endings.) It is, nevertheless, an evidence of Kelly's sense of the appropriateness of such endings that they usually serve an additional function. The end of "You Can Count on Me" emphasizes the fact that Lucy (Alice Pearce) does not fit in with the rest of the group. She is both figuratively and literally beneath them: Gene Kelly is lying on the table while Jules Munshin, Frank Sinatra, Ann Miller, and Betty Garrett, each holding an arm or a leg, twirl him around; but Alice Pearce is sitting on the floor almost underneath the table. At the very end of the number, the five of them climb on to the table but when Alice Pearce gets on, the table collapses, leaving them in a disarrayed final tableau image.

It is difficult to isolate every aspect of Kelly's work because he was involved in so much. Furthermore, there is a sense of integration with everything he did in film. His preparation of dance material for the camera involves both dance and cinematography, of course, but also involves his reasons for doing the dances in *that* particular way. His awareness of screen space and his explorations of it included explorations of dance from within that screen space. Not the least of Kelly's explorations were those involving his own persona, the personality he projected as a character in the films, and this persona, too, was closely linked with his other explorations into the film medium and its relationship with dance. Kelly was aware from the outset that he had a certain physicality which dictated a certain association with dance in his films.

> The reason I liked to play prize fighters or sailors or soldiers is, number one, that you usually have a uniform on, and you can dance better in it. When you dance in clothes, your dancing has to—well, let's take it at its greatest with Fred Astaire. If Fred's dancing with a suit on, it fits his style because his style is *intime;* it's intimate and it belongs with a tie and a suit—whether it's white tie or not doesn't matter. It's an elegant, very graceful, very intimate style. Mine is certainly just the opposite. I put on a suit, and I have a tendency to look like a truck driver going to mass on Sunday.

Almost always playing characters who are figures of American popular culture, Kelly has created a recognizable image for himself. "Kelly has an American-baseball personality," Kyle Chrichton wrote in 1945 (almost prophetically in light of later Kelly roles).

> On the screen it reveals itself in a slow, meaningful manner that shows depth, seriousness and even a trace of menace. In a lighter way it may be pictured as hot dogs, peanuts, hot afternoons in bleachers, smoky fight clubs, pick-up games on corner lots. If you have imagination, you think of Kelly in terms of the corner drugstore, the pool room, the basketball shot from the middle of the floor that wins the game.[11]

Yet it is an image which is extraordinarily diverse, drawing upon myth and history to give dimension to his characters and to his dances. Richard Griffith has recognized a development in the Kelly persona:

> And while he was experimenting with film form, Kelly was also ransacking the history of the dance for imagery which, though traditional, was still usable. . . . The early images of Gene were the straw-hatted song-and-dance-man, the amorous sailor, the cheapjack con-man, but soon the Clown and the Harlequin appeared.[12]

The Clown and the Harlequin were present in earlier roles, however, and just became more overt when he specifically adopted their traditional costumes (at the end of *The Pirate,* for example, or in *Invitation to the Dance*). As Albert Johnson recognized: "one can identify in the sailor Kelly's personal screen creation of contemporary man as a bell-bottomed Pierrot."[13] Kelly also drew on film itself for identification. Jean-Louis Caussou has said that Kelly's characters are a *pastiche* of the myths of American cinema: the gangster, the cowboy, the star, and Charlie Chaplin.[14] Douglas Newton suggests that "the musical film performs the important function of creating a modern myth,"[15] and Kelly combines numerous aspects of that modern myth into his persona.

John Russell Taylor has a generally negative reaction to what he perceives the Kelly screen personality to be.

> Kelly is the open, confident, brash . . . , straight-forward American male, with a smile on his face for the whole human race, as one of his songs puts it. The personality is not altogether appealing. There is sometimes the feeling that the charm is laid on a little too thickly, that the smile is a trifle synthetic, that, to quote another of his songs, he may like himself just a fraction too much.[16]

Taylor's comments, however, do not recognize the great variety of Kelly's roles, nor do they relate the ways in which he presents his personality through dance, for it is precisely through his dance roles that the persona is revealed. The Kelly persona incorporates characteristics of the *alazon* or impostor from Greek comedy who pretends to be something other than he really is, and Kelly does often play a guy who feels that the best way to get what he wants is to impress people: thus he adopts brashness and self-confidence as the means toward that end. He almost always realizes, however, that, instead of impressing people, he is alienating them and that by being himself he will succeed far more readily. That true self is not necessarily less confident but is less egotistical and less aggressive; he is charming and clever and capable of wittily expressing himself through song and dance. Indeed, in many of the films a major number reflects that change in the Kelly character: previously brash and assertive (during which period he generally neither sings nor dances), he has become aware of being able to be himself—at which point he then becomes free to express himself musically.

This is true from his first screen appearance on. Playing a seeming cad in *For Me and My Gal,* Kelly changes attitude twice. Initially he changes from a character with considerable bravado in order to persuade the Judy Garland character that he is sincere about her. Having convinced her of such, he is drinking coffee with her in an all-night restaurant when they have their first love duet, "For Me and My Gal." Ostensibly Kelly is showing Garland some pointers about how to perform the number, but their dancing takes on broader meanings and plays the same metaphoric courting roles as "Main Street" in *On the Town* and "You Were Meant for Me" in *Singin' in the Rain.* (The second change in *For Me and My Gal* occurs when the Kelly character realizes his mistake in purposely avoiding the draft and then makes amends, finally winning July Garland so that they can resume their combined singing and dancing career.) The comparison with these latter two numbers is appropriate, for they are the numbers which the Kelly character performs after he has changed his approach. When the down-home boy from Meadowville, Indiana, prevails over the worldly-wise sailor in *On the Town,* then Kelly and Vera-Ellen can dance together down "Main Street." And beneath his star's trappings in *Singin' in the Rain* lies a down-to-earth guy who convinces Debbie Reynolds that she was, indeed, meant for him.

Certain roles epitomize the conscious adoption of role playing within the films. In *The Pirate* the actor Serafin becomes Mack the Black in order to fulfill Manuela's fantasies, but it is *as* Serafin that he wins her. In one of his minor roles, that of husband number four in *What a Way to Go,* he even apologizes for his brashness at one point, saying that it is "just my way." And in his dance in the night club he becomes a success only when he abandons his role as a clown and performs *sans* costume, *sans* makeup. These changes in the Kelly characters are manifest in other films: Jerry Mulligan is initially aggressive in pursuing Lise (Leslie Caron) in *An American in Paris,* but once he has toned down his approach, they get together and dance "Our Love is Here to Stay"; similarly, Ted Riley first tries to impress Jackie Leighton (Cyd Charisse) in *It's Always Fair Weather* with his cool, New York glibness, but ultimately it's his true self (realized as part of the film's narrative) which attracts her (since this self-realization comes about over a longer period of time within the film, there is no courtship love-duet).

The Kelly persona is complex, drawing as it does on such a wide variety of sources. Indeed, the complexity and eclecticism of his dance style are reflected in the Kelly characters, for they manifest the diversity of his approach to all aspects of dance and of filming dance. In addition, the costumes he wore also represented the wide background Kelly brought to those roles, and his figures of popular culture and modern myth incorporated aspects of high culture and ancient myth. The vaudeville song and dance man of *For Me and My Gal* and *Summer Stock* is a hoofer—his principal dances are tap routines. The introspective Pierrot of *Invitation to the Dance* as well as the Pierrot sailor of "A Day in New York," both coming directly from Italian *commedia dell'arte,* is a more balletic dancer. (Not insignificantly, the costume which Jerry Mulligan wears to the ball at the end of *An American in Paris* and in which he "dreams" the final ballet seems a combined Pierrot-Harlequin outfit—black and white with large diamond shapes on it.) And the swashbuckler of the dream dances of *Anchors Aweigh* and *The Pirate* is an athletic performer, combining the grand gestures of *tour de force* ballet movements with acrobatic and gymnastic stunts. In *all* these roles, furthermore, Kelly dressed to provide identifiable characteristics, for not only did the costumes become signs of character, but also they were perfect outfits in which his popular culture figures could dance.

You can't play a *part* and come out in ballet slippers, and you can't come out in regular shoes, [Kelly has said] so I sort of invented the wearing of moccasins (which bend like ballet shoes) and white socks, and made sure that the pants were very tight and rolled up a bit, and wore a shirt or a sweatshirt or something that would show the figure. . . . a sailor suit was ideal. . . .[17]

There has been a recurrent fascination with sailors in musicals (Arlene Croce notes their indebtedness to the play *Shore Leave* and the musical *Hit the Deck*,[18] but they surely hark back to Gilbert and Sullivan's *H.M.S. Pinafore* as well), and Kelly extended the sense of camraderie of those sailors to his other popular culture figures—the show-biz mates of *Cover Girl, Summer Stock,* and *Singin' in the Rain,* the expatriate pals of *An American in Paris,* and, of course, the three ball players of *Take Me Out to the Ball Game* and the three soldiers of *It's Always Fair Weather.* Moreover, having those buddies dance together " 'seems to be a very effective masculine way to approach things. It was done in ballets *Les Matelots* (1925) and in *The Three Ivans* (1921): historically, it goes way back to the nineteenth century. Things grow better,' Kelly philosophizes, 'if they have roots. So the three sailors dancing together, the fact they were American, and that it was American music, delighted all of us.' "[19] In a sense, then, Kelly's roles frequently redefined older or mythical character types in American terms.

The " 'lonely' hero" of the modern musical, as Douglas Newton suggests, exists "in situations and has attitudes we think of as essentially modern,"[20] yet that lonely hero is an American adaptation of an ancient character type. Pierrot is the lonely figure of *commedia dell'arte,* beset by Fate and harrassed by the other characters, but he is one who endures, finally gaining the audience's sympathy and the favor of a Pierrette or Columbine. In spite of his aligning himself with buddies or companions, Kelly's characters are also frequently alone, and significant dances are soliloquies—almost meditations on the essential loneliness of his role at that point. Gaby realizes that he must find Miss Turnstiles by himself, and, having lost her a second time, he wants to be by himself—first, at the bar and, later, when he dreams the "A Day in New York" ballet in which the separateness of his role is emphasized both by the anonymity of the other dancers and the disappearance of Vera-Ellen. The ballet from *An American in Paris* is almost the same in its diegetic motivation and in its serving as a microcosm of the rest of the film. Jerry Mulligan has been abandoned by Lise and consequently dreams the dance replay of their relationship. Though far more elaborate than the one in *On the Town,* the ballet does perform the same function, for ultimately the Kelly character is left alone within the dream/dance. There is a somewhat melancholy aspect to almost all the Kelly roles, for it is the character's nature to brood about his loneliness. The "Alter-Ego" dance in *Cover Girl* is a soliloquy in which he is worried about losing his girl friend; his squeaky board number in *Summer Stock* is a meditation on his new feelings for the July Garland character; and, to a certain extent epitomizing the roles in the musicals, his Pierrot in the first section of *Invitation to the Dance* even dies while trying to overcome an unrequited love.

Certainly one important aspect of Americanizing older material is its incorporating that material—those myths—into contemporary urban settings, and Douglas Newton has also recognized the significance of "city" in musicals.

> The city is of course one of the great elements of the musical. Because audiences have been brought up on the happy, however mistaken, belief that films reproduce reality, the musicals also must have ostensibly "real" settings. The characters have to be based on the modern world, or a familiar period of the past; and as a result the musicals are among the rare poetic works so far to accept big city life without using it simply as decorative detail or a satirical target.
> A good deal of the quality of *On the Town* springs from its joyful acceptance of taxis, apartment life, and the lyrical aspect of townscapes. The wonderful slow opening of the film, New York in the early morning sunlight, is intensely idyllic in mood and poetic in quality. The premise of *On the Town* is that God's in His Heaven, all's right with the world, and the world's New York. It is as valid as the more detached view of *The Naked City,* because it manages to transform the facts into raw poetry. The images of *On the Town* show that its creators are the Poets Laureate of New York. . . .[21]

The Kelly character is often a city character, though one with a small town soul, so to speak. The brashness, the aggressiveness, of his assumed persona within the films is very much a city-oriented persona, but just as that persona hides a more likeable person, so does that characteristic suggest that there is a more personal and friendly nature hiding beneath the outward appearance of the city. This is true of *Cover Girl* and *It's Always Fair Weather* as well as *On the Town*. (And in *Summer Stock* he comes from the city, perpetuating his city personality but revealing his true nature beneath it.) In some respects Ted Riley of *It's Always Fair Weather* particularly represents that Kelly persona. He stays in New York after the war and becomes a fight promoter and con man, a hard-boiled man-about-town who hides the fact that he can recite Shakespeare and is a sensitive spirit, but ultimately he realizes that he cannot continue leading his life that way. The city even becomes a redeeming factor for all three guys in the film; each one comes to a self-realization partly owing to the role of the city as catalyst. Furthermore, the iconographic presence of the city is celebrated in certain of the film's musical numbers. A bar-hop montage early in the film leads directly into dancing in the street, at one point integrating a taxi into the dance and using the Third-Avenue El as a backdrop to the shenanigans. An expensive restaurant, a boxing gym, a roller rink (and more importantly the street outside the rink), and a television studio are all city-identifiable settings in which the characters work out their problems. The lonely Pierrot figure almost becomes corrupted by contemporary society, but working and dancing within that society, within a city setting, he nonetheless comes to conclusions about himself and succeeds in regaining his self-respect and winning his girl.

Among other popular culture aspects of Kelly's work was his incorporation of images and characters from the movies into several of his films. He recognized the nature of film as a medium which often draws upon itself for reference and used earlier films as a source for those roots which he found helpful in identifying his characters. Kelly used other films as choreographic inspiration, as objects to satirize, and as *homages* in the French sense. Most obvious is *Singin' in the Rain;* its self-conscious parody of film made references to Busby Berkeley films in "Beautiful Girl" and to George Raft's coin-tossing *Scarface* gangster in the "Broadway Ballet," for examples, particularly appropriate. But Kelly also worked film references into his own characterizations, subtly (as in "I Like Myself" from *It's Always Fair Weather*) and overtly (as in *The Pirate*). *Singin' in the Rain,* of course, satirizes a number of aspects of the film industry, the star system, and, particularly, the advent of sound film, and the film is filled with specific and general references to early sound films. Several of the songs were written originally for early musicals (as covered in detail in a preceding chapter), most specifically "Singin' in the Rain" *(Hollywood Revue of 1929)* and "Broadway Melody" and "You Were Meant for Me" *(Broadway Melody).* Although the film was designed around the Brown and Freed songs, other film references had to have been Kelly's specific contribution. One such is an imitation of Charlie Chaplin's walk (with Kelly swinging an umbrella instead of a cane) as part of the choreography of the title song.

There is indeed a strong affinity between Kelly's characters—usually as they appear in the dances—and certain silent comics. Kelly's tendency to fit his dance into a diegetic situation, overcoming obstacles present in the pro-filmic space and incorporating them into the routine, is reminiscent, particularly, of Keaton. His use of props of various kinds fits this pattern; furthermore, most of these dances are performed "silent." Dancing with a broom in *Thousands Cheer,* on beds in *Anchors Aweigh,* on the scaffolding of an unfinished building in *Living in a Big Way,* with museum artifacts in *On the Town,* with a squeaky board and a newspaper in *Summer Stock,* on top of a piano in *An American in Paris,* and with trash can lids and on roller skates in *It's Always Fair Weather,* Kelly projects an involvement with the "things of this world" which reflects a similar involvement from Chaplin or Keaton, though without their "battles" with those objects. Indeed, "I Like Myself" seems to be a specific *homage* to two earlier roller-skating sequences, one being Chaplin's scene in the department store in *Modern Times* and the Astaire-Rogers duet to "Let's Call the Whole Thing Off" in *Shall We Dance* (released, incidentally, the year after *Modern Times* and perhaps also drawing on the earlier film). The Kelly character, like many silent comics, is always somewhat ingenuous, expressing a certain joy and innocence as he confronts the "things of this world" and makes them part of his dance. Having escaped from the roller rink wearing the skates, he doesn't at first realize that he is still wearing them. When he becomes conscious of it, he shrugs and accepts it and continues dancing. When the cop confronts him at the end of "Singin' in the Rain," he initially acts guilty, shrinking away from the policeman like a little kid having done something wrong, but as the number fades out, he seems to become proud of his actions, stands straight and tall, gives away the umbrella to a startled passerby, and tips his hat to the officer.

Kelly's most self-consciously film-based characterization is his role as Serafin in *The Pirate* (the role prefigured somewhat by the swashbuckler dream dance in *Anchors Aweigh,* though that seems modeled more on Valentino).

> From the start, Gene's idea of the part was to poke some affectionate fun at his childhood heroes, Douglas Fairbanks in the swashbuckling scenes, and John Barrymore in the romantic ones. Minnelli, too, was charmed with the idea of satirizing the entire myth of the adventure yarn.[22]

> Gene Kelly's uncomplicated, Vaudevillian movie persona was . . . severely altered in *The Pirate.* His performance is a carefully worked-up pastiche of Douglas Fairbanks romantic heroes and that latter period John Barrymore specialty, the matinee idol as the height of narcissistic self-parody. This theatrical joke of a character was . . . not the foot-loose sailor-suited Kelly. . . . The parodic posturings, the luxuriant mustache, the finger-waggling and eye-rolling were often criticized as overacting.[23]

In "Niña" and the "Pirate Ballet," particularly, Kelly's characterization manifests these two influences. Swaggeringly romantic in "Niña," he jumps—sometimes literally—from woman to woman with an air of nonchalance and a typical Kelly bravado, but—as with most other Kelly roles—once committed to Manuela, Serafin reveals himself—though ironically here—to be not quite so brash but nonetheless clever and ingenious in accomplishing his goals and achieving a victory over his adversaries. And doing his own stunts in the ballet (as well as actually walking a tightrope at another point), Kelly revealed himself capable of great athletic skill and swashbuckling stunts à la Fairbanks. (Minnelli noted that they conscientiously filmed certain parts of the ballet in single takes to emphasize that no stunt man was being used: "Gene is very athletic, and the great thing in this was the slide up this enormous pole, but you had to show that it was he who actually did it and not a double. As he came down, then, this tiny figure stopped right in front of the camera, so that you saw this was in the same shot.") Kelly's character in *The Pirate* serves to emphasize the reality/fantasy-life/art dichotomy which is the theme of the film. Furthermore, there are other film references which make the Kelly characterization fit into a total pattern: Judy Garland's earlier role in *The Wizard of Oz* becomes a source of humor at two points, once when Aunt Inez tells her, "You can make anything come true if you wish for it hard enough," and again when her cry, "Aunt Inez, Aunt Inez," is made to sound particularly like "Auntie Em, Auntie Em."

The Kelly characterizations are, most significantly, all of a piece within the individual films. Certainly part of the process of integration as Kelly viewed it was to move easily and naturally from the regular narrative portions of the films into the numbers and back again; that required a dancing persona, though not necessarily a character within the diegesis who is explained to be a dancer. True, many Kelly characters are entertainers (in *For Me and My Gal, The Pirate, Take Me Out to the Ball Game, Summer Stock, Singin' in the Rain,* and *Les Girls,* for examples), yet they are rarely established initially as professional dancers; nor do the numbers serve, as so often in Astaire-Rogers films, as entertainments within the film. Instead, the impression is given that this person dances naturally, and, as a result, the character in the numbers is the same character as in the rest of the film. Even those numbers which are performed on stage for an audience reflect the characterization of the moment. In "Fit as a Fiddle" from *Singin' in the Rain,* for example, his assumed movie star image of sophistication and class is being ironically debunked by the "truth" revealed in the number. (It is significant, also, that in two films in which he performs as part of an obviously artificial onstage show—"Slaughter on Tenth Avenue" in *Words and Music* and "I Love to Go Swimmin' with Women" in *Deep in My Heart*—he is not a character in the rest of the film.) More often the character sings and dances to reflect his feelings of the moment. Don Lockwood is joyful and therefore sings and dances in the rain; Danny McGuire is battling his conscience and therefore dances with his "alter ego."

Throughout Kelly's career, his persona has grown and developed, though many aspects seemed present from the beginning. The song and dance man (itself a figure of American popular culture going back to nineteenth-century minstrel shows and also an important part of American musical theater) became incorporated into other popular culture figures, giving the impression that everyone is a song and dance person to a degree: sailors and soldiers and baseball players are also capable of singing and dancing. He gives the impression, in other terms, of being a low mimetic character as defined by Northrup Frye: " . . . superior neither to other men nor to his environment, the hero is one of us: we respond to a sense of his common humanity. . . ."[24] Certainly part of that impression comes from Kelly's singing and dancing style. It has been suggested that Kelly's "dances are the kind of dances that make . . . a non-dancer, think, 'Well, I can't dance, but if I could dance, I'd dance that way.' "[25] Kelly was very much aware that his style required a recognition of popular roots and should be part of a general popular culture.

Innately I was a kid from Pittsburgh, and I wanted to dance to Cole Porter, Gershwin, Kern, Irving Berlin, Rodgers and Hart. . . .

I very definitely wanted to get out and use popular songs and the popular idiom for what I had to do.

In the everyday world you can't jump out of a truck, being a truck driver, and go into fifth position. It looks silly, and you also can't wear ballet slippers. You've got to do something that fits your outfit. You've got a sweatshirt and rolled-up sleeves, so the characterization determines a lot.

Kelly was also aware of the limitations—but the appropriateness—of his voice, and he always sang for himself.

. . . Fred Astaire has a better voice than I, but we both have tiny voices. . . . . We sing, usually, to set up the scene, to set up the dance. Neither Fred nor myself . . . pretend that we can put ourselves in league with the good, popular singers, and we don't try. But, like every song and dance man, we tell the lyrics, we speak them as they were written and give them whatever nuance the lyricist intended.

But while that song and dance man remained at the roots of Kelly's characterizations, nonetheless those characterizations took on greater dimensions. They began to include the Pierrot figure, for example, and they started using other dance forms in an eclectic way that also made them part of his general popular culture image. His persona is an identifiable one, partially because, as an article in *Dance Magazine* suggested, "Kelly . . . dances about everyday things and people."[26] His characters often act archetypally, experiencing situations which are common to human experience and which are, indeed, modern myth. Though the characters act metaphorically, the metaphors are never far removed from that common experience—city living, falling in love, assuming attitudes not necessarily reflective of one's true nature. Most importantly, perhaps, those metaphors are manifested particularly in dancing which draws upon various sources. The Kelly persona is at its most complete when it dances that human experience.

Certain important factors must be considered in analyzing Gene Kelly's dance style. First, Kelly is both a dancer and a choreographer, and in most—perhaps all—his films he choreographed his own dance material; furthermore, he never choreographed a film in which he did not appear. (Though Kelly directed the musical *Hello, Dolly!*, Michael Kidd did the dances; Kelly said that he did little more than help rehearse some of the material.)[27] But Kelly did work with a number of other choreographers and directors, and questions arise as to the nature of their influence on his style. Second, Kelly did much of his important work in collaboration with Stanley Donen, and the nature of that collaboration is also open to considerable speculation. It is a truism, of course, that film is a collaborative medium and that the success of any individual film is the result of ideas from many people. There is a consistency in Kelly's style, however, which makes it possible to infer his choreographic authorship. Although he was constantly striving to improve himself, to create different dance material, and to achieve increasingly ambitious projects, nevertheless, he retained certain foundations, certain fundamental dance patterns, and they were always strongly related to the Kelly persona and to the ideas projected by the particular films. His style was rooted in tap and musical comedy dance, but it incorporated other dance styles to a degree that makes him somewhat more eclectic than any other dancer and choreographer working in Hollywood. Ballet, modern dance, jazz, and gymnastics were as much a part of Kelly's choreography as the time step and the buck and wing. Although he used all kinds of dance interchangeably, he also seems to have consciously designated them for specific purposes. As suggested earlier, the simple, down-to-earth part of Kelly's characters was manifested in more popular dance styles—he emphasized tap routines—whereas the more pensive and soulful part was manifested in so-called "expressional" forms—ballet particularly. The more flamboyant dances were usually used humorously and ironically. Kelly's eclecticism probably made it possible for him to work successfully—if not easily—with a great variety of people. Certainly it made it possible for him to develop a broad range of dance expression which could interact with and become part of the entire filmic system; for with Kelly dance was as integral a filmic code as editing or camera movement, and it is usually impossible to separate those codes in most of his work—irrespective of the collaborators with whom he made the specific movies.

Besides Stanley Donen, Kelly's most frequent major collaborator was Vincente Minnelli, who directed three of Kelly's films and one number with him in *Ziegfeld Follies*. Minnelli has spoken at length of their work together.

DELAMATER: You directed the Kelly and Astaire number, "The Babbitt and the Bromide." Could you tell me something about how they worked together in creating that number?
MINNELLI: It took a long time in rehearsal because they both had such respect for each other that they would Alphonse and Gaston each other all over the place. One would say, "Well, do you think we might at this point do so and so or this kind of step? No, I guess not." "No," the other said, "we'll try it." Well it took *so* long. Astaire was the grand old man of the dance. He was the greatest, the star, and Kelly was younger. That condition conditioned them. They were both so anxious to please each other that it took a long time. We thought we'd never get it on.

DELMATER: Did you work closely with them in deciding things like camera angles?
MINNELLI: Yes. Gene and I think very much alike about those things. The dance is terribly important to him and also the continuity, keeping the ball in the air.

DELAMATER: You said . . . that Astaire didn't worry quite so much about the camera the way Kelly did.
MINNELLI: Kelly was much more conscious of the camera. With Fred, he'd put himself completely in your hands. He knew that you knew your business. With Gene you'd have long discussions about it, because Gene loves to discuss; so do I.

DELAMATER: Would you tell me . . . about some of Kelly's other work with you? Perhaps the joint work which Kelly and Robert Alton did for *The Pirate;* what was the nature of their collaboration?

MINNELLI: They would both make suggestions. Bob Alton also was from New York and was very resourceful. He could change a whole dance within minutes. He had this faculty, if he didn't like something, of changing all that, a whole section. Gene is much more deliberate. He knows himself so well. He patterned the character on John Barrymore and Douglas Fairbanks, which was absolutely right, because it was an actor; he was showy and aimless. In "Niña," for instance, which was all Gene, he was always the center of everything. All three of us worked very hard on that. The set was designed for that because he had to jump up on balconies and stick his head out of windows and go across and slide down and so on. The set was very Spanish. It's very difficult to differentiate who did what because it's completely a matter of collaboration, and we all got along so well.

DELAMATER: In the number later in the film, "Be a Clown," which Gene Kelly does with the Nicholas Brothers, how much did the Nicholas Brothers contribute?

MINNELLI: I think it was mostly Bob Alton and Gene. There are a lot of typical Gene Kelly steps in that, because it was a rabble-rousing number. It was an audience number and quite acrobatic. But it also suited the style of the Nicholas Brothers, the dances they did in their acts; splits and handsprings and turnovers and so forth were incorporated. You use the people to their best advantage. But there were an awful lot of Gene Kelly steps in that, good old standby, flag-waving steps.

Cinematographer Joseph Ruttenberg compared the work which Minnelli did with Kelly on *Brigadoon* and with Jack Cole on *Kismet:*

[Minnelli]'s quite an artist himself, and he's very particular. He was better able to talk with Cole than with Kelly because Kelly was quite set on his ideas, and he insists upon things he wants, and quite rightfully for that's his job. In *Brigadoon* Kelly had his way, but in *Kismet* Minnelli had the most to say. Minnelli has a lot of fine ideas and was very artistic. As a matter of fact, Vincente could probably have choreographed any of the dance numbers as well as anyone else. But Kelly has his mind set on the way he wants the things done. He gives it a lot of time and a lot of rehearsal and feels this is his number; this is the way he wants it done, and so it is done that way. Most directors who work with Gene Kelly give him his way. They will discuss things with him, of course, but, after all, the dance is *his* business. Gene Kelly is a nice guy and I like him; I love him, but he is stubborn. This is the way he wants it, and this is the way it has to be: no matter how much it takes, no matter how much it costs. This is what he was being paid for, I suppose.

I think that in most of the numbers in all the great musicals, it was *all* done by the choreographer, throughout. He was in full charge; the directors didn't interfere much at all.

Kelly himself speaks very positively about his work with Minnelli:

. . . the great joy in working with Minnelli is his marvelous eye not only for color—because he started out as a scenic designer, that was his background—but he welcomed innovative movements of the camera and innovative dance movements and innovative ways to stage things. And he was a great man to collaborate with, also; because he would take care of this one end of the—let's call it—overall design, you were a little freer to work on the other end. We complemented and supplemented each other quite well.

> . . . Minnelli and I came together as two mature men head on and found this wonderful collaboration.
>
> . . . when we collaborated it was always a happy thing because we didn't have to sacrifice his taste of color and style, but at the same time we did get some kind of vigor from me. . . . Often it's a plus to have someone who has a different style than yours in working together with him, because if you kick it around you get the best. I know that you must be thinking you often get the worst, but I always felt that Vincente and I brought out the best in each other.

There *is* a difference in the Kelly-Minnelli films that sets them off from those films which Kelly did with other directors. *The Pirate, An American in Paris,* and *Brigadoon* are all more exotic than most of Kelly's other work. Though they do rely heavily on the Kelly persona, they are removed in general from contemporary popular American culture. *The Pirate* is set in another culture in another century, and, in spite of its use of ironic caricatures of silent film personalities, the film employs dance styles conventional to its setting, as does *Brigadoon,* set as it is in the Scottish highlands. Kelly has remarked that "As far as the style goes, I have a strong hunch that if Minnelli and I had done *On the Town* that it would have turned out the same way, because I was influential in getting it on the screen." *On the Town* differs from *An American in Paris*—the only contemporary Kelly-Minnelli film—in major ways, however, and comparing the ways in which the two feminine leads are introduced displays some of those differences. Each is seen in the imagination of another, but Miss Turnstiles performs against a plain yellow background with simple sets which merely suggest her personality and activities—a doorframe, an ironing board, an easel—whereas the Parisian girl dances in complete rooms, each color coded and fully decorated. Although Kelly does tap with the children to "I Got Rhythm," his style is, in general, based less on popular modes in *An American in Paris.* The courting love duet, "Main Street," in *On the Town* is primarily a soft shoe; "Love Is Here to Stay" has the same function in *An American in Paris,* yet it is based more on an exhibition ballroom dance style with a considerable amount of interpolated ballet. And, finally, the relatively simple New York skyline set of "A Day in New York" gives way to the numerous, detailed, Impressionist-inspired sets of "An American in Paris" with an athletic Kelly in the former becoming a balletic Kelly in the latter. Each style, however, seems appropriate for its film, and in one sense Kelly's eclecticism made it possible for him to be comfortable in any film making style. He could work as easily within the overall impression of Minnelli's *oeuvre* as he could in a simpler, more popular idiom.

Kelly's relationship with Stanley Donen is, perhaps, somewhat more problematic because their work together seems to have been strongly collaborative. Though trained as a dancer, Donen appeared in only one film, *Best Foot Forward* in 1943. He did direct the dances in a few films in the

forties (e.g., *A Date with Judy, The Big City*) but did no solo choreography
after 1946. Donen co-directed and co-choreographed three films with Kelly,
and, of course, he has subsequently achieved a considerable reputation as a
director on his own, but of the films he has directed, he has choreography
credit (shared with Gower Champion) only on *Give a Girl a Break*. Much
evidence suggests that the Kelly-Donen collaboration was a strong one in
which it is difficult—and probably unnecessary—to discern or to determine
who contributed what. It seems fairly clear that Donen was not just Kelly's
amenuensis as has been suggested about Hermes Pan and Fred Astaire. Betty
Garrett, who worked with them on both *Take Me Out to the Ball Game* and
On the Town, has said that there was no really discernible division of labor
during the shooting except that during actual takes Kelly was in front of and
Donen behind the camera. Art director Randall Duell, on the other hand,
said, "Stanley was sort of an assistant choreographer to Gene.... Gene ran the
show. Stan had some good ideas and worked with Gene, but he was still the
'office boy' to Gene, in a sense, although Gene had great respect for him. But
they made a good team, because they were very compatible." Donen himself
has said:

> ... we really worked as a team—we didn't say, "I do this and you do that." No, not a bit.
> Even through rehearsing the numbers, when everything would really get complicated I
> would be with him. When there was real pressure to get a lot done in terms of rehearsal, I
> would rehearse in one hall and he would rehearse another number, but then we would
> switch and I would go supervise his number and he would come to do mine. So it really was
> a collaboration. There was no question about it.[28]

What began for Donen as an assistant's position grew into one of genuine
collaboration; certainly this is the impression inferred from Clive Hirschhorn's biography of Kelly. By the time they made *It's Always Fair Weather,*
however, their relationship had changed.

> It was ... the last time Gene was to work with Stanley Donen, who recollects the making of
> it as one of the most wretched experiences of his life. The two men rarely saw eye to eye on
> matters of artistic policy, and incompatibility developed between them. What, according to
> Donen, had once been a workable and productive partnership had, by 1955, irrevocably
> deteriorated.[29]

Inasmuch as Donen did little choreographing on his own, one can hardly
determine the nature of his input. His later films, with their frequent use of
montage sequences, special effects, and split-screen experiments, do suggest a
certain potential contribution on his part. In *Indiscreet,* for example, Donen
has the Cary Grant and Ingrid Bergman characters in the same screen space—
seeming almost to be lying in the same bed—though diegetically one is in

Paris, the other in London; the general impression of shared screen space is the same as the split-screen dance in *It's Always Fair Weather*. In terms of dance specifically, however, there is insufficient evidence to determine Donen's contribution. Kelly's dances are so strongly tied into his performing that it is almost impossible to separate the two. (Even in those rare dances in which Kelly doesn't perform or is not the main dancer [e.g., "Make 'em Laugh" with Donald O'Connor or "Prehistoric Man" with Ann Miller], the performer's and not the choreographer's abilities seem paramount.) The choreography for *Give a Girl a Break,* despite the film's credits, seems quite easily divided between Bob Fosse's acrobatic jazz style (e.g., "Our United State") and Gower Champion's exhibition ballroom style (e.g., the Champions' dance on the roof patio). Whatever the nature of Donen's contribution, Kelly's style can be discussed on its own terms, for not only did he work with many different people, but also he manifested a consistency within a diverse dance style which suggests that the Kelly style can be considered abstractly and structurally.

Kelly has described his dancing style as "a synthesis of old forms and new rhythms,"[30] and he recognizes its eclecticism:

> . . . I don't have a name for my style of dancing. I'm sorry, that would be very convenient. My form of dancing . . . I wouldn't know what to call it; it's certainly hybrid and, if you'll allow the term, it's bastardised. I've borrowed from the modern dance, from the classical, and certainly from the American folk dance—tap-dancing, jitterbugging. . . . But I have tried to develop a style which is indigenous to the environment and locale in which I was reared. . . .[31]

Writing in 1948, Mary Jane Hungerford said of Kelly's dances, "They may have a tap base, but they definitely convey meaning, ranging all the way from a vague mood to very specific ideas."[32] And perhaps this is one way to distinguish and characterize Kelly's work, for otherwise he does not have so easily discernible a set of patterns within his dances. Whereas one can relatively easily describe the patterns to certain Astaire routines (particularly the Astaire-Rogers duets), one can only assume that Kelly acquiesces somewhat more obediently to the material of the film and the place of the dance within that film. In other words, Kelly's eclecticism is not imposed on his material; it grows out of it.

> Each number practically dictates the method [of creating a dance for film].

> This music is king. If you're doing musical comedy, you're often faced with the fact that just before, you've said, "Well, I don't want any of this, and I'm going off alone." Now you can't write in Mozart or Stravinsky or somebody there. Let's say the music you're using is Rodgers and Hart. You have to take a theme from Rodgers and Hart and do variations on the theme, and you have to do that in close association with the arrangers of the music. To do a number like that you sit down like a writer, alone, in a chair, and you start thinking,

"How do I further the characterization by the use of dance?" Since you also have words to help you, it isn't always as tough as it sounds. You write yourself a little story or what might, in some cases, be a series of impressions, but they're in your head. At least you have a beginning and an end; the middle is never a problem. That's one way to choreograph a number.

The easiest way—it's not always the best way, depending on your luck—is when the number flows out of a situation. If you're stopped in the street by a bouncing ball that children have been playing with, and you pick it up and you throw it back and they throw it back at you, the situation becomes a dance with a ball and children's games, which I've actually done. That keeps the scene in character and makes the dance very much an integral part of the motion picture, the story, and the characterization.

By far the best results are usually gotten by having a song which you can interpret; for example, "Singin' in the Rain" is an obvious one. I kissed the girl goodnight, and it was raining. Of course, we made it rain. We write the scene expressly for it. And we've made jokes about the California weather. . . . So I decided to walk in the rain, which everybody at one time in his life has felt. You had a universality of feeling there. In presenting the song as a thesis—I'm singing in the rain, I'm happy again—you elaborate on that thesis by dance. You become happier and happier as you dance.

Kelly was attempting to create meaning through his dances, not just through the "stories" of the numbers but through the very dance steps. He also recognized the conventional applications of dance forms (he went on to say " . . . if you look at popular dance, it's usually done when people are happy"), and his dances do follow certain conventions. The dances showing *joie de vivre* are usually tap numbers or use other American popular dance idioms; the "mood" numbers tend to be more of a concert dance variety, using ballet or modern dance—both of which Kelly felt had influenced him greatly. Moreover, there is a general integration of all dance forms; for, though Kelly did use the audience's expectation of dance conventions, he also attempted to create new dance conventions, to give new meanings to older dance forms and to use them in different contexts, juxtaposing dance styles when he felt them appropriate or when, for example, a particular dance partner's style dictated the direction in which he should go.

Playing himself in George Cukor's *Let's Make Love,* Gene Kelly, trying to teach the Yves Montand character to dance, says, "a dancer expresses with his body what an actor does with words." This may well be the underlying idea of all Kelly's work because he attempted to achieve a full range of dance expression in order to fit his material into the context of his films, and the dance was for him *the* method of expression. Furthermore, working during what may have been the period of culmination of Hollywood musicals, he combined dance forms into an eclectic style which is difficult to describe and categorize because of its breadth and range. Unlike most Hollywood dancers and choreographers whose styles were unique because of certain recurrent patterns and forms, Kelly's style was unique because it incorporated so many different patterns and forms. Kelly used tap dancing throughout his dancing/choreographing career, but it seldom predominated in his style. Strictly speaking, Kelly used very little "pure" tap in the sense that Bill Robinson, for example, did. More commonly, tap was incorporated as part of a general musical comedy style. Even as early as "For Me and My Gal," which does include a considerable amount of tapping, Kelly and Garland end in a ballroom style à la Astaire and Rogers. Furthermore, though he did seem to prefer tapping in his *joie de vivre* numbers like "Singin' in the Rain," at the same time he would also use it in his more pensive moods such as in the squeaky board/torn newspaper routine of *Summer Stock*. In other words, even if, as Hungerford has suggested, Kelly's dances have a tap base, tap was only one aspect of his style, and as he became more ambitious, other aspects— particularly ballet—would become more significant. Kelly's style was also an athletic one; it lacked Astaire's refined elegance, partially, as has been noted, because of the differences in their physicality. Kelly's movements tended to be broader and to seem more muscular; he included more jumping and lifting; he bounded between different levels of a set; he seemed to occupy—indeed fill— both the pro-filmic and the filmic space with his movements. It has been stated before that, by the time Kelly appeared in films, certain combinations of dance forms had become standard, and the blurring of distinctions among various kinds of dance had been manifest for some time. Every dancer used turns which were based on ballet principles, for instance; rarely—if ever—did hoofers tap with only the feet, for now arm movements were integral—the entire body had become the dancing instrument. And Kelly, rather than really creating anew, fulfilled all those aspects of dance within a cinematic context. He did prove to be the complete performer, in a way, because he used all different dance styles, performing with his own dance instrument but at the same time making that instrument a vital form of film expression.

Kelly may have overstated his position in regard to ballet in the early forties (". . . I was a ballet dancer mainly, and I was a good one." "I love the classic style, but I knew if I went into Monte Carlo Ballets Russes, for example, which was then touring and which would have taken me, that at forty years of age I'd be dancing *Swan Lake* again and again. . . ."); the evidence doesn't support these statements made thirty years later. He was not at all involved in ballet work when he was in New York, and ballet doesn't really enter his film work to any extent until later—first, limitedly, in *Anchors Aweigh* and then, more fully, in *An American in Paris*. But Kelly's interest in ballet and its influence on him is always evident even if in minor ways; he seems a much more controlled and disciplined dancer as a result. The rigidity of ballet manifests itself in Kelly's control of his entire body. His arms never flail, so to speak, but are choreographed as intentionally as his feet and legs. His body movements tend to be symmetrical and parallel (he rarely—if ever— employs the isolation technique of Cole or Fosse), each movement duplicated first on the right, then on the left. Duplication of movement is also important when Kelly dances with someone else. He and Vera-Ellen in "Main Street" and he and Debbie Reynolds in "You Were Meant for Me" often match each other step for step, suggesting, to a certain extent, the equality of their relationships at those points. Donald O'Connor and Kelly in the otherwise almost completely vaudeville-oriented routine of "Moses Supposes" dance like twins, rarely doing anything different and in synchronization throughout; when they do perform different steps, it is with an obviously intended contrasting or counterpointing of their movements. Kelly, following Astaire's lead in tapping into and out of ballet movements, taps into and out of ballet "scissors" jumps during the Spanish dream-dance of *Anchors Aweigh,* but Kelly did it more often and also used more specific and more difficult ballet steps. He does large *jeté* turns around the horse to end *The Pirate* fire dance, for example. The most basic ballet steps underlie much of Kelly's work as well. Customarily in a soft-shoe or musical comedy number Kelly moves through ballet positions or steps; even simple walking movements are ballet flavored, so to speak. He generally uses *balancé* steps to dance to the side and back again, and a walk includes a slightly exaggerated bend of the knee and spring of the foot as in the beginning of "Sinbad the Sailor" in *Invitation to the Dance.* This use of ballet is certainly not exlusively Kelly's, but it is fundamental to all his movement in a way that seemed true of no other star during that period.

As with most other choreographers and dancers, Kelly took much of his inspiration from the music of a number, and he seems to have been limited by no type of music. Certainly one reason for his dance eclecticism is the broad range of musical sources for his dances. He did dance to the popular songs of Rodgers, Porter, and others, but he also danced to more elaborate material: Gershwin's symphonic poem "An American in Paris"; Jacques Ibert's commissioned score for "The Circus" in *Invitation to the Dance.* This range of music, coupled with his intention always to make his dance material conventionally appropriate and integrated into the film, gave him the opportunity to perform an Irish jig as part of "The Hat My Dear Old Father Wore," and Spanish *tacaneo* in *Anchors Aweigh* as well as his more usual tap routines and dream ballets. Moreover, the movement of the camera in relation to the dance also frequently seems determined as much by the music as by the dancing; the three are completely interdependent. In "You Were Meant for Me," for example, the volume and the orchestration imply movement, and the camera "sweeps," so to speak, as Kelly and Reynolds move to similarly "sweeping" music. There are few breaks and poses in Kelly's choreography (and none at all in "You Were Meant for Me"), and breaks in the music—at the end of a phrase, for example—are often used to cut from one shot—one camera set up—to another. In this regard, too, it is rare for Kelly to dance when there are tacits in the music; he is much more inclined to "punctuate" the movement with the orchestration: the musical "sweeps" are usually emphasized by the strings, for example; or, more specifically, those movements which Kelly makes with his hat in "Singin' in the Rain" are accompanied principally by the brass. It is customary, as well, for Kelly to use the reprise of the major melody line as a source for an important dance movement; usually it is preceded immediately by a cut and the full orchestra resumes playing as the camera, often on a boom, follows Kelly (and Debbie Reynolds—to use "You Were Meant for Me" again as example) as he dances with large movements around the set.

Kelly was conscious of this interaction of codes as he prepared his material; " . . . when I start putting the dance on its feet," he has said, "I start immediately about the camera." He also gave considerable praise to the musicians responsible for the sound that accompanied the dances. When asked who the important people in the MGM music department were, he replied, "The arrangers. Conrad Salinger was most important to the dancers, because he could do things with the mood numbers that nobody else has done before or since." Kelly continued:

> . . . there were two men who were most important to all of us. They were Roger Edens and Saul Chaplin. They were the translators, the interpreters between the dancers, the singers, . . . and the arrangers. They'd say to the dancers, "I hear flutes here," and they'd say why; they'd look at the number and say, "Wouldn't it be better if you had a clarinet in here?" or whatever. They'd work with you when you were constructing things out of thin air. Often when you just heard something in your head and you couldn't say, "These four bars should be a mixture of this instrument and that instrument . . .," they would translate your thoughts for you.
>
> The conductors Lennie Hayton and John Green, of course, were important, because they always wanted to get our tempi right, and they were dedicated motion picture men.

For Kelly the contributions of all the members of a film making team were essential.

> . . . we did a lot of the work in very close collaboration which . . . was an important thing for me . . ., because in making a big musical you must collaborate with people. The auteur theory is non-existent, you know, if only that you have to work with musicians and lyricists.

Nevertheless, Kelly coordinated those contributions and applied other people's ideas to his dance routines in much the same way that he used diverse dance forms to make up his dance style.

The squeaky board routine from *Summer Stock* serves particularly well to illustrate and exemplify certain important facets of Kelly's amalgamation of dance, music, and film. First, the number grows out of a diegetic situation.

Kelly having recently become involved with Garland, is brooding about the problems this potential relationship could cause. Second, it shows how he "naturally" uses props and devices as an essential dance item with which he can interact. Finding himself alone on the stage, he begins to dance when a squeaky board he has walked on inspires him to create steps incorporating that sound; subsequently, discovering a newspaper on the stage, he brings it, too, into the dance. He starts experimenting with a four-beat tap with a fifth-beat squeak. He does that twice, then elaborates on the tap and ends on the squeak. He discovers the paper and begins the music as he puts all three together. At the end he tears the paper into bits with his feet as part of the dance movement. Third, the music doesn't simply accompany the dance but interacts with it on all levels. The music to the song "You, Wonderful You," which Kelly has just sung to Garland, is also the music for the dance, suggesting a carry-over of the Kelly character's feelings from one moment to another in the film. The number begins unaccompanied; when Kelly actually starts to dance, he whistles his own accompaniment. A piano softly picks up the melody, and the full orchestra comes in just as Kelly makes a typical"full" dance gesture—he runs to the top of a riser that is on the stage. Finally, the camera work and editing are similarly "choreographed' and "orchestrated." The camera initially films in high angle long shot, but there is a cut to medium shot as Kelly experiments with the board. The entire number has generally been photographed in long shot, but the cuts facilitate movements into different areas of space. Even though the pro-filmic space is restricted to the stage set, Kelly makes the filmic space diverse by using areas of that set as seen from different camera positions. The cuts are also made by musical and dance cues, so to speak, for they are almost always made at the end of a musical phrase which also happens to be the end of a series of dance steps.

Other numbers show the diversity of dance forms in Kelly's work as well as that integration of codes. Though he seldom uses any dance style "pure," as it were, he seems to favor certain styles for particular dances. "I Got Rhythm" and "Tra La La" from *An American in Paris* are principally tap routines; indeed, in the former he self-consciously refers to the dance itself, introducing the children to the time step and the shim-sham as part of *"la danse américaine";* and in the latter he makes use of available material and space by tapping on top of Oscar Levant's piano. Specific ballet routines emerge in *An American in Paris, Brigadoon,* and *Invitation to the Dance,* among other films. The lengthy ballet "An American in Paris" more fully exploits ballet technique—for Kelly both as dancer and as choreographer—than in any other preceding film. Isolated movements were present in *The Pirate* fire ballet and "A Day in New York," for example, but other styles predominated. In "An American in Paris," however, Leslie Caron dances primarily on pointe and the Kelly-Caron *pas de deux* in the flower market section displays a typically balletic dependent relationship in which the male turns and lifts the female. Similarly, Kelly and Cyd Charisse dance balletically to "Heather on the Hill." Though Charisse does not dance on pointe, Kelly does lift her, and both of them assume ballet positions throughout. The first movement, "The Circus," of *Invitation to the Dance* is a ballet, very much in the nineteenth- and early twentieth-century sense. There is a mime role (Kelly's Pierrot) and exhibition dancing in which Igor Youskevitch goes through the repertoire of male *tour de force* steps. Although Kelly has said that he was influenced by Martha Graham and others of the modern-dance school, there are only a few of his dances which actually manifest that influence. The generally somber mood of "Slaughter on Tenth Avenue" in *Words and Music* comes through partially because of Kelly's use of modern dance, and in *Les Girls*—for which, perhaps significantly, Jack Cole has dance credit—Kelly's "Rope Dance" with Taina Elg is similarly modern-dance inspired. In both numbers Kelly abandons a quality of lightness, characterized through jumps and tends to perform in more conventional modern dance poses on the knees or lying on the floor. There is some evidence, too, of modern dance in the ballets in *On the Town* and *Singin' in the Rain*, though each also includes more material that comes out of a general musical comedy dance tradition. He uses the floor more significantly in both numbers—sliding on his knees to the Miss Turnstiles poster, for example, or incorporating the colored floor patterns into his dream dance with Cyd Charisse; neither number ,however, has the sustained moodiness which has become associated with modern dance, and it is probably a sign of Kelly's awareness of how appropriate certain dance conventions are that he used modern dance only when that moody quality was intended. Kelly's roles often required him to use some semblance of ethnic dance, though what he did perform and choreograph was always a conventional ethnic—perhaps pseudo-ethnic—form rather than a true ethnic one. Such numbers include the dream dance in *Anchors Aweigh* (for which he did employ the Spanish heel and toe work), a bolero style for part of "Niña" in *The Pirate*, and the pseudo-Scottish "I'll Go Home with Bonnie Jean," in *Brigadoon* (during which he and Van Johnson tap, thus setting them off via dance from the rest of the characters). Finally, Kelly's athleticism suggested that a gymnastic/acrobatic style—certainly present in his many dance styles—should predominate at times. His "dance" on the scaffolding in *Living in a Big Way* and his swinging on the rope in *The Pirate* are two of his more obvious athletic feats, but certain smaller numbers also call for this skill. In "Be a Clown," also from *The Pirate*, Kelly performs with the Nicholas Brothers, using some material suggested by their routines (sliding into and out of splits) as well as material of his own (hopping sideways in "push-up" position) which he used in other films. In "Thanks Alot But No Thanks" from *It's Always Fair Weather* he choreographed (though did not dance) material, strongly suggestive of Kidd or

Fosse, which showed backward somersaults and cartwheels. As both dancer and choreographer Kelly managed a broad spectrum of dance forms, but it seems evident that they were never meant to be isolated from the rest of the film; instead they were intended to interact with the totality of the work and to suggest ideas which could be suggested only through different kinds of dance.

The principle of integrated musicals has generally meant that the song and dance numbers grew "naturally" from the narrative, that the films adhered in one sense to the Bazinian theory of realism because the numbers were not set off from the rest of the film but were made to seem as real, so to speak, as the rest of the film because the characters sang and danced as a natural part of their existence. A number of films—and particularly the ones Kelly co-directed with Stanley Donen—took the principle one step further. There is a definite style to certain integrated movies which suggests a ruling principle—if not a ruling power—of choreographing for the camera, not only in the dances but also in the general movement of the film and in the camera work and editing. In other words, the film is a total piece in which the numbers not only evolve from the narrative but also, in turn, influence the narrative.

On the Town, for example, seems a film in which the creators were aware of this notion, for even simple walking sequences convey a dance-like grace. Indeed, the performers often seem on the verge of dancing, and in certain instances they actually walk into dance. Kelly and Vera-Ellen begin "Main Street" as a walk, the next logical step to which is a dance step. Even when not leading into a dance, the film presents the performers in montage sequences which seem choreographed with the camera and through the editing. In "New York, New York" short scenes presented in rapid succession of the three sailors, almost always standing still, against a background of the Statue of Liberty, Grant's Tomb, or Rockefeller Center or of the three taking a carriage ride through Central park give a *moving* picture tour. The museum-search montage is much the same kind of choreographed movement with shots of museum names intercut with bits of action at each museum. And certainly the chase sequence reveals the film makers' awareness of arrranged movement of objects, for the taxi, the police cars, and the motorcycles are all choreographed as precisely as "A Day in New York." Furthermore, the camera is also included in this choreography. As they cross Brooklyn Bridge, for instance, the camera views part of the scene from a high angle; the camera's point of view shifts: part of the chase is shown objectively from a distance; sometimes the police car is seen from the taxi (usually as Jules Munshin sees it when he is standing up through the sun roof); other times the taxi is seen from the police car. (Interspersed among all this, of course, are scenes of dialogue and repartee with the characters.) Finally, the highlight of the choreography of the cars occurs as the taxi, having arrived in Brooklyn and having picked up two or three extra police cars, moves head on at two motorcycle cops. In a visual pattern as controlled as any ballet, the motorcycle screen-right crosses to screen left as the motorcycle screen-left crosses to screen right. The taxi, followed by the police cars, moves down the center of the frame between the two motorcycles as they circle around to follow.

Other films in which Kelly appeared or which he co-directed also manifest this sense of "total choreography." A walking into dance begins "You, Wonderful You" with Judy Garland in *Summer Stock* and "You Were Meant for Me" with Debbie Reynolds in *Singin' in the Rain.* Every time Gene Kelly walks through the streets in *An American in Paris*, he is accompanied by the theme music of the title piece, and he dances in the street not only with the children in "I Got Rhythm" but also with the old women in "By Strauss." And different types of diegetically-motivated action become dance as well. Kelly's fight with the mayor's henchmen—itself choreographed—leads directly into *The Pirate* ballet. The fight at the end of *It's Always Fair Weather* is not only choreographed but also seems an extension of the dances which the three ex-soldiers have participated in together since the beginning of the film. In that same film the "March, March" montage becomes a form of ritual dance that carries the men through the war, and the bar-hop montage leads directly into their first big dance routine together on the streets of New York.

Another aspect of integration is that the dances contribute to the multiple levels of meaning in the film; the dances, in other words, become signs of courtship and love, joy and sadness—exterior manifestations of a character's interior feelings. In addition, at times the numbers can take on even greater significance. In *Singin' in the Rain*, for instance, almost every number furthers the narrative but also plays a part in the film's satire of Hollywood and general show business traditions. "Fit as a Fiddle" emphasizes the irony of the Kelly character's current position and also suggests that he isn't the person he presents himself to be. As he tells Dora Bailey and the crowd that his background was one of "dignity, always dignity," the musical numbers show the true origins of his training and talent: burlesque and vaudeville, not high society and the music conservatory. The appreciation of show business and entertainment values is important throughout the film and comes across most readily in the numbers. "Make 'Em Laugh" is a *paean* to vaudeville tricks and stunts, emphasizing them as a source of pleasure for the audience. Likewise, the "Broadway Ballet," presented as a potential source of audience pleasure in the film they're making, also illustrates the lead character's humble beginnings. He is someone who has "gotta dance" and will do it anywhere. In a concise encapsulization of show business roots, the dancer rises from burlesque through vaudeville to *The Ziegfeld Follies* and stardom, each routine using the same music and basic pattern but becoming more sophisticated and pretentious each time. All the numbers serve as a sign of show business ability, and Lina Lamont's inability to dance and sing—or even talk—is emphasized by her not doing any of the singing and dancing. Indeed, "Moses Supposes" particularly points up how competent Don and Cosmo are compared to her; the juxtaposition of two speech lessons—Lina's disastrous, Don's perfect—is followed by the dance, which reflects their linguistic ability. The whole film encompasses the styles of many musicals and has numbers that work like Berkeley's ("Beautiful Girl"), MacDonald-Eddy operettas (*The Dancing Cavalier* sequences), and even Astaire-Rogers (the ballroom movements as part of "You Were Meant for Me"). Finally, the Kelly character's fulfillment as a performer and as a person coincides in the film, coming together in the title song and dance. Don Lockwood has been brash and overbearing, but, revealing his true self, he has won Kathy Selden. In *The Dueling Cavalier* he also presents some of that image, but the failure of that film ultimately leads to greater success. After Don, Kathy, and Cosmo realize how they can save the film, new worlds are opened to him as a performer. His *joie de vivre*, then, which causes him to sing and dance in the rain, has multiple causes. He is happy in love and happy because his career has been saved; and both developments result to a certain extent from that change in character which is so much a part of the Kelly persona.

Gene Kelly's contribution to film dance has been appreciated on many levels. Walter Terry has written in *The Dance in America:*

> That motion picture dancing has progressed as far as it has is due, in no small measure, to the efforts of Gene Kelly. For Kelly was not only a first-rate tap dancer and a skillful choreographer; he was also a willing and imaginative experimentalist. Although he was unquestionably the star of his motion pictures and the center of dance interest, he saw to it that his own dancing was supported and extended by the dancing of others, sometimes soloists, sometimes groups of dancers. He knew, obviously, that movies could create fantasy and aspects of spectacle better than any other medium and he did not hesitate to explore the possibilities. Not content with simply photographing dances, he used the camera's inherent mobility and almost magical perceptiveness to seek out dance details or, through absolutely appropriate fantasy, make the dancer a part of the wind, the rain, the sky, just as the dancer really is in his own dreams.[33]

And Richard Griffith has more specifically recognized aspects of Kelly's work.

> He uses the conventions of the musical, familiar to and instantly accepted by audiences, as his own invisible platform from which to take off in contrapuntal flight. Like the silent film comedians, in whose tradition he stands, he uses his physical surroundings as the basic *material* of his dances: to "say it with props" is still the best way.
>
> No doubt his solo inventions would be just as effective danced on a bare stage before a curtain. But it is his instinct, and a truly cinematic one, to use everything he sees, touches,

passes around or through, as part of the mimetic or terpsichorean configurations which he creates. When Kelly is on, everything dances.[34]

It is, then, Kelly's imbuing his films with dance which distinguishes him from the other dance figures in film. That is not to judge him qualitatively better; it is simply to recognize him as both a culminating figure and as a contributor in a variety of ways. He realized the importance of the performer, but he also found it necessary to choreograph and direct, to guide the film, so to speak, into a totality in which dance was the motivating force. Musical films had been moving in the direction of integration since their inception, yet Kelly seems to be the figure who fulfilled that movement. He could hardly have achieved such on his own, and, indeed, many others contributed, but he had the fortune to be at the right place at the right time. The repertory company which existed at MGM made it possible for him to create within a form but also to extend that form. He was able to work with many of those—like Berkeley and Astaire— who had helped to develop the genre. He was also able to influence, directly and indirectly, others working at MGM, those who would continue making musicals beyond the mid-fifties—particularly Stanley Donen and Bob Fosse. Furthermore, Kelly fully exploited varieties of dance forms and strove always to fit them into a film context. Aware of the conventions of both dance and film, he attempted to combine the two within the integrated musical. He experimented with dance and with film in order to extend the limits of both, yet he seems always to have recognized that point beyond which he should not go. In most instances that point was determined by the nature of the particular film, for Kelly also used the nature of each film as both inspiration and guide.

The last musical Kelly made at MGM was *Les Girls,* and it seems significant that it was directed by George Cukor with whom Kelly had never previously worked and who had done relatively few musicals. Jack Cole was assigned as choreographer, and not only had they never worked together before but Cole was rather disdainful of Kelly's abilities. Kelly's preceding two musicals, *It's Always Fair Weather* and *Invitation to the Dance,* had not been particularly successful (*Weather* barely broke even; *Dance* lost money), and Cole said that the studio wanted someone to oversee Kelly.[35] In a sense Kelly went the way of the original film musical. Having brought it to something of an apex, he stopped making musicals for what appears to be the same reasons that the studios phased them out. The repertory company at MGM was disbanded, and those very people with whom he had worked so congenially were no longer under contract. Kelly seems also to have made a connection between choreography and performing. Once he stopped dancing on the screen, he also stopped creating the dances. Although he has continued to direct—and to direct a major musical, *Hello, Dolly!*—he has not continued to choreograph. One can only infer—but it seems a fair inference—that the totality with which he considered musicals required his performing in them as an assumption which underlay his involvement on other levels. Other musicals have been made but no other complete performer has emerged, for the combination of people and factors which made Kelly's work possible has disappeared.

8

The Decline of the Musical

The musical as a film genre was always extraordinarily dependent on the Hollywood studio system. The available resources on every level made the necessarily additional expenses of the musical possible. With dancers, singers, musicians, costumers, technicians, and others under contract, the studios could call upon experts to provide material at a moment's notice. Although speaking disparagingly of the system, Jack Cole probably characterized it accurately when he said: "They were in the business of making scenery, and they were in the business of making costumes."[1] Art director Randall Duell spoke at length during my interview with him about the sculptors and modelers under contract at Metro and also about the backlog of stock units which could be modified and redesigned in order to keep a project moving. The system fed on itself, so to speak. It behooved studios to make films in order to keep the internal businesses operating; at the same time, the internal businesses made it possible to produce films with efficiency and expertise. An article in *Life,* April 14, 1952, pointing out that MGM had made eleven musicals in 1951 and had scheduled thirteen for 1952 said:

> Metro's moguls make no secret of how over the years they have succeeded in making their company's name practically synonymous with a glossy, brassy, cornily plotted, elaborately staged, expensively produced extravaganza. They have 32 stars who have received special training for musicals, including solid old names like Fred Astaire and bright new names like the Champions. They have the most grandiose sets in Hollywood and a wardrobe department so vast they did not have to send out for a yard of tulle or satin to outfit the 450 waltzers in *The Merry Widow.* They spend upwards of $1.5 million on each film, and when they want to do something really big and eye-catching they are ready to shell out for it. They paid over $400,000 just for one colossal fashion show episode in *Lovely to Look At.*[2]

But it was to be their swan song, for the studio system as it had existed was moribund by 1956. Writing about Arthur Freed, Hugh Fordin notes:

> As the last of the major studios, Metro was falling apart. Producers were no longer under contract and only a handful, including Freed, were in the process of legally setting up their own companies. The famous MGM roster of stars no longer existed. Less than a dozen stars

were retained for one picture a year, among them Charisse, Astaire and Kelly. If at all, audiences by now were only attracted to musicals with the marquee value of a hit Broadway show.[3]

In addition to the general depression of the film industry at the time, there seemed, indeed, to be a decreased interest in musicals specifically. Betty Garrett, for example, noticed a considerable change in attitude.

I went on a publicity tour for *My Sister Eileen*, and every time I'd get into town, the distributors and the theater owners would give a cocktail party and they'd say, "Don't mention that it's a musical. Musicals are out now." And the picture, I understand, laid a bomb the first time around. The American public did not want musicals at that time. It was very strange; I don't know why, but they were just kind of down on them.[4]

Furthermore, one need only compare the gross receipts of several Freed-produced musicals to realize that the mid-fifties were not banner years: *An American in Paris*, 1951, more than $8,005,000; *Show Boat*, 1951, more than $8,650,000; *Singin' in the Rain*, 1952, $7,665,000; *The Band Wagon*, 1953, $5,655,505; *Brigadoon*, 1954, $3,385,000; *It's Always Fair Weather*, 1955, $2,485,000; *Kismet*, 1955, $2,920,000; *Silk Stockings*, 1957, $4,417,753. *Brigadoon, Fair Weather,* and *Kismet* barely recouped their investment. In 1956, Metro operated at a three-million dollar deficit.[5] The musical—that is, the original, studio-product musical—was not to be seen again. A few original musicals would be produced in subsequent years, but dance would seldom be one of their major components.

The adaptation of Broadway hit musicals has become the major source of film musicals since the mid-fifties. The studio system, while ideal for musicals, has given way to a system which seems controlled by the commercial adaptations appealing to audiences "pre-sold," using John Cutts's and John Russell Taylor's term, by success on the stage. Cutts also notes that formerly the star—not the property itself—drew the audience, whereas later the property became the attraction, thus reflecting a change in the audience's attitude.[6] One result of this was a general feeling of obeisance to the property—an attitude that what had worked once should work again, and many of the films were transferred to the screen without consideration of their potential as films. In an interview with David Austin, for example, director George Sidney reveals that he held the material of stage musicals almost sacrosanct, that he believed they shouldn't be changed much.[7] Significantly, much of Sidney's work had been in adaptation—even in the forties; *Annie Get Your Gun, Show Boat, Kiss Me Kate, Pal Joey, Bye, Bye Birdie,* and *Half a Sixpence* had all seen a prior existence on the stage. On the other hand, some people recognized that the trend was not necessarily a positive one. Composer and music director Dimitri Tiomkin has said, "Adapting large scale Broadway musicals intact . . ., duplicating their success formula by slavishly adhering to their original theatrical presentation, hardly strikes me as right, healthy or forward looking."[8] Freda June Lockhart observed in 1957 that these trends were "combining to bring dancing musicals once more to a standstill, to take us to another age of stationary singing spectacle."[9] Although filmed adaptations had always been important to the medium, they did not always predominate in the genre; at their best they had had the qualities of cinematic inventiveness associated with the original film musical. Several Broadway shows, however, had become institutions, so that when they were transferred to film they were treated with the respect usually given to Hollywood versions of Shakespeare. In many respects, this handling was the result of the Richard Rodgers and Oscar Hammerstein collaborations and their development of the integrated musical, for, on the stage, the idea of integration had become inviolable principle: ". . . this alone was the proper, the only admissible way of putting together a musical. The motive for this hardening of attitudes in, and especially after, *Oklahoma!* seemed to be the somewhat dubious one of a desire to lend dignity to a form which up to then had not always enjoyed it."[10] The result, as John Russell Taylor also points out, was a kind of folk opera that eventually led directly back to the operetta through musicals like *Carousel, The King and I,* and *The Sound of Music.* Simultaneously there was an attempt to deal with social issues and serious themes: racial oppression in South Africa *(Lost in the Stars),* gang war in New York City *(West Side Story),* the advent of Nazism *(Cabaret).* All this was bound to have an influence on the film musical.

The attempt to achieve a musical with a social conscience presented certain problems in regard to a so-called "realistic" musical. The relationship between socially-conscious themes and cinematic realism is a strong one, and the desire to get musicals out of the studio and into the streets, as it were (represented, for example, by the "New York, New York" montage of *On the Town* or by "June Is Bustin' out All Over" from *Carousel* as well as by the film makers' original attempts to film *Seven Brides for Seven Brothers* and *Brigadoon* on location), became manifest when those serious musical plays came to film. Musicals seem stylized almost by definition on the stage, but the superior production resources of film present the possibility of greater realism. As a result, many of the filmed adaptations, shot on location, incorporate a conflict between the innate stylization of the musical genre and the realistic milieu supposedly necessitated by the serious issues of the material. And surely the problem becomes multiplied in regard to dance, for unless the dance is grounded in and explained by some diegetic source such as a social dance ("Shall We Dance?" from *The King and I;* the dance at the gym in *West Side Story*), a folk or religious ritual (the boar's head ceremony on Bali Ha'i in *South Pacific*), or part of an on-stage show ("Honey Bun" from *South Pacific;* "The Small

House of Uncle Thomas" from *The King and I),* the dance is a stylized presentation of some diegetic situation. And this stylization frequently lies uneasily with an unstylized setting.

West Side Story, directed by Robert Wise and Jerome Robbins, using Robbins's stage choreography, may well serve as a prime example of the adaptation, the serious musical play, and the frequent approach to dance in the musicals of the period. The general attitude of the film makers is probably fairly accurately presented by the comments of John Green, music director on the film.

> Jerome Robbins' dances for the film were obviously and unabashedly derived from his work for the stage show, and *derived* is precisely the correct word. Everything we did on the film was derived from the stage show. The objective of everybody concerned in the making of the film was to carry over into the film medium the essence—the communicative essence—of the stage play. There have been instances in which a stage play has been either an indifferent sort of half-baked success (or in some instances not a success at all) but one in which there may have been a hit tune or two or something else that was attractive to the film makers. Or something about such a play made its film purchasers feel that there was the possibility of a viable motion picture in it, and therefore they bought it. That wasn't the case with *West Side Story.* With *West Side Story* we had a towering, monumental theatrical work, a work in which, whether the songs made the hit parade instantly or not, there was no doubt in the minds of anybody that Leonard Bernstein had written one of the great scores of all time musically for the theater—*of all time.* Stephen Sondheim's lyrical job was hailed by anyone and everyone who knew anything as one of the great achievements in its field. And I think somewhat in error—or definitely in error—the general kind of smart talk around everywhere was that the show had been a success because of Jerry Robbins' dances. Well, if there's any truth to that statement at all, then naturally one of the things that one would try to recapture in terms of the screen would be those dances, that choreography that had allegedly in so many people's minds been what was great about the original stage production.
>
> The musical team for the picture was myself and Saul Chaplin, with whom I had collaborated many times at Metro, and, at Leonard Bernstein's behest, we brought out from New York Sid Raymond and Irwin Kostal, who had orchestrated the original New York production, to work with us on the film. Well, just think of the opening of the picture and think of using the streets of New York as a stage upon which to mount choreography as against the stage of a theater. Right away you have questions of dimension, you have questions of direction (by direction I mean compass direction), you have far greater latitude from the point of view of spaciousness, and you have the attribute of reality. Of course, you can say that nobody dances in the streets, certainly not Jerome Robbins' choreography, but I mean the reality of setting.[11]

There was, of course, some awareness of the potential discrepancy between two styles. Robert Wise has said:

> Jerome Robbins was intrigued with the notion of filming dances on New York streets, but he felt it was a great challenge because we were putting his most stylized choreography against the most realistic backgrounds we'd have in the whole film. You couldn't say it was

completely real, because the usual crowds weren't there. We just had a few people and an occasional car going by, and we chose places that had a certain shape to them which might call to mind the formality of a stage backing.[12]

In spite of the apparently strong feeling toward keeping the staged dance material in the film, neither of the stars of the film was a musical performer—neither danced very much within the film, nor did they do their own singing. (Dubbed voices had been used occasionally before but had become more frequent.) In spite of the general approbation of *West Side Story* as a dance film, it differs significantly from the earlier dance musicals in that dance is relegated almost exclusively to a supporting role.

The major dance sequences in *West Side Story* are ensemble numbers: "The Jet Song," the dance at the gym, "America," and "The Rumble." The love songs ("Maria," "Tonight," "One Hand, One Heart") are not dances, and, given the general tragic nature of the film, there are no traditional dance expressions of *joie de vivre;* the one humorous routine, "Gee, Officer Krupke," is a cynical look at the social situations which have caused the characters to be what they are. The four ensemble numbers are all in the stylized dance format, associated with Robbins, which has come to be called "jazz dance" in modern dance parlance. Its relationship to true jazz dance has been charaterized by Marshall and Jean Stearns in writing about Robbins's *NY Export: Opus Jazz:*

> . . . Robbins . . . employs movements that are *derived* from the vernacular, changed, molded—quite properly—to fit his own notions. That they are not particularly authentic is of little importance; that they lack the rhythmic propulsion which is at the heart of jazz is less fortunate, since it could create additional force and flavor.[13]

Robbins's work for *West Side Story* is probably called "jazz" more for its qualities of asymmetry (coupled with a moderately dissonant musical score at times) than for any truly improvisational jazz aspects. Indeed, there is an evident ballet base to most of the movements. The ensemble members in "The Jet Song," for example, usually move together with some general unanimity of body position. Each specific individual, however, does something different. At one point they all jump with their legs tucked beneath them and their arms outstretched. Each one is facing a slightly different direction, though; their legs are positioned differently, and their arms are also stretched in dissimilar ways. At another point they taunt their rivals, the Sharks, by forming a phalanx, arms stretched in front of them, palms facing each other; their body stances, however, are all different.

West Side Story does have a considerable amount of exploration of film space, however, which adds to the sense of disorientation created by the dances. During the opening number the dancers, by means of the jump cut, move around New York City much as Kelly, Sinatra, and Munshin do in *On the Town*'s "New York, New York" montage. But the dance steps themselves are not contained within a shot; they carry over from one location to another as in Maya Deren's *A Study in Choreography for Camera.* Furthermore, later in the film colored filters are used to help make the transition from Natalie Wood's room to the dance at the gym, and at the moment when she and Richard Beymer meet, the image around them is put into soft focus in order to isolate them from the other dancers. While it is probably true that much of *West Side Story* as a film relied heavily on its stage material, it is also true that it used certain strictly cinematic effects to complement that material.

This broader scope provided by film plus a variety of cinematic devices became the major attribute of many adaptations. *South Pacific* also used colored filters to create mood during several musical numbers, and the extended screen space made available by location shooting and aerial photography became an essential in the song "Don't Rain on My Parade" in *Funny Girl.* Such explorations into the possibilities of both the genre and the medium would characterize the adaptations of most Broadway musicals. Some would even extend those explorations to the point where the adaptation would be as "original" as *On the Town,* itself an adaptation. Some of Bob Fosse's work has, indeed, been with adaptations, yet the musicals he directed made the musical adaptation into something peculiarly cinematic, by using both intended realism and the serious theme to advantage. The dance montage of "I'm a Brass Band" from *Sweet Charity* exploits the reality of New York locations but stylizes them through the jump cut, and in *Cabaret* Fosse makes the conflict between styles of realism and fantasy essential to the film as the musical numbers comment on the narrative. By eliminating several songs from the stage production, and concentrating on a prolific use of close-up, *Cabaret* becomes Fosse's film, not just another adaptation.

John Baxter in his book *Hollywood in the Sixties* noted that finances were one major reason for the change in production of musicals.

> Among sixties musicals, one missed most the ebullient mid-budget originals which had always been a backbone of the *genre. Singin' in the Rain* and *The Pirate* had few counterparts, and graduates of this lively school were the recession's saddest casualties.[14]

The studio system had in many ways been ideal for musicals because it allowed for experimentation, but that experimentation would become prohibitively expensive in a system where people were hired on an *ad hoc* basis. In addition, the purchasing rights for shows like *My Fair Lady* and others cost in the millions of dollars, thus putting an initial high cost on to an increasingly expensive film making process. An occasional original musical would be made: *Dr. Dolittle, Mary Poppins, Funny Lady,* but they, too, were big-budget films, and more customary was the very-high-budget adaptation: *Oliver!, Paint Your Wagon, Hello, Dolly!, The Unsinkable Molly Brown, My Fair Lady.* Another feature was that the roster of directors usually associated with musicals would be replaced, so to speak, by directors who were established in other genres and did musicals for the first—and sometimes only—time. Robert Wise had never directed a musical before *West Side Story,* nor had Fred Zinneman done one before *Oklahoma!* Others in similar circumstances were Otto Preminger with *Carmen Jones,* Joseph L. Mankiewicz with *Guys and Dolls,* William Wyler with *Funny Girl,* Carol Reed with *Oliver!,* Richard Fleischer with *Dr. Dolittle,* and Francis Ford Coppola with *Finian's Rainbow.* Although this switch to non-musical directors for musical films was not in itself necessarily bad, it did reflect an attitude toward production of the genre. Always a staple of the system with its own committed personnel, the musical became a luxury item of the industry, more expensive and less open to innovation.

Two other factors, perhaps related, may have contributed to the decline of the musical film; they certainly contributed to the diminished use of dance within the genre. One was the advent of rock music, coincidentally corresponding roughly to the end of the studio contract system. There had always been a close relationship between popular music in general and music written for the stage and screen. Alec Wilder's *American Popular Song* establishes quite strongly that the great majority of standard popular songs were originally written for musicals—both on stage and in films. With rock music, however, that symbiotic relationship would change. (With certain exceptions, of course, the music for musicals would continue to be written in styles no longer popular with the general audience.) With its emphasis on beat and rhythm over melody, rock music also caused a change in popular dance. The image of couples dancing arm in arm would be replaced by groups of individuals— rarely touching—moving to the insistent and repeated drum beats predominating within the music; the Stearns even suggest that it is a return to certain tribal dance elements. The kinds of song and dance generally used in musicals, then, were no longer popular in the same sense that they had been. A different kind of musical and dance taste had developed, and the musical film did not really change with it. Those films that did star rock music stars and feature rock music were seldom really musicals. More teen-age romance films, they almost never confronted the issues inherent to the genre, seldom integrating the music into the diegesis, seldom using dance except in social situations within the film. (One possible exception is John Badham's *Saturday Night Fever,* which attempts to use the social dancing at the 2001 Disco as a means of character and plot development. The Bee Gees' music is not integrated in the traditional sense, yet it provides John Travolta's Tony with a process of self-realization. In contrast to his everyday life, Tony is admired as a disco dancer; moreover, his preparations with Stephanie for the dance contest are courtship rituals not unlike those of Astaire and Rogers. Finally, winning the dance contest—his goal throughout the film—makes Tony aware of how limited his world really is. *Saturday Night Fever* seems unique, however, and has not become the prototype in another era of dance musicals.)

The second factor that contributed to the decline of the musical film was a conscious decision that dance was not a necessary element to the genre. With the trend in stage musicals toward a kind of folk opera, dance became less significant, even though it did have persistent manifestations. By the late fifties film makers were rationalizing not using dance in films. Vincente Minnelli has said of his later work:

> Alan Lerner started that kind of school of musicals that had very little dancing, and the lyrics are like dialogue. It was the same thing with *Gigi.* It's of the same school. It didn't call for dancing . . ., it didn't even have a ballroom number like *My Fair Lady.*[15]

And of *Bells are Ringing:*

> There were just bits and pieces of dance in that. The number on the stairs, "Drop that Name," for instance, but mostly they were character things.

Minnelli's latest musical, *On a Clear Day You Can See Forever,* an adaptation by Alan Jay Lerner of his stage original, has dancing only as part of ballroom sequences in the period flashback sections. Significantly, the very short dance routine in *Gigi,* "The Night They Invented Champagne," while staged by Charles Walters, goes uncredited on the film, and Charles O'Curran, relatively unknown as a choreographer, had never worked with Minnelli before *Bells Are Ringing.* Of O'Curran Minnelli said, "I . . . only know him as a charming fellow who is very professional."

This period of decline in the musical—and more specifically of the decline of dance in the musical—has been accompanied by a resurgence of interest in dance on the stage and of interest in those very dance musicals which are the subject of this study. Dance has become big business in a way. Many students are showing their interest in dance by actually learning ballet, tap, and modern dance; and one result has been an increased amalgamation of dance forms. As Richard Kraus has observed:

> On television, in movies, and on the musical stage, the quality of dancing has grown immeasurably. Years ago, dancing in Broadway shows . . . tended to offer little more than a lineup of attractive "hoofers." Today, few dancers are hired for musical shows, movies, or television programs who have not had extensive training in ballet, modern dance, jazz, ethnic, and tap dance. . . . public taste with respect to dance in popular entertainment has become increasingly sophisticated.[16]

Also recognizing this trend, the Stearns have speculated on the future of dance forms:

> . . . it seems clear that art dance and vernacular dance will combine more and more effectively as time passes. They have already blended in theatrical dancing. Their merging has progressed for some time—like the blending of classical music and jazz—and the extent of the mixture is a matter of degree, for neither tradition can assimilate the other completely, and for the same reason, the resulting blend will always be new, different, and perhaps fine art.
>
> The fluid spine and flexed knees of tap dancing, for example, wreck ballet posture, just as pointing the feet at a forty-five degree angle in the ballet tradition makes tapping impossible. But different approaches of the two traditions, such as strict or casual displacement in person and on the stage, traditional or improved movement, and contrasting or repeated gestures, have merged to varying degrees.
>
> Perhaps rhythm is the key to future mixtures. Employing the free meter of art dance in the over-all structure, with insertions of the strict vernacular beat as contrast, might unite the best of both. The problem is to find dancers (and musicians) who are expert in both idioms and can modulate back and forth between them.
>
> Nevertheless, we are witnessing increasingly successful borrowing and blends from both the art and the vernacular dance traditions by such choreographers as Donald MacKayle, Jerome Robbins, Jack Cole, Peter Gennaro, Alvin Ailey, Robert Fosse, Michael Kidd, and Gower Champion—to name a few of the best. The blending has been going on for years, and although no one blend pleases everybody, the process is time-honored and the result— at any moment—may be truly great.
>
> The sixties, then, were a transitional era in which the old was dying and the new struggling to be born. There is little reason to believe that the great tradition of American vernacular dance has vanished forever, and much evidence to support the belief that a new and perhaps more remarkable age of highly rhythmic dance will arrive in the not too distant future. Not the least of our problems is to recognize it when it appears.[17]

The evolution toward integration of all elements within the musical contributed to making dance important in film and film, in turn, important to dance. One can only hope that the musical film will play as important a role in the presentation of possible new dance forms (within, perhaps, possible new forms of the musical itself) as it has with older ones.

9

Conclusion

In general this study has considered three areas in analyzing the use of dance throughout the history of the Hollywood musical: one, the actual forms of dance employed in the choreography; two, the various approaches to filming dance that have been manifested in the genre; and three, the relationships that the dances have to the totality of the films. It is relatively easy to give a general history of the dance in film, but one thing my research has suggested is that a too-easy analysis presents simplistic conclusions. The use of dance in film is complex and involved; unfortunately too much criticism of the form has been simplistic. Various choreographers, directors, and, of course, films, are given credit in most instances for certain contributions to the development of dance in the musical. As with most art forms, however, giving credit for firsts is subject to the assumption that one is aware of everything—a physical impossibility; thus in criticism of the musical, Busby Berkeley has always been credited with discovering the "top-shot," whereas, in fact, such overhead shots were used in at least one film before he ever was in Hollywood. His exploitation of that shot, however, certainly made him its most well-known user. Similarly, criticism, perhaps of necessity, has usually broken the form down into isolated units: Berkeley at Warner Brothers, Astaire-Rogers at RKO, and Kelly at MGM, to name the three major ones. Films are not created in a vacuum, however, and there is constant evidence of the interaction of their work. Elaborate routines in certain Astaire films show Berkeley's influence, for example, and then certainly there is a development in Astaire's style of filming dance as he moves to different studios; at MGM later in his career he shows some evidence of an awareness of what Gene Kelly and others were doing at the same time in making the camera a more vital part of the choreography than Astaire himself had seemed interested in doing at RKO. Minor—and hence overlooked—figures occasionally play important roles as well. Criticism has also overlooked or at least given limited attention to certain analyses of dance that seem fruitful when given serious consideration: Berkeley in many respects seems the consummate surrealist of American film, yet little attention has been paid to that facet of his use of dance. (Although surrealism is occasionally mentioned in passing in works about Berkeley himself, Ado Kyrou's book on surrealism in film does not even mention his name.) This study is not definitive; it is more an exploration, yet the poverty of serious analytical criticism makes it a necessity. My conclusions are largely tentative, yet I have tried to base them on analysis and not on dogma.

Perhaps no form of dance has ever been excluded from the screen, but there have always been predominant forms. From the early days of the genre when dance directors from Broadway gave little more than duplications of the kinds of dance popular on the New York stage to the later attempts of such people as George Balanchine and Eugene Loring to open the movies up to an acceptance of ballet itself, dance in the musical has become increasingly accomplished. Although Berkeley never cared if his girls could dance, today it is uncommon to have dancers who cannot move easily into all forms of traditional theatrical dance: tap, musical comedy, modern-expressional, and ballet. Various forms of social dance—ballroom, ethnic, folk—have also been prevalent in the musical film, but they too have become increasingly complex. In the early days, social dance, particularly ballroom styles, played an important role in displaying a screen dancer's abilities, but as the dancers became more skillful their use of ballroom styles became increasingly less social in orientation and increasingly more theatrical. The Astaire-Rogers ballroom numbers, always an important part of their films, could never be duplicated by the average dancer, and even in certain audience-oriented numbers, such as "The Varsity Drag" in *Good News,* no person without considerable training would ever be able to attempt the steps; furthermore, the intricate patterning of the ensembles was designed as choreography to be watched—not imitated—by the audience. Ultimately what seems most obvious is that barriers among dance forms were eliminated on the screen just as they were on the stage. Ballet uses tap and ethnic forms now just as musical comedy dancing uses a great deal of ballet. This change in stage performing has, of course, been reflected in film. There has also been an increased use of athletic styles—indeed, of gymnastics itself—in all forms of dance, thus moving away from the somewhat effete nature of some dance and incorporating the robustness of black dance. In almost all respects the work of Gene Kelly seems the natural culmination of dance exploration in the film because as much as anyone else—and more than almost everyone else—he seems to incorporate all the dance styles that preceded him and to suggest many of those that would follow him. In addition, he also was interested in the medium of film and the means to incorporate dance into film in a way that had not been completely accomplished prior to his work.

The general trends in dance forms in the musical film in many respects mirror dance as presented on the stage during the same eras. The revues of the twenties were best known for their spectacular displays of chorus girls going through fundamental dance movements in elaborate arrangements using extraordinary technical stage facilities. This influence, probably the strongest in the first years of sound film, has given early film musicals their stylistic image. Made more spectacular through the superior technical facilities of the Hollywood studios, the chorus-girl dance was, in general, the predominant form of the early musical. Receiving their most elaborate treatment for the longest period of time by Busby Berkeley, such dance forms have been given his name. Although he was neither the first nor the only dance director to elaborate on Ziegfeld-type dance forms in Hollywood, he is certainly the best remembered.

One trend in dance that has been manifested throughout the history of the musical has been that of a move from popular, vernacular dance to ballet. This movement has been evident, among other ways, by the change in the use of terminology: *dance director* has become *choreographer*. And just as in dance on the stage there has been a gradual incorporation of jazz and popular elements into ballet (and ballet into musical comedy and popular dance) so has there been this elimination of distinctions on the screen. Fred Astaire was among the first to incorporate these elements into his work. Although Astaire was in no sense a ballet dancer, he did have some ballet training and did use some ballet in his work. In general Astaire used tap and soft shoe, ballroom dance, and ballet, and during his period at RKO Astaire always included an elaborate partnering number based on social dance/ballroom steps (a waltz or, more commonly, a fox trot) but which manifested some evidence of ballet. Ballet in its "purest" forms, however, came into use in musical films when George Balanchine was invited to Hollywood by Samuel Goldwyn. Balanchine had just finished his work in *On Your Toes* in New York when he went to Hollywood to do the choreography for several films, both musicals and non-musicals, which had dance numbers of some kind. His influence as such, though, seems to have been more through his stage work than his screen work. His opening up of stage musicals to ballet was followed by such people as Agnes deMille, and choreographers who later became well known for their screen work—like Michael Kidd—often studied with him or performed with the New York City Ballet and seem to have been influenced by his dance forms. As a figure of the contemporary dance world, Balanchine's influence has been profound and is constantly evident both on the stage and on the screen, and whatever ballet is present in American musical films during that period can be traced at least indirectly to him.

Various ethnic and folk dances, usually employed in films using settings or characters of a particular nationality, were introduced into screen dance and integrated into the general image of dance as well. Such dancers as the DeMarcos and even a more popular actress like Dolores Del Rio helped acquaint Hollywood with Spanish dances, and subsequently other dancers and choreographers would find ways to use those dance forms in their work. (Kelly's Spanish number in *Anchors Aweigh* shows his awareness of *tacaneo*, flamenco heel and toe work, for example.) Similarly, modern-expressional dance, as a result of Jack Cole and others, would also begin to show itself on the screen toward the end of the thirties and in the early forties. Modern dance—using the body without restrictions in style and method, almost spontaneously—had become a means of psychological expression through movement.

Perhaps the most important aspect of the integration of dance forms into the filmic system, however, lies with the conventional application of those forms as signs. Criticism of dance in film has often been directed at the "inaccuracy" of certain dances. Although there may be some validity to the charges of inaccuracy, all too often such criticism ignores the dances as conventional signs: folk and native dance sequences, for example, generally fulfill an audience's expectations of how those dances should look. Social dance forms in film represent the society they are a sign of and connote the *impressions* of what those dances were rather than denote the historically accurate movement. As a result, eighteenth-century court dances are formal whereas folk dances are boisterous; the waltz is romantic whereas tap dancing is good humored. By extension other dance forms have also become conventionally applicable. Ballet has most often been used to represent the exotic and the ethereal, modern dance to represent the "disturbed" and "tortured," the psychological. This conventional application of dance is closely linked, too, with the dances as signs of rituals. With the evolution of the integrated musical, the dances increasingly became exterior manifestations of the characters' interiority; they sang and danced their feelings— usually in a conventionally appropriate manner. The fox trots of Astaire and Rogers expressed their characters' growing love, for example, and Kelly tapped his joy while "Singin' in the Rain."

Indeed, Gene Kelly's awareness of the conventions is combined with his exploitation of multiple dance forms. He moved easily among dance forms in both his performing and his choreography. As his characters worked through a situation by means of dance, he changed their dance forms according to the conventions. In *An American in Paris* Kelly expresses Jerry Mulligan's exuberance through tap, his love for Lise in elaborate ballroom numbers, and his dreams through ballet. In this same regard it is not unusual that Cyd Charisse should end her number in Stillman's Gym in *It's Always Fair Weather* with *chaîné* turns, for the number has used a combination of ballet, modern dance, and, appropriately, gymnastics. This combination of forms is manifested throughout all of Kelly's work: tap, softshoe, ballet, modern, ethnic are all present yet are combined as well with the film itself to become genuine forms of cine-dance and not just records of dance routines. Furthermore, they are all presented in a popular mode, as an integral part of the musical genre. Even when he attempted to employ dance in a more serious vein, as in the ballet at the end of *An American in Paris* or in the all-dance film *Invitation to the Dance,* he nonetheless included popular forms and integrated them with the more conventionally serious forms. There are tap and jazzy musical comedy routines juxtaposed with ballet and modern in each of the films.

In summary, the approach to dance, per se, in film has increasingly eliminated barriers among dance forms; furthermore, there has been a greater accomplishment on the part of dancers and an increased seriousness[1] of the purpose of dance, including the awareness of dance as a cinematic code manifesting conventional signs—a field of expression with fields of meaning arising both from an audience's expectations of how dance should be used and from film makers' changing applications of dance over three decades.

The possibilities of film-dance (not just filming dances that already exist) have become increasingly important, as well, for dance as a cinematic code functions in relationship to all codes of the film system. Naturally Berkeley is given a great deal of credit for attempting to create something that is not just stage dance on film; however, he was not really interested in *dance* and, therefore, becomes less significant a figure than one ordinarly assumes. Astaire, on the other hand, was concerned about filming dance, perhaps in a manner which is the exact opposite of Berkeley, because for Astaire the dance had to predominate—at all costs. His aim to keep the full figure showing at all times and never to violate the integrity of the dance as a whole led him to use the camera primarily as a recording instrument. He removed the dance from the artifice of a stage performance in his films and thus made possible a use of dance in which a character danced wherever and whenever he felt like dancing, a use exploited in the subsequent musicals of someone like Kelly. Kelly, then, seems to fulfill his forerunners' explorations into the ways of filming dance. For him there was always an obvious attempt to choreograph for the camera—indeed, to choreograph the camera as part of the routine.[2]

Although it is a cliché of the early musicals that they were rigidly stagebound in their use of the camera in relation to dance, there were, nonetheless, a few attempts to move away from the stage and show dances as they could never be seen on the stage. Occasionally an overhead camera or even an occasional moving camera would lend a more cinematic quality to the otherwise recording aspect of the filming of dance. It is true, however, that for the most part the dances in early musicals were stagebound, not only because they were almost always presented as if they were being danced as part of an actual show on a stage, but also because they were created as if they were being presented on a proscenium arch stage. The camera was always the occupant of the best seat in the house; camera movement usually followed the dancers as the audience would with its eyes. The most radical departure from the full shot was a cut to a close-up of some part of the body—particularly the feet—which was busy with isolated movement. At the same time, though, there would often be cutaways to audience reaction, to non-dancing members of the show, or to close-ups of the dancers' faces. These kinds of interruptions of the integrity of the number were what made Berkeley feel that Hollywood did not know how to film dance when he first went to the West Coast. In addition to his usually recognized contributions, then, he was also instrumental in restoring a certain kind of integrity to the number as a unit. In fact, his routines really could not exist without their unity; each is separate from the rest of the film in such a way that a movement between the two radically different worlds of the narrative and of the numbers would destroy the illusion of each, as indeed seems the case during the "Muchacha" number of *In Caliente* (in which a cutaway to Edward Everett Horton and Pat O'Brien watching the number makes its elaborateness seem ludicrous in a way that is never the case in most other Berkeley films). This integrity took different forms for Berkeley, however, in that he would integrate close-ups and otherwise non-dance aspects of his material into the numbers themselves. Similarly, radical changes in camera angle, abrupt movements between unrelated facets of the number, and, of course, elaborate stage effects were all an integral part of his routines; what might have been considered out of place and unrelated to dance he incorporated into his material in order to achieve the integrity that he found missing in musicals before he went to Hollywood.

This respect for the integrity of the whole number has carried through in film musicals, but for the most part Berkeley's influence has been minimal, particularly inasmuch as most of his successors have been interested in *dance*. There are, assuredly, many attempts to copy the flamboyance of Berkeley routines in other thirties pictures: the final number with the girls on the airplane wings in *Flying Down to Rio,* the "Continental" in *The Gay Divorcee,* the finale of *Stand Up and Cheer,* the parade routines of *Flirtation Walk,* to name just four, all suggest a Berkeleyan influence. Although there was often an elaborate routine in the Astaire-Rogers films, it was specifically Astaire's style of dancing that characterized those films. The integrity of the dance was paramount for Astaire, but it manifested itself for him in an intimacy which had little to do with Berkeley's feeling for integrity. Astaire wanted the body to be seen whole, the camera generally accompanying the dance, rather than participating in it. Long takes and few cuts characterize his dances, the camera moving almost imperceptibly to keep the dance centered in the frame. Astaire's control over his films was such that he could insist on the results he wanted. Although this was not so with most other dancers of the period, nonetheless, there was uniformity to the style of filming dance in the thirties. If they were not trying to copy the Berkeley style, then they generally did maintain the dance documentation quality of the Astaire films. In most of the sequences between Shirley Temple and Bill Robinson, for example, cutaways to Robinson's "educated feet," although occurring frequently, were the only permissible moves away from the totality of the dance itself. Eleanor Powell's dances were shot in a similarly utilitarian manner: long takes with tracking camera show her off during a series of tapping *chaîné* turns, but numerous cuts and changes of camera angle document the numerous changes from ballet to tap to gymnastics which characterize her style. On the whole, however, the participation of the camera in the number, present in some of Berkeley's work, and the intimacy with and respect for the dance itself, characteristic of Astaire at RKO, did not come together at that point.

They did come together, however, during the years of MGM's predominance as *the* musical studio in the subsequent decade, particularly in those films featuring Gene Kelly. Kelly was permitted to do his own choreography almost from the beginning of his Hollywood career, and there is a definite style to Kelly's films, particularly the ones he co-directed with Stanley Donen, which suggests a ruling principle of choreographing for the camera, not only in the dances but also in the general movement of the entire film. First, there is a natural movement from walking into dancing that connects numbers to the narrative. Second, there is a conscious attempt to make the camera work unobtrusive in order to emphasize the dancing, not, as in the Astaire numbers, with a camera from a "front-row seat," but in long takes with elaborate tracking and dollying shots and with match-cutting on action to reduce the noticeability of the editing. The integrity of the number was important to Kelly but so was the integrity of the entire film; for all the people working at MGM the integrated musical was paramount and the cooperation among the various creative personnel was strong. The films Kelly did with Vincente Minnelli have an exotic quality more in the tradition of the singer's musical, yet each film reflects Kelly's presence not just as a performer but also as a choreographer. He was concerned with a cine-dance form viable to the musical genre, not just with a dance form that is recorded documentary-like and inserted into the narrative line.

Integration may be the key word in analyzing dance in the musical, for just as there has been a movement toward integration of all forms of dance and to integrate the camera and the dance into viable film-dance, there has also been a movement toward integration of the dances themselves into the narrative lines of the films. In the early revue musicals there was, of course, no narrative, but as the narrative musicals developed, the numbers seemed to lag behind and became only inserts into the flow of the story on many occasions.

Berkeley's films, again, are the obvious examples, for his numbers were seldom presented except as numbers to be performed during the stage show which the narrative line had been leading up to. Although that may be, in one sense, a form of integration, the fact that he usually worked completely separately from the rest of the film, and that the numbers are stylistically and tonally distinct from the rest of the film, makes it not integrated according to conventional definitions of integration. As the musical progressed, however, there was a conscious effort to create integrated numbers as expressions of inner feelings, manifestations of joy and exuberance, comments on the relationships of the characters, rituals of courtship and love, and even on occasion the actual working out of narrative situations and thematic concerns.[3] The dances thus seem to be given greater opportunity for expression and for exploration into dance forms; the stage show has a somewhat limited range of dance forms whereas the dance unencumbered by stage obligations can use varied and multiple forms as conventionally befit the situations being expressed.

Although there were certainly some attempts to make the dances as presented in the backstage musical relevant in some way to the rest of the narrative, nonetheless, the relationships were always tentative. Rather than expressions of the characters, rather than serving as rituals within the context of the film itself, they generally stood as expressions of the fantasies and concerns of the choreographer and dance director—or, as in the case of performers who were able to develop their own material on the screen, say an Eleanor Powell or even a Bill Robinson, they became expressions of a screen persona without really being part of the character within the film. This is never more true than with Busby Berkeley, for deliberately working independently of the rest of the film in most cases, he created worlds which displayed his erotic fantasies and his surrealistic view of the nature of reality. Blondes with legs spread wide for a dollying camera to move through, dancing pianos, disembodied heads, phallic bananas, and a child-playing midget appearing at lewdly inopportune moments are all manifestations of Berkeley's imagination. The abstract geometric formations so associated with his work, which seem almost forerunners of contemporary computer films, are only one facet of his vision. It seems indicative that one usually thinks of the Berkeley-Warner Brothers films as Berkeley's films; he becomes the auteur even though he was rarely the actual director. His concerns and the manifestations of them are so strong that they carry the films with them; and in one sense integration of the entire film seems irrelevant, for the films function as vehicles for those production numbers.

The backstage story provides an excuse for the existence of the dance numbers, of course, but that is only one way of approaching the problem of the relationship of the number to the narrative. There are numerous others. The dream sequence, for example, has been consistently employed throughout movie musical history. Even within the more sophisticated integrated musical, dream sequences have provided dance with opportunities which might otherwise have been denied. In Kelly's films, for example, dream sequences tend toward ballet and other more skillful forms. Dream sequences provided the opportunity for Astaire and Rogers to kiss for the first time on the screen in *Carefree*. More important to the development of the genre, however, is the feeling of necessity and explanation implicit in the dream sequence. When dealing with a diegetic reality, it seemed necessary to many of the film makers that the fantasy of the dancing and singing had to be separate from the rest of the film—hence the dream escape and the conclusion that this was not really happening to the characters, though it may have been presenting narrative situations, character traits, or emotional outlets necessary for the totality of the film. The excuse for dancing is also often found in the profession of the leading character. Fred Astaire in the thirties films was always a dancer by trade, a fact usually established within the first several minutes. This then gave him the "right" to dance in the films, a right denied characters whose professions were more mundane. This professional excuse, as it were, would be a perpetual holdover even into the forties and fifties. Kelly, for example, was a professional dancer in *For Me and My Gal, Take Me Out to the Ball Game*, and *Summer Stock*, among others; yet that characteristic seemed incidental when the opportunity to dance arose in the films. Kelly's characters were popular manifestations of traditional character types—the Greek Alazon, the *comedia dell'arte* Pierrot—who existed in the "real" world and just happened to be able to act out their fantasies through song and dance as a natural extension of their lives. Jerry Mulligan needed no excuse for knowing how to tap in *An American in Paris;* tapping in "I Got Rhythm," Kelly showed the children *"la danse américaine,"* and it was only natural that he should teach them English and dancing simultaneously.

The integrated musical is as conventional as any other type, yet its conventions have resulted from the experimentations occurring since musicals began both on stage and on screen. Furthermore, the integrated screen musical raises certain questions about film which make the genre seem the epitome of certain problems of film theory: the realist versus formative traditions; the nature of spectacle and its manifestations of the high art/popular art dichotomy; and the principle of authorship within a collaborative art process. Though an exploration of dance in the musical can neither answer all the questions nor solve all the problems, nevertheless it can suggest avenues of further inquiry while at the same time making clear how conventions have developed and how dance in the musical actually functions.

First, the Lumière-Méliès dichotomy, though itself probably an oversimplification, has been present throughout film musical history. Indeed, both the realist and formative tendencies occur within individual films. A character's ability to sing and dance in the streets, as it were, assumes a Lumière approach; moreover, the attempt first by Astaire and later by Kelly and others to move from walking into dancing without a break and within the same shot fulfills to a certain extent the requirements of Bazin's aesthetic as well.[4] Nevertheless, there is still that element of fantasy and its allied "willing suspension of disbelief," for the conventions of the genre have come to mean a combination of the two major theoretical trends.

Second, the nature of spectacle—i.e. performing for others—is related to this dichotomy and has also been important historically in the genre. In the backstage musical the sequences were intended to be spectacles, operating extra-diegetically (often with their own diegesis, in fact) and provided with their excuse for being as part of a stage show. That few of those spectacles could ever have been presented on a stage was conventionally unimportant, but they do raise a theoretical point: though "realistic" in the sense that they occur in a show prepared for in the narrative, they function "fantastically" as isolated units of their own. Spectacle becomes more complex in the integrated musical. The dancing and singing operate primarily as ritual signs, but they are also spectacle at the same time; they are exteriorizations of characters' interior feelings but also serve as performance both to others in the film and to the film's audience in a way not like regular acting. This duality is often emphasized by virtue of the way numbers are shot. The applause-inducing tableau ending or the smiling face close-up ending exists as frequently in the integrated musical as the casual return to walking which would seem the natural conclusion to a number beginning with walking into dancing. The nature of spectacle also reaffirms the conventional roles of popular and high-art dance forms in the musical. Though an integration of all dance forms has characterized the musical in general, when dance as high art has been emphasized—the ballet in *The Band Wagon,* for example, or "Slaughter on Tenth Avenue" in *Words and Music*—it has been presented as spectacle for its own sake, suggesting that popular dance forms are more naturally integrated into the genre.

Finally, film as a collaborative process raises questions of a musical's authorship. The usual designation of the director as auteur seems not so easy to make, for at times certain contributions become more important than that of the director. Many musicals seem the result of either collective auteurs or multiple auteurs. Emphasizing the dance suggests a principle of choreographer as auteur, and the contribution of most Hollywood choreographers has given them at least some claim to such a distinction. But that too raises problems, for the separation between performer and choreography is not an easy one to make in films inasmuch as a dancer's style often became an essential element in a film's numbers. The process is complicated, furthermore, by those performers—Astaire and Kelly especially—who prepared their own material. Only Berkeley among the major dance directors made his dancers individually anonymous; more often the star of a musical could claim a film as his or her own vehicle with the dances serving to show off the star's individual talents. As director, choreographer, *and* performer Gene Kelly was concerned with combining all forms of dance, with making those dances an essential cinematic code, and with making them conventionally appropriate ingredients of the integrated musical. His work seems the culmination of musicals which preceded him and the forerunner of those which followed.

In many respects the musical as a major film genre is now an almost complete body of work; since the late fifties the genre has been moribund as an original film form. Musicals have been made, of course, but as a staple of the industry they were inextricably linked with the former studio contract system. Its decline at approximately the same time as a major change in popular music tastes made it almost impossible to make relatively low-budget musicals not previously established on the Broadway stage. Ironically, as musicals have been phased out there has been an increased interest in dance as both a high and popular art, as manifested by attendance at live performances of dance companies and at revivals of film musicals. But even television—except perhaps in those variety shows which seem heirs of the early revue musicals— has not adopted the musical genre as its own, as it has so many other film genres. Nevertheless, as a body of work musicals seem microcosmic of film in general. Within a period of thirty years they went from a relatively primitive form to a sophisticated genre embodying all aspects of the medium. The manifestations of dance within the musical also seem microcosmic of film, for as dance developed as part of the filmic system it reflected the nature of all other art forms being integrated into that system. To study dance in the musical is to study the nature of film itself.

Appendix

The following interviews have been edited, essentially to make them easy to read. Some material has been rearranged in order to present a logical flow of ideas, and certain unnecessary digressions have been omitted. On the whole, however, the original conversations have been duplicated, though with necessary adjustments to create sentences and to correct grammar.

The material within the interviews is not always directly pertinent to the topic of this study; nevertheless, anyone interested in an analysis of dance in the musical would find the general comments not only interesting but also potentially valuable for further research. By including them as an appendix, therefore, I am making them available for other scholars and am providing information of general relevance to the musical and of specific relevance to dance as a code of the genre.

Music director and composer John Green very kindly answered via a tape recording a series of questions I had mailed to him. His comments were extensive and most informative. At the time, however, he specifically requested that I use the material solely for my dissertation; therefore, I am honoring that request by not including his interview here.

I have arranged the interviews alphabetically within the following categories: Choreographers and Performers—Jack Cole, Betty Garrett, Gene Kelly, Eugene Loring; Art Directors—Preston Ames, Randall Duell, Jack Martin Smith; Director—Vincente Minnelli; Director of Photography—Joseph Ruttenberg.

Interview with Jack Cole

My interview with choreographer Jack Cole took place at his home in the Hollywood Hills on 29 November 1973. Mr. Cole talked freely and openly about his work in Hollywood; a strongly iconoclastic and irreverent person, he was largely disdainful of the motion picture business and everyone in it.

This may well be the last interview which Mr. Cole gave, for he passed away in February 1974, three months after I talked with him.

DELAMATER: You have mentioned your role in urban dance.

COLE: The term I use is *urban dance;* it's a kind of urban folklore, an expression of the way people act.

DELAMATER: Could you give me some information about your background, your dance training?

COLE: I first started at Denishawn and was a member of the Denishawn Company. It was my first experience with dancing. I had never danced in any way; I had never gone to dancing school. I was sixteen, and apparently I was very talented because I was put in the company and got free lessons. It took me a very short time—even though I was in the company and had gone on tour for two seasons—to know that that really wasn't *my* kind of thing. It was such a romantic, sentimental approach, not very real. I used to go at that time to the Savoy and had to do a lot of jazzing and talking to get in. I was very young looking, very blond and blue-eyed, and it was rough for a kid to get into the Savoy. But they were amused with me because I seemed nice; I wasn't like a nut or a freak. Sometimes I'd go with girls and we'd dance, or I'd go by myself and eventually I got comfortable enough. Most of the places in Harlem at that time were slum places to the status people: "Oh, they're so amusing!" They were so stylish, a Carl Van Vechten approach to Harlem. The Savoy was, particularly in the beginning, very much a neighborhood dance hall. It was where people went to dance, buy a drink, and meet each other. It was fun because it wasn't a fixed place, although slowly it became infiltrated with people from downtown. It was where all the good bands were and so everybody wanted to go there. Every once in a while I'd go over to a table if I saw a couple who could dance absolutely marvelously. The only way you can learn that kind of dancing is to dance with somebody who is very good. I'd ask if I could dance with the young lady. I was such a kid, and it was all so improbable that they would usually say yes. So I'd dance a while. Only once did I have trouble. I was walking home and suddenly I was picking myself up out of the gutter; somebody had hit me in the head with a rock because I had been dancing with a Negro girl—very curious and hard to think of that in terms of where we've gotten to now.

I used to talk to Miss Ruth [St. Denis] about it, but she didn't understand. I remember a funny thing that happened. I had bought a new Cab Calloway record called "Oh, You Dog, You Dirty Dog," and I was playing it on a portable phonograph in this great big studio which was right in back of the dining room at the Denishawn house. Miss Ruth was having dinner with Bishop Guthrie, an Episcopal bishop, and they were talking about the ecclesiastical dance and some kind of Masque for Mary which she was going to do for the Christmas season in the church. I didn't know this, and I was in the studio and had the phonograph going with Cab Calloway screaming. I was squirming and dancing, just feeling marvelous, when Miss Ruth appeared in the doorway and said, "Shut that damn thing off." I had never heard her say *damn* before. She was very tall, an enormously beautiful, imposing woman, and she was white with rage because she had tried to talk with Bishop Guthrie through this. I shut it off and got a severe reprimand. Later she went by and another boy and I were doing something, a bit of tap dancing and jazz dancing, and she let out a wail (I didn't even hear her) and went up to her room. All of a sudden the gong rang in the school, which always meant to assemble in the big studio. We were all assembled, and Mr. Shawn came in (he always wore a Japanese kimono). We all sat down on the floor and, looking very serious, he said, "The temple has been defiled." They were always being very earnest about that kind of thing, but I had a sense of humor that often got me into trouble around the school. We were given a bad time and made to listen about all the sacrifices they had made, which was very true. I used to talk to Miss Ruth about jazz dance and the Savoy, and she'd say, "But it's so sexual, dear." She was a very dear, bright woman but in certain areas there were great Victorian blanks.

Miss Ruth never understood my interest in investigating social and erotic intercourse with people, how they flirted, which is what the movement is about. I was interested in many things. I was interested in the Oriental theater, Japanese and Indian particularly. I was always interested in the culture of people and how they expressed themselves. I never wanted to *be*—people are always confusing why you are teaching them; they think you want to teach them to *be* an Indian dancer—but I was trying to expose them to a different attitude, to give them the excitement and the discovery of the thousand ways there are to move that are peculiar and different, totally different, that would never enter your head here. It opens up a new vocabulary of movement, different ways to approach the problem, rather than a balletic way. When I am going to do a certain kind of conflict, male conflict, I always think of Japanese theater because they do that particular kind of thing in a highly successful, very formal, stylized way.

I started doing concerts and had my own concert group which made tours, but there was always the problem of making money. I had been with Doris Humphrey and Charles Weidman and that was the reason I left them. I was making ten dollars a concert for three concerts a year. The rest of the time you were supposed to stay alive even though the rehearsal periods and classes were enormous. One time I used to live at Doris's and Charles's studio and sleep on the floor. Charles used to leave fifty cents every once in a while so I wouldn't starve. We used to walk up and down town. The studio was on Eighteenth Street and we used to walk up to about Forty-third Street where there was a health food cafeteria where you could get a dinner inexpensively. On the way out we'd fill a glass full of sugar from the sugar containers and eat it and say, "Energy."

If it is viable and work, you should get paid for it. I was a great one for the economic factor. If you like it, pay for it. I didn't want to keep on working on the side. If I'm going to do something good, it's going to take all day long, and I've got to be able to live and to live in a certain way, particularly if it's a physical art. There is no reason, if you belong to a proper area of the establishment, why you shouldn't get a wage comparable to somebody else. It used to be very irritating in the early days in the musical shows in New York. The kids in the ensemble used to get thirty dollars a week and no pay at all for rehearsals. You just rehearsed for five weeks, and you didn't get paid until you went out of town. Stage hands who had no skill at all and did their job very badly would be pulling down two hundred fifty to three hundred dollars a week. So I was involved with organizing unions. I helped to organize some of the unions at the night clubs, which was very difficult because of the gangster element. There were very nice gangsters who were always good people to work for. I was friends with them because I was enormously successful in night clubs so they liked me—they liked success. If people produced what they wanted, they'd give you anything. It used to be difficult to organize a line of girls in the night club because the gangster bosses used to be very nice to them: their mothers got sick and they'd pay the hospital bills. At the same time we tried to explain to them that their salary wasn't a gift for being good or pretty. It belonged to them because they worked. There were conditions under which they worked—like the dressing room and the johns—that you wouldn't believe. But they were afraid that the gangsters were going to get them for being disloyal.

I was hired to choreograph Betty Grable in *Moon Over Miami* and also to dance in it. When they wanted me to start the picture, I couldn't get rid of my night club obligations and so they got Hermes Pan to do it. I came out later and did one number which was mostly removed from the picture because of censorship, which was very interesting at that point. They had the most elaborate kind of censorship. One was that my navel showed and you couldn't show signs of physical birth, which was truly idiotic. You were supposed to cover it with transparent tape, put body makeup over it so that you had some strange kind of abdomen. Another was that the man could be on the floor and the woman could stand or the man could stand and the woman could be on the floor, but you both couldn't be on the floor together. That was the most perverse sexual attitude that I had heard in a long time: both people couldn't be prone on the stage at the same time. You couldn't strike a woman. I was doing some kind of betrothal Indian thing where the girl got a crack on the face. It was a very serious distortion of a real Indian ritual. Hermes Pan was a very pleasant man whose main object in life was not to make trouble. He got along very well with people which is why he worked for such long periods of time. He had no strong attitudes to bother anybody. I have always made a lot of trouble. It makes a lot of trouble if you *have* an attitude.

Metro brought me out and paid me an enormous amount of money—unbelievable—which they did everybody. They had the most incredible crafts people at Metro at the point when I first came out, which was 1943; they could do the most miraculous things. They had heard that I was an expert, and I was hired and rushed out here, but they didn't really know what I did. For a long time they just get you to run around the studio and watch people at work, which I did. After a while I got curious because I got tired of watching and wanted to do it. Then they called up and asked if I would teach Ingrid Bergman to waltz for *Gaslight,* and I said, "No." I didn't want them to get the idea that I went around doing cleanup jobs, that I was a dancing teacher. That was necessary. You had to do that at places like Metro, particularly. You had to set it up right away that you didn't do certain things.

Then a little later I came acropper with some of the larger queen bees like Cedric Gibbons, which made things difficult. It is possible to build a set where you direct a scene, and he was given to doing that. He'd smile and say yes to a director and go ahead and do what he wanted to do. The money that was spent at Metro! The business within a business there! They were in the business of making scenery and they were in the business of making costumes. I remember that the costumes for an Esther Williams film, the bathing suits, were going to cost eight hundred dollars apiece. They were in business and the ones who used to get it were the producers and directors who were on royalties in terms of profits. The studio used to make enormous amounts of money in that way before the picture ever started. They were in the business of making scenery and supplying it, and they really charged the picture for it. That was one of the things you had to counter.

I enjoyed working at Columbia rather than at Metro because Harry Cohn let me do everything. I really could get into the cutting room; I could get down on the sets. I got to know the whole bloody thing upside down. I was always in the middle of everything. At Metro it was always very difficult because you had all the queen bees telling you how to do it. When I did the musical numbers there was no director on the stage. Harry told everybody to leave me alone. I could do what I wanted; I designed the clothes and the sets and did the number. He used to tell the producers pretty much not to tell me how to do it. Which is a good way. Good executives give you an enormous amount of freedom and then when you flop, they don't get sore. They just don't want you to do that thing again. Harry was also pretty good about most things when it came to spending money with me because I was very good at demonstrating how I could save him money, which was how I got to develop a dance group. (Gwen Verdon and Carol Haney and all those people came out of this group.) I used to get involved with doing a lot of musicals, and I kept telling Harry that it was much better to have an expert group always ready to work.

DELAMATER: Would you talk about your approach to filming dance, things to do and not to do, when you began working with camera, and so on? COLE: The thing you need most is rehearsal time with the camera because the camera is the most important object and its movement requires a great deal of time. I always wantd to say, "Get away. I'll do it," but you couldn't say that even if the work somebody was doing bothered you. Lighting is also quite a craft to learn for film, and you couldn't do it. You had to depend on the cameramen, and they are not too bright except in relation to looking at an object. As related to theater or what it's about, they did not know anything at all. It is very hard to get what you want because you are working through somebody else. But the most elementary thing I can tell you is that you need rehearsal time and particularly with the camera crew who are handling the camera, moving it.

Busby Berkeley used to do that a lot. But Busby Berkeley had no involvement with dancing. I don't know why one would want to talk about *dancing* when talking about his films. He was interested only in photograph-ing designs and doing long traveling shots, which he did very well. He had the patience to build up a long crane shot forever and then really rehearse it and keep rehearsing it until he got it exactly the way it was supposed to be. He never looked at what the girls were *doing*. He was just watching for marks of the camera in relationship to musical bars. He was just creating wallpaper. But he was interesting as a cultural object reflecting the erotic attitudes of the middle class. He was like a really old theatrical agent in New York who liked girls a lot. He got lots of blonde girls and photographed them in as many ways as were acceptable to the middle class. He couldn't get them completely nude, but he would get them with their legs open and their breasts hanging. It was all about looking at gorgeous women erotically with the camera as a penis substitute. It was very interesting; he'd go to all that trouble to get those Germanic armies moving against each other. LeRoy Prinz, who was also the dance director at Warners, didn't know a bloody thing about dancing either.

But the one thing is the camera rehearsal. One of the good uses of the camera was *Jammin' the Blues*. Mave MacDonald and Archie Savage dance in that the way they did at the Savoy. The choreography isn't very interesting, but they are two very interesting looking people who could dance very well. It is photographed very well because the camera does musical architecture. Their first object is to retreat and then come in slowly with the long phrase, an eight-bar phrase or something. It was an elementary attempt to have some kind of relationship and an attitude. You were being asked to look at the thing musically.

I used to elaborately choreograph for long crane shots, which didn't mean long shots. They were in and out with varying angles which would go in and sink and hold and then move slowly. I had the camera in mind while I was choreographing. You work with somebody like Cukor, who is an old-school man, and he automatically shoots everything long, middle, and close, right, center, and left. It's almost maddening to watch the film go down the drain. I also cut the picture as I'm doing it, and I absolutely know what it's going to be like. When somebody says that we should take protection shots, I say I don't want any protection; if it doesn't come out, we do the shot over again. I know exactly what I'm doing, and it's been designed that way. I'm not going to let a cutter who doesn't know anything about it put the first cut together. I never gave them anything. All they could do is put the stuff together. If the sequence was made up of six shots, then they had six pieces to fasten together, that's all.

DELAMATER: You have dance credit on *Les Girls*. Would you tell me how that came about and what it was like to work on that film?

COLE: Kelly had just done *Invitation to the Dance*, and the people upstairs at Metro wanted somebody to exert some control. I'd known Kelly for a long time. I was the star in the Rainbow Room in New York when my agent brought him in to audition. I came out about two years after Gene did. *Les Girls* was not the most interesting scene for me. Kelly was a really aggressive "get-ahead," and he had gotten ahead with not much. When you get ahead with not very much, you get very protective of how to hide the fact that you don't know how to do very much, that your means are not very great. You do things yourself because you know how to use what little you've got. Which is what he did. He would turn everything you did into Gene Kelly, which is very sad. All the things were turned into the clichés. He'd say, "Well, it feels better on me this way." When it got to a certain point where the footwork got very involved, he'd stop and say, "Don't I stop here and sort of push my hat back?" He was not a very good dancer at all, but he was interesting as a phenomenon. It's a cultural thing that he happened to succeed—which is always the way with popular art. There is always the establishment attitude about dancing and men dancing in the right way. He knew how to use creative people. He would always use what was new or a new attitude very judiciously to bolster what he was doing. I had given his wife Jeanne Coyne her first job. She was a very nice girl and a very good dancer. She told me at one point that he never in a million years could do something that I was choreographing for him, which gave me the idea that his technical means were not very great.

As *Les Girls* worked out, it was interesting for one comedy scene I did with Kay Kendall where she was drunk (which had nothing to do with the music). Kay wanted me to do it with her because she didn't feel relaxed or funny around Cukor, who was not her style. (She was not very fond of Gene Kelly either.) In her big drunken scene we plotted it out as an improvisation, which is the way she worked. But Cukor doesn't work that way. He wants to know everything you are going to do. She told him that she wanted to do it with me, so we went over the day she was going to do it and worked it out. I did generalized geography, what would take her from one point to another. We did it about four times through. I just laughed at what she was doing and by the fourth time she had it down. Cukor had to depend on me; she didn't understand his verbal way.

Cukor is a very bright man, but he has disturbing traits as a director. Actors are emotional people, and verbalizing is very disturbing to them. He yells, "Cut," and then comes up and goes yakkety-yak and goes on talking, and then, as soon as he finishes, yells, "Roll it." An actor is really thrown up in the air by that because he can't get his thoughts together. He has to get ready again. Dancing to a degree is that way, too. And Cukor is not very knowing in terms of music really (I think Gene Kelly would tell you that). But he always hires the best people. He hears that so-and-so is terribly creative and very stylish so he hires them, the best. Taina Elg did a marvelous performance in *Les Girls,* and that was all George Cukor. I watched him do it. He just rehearsed every bloody reading with her—action, breathing, movement. In certain ways he is very good with some people.

It was the same with Marilyn Monroe and Cukor as with Kay Kendall. Marilyn absolutely didn't understand his verbalizations. Not that she was stupid. The people who could get the most out of her were myself and Josh Logan. She had to work in an actor's way—totally emotional. You had to use all the effects to get things out of her. You couldn't articulate the craft because she had no craft. She didn't know how to approach it. Certain kinds of things you had to repeat but if you repeated too much, she would look as if she was getting instructions over the short wave. George had to depend on me because *Let's Make Love* was one of the pictures where she was really coming apart. Only one number had been rehearsed when we finally began shooting and that was "My Heart Belongs to Daddy." It's a very good number and what she looks best at in the picture. The other numbers are rather terrible; they were never rehearsed. We just recorded them. I would rehearse with her before each shot. Some people you could do that with, but not with her; it was very difficult.

That wasn't true of her in *Gentlemen Prefer Blondes,* though, because that was her first really big chance, and Jane Russell was extraordinarily sweet to her, liked her. Marilyn worked like a dog. She didn't have so many personal problems then; she was still pretty much in control of herself. Howard Hawks was a very good director for her because he was very understanding of a young girl who didn't have very much craft. He was very kind, and he never said rotten things about her.

Billy Wilder brought it on himself; he was so nasty. He is a very autocratic man, a little like Harry Cohn: he hated stars. He would just be rude to her and say very personal things. She was pregnant at the time, and she would punish him. He would never learn—he was that stupid. She would say, "I'm feeling a little dizzy," and I would go into the dressing room (he had learned that I could get her out), and she would be sitting there doing nothing. She would say, "Let him sit on his German ass and maybe he'll learn not to be rude and humiliate me in front of everybody." She would ask—which is quite reasonable—for visitors on the set to sit where she couldn't see them. Some people didn't mind visitors—they enjoy having people look at them—but she had a hard time with her concentration, with getting into something. She felt that she was exposing herself, that people would see that she wasn't very good. It made a terrible burden for her, and Wilder was so rude about it.

Marilyn Monroe got me in to do one number on *There's No Business like Show Business.* I did the "Heat Wave" number, that's all. She had done two numbers with Bob Alton and didn't like the way she looked. She had screamed, but they said that they had a contract with Alton and that they were going to have to pay him anyway. Finally, she said that if I didn't do it, she wouldn't either, and I did it. The director, Walter Lang, didn't like her. He'd say, "Try to remember that you are like the girl next door." She'd look at him very hard and say, "No way. I've never been like the girl next door."

Interview with Betty Garrett

The interview with Betty Garrett took place in Hollywood, California, on 28 November 1973.

DELAMATER: Could you tell me something about the rehearsal process Gene Kelly followed on the films you made with him? How did it differ—if at all—from other choreographers with whom you worked?
GARRETT: On almost every musical picture I did we rehearsed dance numbers almost the way you do for a show—very long, intense rehearsals starting at nine or ten o'clock in the morning, and we'd rehearse all day long up to six o'clock at night. I think that on the two pictures I made with Gene we rehearsed all the dance numbers before we ever shot the picture. We rehearsed those numbers and worked them up to "opening-night" perfection before we ever started to shoot the picture. When I did *My Sister Eileen* with Bob Fosse, though, we would work on a specific number until it was right and then shoot it and then start on the next number. It was done one number at a time. I suppose that it's just up to the choreographer (and also up to the producer, as well as whoever is putting out the money) as to the cheapest way to do it.
DELAMATER: Did you have many—or any—camera rehearsals?
GARRETT: No, not until we got on the set. I wish I had been more aware in those days of what was happening with the camera, but I didn't pay much attention to that. I'm sure that Gene and Stanley had in their minds how it was to be shot and choreographed it with that in mind, but as far as *I* was

concerned it was just like doing a dance number on the stage. We would do it through from beginning to end, and then we would find out later that part of it was going to be shot down on the street, for example, and we would do only that part, and then the other part was to be on top of a building, if you recall that in *On the Town*. It was rehearsed as if it were a continuous number but shot in bits and pieces. But Vera-Ellen's "Miss Turnstiles" number would have been impossible to do on a stage. Just acrobatically and physically it would have been impossible to do that number from beginning to end on stage. She'd have had to be some kind of superwoman to do it. Vera's background was in acrobatics, but they had her doing some things where no one could have kept up the pace. So that was geared to be shot in sections. I was around just a very little when it was being shot, but I remember talking about it. "Prehistoric Man," the number in the museum, as I remember, was also done almost like a stage number. They dollied the camera a great deal, and often where there actually were different angles, we didn't stop for them, but the camera would catch us.

DELAMATER: But there are some places in that number where you change costumes.

GARRETT: Yes, but even there I remember scrambling up and putting the teeth in and being ready for when the camera came by. I think it could have been done very similarly even on the stage. Stanley and Gene both came from the stage, and their inclination was to do the numbers that way. Bob Fosse, I think, was the first to really make use of film technique in dancing, where the camera angle and what the camera caught was almost as important choreographically as the dancing.

DELAMATER: In the museum number did Ann Miller contribute anything to choreography at all?

GARRETT: Of course, to her tap sequence; Gene Kelly certainly choreographed it, but it was done in the Ann Miller style.

DELAMATER: How did Kelly work around a non-dancer like Frank Sinatra?

GARRETT: Many of us were "non-dancers" in that we couldn't do things that Gene Kelly could do. Even Annie, who *was* a dancer, was used to her kind of dancing and had to adapt to what Gene did. When Gene worked with somebody like Frank, he scaled himself down to things that the person could do. He didn't give you something impossible to do, but Frank is a natural. Whatever he had to do, he could do very presentably. He's just very quick and had a certain style about the way he moved. I think he looks marvelous in the things he does. And he worked very hard; he was right there with us all the time. It was one of the happiest rehearsal times I've ever had. Lennie Hayton, who was the musical director, used to drop in just to sit and watch. We all had a wonderful time.

They used to work out the numbers with a kind of dance stand-in, simply to save the energies of the people, particularly those who were non-dancers and not used to that sort of thing. They would also figure out things to do so that the cast didn't just have to keep hanging around, although I never minded that. I think that half the fun of working on something is to be right in on the development and the changes. Carol Haney was his head dancer and his assistant, and Jeanne Coyne was his assistant in working with the chorus usually. Carol was a fabulous dancer, just incredible.

DELAMATER: Kelly and Donen share credit in *On the Town*. What was the breakdown in their responsibilities as you observed them?

GARRETT: The first picture I did with them was *Take Me Out to the Ball Game,* and that was directed by Busby Berkeley, but so much of it was choreographed and so much of it was a kind of dancing that Gene and Stanley had a lot to do. Buzz was the overall director, but anything that required a kind of choreography and staging, Stanley and Gene did. In *On the Town* they worked pretty closely together. I don't remember exactly how it was divided except that Stanley was the one behind the camera and Gene was in front of it. And I think that was very wise, because if you're in something you really can't judge what's going on. Gene seemed to leave that up to Stanley.

DELAMATER: Was there much changing of the numbers while the rehearsals were going on?

GARRETT: I think we did work things out as we went along. On some of the complicated routines Gene would work with Carol as his partner or whoever he was dancing with—Frank, Vera, or whoever—and then they would teach it to that person. But in those big chorus numbers I can remember rehearsing just as if we were doing it for a show. We'd try something, and Gene would say, "That's no good." Then he'd make you go over and over it in front of a mirror so that your arms, for example, were together. It was really developing it just as you would for a dance group or for a show. I don't know whether the experiences I had were typical because I didn't make that many films—only five musicals really.

DELAMATER: *Words and Music* and *Neptune's Daughter* are two lesser known films you did. Would you comment a bit on them?

GARRETT: Bob Alton staged the two numbers I did in *Words and Music* (I'd worked with Bob in New York; we'd done a show), and those were done the day before we shot. Bob came in and said, "Now, dear, do this. . . ." And they look it. There's nothing terribly exciting about them. It was almost as if it were an afterthought: "Oh, we'd better do something about staging this."

But Jack Donahue did *Neptune's Daughter,* and he worked ahead of time, too, on everything. We had all those numbers choreographed ahead of time and then shot. We worked in a rehearsal studio just as if we were preparing for a show. I was very lucky to have probably some of the most exciting choreographers: Gene Kelly, Bob Fosse, and also Jack Donahue, who was just the most brilliant comedy choreographer. He was wonderful at staging a trick number of some kind. That was why he was so wonderful in Esther Williams's swimming things. Do you remember the slide into the water in *Neptune's Daughter?* That was terrifying. About two or three weeks rehearsal went into that, and a lot of kids got hurt because it was very dangerous, but Jack wouldn't make the kids do anything he wouldn't do. He'd try it first, and then he had very skilled dance assistants who would try all the things to make sure they were possible. They had a special plastic sheet on the side of the pool, constantly covered with water. And you would literally do what you did when you were a kid: go run and then stand and slide, only at the end of the slide was the pool. You just went ssswish into the pool. It's a scary thing to do if you are not well coordinated. You can give yourself a terrible fall.

Eddie Buzzell directed *Neptune's Daughter,* but Eddie just did the dialogue parts and the dramatic parts. I didn't have that much to do with Eddie Buzzell. The one I remember most was Jack Donahue because he was in charge of the things I was most involved in. He was just marvelous, a delicious man with a wonderful sense of humor.

That sequence with Red Skelton and me on the horse was directed by Ed Sedgwick, an old Keystone Comedy director, and he directed that with three cameras like they used to direct the old Keystone Comedies. He would give us the situation, no dialogue, no nothing, just the situation, and we would improvise for a half hour. Out of that they cut seven minutes of film. The whole experience was just an experience in itself, so much fun to do. He trained three cameras on us with one camera on the horse as backup for protection. Whenever he wanted, when he got to cutting the film together later, in order to skip whole sequences which couldn't be included in the final seven minutes, he would cut to the horse's reactions. That would cover in case we had to be in a different position. There is a funny story about that sequence too. Red Skelton always says he is deathly afraid of horses. He says, "I can't get near a horse. All that stuff has to be done with a stand-in." Then the stand-in would do a trick and Red would say, "No, no, no." And next thing you know Red would be up on the horse completely forgetting that he has this deathly fear of horses. They started this scene where two grooms and I try to get him up on the horse. Well, everything happens: I get up or they get him up backwards or they get him on me. It's just insane. They get him up, and he comes right around underneath. Red swore he couldn't do this because the horse would step on him or he would get a terrible allergy. They said that once we started fooling around they'd get him a phony horse and that settled it for awhile. Finally they settled on a horse they said was the gentlest horse in the world, just absolutely a stupid horse that just stood. Not only that but they'd wire the horse so that it couldn't move, not even its head. Red finally said O.K. When we started, Red forgot completely, and we were just having a ball. Suddenly, in the middle of the thing, Ed Sedgwick yelled, "Cut!" The horse was enjoying this sliding over and under him so much that he had this enormous erection hanging all the way down to the floor. Ed said, "What are we going to do?" The grooms, who actually were the guys who took care of the horse, said, "We'll fix it, we'll fix it." They unhitched the horse and took him back to the stable, with me, the SPCA champion, demanding to know what they were going to do to that animal. When they brought him back, he was fine; nothing happened. I insisted on knowing what they had done to the horse, and they said, "We scotchtaped it." Animal sequences are such fun; it was done just like an old Keystone Comedy.

The "Baby, It's Cold Outside" sequence was choreographed just like a dance, every bit of it, because there was a lot of stuff that was very dangerous. There was that wonderful bit where I hold the coat for Red. He gets into one sleeve and I get into the other sleeve then I turn suddenly and it flips him up onto the bed and me right on top of him. We did it for the Academy Awards about a year later, and in dress rehearsal it knocked me absolutely cold. It had to be choreographed just like a dance, but Jack Donahue was a genius with that kind of thing.

There was one number that Jack and I did that was cut out of the picture (it broke my heart) called "I Want My Money Back." The idea was that I had subscribed to all these beauty aids, had gone to beauty schools, and had done all the things you do in the ladies' magazines, but nothing helped. So the idea of the song was that I wanted my money back. It was done in a room with models who were all putting on lotions and makeup and wigs and stuff, and I had to run over the top of the makeup tables. We had one bit that was done in one shot where I went in one side of the closet dressed one way and came out the other side dressed another way. We literally did that. Nobody believed that it wasn't a trick shot. We rigged something up so that I just walked into it like a quick-change artist. There used to be a marvelous man who did a whole show, a one-act play based on a Dickens story, and he played all the characters. He would walk off the stage and come back on as somebody else. His costumes were made like springs, and he'd walk right into them. It looked as if he were following himself. Well, we did the same thing in the closet. At the end I stood in a doorway that had drapes, and I took the drapes, swept aside, and the whole curtain rod fell down on my head. Very intricately choreographed, a marvelous number, but it was about seven or eight minutes long, and they just sliced it. There wasn't enough time for it. I'd like to know what happened to those pieces of film.

DELAMATER: What was it like to work with Richard Quine, who directed *My Sister Eileen?*

GARRETT: Richard Quine is the kind of director that you don't think is doing anything. He just sits there like a smiling father. Later you realize that Dick is working all the time and that he doesn't let you get away with anything. But the atmosphere is so easy and so warm that it is very encouraging to work on the films, to do your own thing. He'll stop you if it's wrong, but he really lets you express your own particular way of doing things. I loved him. *My Sister Eileen* was a very happy picture, too. We worked nine months on it. The whole first section of the picture dealt with all the parts before Jack Lemmon came in; then when Jack came into the picture, shooting stopped and we went back into rehearsal of all the numbers that Jack was involved in and then shot those. It stretched out over nine months, and we got really close. We were very tired at the end, but all of us said, "Let's start all over again." It's really lovely when you have that kind of relationship with people in the picture. We all adored Bob Fosse, and Janet Leigh and I began to feel as if we were really sisters by the time the picture got through. Jack Lemmon is just the dream of the world to work with. He's one of those people who just hangs loose about everything. Nothing flaps him. He's a very hard worker, really committed and dedicated to what he's doing, and that's a rare combination. People who are easy are sometimes sloppy; you can't get them to work—but not so with Jack.

There was a strange thing about *My Sister Eileen*. I went on a publicity tour, and every time I'd get into town, the distributors and the theater owners would give a cocktail party, and they'd say, "Don't mention that it's a musical. Musicals are out now." And the picture, I understand, laid a bomb the first time around. The American public did not want musicals at that time. It was very strange; I don't know why, but they were just kind of down on them.
DELAMATER: *My Sister Eileen* was Fosse's first full choreographic assignment; how much freedom did Quine give him?
GARRETT: I have no idea what the conferences between them were, but I'm sure there was quite a meeting of the minds about what each number should do and mean. The feeling between Bob and Dick was a very cooperative one. Knowing Dick, I'm sure that he let Bob do a great deal, which was smart of him. I think that the dance in the alley between Tommy Rall and Bob is one of the best things in any film. Dick had a tremendous respect for Bob. Everybody did, and the way the numbers turned out was completely Bob's. Bob is very adept at compiling music or commissioning music for dance numbers. There was a fellow who worked with him for a number of years. I can't remember his name right now, but he would work on an idea, and he could translate that into music. Bob had a marvelous feeling about the relationship between music and dance. He would say, "No, no. What I want is more bass rhythm here and more syncopation," or something like that, and the other guy was able to do absolutely what Bob wanted; Bob's very strong musical sense is a lot of his talent. "Hernando's Hideaway" from *Pajama Game* wasn't like that at all when they got it. I think it was a lush tango

sort of thing, but that wonderful, mysterious, rhythmic thing they did with it was all Bob's because of the way he chose to do the dance. He was marvelous. I just loved being around when he was working on things because he works as much with the music as he does with the dancers. It's that important, exactly what the music is doing.

DELAMATER: Did he direct—shoot—his own numbers?

GARRETT: Yes, all of the dances, the movement sequences. I never worked as hard in my life as I did with Bob. He never stopped. He had one phrase: "Once more." About five o'clock at night, he'd give a little criticism and then say, "Once more," and at 7:30 you'd still be doing it once more.

DELAMATER: Did he have assistants and work in that way as Kelly did?

GARRETT: I'm sure he did, but I just can't remember. I felt always with Bob that it was such a one-man operation that I cannot remember if he had a particular assistant.

Many of the choreographers at that time had a common base—Gower Champion, Bob Fosse—particularly the ones who came from New York. They all went through the ballet training and the jazz training and then musical comedy, and all in their different ways began to combine what they had learned. When they became choreographers, they all used the same thing to varying degrees. Matt Mattox is credited with originating and defining the isolation in jazz movement. Isolation is exactly what it says: you move one part of the body without moving anything else. If you watch really good jazz dancers like Gwen Verdon or Peter Gennaro, every section of their body seems to be self-controlled. They can literally pat their heads and rub their stomachs because they can do things separately. It's not all one piece. That seems to be very important to jazz because in order to get the kind of distortion that jazz has you have to be able to isolate parts of your body and do just what you want with them. Matt Mattox was the first to define it and teach it and put it into exercise. But all your good jazz dancers seem to be able to master that.

DELAMATER: What did you observe about the roles of the films' writers when the films were actually being shot?

GARRETT: Comden and Green were around a lot, particularly when we worked on the musical numbers of *On the Town.* But I don't think that's always true. I take that back, though. Frank Loesser was also around when we did *Neptune's Daughter* (his assistant Jerry Dolan is still my accompanist and collaborator. We work on songs together, and we're very great friends); Frank was there to work on the numbers, and then Jerry worked with us to see that they were done just the way Frank wanted. Leo Robbins and Jule Styne did the songs of *My Sister Eileen,* and they were around at the beginning while we were learning the songs.

DELAMATER: Were there generally many changes made in the scripts themselves?

GARRETT: Every once in a while there would be a change as a result of seeing the rushes or in seeing a rough cut. They would decide that something was missing or wrong, and they would re-do a scene. Then you might get a new script, but all the ones I worked on had a pretty complete script in the beginning. There weren't great changes. Sometimes they would come down and say that we need another little scene here. They found that they needed something, and so they would hand you a script. Larry [Parks] told me that he made pictures—like the Jolson pictures—where he got the pages for tomorrow today. On the first one Sidney Buchman would be up all night writing and send the pages over to Larry, and he would look them over quickly before he went in to shoot it. *The Jolson Story* was a picture that they thought was not going to turn out. They called it Cohn's Folly for a while. It seemed like a dumb idea to make a biography of Al Jolson, but as the picture began developing, everybody started getting excited. They began shooting the numbers, and the numbers looked great. Sidney Buchman is another genius; other people got the writing credits although Sidney did almost everything on that picture. He was there on the set almost all the time, looking over the director's shoulder and rewriting every scene the night before shooting. He was the mastermind of that picture. But I don't think I ever had to do that much where they gave me a new scene just before I went on.

Interview with Gene Kelly

The interview with Gene Kelly was done in conjunction with Paddy Whannel at Kelly's home in Beverly Hills, California, on 20 November 1973.

WHANNEL: Could I begin with asking about *Take Me Out to the Ball Game?* Really what I want to know is how you and Stanley Donen came to write that and conceive it. What were the origins of that?
KELLY: There was a famous old team, Al Shact and another fellow whose name escapes me at the moment, who were actual clowns on the baseball diamond, and I knew the history to the story. They were a little before my time. I met Al Shact; he retired from baseball and had a restaurant in New York City. But I often thought it would be a good idea to make a movie about them, because they were vaudevillians in the wintertime—not in the sense of Babe Ruth who used to go out, used to say hello to the people and swing a bat—but they did good comedy gags. They did them on the baseball diamond. There was a property at MGM, an idea that was the only idea coming up from the studio writers through their channels, that was very bad, and I said, "I can write a better one than that myself." They said, "Fine, let's read it," so I wrote this treatment. I was in New York City at the time, and I called Stanley Donen, who had been my assistant and was becoming my collaborator on pictures,

and I said, "Stanley, come with me and let's kick this around, because I really have to get out of this other picture." I had written it on the train from New York to Washington or vice versa. We talked all about the story, and Stanley had a couple of suggestions to make, and so instead of it being like a ten-page treatment, it was something like a fifteen-page treatment. So I put Stanley's name on it, and we took it to Arthur Freed, and he persuaded the studio to make it, and that's how it got to be made. The chap who wrote the screenplay, his name is Harry Tugend; we didn't do the screenplay. We were busy enough with worrying about the choreography and the staging and numbers. We got Busby Berkeley out of retirement to direct the film. It was a minor bit of nonsense, but it was a lot of fun, and it sure as heck did well at the box office. As I say, it was a minor bit of nonsense, and it didn't hurt anybody. It didn't make any new artistic standards, of course.

WHANNEL: Was it conceived for that particular cast?

KELLY: It was conceived for Frank Sinatra and myself. The idea of having Jules Munshin who was around the studio was not just quickly taken. We thought of having a Jewish lad in between the two Irishmen. I forget whether his name came first or Betty Comden and Adolph Green found that Goldberg went well with O'Brien to Ryan to Goldberg. That, of course, was a play-up on the old Tinkers to Evers to Chance famous double-play combination of the Boston Braves in 1914 that's become part of athletic legend in America. That also worked out well, the two Irish boys, Frank playing one and me being one. It worked out very well.

WHANNEL: It was very much like a "rehearsal" for *On the Town* in the sense of the characters, the relationships, the Betty Garrett-Sinatra relationship.

KELLY: Yes, we found that out later. We didn't have the prescience to know that then, but it certainly was a good rehearsal. It also was the first time in a major film that Stanley Donen was allowed to shoot a number by himself which I thought was a very important thing for our collaboration, because I'd been telling the studio how good he was. He was not just a young man around there working for a visit, he was a comer. He was coming on. So Stanley shot the number with Betty Garrett and Frank Sinatra where they're running around the bleachers and so forth. It had very important things in it that paid off in *On The Town,* of course.

WHANNEL: Going back before that, at some stage you developed ideas about what a film musical should be, beyond just appearing and beyond choreographing. Could you say at what point those ideas began to crystallize? Would it be around about *Cover Girl* or before that?

KELLY: Well, they began to crystallize before that; they began to crystallize during my first film, because I found out that what I would do on the stage just didn't work in films. This was in *For Me and My Gal.* Also, I found out that I was woefully ignorant about the use of the camera. Of course, the director of that first film was Busby Berkeley, and he was a master with the camera. Busby wasn't interested in dancing per se. He was interested in doing things with the camera, and he taught everybody in Hollywood many things about camera movement. But I soon learned that a five-minute number on the stage would last only a minute in the films, and I began to ask questions, and I found out that no one in Hollywood seemed to care. There was one dancer, Fred Astaire, with whom (as Orson Welles often put it, the camera loves some people) you could set up a camera like Chaplin used to do, and as long as he was in full figure everything would be fine. But for the kind of big sweeping [movement] that I wanted to do and the stronger, kinetically speaking, physically speaking, kind of dancing that I had developed on my own, I had to pretty much start from scratch in working out what I wanted to do with the camera. That began very early. I found out that I was in a bit of a contretemps with the studio in the making of *Dubarry Was a Lady* because it was usual for directors of pictures to shoot the numbers, and Roy Del Ruth, who is a fine man, a fine director, wasn't really interested in having dance numbers coming off at all. So I began to set up camera angles, and I'd explain the reasons. The studio was impressed enough to let me go on, but I do think that it didn't come to fruition until *Cover Girl.* The numbers that I was in in *Cover Girl* I choreographed and I shot. So when I came back to MGM they gave me a much freer hand. After *Cover Girl,* I did *Anchors Aweigh,* and did the numbers, wrote and shot them and gave Stanley Donen a full-partnership credit in the choreography.

WHANNEL: Now, that would apply, I would assume, to *Take Me Out to the Ball Game* as well.

KELLY: Oh yes. A free hand, yes.

WHANNEL: Looking at that film, it's very hard for an outsider to say that there's anything of Busby Berkeley in it. And it looks so much like the later work you were to do in *It's Always Fair Weather* even.

KELLY: Yes, well, it was. I shot the numbers in that myself except for the one that Stanley did with Betty and Frank. They were shot by the choreographers, in this case, myself and Donen.

DELAMATER: Would that be general practice with all the films in which you appeared when other people do have credit, like Robert Alton has credit on *The Pirate* for choreography?

KELLY: We shared credit on *The Pirate,* but I would have given Bob Alton credit just out of gratefulness for what he had done for me in the Broadway theater, because he had told producers and directors (I worked under him in three shows) that I was working on a new style of dance and to let me do it. So, for example, in *Pal Joey* where Robert Alton was the choreographer and the best on Broadway at the time, whatever things I did, he'd say, "Go ahead, Kelly. Just let me see what you've got in mind and what you do." He encouraged me greatly and did more than encourage me. He let me have my head, and I give him a lot of credit. In *The Pirate,* he had so much work and so little time he'd say, "Well, you take this over there and see what happens, and I'll take the group around you, and then we'll see if we can put it together." So we did a lot of the work in very close collaboration which again was an important thing for me in the future, because in making a big musical you must collaborate with people. The auteur theory is non-existent, you know, if only that you have to work with musicians and lyricists. It's silly to call yourself an auteur because you have something of a stamp on a picture when Cole Porter writes the music. I'd like to be able to claim that, but it didn't exist. So it helped me in what we would like to think of now as our MGM repertory group. Most of us who had known each other and known about each other in the Broadway theater, like myself, pulled other people into the MGM group and appreciated the fact that this person had specific talents over and above what we did. This didn't mean that we didn't cross lines. (In the olden days they didn't cross lines. The cameraman would shoot, the director would tell him the angle, the choreographer would go in the corner and do the choreography, and the director wouldn't see it most of the time until the day before or the day he shot.) We all crossed lines. *The Pirate,* which was such a fun picture to do, although it wasn't at the time the big success that most of our other musicals were, was strictly a collaboration among as many people.

DELAMATER: You mentioned the word style in Alton's recognition of a certain kind of style you had early on in Broadway. Could you talk a bit about that?

KELLY: Yes, I was a ballet dancer mainly, and I was a good one. I may have gone into the American Ballet Company and just stayed there, because I loved it. I love the classic style, but I knew if I went into Monte Carlo Ballets Russes, for example, which was then touring and which would have taken me, that at forty years of age I'd be dancing *Swan Lake* again and again and other ballets. You're restricted to certain things. Innately, I was a kid from Pittsburgh, and I wanted to dance to Cole Porter, Gershwin, Kern, Irving Berlin, Rodgers and Hart, and you couldn't quite do that. Also, I felt that the musical comedy was coming of age, and if you played a character you couldn't come out and use classic style, because it was un-American. (Of course, in those days a lot of things were un-American, weren't they?) So I felt I had to find a style. Now that was that famous fermenting of the thirties, the modern dancers, Graham, Weidman, Humphrey. They were all looking for a style, but their style was very misunderstood by the general public. They didn't want to use popular songs. They were just groping for a kinetic outlet, and they were dancing to a lot of percussion in tiny places. I very definitely wanted to get out and use popular songs and the popular idiom for what I had to do. I, factually, if you're interested in this, based a lot on athletic movement, you know. I never lost the classic line. I might have broadened it a bit. I did incorporate a lot of things that I learned from my colleagues in the modern dance movement of the thirties which give a dance strength. Nowadays all dancers do this. In Martha Graham's company I see a lot of long balletic, classic line. And in a lot of classic companies you'll see the same thing vice versa.

DELAMATER: Could you say something about the method you actually go through in creating a dance for film, how you conceive it and communicate it to the dancers and rehearse it?

KELLY: Each number practically dictates the method. Let me start with the classic ballet concept. Let's start with a great choreographer, whom everyone interested in ballet should understand, George Balanchine. Balanchine is a great musician, and he will take a piece, let's say a difficult piece by Stravinsky, and he will choreograph the ballet right out of the music. The flutes will be three girls in the corner, and the violins might be the leading lady and the bassoon an old man, which I'm oversimplifying, of course. Sounds like a Disney children's thing. But the brass would, let's say, be the male *corps de ballet* or the male *ballerino*. He'll completely interpret the music. The music is king. If you're doing musical comedy, you're often faced with the fact that just before, you've said, "Well, I didn't want any of this, and I'm going off alone." Now you can't write in Mozart or Stravinsky or somebody there. Let's say the music you're using is Rodgers and Hart. You have to take a theme from Rodgers and Hart and do variations on the theme, and you have to do that in close association with the arrangers of the music. To do a number like that you sit down like a writer, alone, in a chair, and you start thinking, "How do I further the characterization by the use of dance?" Since you also have words to help you, it isn't always as tough as it sounds. You write yourself a little story or what might, in some cases, be a series of impressions, but they're in your head. At least you have a beginning and an end; the middle is never a problem. That's one way to choreograph a number.

The easiest way—it's not always the best way, depending on your luck— is when the number flows right out of a situation. If you're stopped in the street by a bouncing ball that children have been playing with, and you pick it up and you throw it back and they throw it back at you, the situation becomes a dance with a ball and children's games, which I've actually done. That keeps the scene in character and makes the dance very much an integral part of the motion picture, the story, and the characterization.

By far the best results are usually gotten by having a song which you can interpret; for example, "Singin' in the Rain" is an obvious one. I kissed the girl goodnight, and it was raining. Of course, we made it rain. We wrote the scene expressly for it. And we've made jokes about the California weather, you know. So I decided to walk in the rain, which everybody at one time in his life has felt. You had a universality of feeling there. In presenting the song as a thesis—I'm singing in the rain, I'm happy again—you elaborate on that thesis by dance. You become happier and happier as you dance. Dance is usually done as a happy thing—not always but that's mostly in dance concerts—but if you look at popular dance, it's usually done when people are happy. If I'm very sad I don't go to a discotheque and dance; I walk around the block hanging my head. It's a natural thing to do. You can follow a number in that way until you've filled it up, and finally you revert to childish humor where you're stamping in the puddles and getting yourself soaked and wet, and you just don't give a hoot about anything. That number, for example, was very simple to put on. Arthur Freed, the producer, also wrote the song and said, "What are you going to do with it?" I said, "Well, it's going to be raining and I'm going to be singing." And he said, "Well, that's logical." The number was constructed very quickly and done very quickly.

WHANNEL: It looks simple and very beautiful. At which point in the process of thinking about the choreography do you think about where the camera might be?

KELLY: Every time I do a step. (When I say do a step it should be properly called, in dance terminology, an *enchaînement*—a linkage together of the steps.) As you put one step after another, you have a chain linking, and you go back and say, "If I shoot that with the camera here as I started out to do to make the cut on the other one, it would not work well because they'd be shooting my derrierè instead of my front or instead of my side if I wanted to make a line to make a particular point or a particular look." When you start with the idea—let's call it the libretto or the story—I don't worry about the camera there. It's when I start putting the dance on its feet, I start immediately about the camera. What I did in "Singin' in the Rain," why it fell into place so quickly (which cost a little more money, because they had to make more rain pipes down the street), was to take the whole street and keep the dance moving down the street so that forcing the camera back all the time didn't decrease the kinesthesia, the movement in the camera, which is always the strongest one you can do in a two-dimensional medium (which is film, like paintings, whereas a sculpture, any kind whether it's an egg or anything, is three-dimensional). And on the stage you get this kind of kinetic force. You get it easily by thrust of your body, because you have it in three dimensions. Also you had the environment around it. On the screen you just get the tiniest bit of environment around the dancers, so you have to make a choice of moving back further, that way making your figures smaller, or coming in closer and cutting down the environment. If you shoot down a street, for example, you have the best advantage, because you usually get both. I often use streets. I often dance outdoors. That wasn't done much before.

WHANNEL: Is that partly why there are so many numbers you do in streets?

KELLY: Yes, definitely. If you're on a stage, let's say this room—in *An American in Paris,* I just looked at the piano and thought of Oscar Levant playing—now, it's easy to do a number there. We centered around the piano and practice shot it like Chaplin would have shot a number of his own in the old days with the camera just almost there and the two fellows there. The obvious need of cuts to underline, the same as you do in any kind of scene, comedic or dramatic, you use the close-up or the change of angle to underline a point. If in the usual set which is, let's say, about maybe twice the size of these two rooms, you do have a problem of panning and every once in a while panning and moving toward the camera, and the camera has no place to go, because you've run out of space. So eventually you have to lose some of your physical force by going backwards away from the camera. So those are the most difficult, I've found, to set for the camera without dissipating the forces that are most important, because the dancer "writes" with his anatomy.

DELAMATER: Did you generally use just one camera or did you ever use multiple camera set-ups?

KELLY: I used only one camera so I could have control. There have been instances where I've used several cameras. In doing a picture like *Hello, Dolly!* where we had thousands of people, I had several cameras. I picked up all the shots in half a day of all the crowds by using at least five cameras on that, but that was a parade. It wasn't a dance number. I can't think of any other time. Most of that is because you want to control the look. You want to control the lighting. You want to control the movement. Since you've ended it in your head already, you might have ended it in the middle of a turn, shot to match on a certain beat of the playback. There are axioms in the use of the camera that one shouldn't forget, and someday maybe I'll put them all down in a little book for fledgling choreographers. Axiomatically, let's say you're dollying alongside the dancer; no matter what the dancer does he's standing still. If you have two cars going at sixty miles an hour, I can be talking the way we're sitting now. You lose speed if you're dollying like this by a dancer, unless you want to slow everything down. The dancer usually wants to push it up the other way. As an axiom, I would say don't do that. Another axiom, which I mentioned before, is the more you can go into the camera the more force you'll get, the more impression of a third dimension you'll get. You won't make it three-dimensional, but you'll get force. As he goes away from the camera, he decreases that force. So he should go away from the camera as little as possible, but he should construct a dance so that if he doesn't move, the camera is making a move. There are many differentiations of this kind of thing. For example, in *Singin' in the Rain,* I lift Cyd Charisse up, and I had the camera go down. There are many different ways to make the camera interesting. And those, and I'm sure that must be what you're thinking of, will depend on the particular movement itself. But there are some axioms you can apply that you should always watch for. If the camera is too high, you'll foreshorten the dancer. A dancer works all his life for a long line. If you use the camera high, you'll foreshorten the dancer and get a stunted line. That's another thing that's pretty axiomatic. If you want to do a Busby Berkeley shot and you don't want to do an overhead right down and make a pattern—which isn't very much dancing, but it's an interesting pattern—then you certainly could do that. But in between is not a good way to photograph a dance.

WHANNEL: Could I switch back a bit to studio style? You mentioned about MGM being, I forget your term, I always think about it as a creative workshop.

KELLY: Repertory company is what I called it, because we all worked together in and out in different things, kept doing different things.

WHANNEL: What I was wondering is did you, before you came out and went into films, did you have thoughts when you were on the stage of going into films?

KELLY: No, not very avidly, because I remember very vividly that I turned down twice an MGM offer to come out with MGM. And when I did come out for David Selznick it was to come out as an actor, not as a dancer, because Mr. Selznick said, "You're a good actor, and I'm not interested in making musicals." I had an agreement with him that I'd come out and do a film and go back to Broadway. I stayed out here for several months, and he didn't make a film at the time. We became great friends and had a lot of fun and several good drinking bouts every month, but he finally loaned me to MGM to do a film with Judy Garland. And then I began to realize that there were some very enchanting things that were completely unexplored here, completely. And nobody cared, you know.

WHANNEL: If you'd gone to a different studio, not Metro, somewhere else, do you think that would have altered your career and what you've done?

KELLY: I think so. I think that, for example, let's say I went to Columbia, I think that I would have done more dancing with Rita Hayworth. I certainly would have been allowed to experiment, because in *Cover Girl* Harry Cohn allowed me to do that. I think that if I'd gone in Warners or Fox, I could have persuaded the brass there to hire a lot of the people I persuaded them to hire at MGM. There *was* an MGM style but it came out of a group of people. We were all very aware of the fact that things could be done quickly and badly or worked on very hard and come out a little better. That's a hard question to answer, really. Would Jack Warner have said, "All right, you can bring in these young people," at least some of us, you know, from the theater? That's hard to answer.

WHANNEL: You mentioned about there being an MGM style, now I know what you mean by that, but even within that, do you think that your work—and I mean this in the broadest sense—that the work you did with Stanley Donen differs from the work that you did with Minnelli?

KELLY: Yes, the great joy in working with Minnelli is his marvelous eye not only for color—because he started out as a scenic designer, that was his background—but he welcomed innovative momements of the camera and innovative ways to stage things. And he was a great man to collaborate with, also; because he would take care of this one end of the—let's call it—overall design, you were a little freer to work on the other end. We complemented and supplemented each other quite well. Working with Stanley, for the first several years, Stanley started out in the chorus in *Pal Joey;* then I gave him a job in *Best Foot Forward* when I did the choreography for that on Broadway. He came out here, and he was my protégé. There's no doubt that he was influenced by me a lot more, whereas Minnelli and I came together as two mature men head on and found this wonderful collaboration. As far as the style goes, I have a strong hunch that if Minnelli and I had done *On the Town* that it would have turned out the same way, because I was influential in getting it on the screen. I wanted to take it into New York proper, into the city, and, of course, people thought that was crazy and ridiculous and spending a lot of money foolishly. To do a song with a series of cuts right in the middle of it; it made no sense jumping from Grant's Tomb to Mulberry Street to Radio City—they couldn't see it, thought it was silly. But it had a great influence. It certainly had a big influence in starting the *nouvelle vague* in the French cinema, unless they're just being nice to me by saying that. I think if Minnelli had been on that we would have approached it the same way because of our common goals. The MGM style did not come from the executives of MGM, it came from the group of people who were working there together and who enjoyed their work. We ran around together. We'd go to each other's houses and play games and drink together and laugh together. It was quite a group.

WHANNEL: Could I ask you further about that? It would seem that in the Minnelli films there's a more Baroque effect.

KELLY: Largely, that's a scenic designer's background.

WHANNEL: I think in your films with Donen, they have an equally distinctive visual style which is actually taking things away from the image or paring it down like in the "Miss Turnstiles" ballet.

KELLY: I agree with you, but, also, one must remember that in doing these kinds of films, we often were cast or cast ourselves. I might say, "Well, that's not my particular cup of tea, somebody else would do that better." I don't think anyone else could have directed *Meet Me in St. Louis,* which happens to be my favorite musical, I guess, of all, and I had nothing to do with it except come down occasionally and smile and applaud while they were shooting it. I don't think any director could have done it as well as Minnelli. Minnelli and Charles Walters and myself were protégés of John Murray Anderson on Broadway in different ways; nonetheless, we all worked with him. We had learned a lot about timing and taking time and mood. John Murray Anderson would take a scene in a revue and instead of having the ballad singer just sing and the lady pirouette or something, he might just have them hold the lights and walk for a couple of minutes, things that other people weren't doing. The three of us, I know, learned a lot from him which helped us to do that in motion pictures. I think the supreme example of it was what Minnelli did in *Meet Me in St. Louis.* The fact that Stanley and I were younger and he did grow up under my wing certainly contributed to that; we had a mutual outlook. And it was more vigorous. Minnelli and I, when we collaborated, it always was a happy thing because we didn't have to sacrifice his taste of color and style, but at the same time we did get some kind of vigor from me; for example, in *An American in Paris* it worked out very well. Often it's a plus to have someone who has a different style than yours in working together with him, because if you kick it around you get the best. I know that you must be thinking you often get the worst, but I always felt that Vincente and I brought out the best in each other.

WHANNEL: Does that relate at all to the fact that in *Singin' in the Rain, It's Always Fair Weather, On the Town,* and *Take Me Out to the Ball Game,* you tend to play more popular characters? They're usually in popular settings. You play a prize-fight promoter, a sailor, a baseball player.

KELLY: I always liked to play those characters, because I thought they were more *au courant* with what was going on at the time. For example, in *An American in Paris*—I haven't seen it for a while, it must be a bit dated now—at the time I was playing a fellow on the GI Bill of Rights. The war was just over, we were right on the time.

WHANNEL: But you were also playing a painter and it was set in Paris.

KELLY: Yes, I studied painting in Paris. It seemed natural, too, that these people, full of life in this city, should think and act the way they did. It was certainly a romantic piece. Now, Vincente has done pieces—for example, *The Band Wagon,* which he did with Comden and Green and Fred Astaire and Cyd Charisse, was a very modern and up-to-date show and had no sense of the Baroque about it. Whether it was more "sophisticated" because of Fred and Oscar Levant and the combination with Minnelli, or not, I don't know.

WHANNEL: Perhaps it was the script of Comden and Green.

KELLY: I always worked very closely with Comden and Green on the scripts. We always sat down every night and went over everything they did and kicked things around. How closely Vincente worked with them on that, I don't know. I have no way of knowing. But there were times when we would do things. If you would cast Kelly and Donen to direct it and Kelly to play it, you know, it was on the brash, popular side. The reason I liked to play prize fighters or sailors or soldiers is, number one, that you usually have a uniform on, and you can dance better in it. When you dance in clothes, your dancing has to—well, let's take it at its greatest with Fred Astaire. If Fred's dancing with a suit on, it fits his style because his style is *intime;* it's intimate and it belongs with a tie and a suit—whether it's white tie or not doesn't matter. It's an elegant, very graceful, very intimate style. Mine is certainly just the opposite. I put on a suit, and I have a tendency to look like a truck driver going to mass on Sunday. I preferred it for very definite and obvious reasons.

DELAMATER: How, in general, did you prepare non-dancers to dance? I'm speaking, most specifically, of Frank Sinatra.

KELLY: Very hard work and a great willingness on their part to be beaten and insulted a lot. In other words, when they wanted to move and broaden their outlook you had no problem. With the younger people who don't understand what's going on, it was a little more difficult, because you'd just have to say, "Now, you do it, because you're in the picture and you're getting paid a lot of money just to do it, to do what you're told." A fellow like Frank, he had made two pictures and had really not unglued his hands from the microphone yet, and he was anxious to move around and improve his motion picture image. He certainly was the idol of teen-age America. We all know that. He was an avid worker. He practiced very fervidly. It's very tough for a non-dancer. It's like trying to play the piano if you say, "You have six weeks, learn to play the piano."

DELAMATER: How did something like that—as well as other people— affect your choreography?

KELLY: You have to simplify to a great extent, but the trick, when every choreographer is faced with a non-dancer, is to make it look good and fit it right on him and do whatever looks good on him. Actually, when you're choreographing for leading leadies in films—I always take that position—do what looks good, do what looks good on them. But then your horizons are broadened if they're trained dancers; that's the difference.

DELAMATER: How do you accommodate yourself to specific people like Rita Hayworth or a different kind of dancer, Vera-Ellen or Cyd Charisse?

KELLY: Actually, that wasn't as difficult as it might seem, because we would always try, at least at MGM, to cast the right girls for the right parts. People ask me, "Who was your favorite leading lady?" That's usually the bluntest way it's been put to me. I, in all honesty, didn't have one favorite, although I might have been attracted socially more to one than another and thought one might be more charming than another, but as far as dancing goes we tried to cast, I say we—anybody connected with the picture—the girl to the role in the same way as the director of the studio would cast me to the role. No differentiation there. When we started doing *An American in Paris,* the studio permitted me to go and hire a little French girl, whom they had never seen, Leslie Caron. I had seen her in a ballet when she was just fifteen. I said, "This girl can speak a little English, she's perfect and she's French, you see. So she'd be better than all the girls that we have here in America." It wasn't a question of who could dance better than the other one. It was a question of casting for the role. Of course, they're all good dancers. So I think the script dictated what we had to do.

Brigadoon was a very circumscribed script, and when the studio bought it from the stage play it was certainly done for singers. The only big dancing in it were the Scottish dances and sword dances, something which, on the screen, would tend not to be as exciting again with this kind of transparence. Minnelli and I and Arthur Freed were very upset about *Brigadoon* when we went into production, because when we bought it, it was pre-television competition, and the studio had told us we could shoot it outdoors, even in Scotland, using the CinemaScope technique at its best, the way John Ford would shoot a Western. So when the clans would come over the hills—again going back to *On the Town*—they'd be real hills, and they'd gather. The high shot would see them marching in, the bagpipes skirling and the drums and the fifes going, and it would have been, maybe, one of the great pictures of all time. It was moved to a stage set, and a lot of our enthusiasm was dampened. But we did the best we could with it. I believe, if I'm not wrong, that Cyd and I had another number in that—or were rehearsing another number—which we cut from the film because of length, just slowness. But the music in *Brigadoon* generally was on the slow side, and the solo numbers were excised.

WHANNEL: You think there is a problem with shooting indoors?

KELLY: Yes, if you're going to shoot the highlands of Scotland and you shoot it in this room, I think there's a problem immediately.

WHANNEL: Is it a problem only when you're shooting, as it were, natural things and country? If, for example, it's in a very urban setting, is that a problem?

KELLY: Yes, I think that's generally the only problem with it. Everything then had to be in CinemaScope because the thinking was it won't be like TV, it will be *this* way. That's not good for dances, because here the two dances were, and all this is wasted. So the idea is not to waste it, to see the environment around it, whatever ambiance that can give you extra, fine. If you're in a studio set you still have this and all this wasted on the side. In *It's Always Fair Weather,* we got an idea to have Dan Dailey and Michael Kidd and myself do three numbers at the same time and divide the frame up. That was scarcely seen, because we found out that most of the houses hadn't invested in CinemaScope mattes and poor Dan and Mike were cut in half.

DELAMATER: May I ask you a quick question about your own use of CinemaScope? That particular number is one that I admire very much as a way of making CinemaScope work for dance. I think that in the "I'll Go Home to Bonnie Jean" number in *Brigadoon,* you also seemed to me to be trying to fill the CinemaScope screen, using things moving back and forth. Are there other ways?

KELLY: Yes, I've always felt that no matter what scope in which you're working you should use the details and your techniques as best you can. The obvious thing about CinemaScope is all that extra space left over. The fact that we broke it up into three and used that was a purely cinematic device. I think what has colored most of my thinking since the first two musical films I made—and we mentioned earlier starting in *Cover Girl*—was to take the motion picture and utilize it as a free art form, as a different art form—in other words, let me state it more simply and succinctly—to do what you cannot do on the stage and to just break away from the proscenium arch. For instance, on the stage I certainly couldn't dance with myself and talk to myself and throw a chair through a window with myself, and I couldn't jump over myself. That was completely cinematic. Dancing in a cartoon is completely cinematic. Having three of us at the same time doing different things to the same tune and then dancing together, that was completely cinematic. There are a lot of things that can't be done on the stage. We certainly couldn't do *Singin' in the Rain,* because we'd wash out the orchestra pit the first time through. There are quite a few things that have now become a bit stale, I think, because they have been over used and repeated instead of new things being thought up.

DELAMATER: I read an interview that you gave in 1958, and you said that you really hated CinemaScope. I wonder if you've revised that to any extent.

KELLY: For dancing?

DELAMATER: Yes.

KELLY: No, for dancers it's an abomination. I'll amend it in one way. For a single and a duo, it's an abomination, and for a trio. If you get a group, you could fill it out. It's all right. But group dancing on the screen—the public really isn't interested in it very much.

WHANNEL: Are there any other technical problems you faced at the time? I'm thinking, now, back to the earlier period. For example, did you have problems with the Technicolor process in any of those films?

KELLY: No, as a matter of fact, the Technicolor people were always delighted to experiment with new things. The old three-strip process where you would come out with a matrix and you'd pull up your red, push down your green and so forth—we'd go down to the Technicolor lab with the fellow and sit in and talk about them, so we got truer prints. We had some problems, of course—the camera, which weighed about forty million pounds. I got them to build me what they later called a Uhangi because it was a huge wooden lip at the bottom of a moving crane. It was just a few inches off the ground, and we put a mirror on it so the camera would shoot into the mirror and shoot up so you could get lower shots and still move the camera. We made little inventions like that at MGM. The Technicolor head to support the camera would still push it eighteen inches off the ground. That's why we finally thought of the idea of shooting through the mirror. But the Technicolor people did help us in many ways to try to improve that. In a scene in "Slaughter on Tenth Avenue," I remember, we just put a camera in a pit. We happened to shoot that where there was a pit. We put it down for when Vera-Ellen came down the stairs, and we used a wide-angle lens. They never do on women, or they didn't up until that time, because it distorts the face. Those were the old movie rules and laws. You couldn't, at MGM, use a twenty-five or twenty-eight inch lens on a girl, because it would flatten her face out. But in this case we used it and, the studio, I never heard them say anything about it. The Technicolor people were always cooperative. When the time came to do the "Alter-Ego" dance in *Cover Girl,* nobody had ever panned or dollied a camera in double exposure. I said, "We can do that." They said, "We've never done it." So I said, "Let's make a test," and we went to Harry Cohn. The Technicolor people said, "Yes, we know we can do that. If he can show us a way to pan and dolly in double exposure, we can get the prints for you." And they did. Because the studio executives certainly had to listen to the technical men, I was willing to listen on that.

WHANNEL: When you came to shoot *It's Always Fair Weather,* that was in Eastman color. Was that an aesthetic choice in any sense?

KELLY: No, economics—cheaper, one strip. The Eastman color had some drawbacks to it. Most gray suits went blue. When Gregory Peck played the man in the gray flannel suit, he was in a blue flannel suit. They had some problems with their dyes. Later on they got around that; they were using one strip and having Technicolor develop the picture. Technicolor kept that a secret. They could make superior prints. They also make superior black and white prints to this day. The old three-strip is gone. The studios just won't fool with it any more because of the expense. As I recall, even twenty years ago, it was forty cents a foot developed. A lot of money.

WHANNEL: I asked the question because *It's Always Fair Weather* has slightly more somber tones than the earlier films.

KELLY: We're still having a lot of trouble with the prints, especially the one you're probably seeing which is a print of a print of a print. They take the original negative, and they put it in the can somewhere for posterity, and posterity never sees it. It's the backup negative; it's their insurance policy.

WHANNEL: When you were working at MGM, the studio at that time was going through lots of financial problems and internal battles. In fact, Louis B. Mayer resigned, I think, somewhere between *On the Town* and *Singin' in the Rain.* Were you and your collaborators affected by any of that?

KELLY: Only because of the affectings, if I may use that term, that television forced upon us, because people were staying home and watching *I Love Lucy* and so forth. Pictures had to be made more cheaply because of the drop in box-office attendance. Yes, it hit a new low, and there were some years when you couldn't even give a good picture away with china or anything. But as far as L.B. Mayer went, as far as his demise went, it had no effect on us at all, because I never talked to him about any creative or aesthetic point in my life. As far as I was concerned, he was more interested in his race horses. He never criticized. How much of the rushes or how many films he saw, I don't know, but I never talked to him about anything creative.

WHANNEL: Do you think he was generally supportive of Freed?

KELLY: He was very supportive of Arthur Freed, yes. He admired Arthur Freed, and that was a good thing.

WHANNEL: That would sustain Freed? Would Schary coming in after that have made a difference to Freed's work?

KELLY: No, we came to Schary with the biggest budget ever for a musical number with the ballet in *An American in Paris,* and Schary approved it in fifteen or twenty minutes, on faith alone. When you say you're doing a ballet about a man's impressions of Paris and the painters, it's pretty hard to write it down. We showed him costume sketches and color schemes, and that's about all. He said, "I have faith in you gentlemen. Go ahead and do it." When Schary came in we did have creative meetings with the head of the studio that we didn't have with L.B. Mayer—*I* never did.

WHANNEL: Everyone obviously admires Freed and what he did. Could you say something about what he did on any particular productions? I know that he was supportive of people and would approve ideas.

KELLY: That was his big talent. He could smell out talent, and, I guess, because he had been a songwriter himself, he knew the vagaries of the upper echelons, and since the producer did have the power to say go ahead on a picture—unless he was overruled, which quite often happened—he would usually take the role of *amicus curiae* in favor of the aesthetic person, the creative person as against the fellows who say it costs too much. Freed had enemies in the studio who kept saying, "Are you going to let those kids try that? That will never work." He'd say "How do you know it won't work? We've never done it." He was very helpful. I must say Joe Pasternak was the same way. When we did the cartoon dance in *Anchors Aweigh,* he was overruled by the head brass, and he said, "Go up and talk with them yourselves. I'm stymied. I'd like to see you try it." But he was very helpful. Joe's interest was not very much in dance. He was interested in opera and opera singers. For example, Mario Lanza, he brought him along, and Kathryn Grayson, and people like that.

WHANNEL: Deanna Durbin before that.

KELLY: Deanna Durbin. Actually, he made her a big star when she was a little girl—*A Hundred Men and a Girl.*

WHANNEL: Were these very distinct units? The word unit is often used in talking about Freed and Pasternak.

KELLY: Joe wasn't that worried about having a unit. He'd use more or less the people who were at the studio. I'm sure he'd cast them the way he thought best. I certainly had a pleasant relationship with him and admired him a great deal. His pictures tended to be very big hits, but he always felt, I believe—I don't want to put words in Joe's mouth—that as a creator when you pleased the public you did your best. For example, when he made that huge picture with all the stars, not *Ziegfeld Follies* but the one I played in with Kathryn Grayson and John Bowles and Mary Astor—

DELAMATER: *Thousands Cheer?*—

KELLY: *Thousands Cheer,* which was the title of an old New York revue that MGM owned and they put it on this, started out as a little picture and became a big picture because he knew that it would charm all the boys in the army camps—seeing the pretty girls and the stars. And he was right. The original picture was more a story about this young man and Kathryn Grayson and her father and mother, but he opened that up. That was his main belief. I think Arthur Freed's was more of a self-satisfaction if he could produce a picture with innovations, a different kind of thing.

WHANNEL: Did Freed make specific creative contributions on a picture? I mean apart from being supportive.

KELLY: Both Freed and Pasternak's contributions were negative, were saying what they didn't think you should do. But I can remember a very important instance when Arthur Freed made a quite constructive contribution. In the first place, *An American in Paris* was Arthur Freed's idea. He was in a concert with Ira Gershwin and they were doing "An American in Paris," playing it, and he said, "That would be a great title for a film. Why don't we see if we can get one?" He called us into a room and said, "Let's work on it." So we all got together and started working on it, and he got the Gershwin catalogue. Now, that's a big contribution. In the middle of the picture, our big ballet was supposed to be another song with great variations on the theme and take place in the middle of the picture. We were going to do what we did in *On the Town,* just go all over Paris, but we found that shooting in Paris was economically prohibitive then. The studios were beginning to pull in a bit. So we talked about doing a ballet to "An American in Paris." We wanted to do it in the middle of the picture at this spot that we all had agreed upon. After we started to talk about it, Freed said, "No, it would be better at the end of the picture." We all said, "No, you're wrong, Arthur; it's better here." So, finally, he just said, "No, it's got to be at the end of the picture." He was right; it was better. It took us quite a long time to see that. I must say that Minnelli and myself and Alan Lerner, who wrote the script, all wanted it in the spot it was before, but as it grew, Freed saw it at the end. Actually, it was a big switch to make in the middle.

WHANNEL: That was well into production?

KELLY: Oh God, yes. We were practically finished.

WHANNEL: So it might have been scripted. We saw it recently, and we were wondering—you were painting a portrait of Leslie Caron, and it seemed that something might be made of that in the script which doesn't actually happen in the film.

KELLY: Well, all that was made was that I was painting her portrait and thinking of her and the lady would come in, and I didn't want her to see it. I was between the two women.

WHANNEL: There wasn't something there in the original script which you dropped?

KELLY: No. That script is not given as much credit as it's due. When we'd come up with a song we'd want to use, Alan Lerner would have to lead in and out of it pretty cleverly. He did the hardest kind of a job, because, when you have less meat and less content, it's more difficult than when you have more. I always made the point that it's harder to play comedy than tragedy. It's harder to play a very light role than to do, let's say, one of Tennessee Williams's roles, because the lighter the material is the more the actor has to bring to it. This is not generally believed. You'll find that stars like Cary Grant go through a whole career, and everybody writes the picture and works till someone gets an Oscar. And it's another challenge. There are quite a few like that.

WHANNEL: Would this generalization—this is probably very wild, but see if it's anywhere near the truth—in the dances, the numbers you do in the everyday world, you will frequently draw on popular sources—tap, soft-shoe and so on?

KELLY: Yes.

WHANNEL: In the numbers you do in, say, dream sequences you tend more to draw on the balletic sources?

KELLY: Of course.

WHANNEL: Why should that be so?

KELLY: In the everyday world you can't jump out of a truck, being a truck driver, and go into fifth position. It looks silly, and you also can't wear ballet slippers. You've got to do something that fits your outfit. You've got a sweatshirt and rolled-up sleeves, so the characterization determines a lot. In the world of fantasy and make-believe, you can move another way and make it look fantastic in the sense of fantasy.

WHANNEL: Do you think that's one of the roots of the appeal of that kind of musical, that your dances are the kind of dances that make someone like me, a non-dancer, think, "Well, I can't dance, but if I could dance I'd dance that way?"

KELLY: I hope it is, but I can't answer that. I'll have to leave that to the critics and writers like yourselves. I can't answer that, but it certainly was what I tried to do, yes.

WHANNEL: I feel that way about the fact that both you and Astaire sing for yourselves.

KELLY: A lot of that is due to the fact that, although Fred has a better voice than I, we both have tiny voices, and we're song and dance men. We sing, usually, to set up the scene, to set up the dance. Neither Fred nor myself—and we've told people this and we've talked about it ourselves—pretend that we can put ourselves in league with the good popular singers, and we don't try. But, like every song and dance man, we tell the story, we tell the lyrics, we speak them as they were written and give them whatever nuance the lyricist intended. As a result, a lot of songwriters like us to do their numbers, certainly not for our mellifluous tones.

WHANNEL: Was your singing style fully developed before you came into films?

KELLY: I did a little better on Broadway, I believe, than in films, because I had to do it every night, and I was constantly having to reach the fourth balcony. We didn't have microphones in that day, so I worked more assiduously at it. I'm afraid when I came to films I never rehearsed singing much. I'd get ready the day before on the song—things like that. I was careless about that. I'd pay more attention to the dance, but, looking back, I wish I had done more singing during the rehearsal periods. But I've never felt that the world has lost anything on that account.

WHANNEL: Who were the most important people in the MGM music department? There are a number of names that you always see mentioned there, but it's hard for an outsider to sort out.

KELLY: The arrangers. Conrad Salinger was most important to the dancers, because he could do things with the mood numbers that nobody else has done before or since. Of course, they've copied him a lot. Everybody has copied his style. He was just one of the arrangers. I can give you a whole list, but there were two men who were most important to all of us. They were Roger Edens and Saul Chaplin. They were the translators, the interpreters between the dancers, the singers, whoever it was, and the arrangers. They'd say to the dancers, "I hear flutes here," and they'd say why; they'd look at the number and say, "Wouldn't it be better if you had a clarinet in here?" or whatever. They'd work with you when you were constructing these things out of thin air. Often when you just heard something in your head and you couldn't say, "these four bars should be a mixture of this instrument and that instrument and that instrument," they would translate your thoughts for you. They were the most highly skilled men I've ever met. (Saul Chaplin is still living here in Beverly Hills.) They worked the hardest, and they worked on more pictures than anyone else. The conductors Lennie Hayton and John Green, of course, were quite important, because they always wanted to get our tempi right, and they were dedicated motion picture men. There always were a few conductors who just were interested in the conducting and the music, and they didn't last very long. André Previn was just a kid when I first worked. He came there, I think, when he was nineteen and he was a movie man, although he's also—they were all great musicians. There as a whole body of men, but I think the heroes unsung were the arrangers. They did fantastic jobs.

WHANNEL: I suppose you would have more connection with all the music people than with the art department. Or would that be so?

KELLY: No, I met with them oftener, depending on what I was doing. If I only had two or three numbers to do and I was doing the choreography, I'd have fewer meetings with the art department, but if I were directing a picture, I'd meet with the art department constantly. You see, in color films, the color of the set can certainly affect the mood. When Vera-Ellen and I, in *On the Town,* were dancing, she had on all black and I had on a white sailor suit against a red background. Color meant everything. If you saw that in black and white, it would just be blah.

WHANNEL: In that particular case, was that your conception or was it one jointly worked out with the art department?

KELLY: In that particular case, it was my conception. In the case where I had Vera dance out of the yellow and then change everything—we had a yellow poster and a yellow background and then we devised the first curved cyclorama ever used, so it all seemed to be structured like she was on a poster which gave her sort of a printed look in that—that was collaboration, because I said to the art director whose name was Smith, Jack Smith, "How can we get rid of that line?" He said, "I can get rid of it if they'll give me the money." You see, I didn't know technically how to get rid of that and he did. He started way out here and went clear up into the wall. That was the beginning of "Cove cycs." I think he made the first one ever made. I said, "I just don't want to see the line." That's all I said to him. So these collaborations were very valuable.

WHANNEL: Was it your idea to have it very stylized, very simple when she moves out of the painting?

KELLY: Oh yes, purely movie technique again—cuts. She'd pass a pole and come out the other side like an old fashioned silent film. That's part of the choreography.

WHANNEL: It's somewhat similar to the way that Leslie Caron is introduced in *An American in Paris,* when the camera pans around to the frame of the mirror and she is seen in various styles or personas. And yet it seems to us still very different visually, that style of *On the Town.*

KELLY: In that case, you could say, "They did that in *On the Town,*" but you're right; it was different. To use the mirror was a way to help Oscar Levant sort of shake his head and help him build up his characterization. Oscar was sort of a one-dimensional actor. He was very witty and very brusque and brisk, but, as far as any depth to any role he played, he was playing himself, as everyone knew and you all know, of course, having seen him in different films. But to give that more, it was Vincente's idea to go in—and I never said to

Vincente, "We did that in *On the Town*," because I knew he'd find a way to make it different. The way also came from Minnelli to use the different kinds of furniture. It was my idea to put her in certain costumes. Of course, I put her in the kind of different things that suited Leslie and her dancing. When she was the student, I knew she could do these acrobatic tricks *adagio*, you know, very slowly, and that this would give the look of a great, concentrated study on her part, at the same time doing outlandish things with her body. The using of the whole color, of course we did it in *On the Town* before that, but Vincente did one better. He said, "We'll give each room a separate kind of furniture." So there's Jacobean furniture with her in an all black leotard and black cap and a white collar with great big furniture all paintd yellow which, if it were in another place, would have been ugly and brash, but with Vincente's ideas and taste it became quite something. Although, basically, you could say that that's the same thing, it's not. It helped the whole picture; it kept it going. Again, these collaborations. . . . Let's say I was directing the picture and doing the choreography myself. I might not have done that. I might have said, "I did that in *On the Town;* we had the same situation." Only this time we were talking about a girl. This time we saw her in a subway. She was in a subway. But, basically, you're right; it's the same idea.

DELAMATER: We've read about *The Pirate* ballet, the big one, that there had, in fact, been another one prepared and, for various reasons, considered too erotic or whatever, it had been eliminated. Can you tell us anything about that?

KELLY: I don't remember the exact details of that, but, yes, there were some cuts made there.

DELAMATER: It was just cuts in the number that is there?

KELLY: If I remember correctly, there were big cuts in the number. That's what it amounted to.

DELAMATER: It wasn't a new number altogether?

KELLY: I think it was all based on "Mack the Black Macoco." That went on for quite a few years, not only at MGM but all the other studios. In the dance with Cyd Charisse, we had to make a couple of cuts where she'd wrap her legs around me, which they do in ballet on the stage all the time. The movie censors were still very active and just said, "Don't allow her to wrap her legs around your middle." In Spain, they excised the part where I kissed her in the white thing—which we thought was very lovely and charming. They just excised that from the picture, because they thought it was very symbolic of love-making. A Catholic country. I remember writing them a letter saying, "I'm a Catholic; I don't understand your attitude." But it didn't do any good. That's what you'd run up against. They used to come down and measure the height of the girls' panties from their legs. Zizi Jeanmaire did a picture in France, and her outfit was cut up here like that, which gives a girl a longer line, and we'd try to sneak them up a little longer to make the girl have a longer line. They'd come down and measure and say, "Well, you have to change that." That was done all the time.

DELAMATER: How about "The Babbitt and the Bromide" sequence from *Ziegfeld Follies,* talking about the nature of the collaborative relationship between you and Fred Astaire?

KELLY: That was as pleasant as it could ever get.

DELAMATER: Did you work the choreography out together?

KELLY: Arthur Freed wanted us to do the number, because he'd seen Fred and his sister Adele do it in the original *Band Wagon* on Broadway. Naturally, I couldn't play Adele and neither could Fred, so we had to do a whole new idea. The thing evolved as a story from one year to the next and getting older and older and still making the same kind of bromides to each other. I originally wanted to do a more "up" kind of number. I guess it was purely because I wanted to do something more in my own style than this. But Arthur Freed said, "No, no, let's do this; I know this is good." I said, "Fine." The collaboration was just fun. We just had a lot of fun. We did our best to make each other comfortable.

WHANNEL: There's no choreographic credit on the film, is there?

KELLY: I think Bob Alton got credit.

DELAMATER: In the titles of the whole film.

KELLY: But he let us alone, and we worked it out.

DELAMATER: The two of you directed that sequence as well?

KELLY: No, Minnelli shot it, but it was head-on like a stage. It was a very simple number. There were no camera problems, no problems at all. I wish we could have done a lot more and tried to dance against each other in our own style instead of trying to amalgamate our things. Nevertheless, it was fun, and it didn't do anybody harm.

DELAMATER: How much of your choreography was retained for *Easter Parade?*

KELLY: What Fred had to do, when I broke my ankle and we got him to come out of retirement and go into it, was adjust the steps. But he kept pretty much the same kind of ideas, like the drum dance I had all finished. But he changed the steps so they'd look like his style. I don't think he kept all the camera moves. In "We're a Couple of Swells," it was such a simple thing, I don't think they ever changed anything. The way it was set originally with Judy—that was the same. I did not work with Ann Miller. I think Fred did a number with her at the beginning. He did a little thing where she got mad or something. I hadn't rehearsed that. I think pretty much most everything was what it was but *not* the actual steps themselves. There he recharged and redid. But don't forget that he walked into a thing that had been rehearsed for six weeks, and they said, "Come on, Fred, get in," and he had to move right in. In very little time, he put his own style on that. As far as that goes, everything he did was his own, but the stuff was laid out musically and pretty much on pattern. I'm trying to think of the other numbers. We had just started working on the little trio of "I Love a Piano and I Hear a Violin," but there, again, that wasn't a real dance number.

DELAMATER: Had you seen the Broadway production of *On the Town?*

KELLY: Oh yes, I loved it.

DELAMATER: Did you follow anything at all as far as Robbins's choreography is concerned?

KELLY: No.

DELAMATER: You completely changed the choreography?

KELLY: Completely made to be cinematic, yes. There were other problems too, by the way. Louis B. Mayer, after they bought it, saw the show, and he hated it. He didn't like the blacks and the Japanese girl being the heroine and blacks in the chorus. He just ignored the fact that New York is supposed to be the melting pot. I believe it was Arthur Freed who got to him and said we're going to change some of the songs that weren't hits. "We don't even have a hit album." So we took some of Bernstein's songs out, and Roger Edens and Comden and Green wrote new songs. That was sort of to assuage the studio. The whole picture was done with one eye on how quickly we can get it done before Mr. Mayer wakes up and says, "Let's forget this now and count off the past."

DELAMATER: What was the nature of your contribution to the choreography in *Hello, Dolly!?*

KELLY: Not much. Naturally, having worked with Michael before and his being one of the gang at MGM, I talked with him a lot about it, but, when we got into the real big numbers, it seemed that I was not there as much as I could have been or should have been. When we went to Garrison, New York, on location, and Michael and we had agreed we wanted to stage a lot of those numbers right on the terrain, it rained about twenty-one days of the thirty that we were allotted. There I helped him out. I'd go in and rehearse some of the gang over here while he was doing that. That's pretty much all I did on that.

DELAMATER: Did he shoot those numbers too, or did you?

KELLY: We took turns. No, he shot. Michael knows how to shoot numbers. There was no problem. The parade sequence—I would have liked Michael to have helped me more in that, just physically, because it was a very simple thing; it's just that there were so many masses of people. But he was very busy catching up on a number we had to shoot right after that with all the kids in the park. We didn't have as much collaboration as we would have liked. He came in quite late, because he was finishing up *Star,* the picture with Julie Andrews. He finished that one day and walked in the next day. The first week he was so tired, I remember, he had to try to get himself straightened out. We wanted him very much on the picture.

Interview with Eugene Loring

My interview with choreographer Eugene Loring took place in Hollywood, California, on 30 November 1973. At that time Mr. Loring was dividing his time between the University of California, Irvine, where he was chairman of the dance department, and the School of American Dance in Hollywood, which he had founded and run for many years.

DELAMATER: Would you please elaborate on how you initially became involved with motion pictures and on your approach to filming dance?
LORING: I've always been interested in film. When I went to New York, I tried to take a film editing course at New York University, even though I was involved in dance, because I had always been interested in the use of cinema *with* dance. I couldn't get one, but I took another course on film and we learned about the difference between stage and film, how the frame is different with cinema. Dissolves and montage and all the means of passage of time that film can do always have interested me, and some cinema technique influenced the way I did my ballet *Billy the Kid.* The street scene is like a montage, and in the case of the dancers moving downstage, I wanted to give the impression of a camera moving in, trucking in.

Since I was not busy right away when Metro-Goldwyn-Mayer brought me out here, I made it my business to get around and watch all the shooting that I could, to learn as much as I could about lenses and the whole business of the use of the camera, the booms and all that. Then when I started to choreograph, I would choreograph with the camera movements in mind. I don't understand the other way of working, where you choreograph and then a director comes in and photographs it, and there has been no idea beforehand in the composition of where the camera would be. As a matter of fact, I can't choreograph with that kind of director. I have to know where the camera is going to go in order to make an interesting composition. The other way the directors are always getting off on an oblique angle which has nothing to do with the original composition.

The way I worked with a director was to talk it all over with him first. Then I always consulted with the editors whether or not I was doing something that was wrong editing-wise. My method of shooting is editing at the same time—instead of taking long shot, medium shot, close shot and letting the editor sew it together, paste it together in some manner. (They don't know what is important, really.) After talking it over with the director and the editor and when I had the work rehearsed, I asked the director and the editor to come in to see whether they were happy with what I had done. That way we could make changes before we got on the sound stage to rehearse it for the camera.

Some directors gave you more freedom than others. Some directors don't like to have you do all that, and they will suddenly change their mind on the sound stage and ask you to make changes. Then it's a matter of whether you agree; sometimes it's very hard to convince a director that he's wrong. They *are* in charge of the picture; they'll do what they want and that's their prerogative. Then again you'll have a different kind of director. In *5000 Fingers of Dr. T.,* the dungeon ballet was a very tricky thing to shoot and tricky in its planning. There were sixty-four boys who had to appear like one hundred and four, and we had to shoot out of sequence (you usually do that anyway) because of cost. We couldn't have sixty-four boys sitting around while we took a small section. I had to plan it so that we used all the people, then most of the people, then gradually let people go. Also, on the dungeon stage there were all those different levels and all those crazy Dr. Seuss instruments. I laid it out and then Roy Rowland and I went on the sound stage, on the set itself, and I started telling him that people come from here and that this kind of lens will do this, etc. When we got about halfway through, he said, "Oh, you know what you're doing. Why don't you direct it? I'll stand by in case you need my advice." So I did. I did the *actual* shooting. He was marvelous to work with.

DELAMATER: You also worked with Roy Rowland on *Meet Me in Las Vegas.* Did his attitude follow through then with that film as well?

LORING: Yes.

DELAMATER: What does it imply when you have joint dance director credit as you did on a number of your films? Does that mean that you did some of the numbers and not others?

LORING: Yes. I did two pictures with Fred Astaire, for example, and when we got to *Silk Stockings* and I was asked to do it (I had done the stage show), I said I would prefer not to choreograph for Astaire again. He's very difficult to work with. By that I mean it's hard to create for him and get something new and fresh that also pleases him. He's very set in his ways. Hermes Pan choreographed everything that Fred did, and I choreographed all the rest of it.

DELAMATER: Was that true of *Funny Face* as well?

LORING: No, I did all of *Funny Face,* and I did all of *Yolanda and the Thief.*

DELAMATER: How did you work with Astaire? What was the method? Obviously, he, having come from a long tradition of film work prior to that, must have had his own ideas.

LORING: *Yolanda and the Thief* was the first one I did with him and we sat one evening. He asked me to see all of the numbers he'd ever done in motion pictures, and he had them magnificently edited. We sat for about six hours, and it was marvelous to see Ginger Rogers when she could hardly walk and then later really develop. He said he didn't want to repeat himself. And yet I had to think of what would look good on him and yet not be hoofing. He was very amenable. The only thing I couldn't do was use my ballet terms. If you say arabesque, then he doesn't want to do it. Ballet to him is sissy. I'd always have to say, "When you stick your leg out in back." I had to be very careful not to use ballet terms with him. He has peculiarities, you know.

But he is an absolutely exhaustive, tireless worker. He would come into the studio at nine o'clock in the morning and rehearse until six. He is a meticulous worker; he's like he's doing it for the first time when you see it on film, and it isn't that way at all. He's a craftsman.

DELAMATER: Vincente Minnelli directed *Yolanda and the Thief.* How was it working with him in creating dance numbers?

LORING: Minnelli kept changing his mind all the time, and that was the most disconcerting thing. There were times when Fred had to put his foot down about changes on the set. Vince would get an idea about something pictorial—interesting—but Fred, being such a careful and meticulous worker, it isn't easy for him to change quickly and be comfortable and sure of himself. It wasn't always the happiest situation.

DELAMATER: Were you able to shoot your own numbers with Minnelli?

LORING: No, we'd have to do a lot of talking, a lot of planning, and then when we'd get on the sound stage, he'd tell us no and there were times when *I* would have to say no, that's really a bad, bad angle.

Of course, a choreographer can't do the shooting unless he belongs to the director's union. With Roy Rowland it was a little bit different because he was on the set.

DELAMATER: What do you think about Gene Kelly's contribution to the musical and the filming of dance?

LORING: Very exciting. I think he's made some marvelous contributions cinematically—particularly with the use of the camera. Of course, he and his assistant Stanley Donen (and then Donen went on to become a director of his own) were dancers. Stanley having been a dancer and Gene having been a dancer, they really worked well together—Gene and Stanley and Jeanne Coyne. Anyway there was a lot of pre-planning and pre-discussion in anything they did together. I think that the "Alter-Ego" number in *Cover Girl* is marvelous.

DELAMATER: In your work with Stanley Donen, what kind of contribution did he make, if any, to the dance numbers?

LORING: The marvelous thing about Stanley Donen is that he understood where the camera should be, and he had a memory for what the dancers were doing, which other directors don't always have. They don't know movement and it's hard for them to know when to direct the cameraman to move the camera at a certain point, but Stanley would know because he had been a dancer. He could think; he knew what they were doing and what to do when.

We were very compatible. I did learn that it was very important who your director was.

DELAMATER: Which directors—besides Stanley Donen—did you find most able to visualize things the way you wanted them visualized?

LORING: Rouben Mamoulian was one. I virtually did all my own stuff on *Silk Stockings*. Mamoulian merely followed my pattern. There was no problem with him. He understood the "Red Blues" number. When you see the number on film Cyd Charisse looks like a human dynamo, but in those days Cyd tired very easily. You had to shoot the most difficult physical things in the morning and try not to take any of the really difficult things in the afternoon. Mamoulian understood that, and he didn't quarrel with anything I asked for. He was very compatible; I never worried about working with him.

DELAMATER: What performers did you find were particularly capable of expressing the kinds of things that you wanted expressed through film? Who seemed to contribute more than others to what you were doing?

LORING: The most compatible person I knew, the happiest, shall I say, experience I had working with any star was with Audrey Hepburn. She would try anything. She never said, "Oh, I don't look good doing that." Never. She would sometimes say, "Do you think that I look good enough, am I doing this well enough, do you think this is right? Somehow I don't feel right." She was not just one of those people who did everything you said. She had opinions. But never unhappy. She would try anything. There were often times when I'd say, "No, let's cut that out. That will never work." And she'd say, "Maybe I'm not doing it right." It was just divine working with her.

DELAMATER: Were there particular performers you had to accommodate yourself to?

LORING: That's a hard thing to answer. Cyd Charisse doesn't look good doing just anything. She has to be used in a certain way. You have to be merciless with yourself in trying to keep the star in mind while thinking of movement. Cyd does ballet best, but even there, there are some things she doesn't look good doing. I had to keep in mind that body—those legs—and knowing what would look good on that body.

DELAMATER: Did you find that conditions at various studios affected your work in any way?

LORING: The assumption is that at Metro things were always lavish. There were boundaries on what you could do but never like at Universal. (Of course, Universal has changed now.) Paramount was pretty good, but Columbia was always doing things on a tight budget. Things were small. You couldn't have the scope you did elsewhere.

DELAMATER: Did you find the studio system itself amenable to work in?

LORING: I didn't like working at Columbia. Mr. Cohn put his finger on everything. He inflicted his taste, and you really had to argue with him. At

Metro I was always involved with glamorous musicals so I didn't have the problem of being realistic, which Mr. Mayer didn't like. He wanted everything—the women—always to be beautiful. Lana Turner, pregnant, goes through an earthquake and ends up with a little sweat on her face. No matter what, no matter how, the women all had to be very feminine, very beautiful, clean and glamorous.

We did have one problem when we did *Funny Face,* but Stanley Donen and Roger Edens took care of it. We wanted the number in the cave with Audrey and the two guys purposely smoky and for the spotlight to hit the lens of the camera—directly into it. When they brought the prints back, the dailies, Paramount had leveled it off in the development of the film. Instead of being dark and smoky—that kind of thing—they had it all lit up, printed very light. It just was all wrong. But the director and producer took care of all that; I didn't have to do anything. Studio policy sometimes did affect [artists' decisions] but mostly I'd say financially. I didn't like Columbia.

DELAMATER: Did you work with Jack Cole at Columbia at all?

LORING: I was there at the same time. He did some numbers on one picture, and I did a number—*The Thrill of Brazil.* As a matter of fact, he suggested that I do the number.

DELAMATER: Did you generally rehearse all your numbers before the film was shot or while the film was being shot?

LORING: I can't think of an instance when I rehearsed all the numbers of a film and then shot them. No. Usually what you would do is rehearse a number and then shoot it, rehearse another number and then shoot it. Except on *Funny Face.* . . . I think we had a couple of things going at one time. The numbers were generally done during the rest of the film, simultaneously with the other parts of the film.

One experience with Fred Astaire on *Yolanda and the Thief* was quite different. There was a number prepared for *Yolanda* called "Bananas." Both Fred and I hated it, and we wondered what we were going to do with it. Now, sometimes when you are doing a film, you have extra time, a number is not ready to go into production or whatever. At one point during *Yolanda* I had nothing specific to do. I had always wanted to do a number that was jazz in five, where every step had five counts but the music is in four so your accents create a secondary syncopation. What I did was work out three different dances, no idea where I would use them or whether I ever would. I just did a moderate one, a slow one, and a fast one—a suite, and my assistant and I learned them. Harry Warren, who wrote the music for *Yolanda,* came by one day, saw what we were doing, and said, "You know, I have a hell of a tune for that sort of thing," and he sat down and played it. We called Arthur Freed down, and my assistant and I did these dances, and Harry Warren sat at the piano and played. Arthur loved it, wrote the lyrics, and called it "Coffee Time." We didn't have to argue about "Bananas." It was just one of those tricks of

Fate. "Bananas" was not up Fred's alley, but he loved doing "Coffee Time."

DELAMATER: Do you have other numbers in your various films that you think are especially successful as film dance?

LORING: The dungeon number in *5000 Fingers,* the thing Cyd Charisse did in *Deep in My Heart,* Audrey's number in the cave. I showed *Yolanda* down at the University in the spring. I did three evenings of anecdotes sacred and profane about show business personalities I've dealt with, and Metro let me show the numbers from *Yolanda,* and, you know, it stands up. The ballet stands up very well; I wasn't a bit embarrassed.

DELAMATER: Did you generally prepare things with assistants and then go to the performers with it?

LORING: Yes. Sometimes I had a skeleton crew, too. In *5000 Fingers* I had five guys who worked in the picture on almost all numbers, and then between numbers we would work on getting other ones ready. In both *5000 Fingers* and *Yolanda* I was in on the writing. I didn't write any of the script, but I was in the story conferences so that I could make the scene take the plot along instead of just having a number. That generally was not the case, though. *5000 Fingers* was marvelous to work on, particularly in the beginning, and that dungeon ballet came about because originally they were going to get somebody like Benny Goodman. When I got in on it, I said, "Oh, let me do that in dance." Stanley Kramer said, "Do you really think you can?" I worked on it with the five guys and mock-up props and those crazy instruments. Then there was a point where we weren't going to shoot it because we ran out of money. Roy Rowland saw me rehearsing and saw parts of what I had done and told Stanley Kramer, "You've been paying for these guys to rehearse over there, why don't you go look at what they are doing?" He came over, and with these funny mock-up props we had a rehearsal. He said, "We're going forward. This is entertainment," and went out and got fifty thousand dollars somewhere. It almost wasn't in the picture.

I don't feel good getting on the set and then starting to think with the dancers sitting around. I want to know where I am going so that all they do is come in and learn it. I might change something, but generally I know where I'm going. I still do that.

Interview with Preston Ames

The interview with Preston Ames was held at the Burbank Studios in Burbank, California, during November 1973. Mr. Ames was then and is still an active art director, working regularly on many films.

DELAMATER: Let's start in a general kind of way. A couple of years ago Betty Garrett spoke at Northwestern University and said that she felt that the art director was probably the most underrated creative force in filmmaking. I wonder if you might want to comment on that.

AMES: Strangely enough, it all depends where you are. The British art director is probably as strong a character in the picture as the director. They're equally balanced. Somehow or another they have created their own image, and believe me, it's been brilliant. They've done great, great things, and I have no quarrel with it at all. Somehow or another we must all be modest. Maybe we don't push ourselves enough. I don't know. Maybe it's because of the way we started. We came out of nowhere. You work with some directors like I did, for example, on *Lost Horizon.* We worked hand and glove like you couldn't believe. The communication was tremendous, but he had been accustomed to working with British art directors, so he was treating me as an equal, which was great. I've never been so flattered in my life, to be on that pedestal with him, which really wasn't a pedestal, but I felt that I was appreciated, and, as I said, the communication that went between the two of us was great, and we did things together. Some directors in this country, and I'm sure elsewhere, have a complete disdain for art direction. It's generally the younger men who don't appreciate the potential of working with somebody. They're a little afraid that somebody is going to be telling them what to do, which is the last thing we want to do. We used to have the reputation we're the guys that put up the walls, we're the guys who do the blueprints, we're the fellows that are just the little back seat pinned on, peons. That's not a general thing at all, but there are certain of us, and I'm not one of them by any matter of means, who are brilliant designers. John DeCuir is a case in point, and John is as versatile a person as I know in the industry, and we have two or three just like him. It all depends with whom you're working and what your particular assignment is.

DELAMATER: When, in general, did you, in most of the musicals, actually start to get involved with the specific film, very early in the screenwriting process or later, after the initial scripts had been written?

AMES: The best case in point was *An American in Paris.* That was the first musical that I did. I got involved long before I met the director—he didn't know me and I didn't know him. I was assigned the production with the idea of a first meeting with producer, director, choreographer, whoever else was involved, to lay out a thought, a theme, or whatever you want to call it. On that show, I was a whole year on the actual production, and I suppose I was on there, not before *anybody,* but certainly before the cinematographer, before a lot of people. Preparation on that was terribly important. All musicals take a tremendous amount of preparation. You have to be able to give an awful lot of people the thought behind it. Your choreographer has to know his acreage and where he's going to operate. Your costume designer must know how you are working, and your director must know in what field are we, and then all the communication with all the . . . it isn't just me; it's the group. If you don't work with a group, you're not making a picture, you're just making a thing. To answer that question, I would say that it's an abnormal amount of preparation which is highly essential.

DELAMATER: One of my major concerns is exactly the preparation that went into the dance sequences and the dance numbers. You mentioned the acreage, for instance, that the choreographer has to know specifically. Could you give me some details about location versus studio shooting, for example?

AMES: When you start doing a number, for example, like one in *The Unsinkable Molly Brown,* in the Dallas Divides in Colorado, 14,000 feet up in the Rockies, that's a whole area, so you say, "Here's a stage, do it." In *Gigi,* it was a question of doing it in whatever that room was or wherever that area was, or wherever Maxim's was. It was smallish, so that you could do that in a rehearsal hall. In *Jumbo,* you had to do it with a circus tent, because you are involved with that. Each one has its own specific problem. A lot of times, you have stage numbers. In the studio where I was working at MGM, they had a fantastic stage. In other words, it's a theater in a motion picture stage, so that you could create all the feeling of an actual theater, ballet, opera, call it what you will. That's gone, that's finished, we don't have it anymore, so you go to a theater and do that. It's terribly hard to say what, actually, you would do. On *Lost Horizon,* we had areas that were a library, and we designed the library on the rehearsal hall before we actually designed the room itself, because there were so many physical things that were required by the choreographer that you had to set up the props or set up whatever was required for the action that was involved, and then we'd build around it. There's really no set rule. Again, you're working with people and communicating with people and providing help for anything that you can.

DELAMATER: You've worked with Vincente Minnelli on a number of films.

AMES: Yes, I have.

DELAMATER: I infer, from watching the films, that there is something that I would call a Minnelli style. I was wondering if you might want to elaborate on that a bit, say how much he is actually responsible for that style.

AMES: Yes, I think he is. He's a very unique individual, very difficult to work with, because his lack of communication is unbelievable. And then, on the other hand, he knows what he wants, and sometimes you can figure out what he wants, sometimes you can't. I met Mr. Minnelli, and he, obviously, had no knowledge of what I could do, and I had no knowledge of this, so it took months to get accustomed to this man's operation. He has a wonderful preconceived notion of what he wants to put in a film, which is a very rare trait in my book. He knows exactly, when he sees it, what he wants, and he'll drive everybody up a tree to get exactly what he wants, and it's ninety-eight percent brilliant. Sometimes the brilliance becomes fiasco, from the point of view of monetary return, but those are the things that we used to call artistic flops. We catered to that for many years and now that's disastrous. But Vincente Minnelli, in my book, is a very brilliant, extraordinary person who has his own style and would copy nobody. He has no desire to copy. He's a brilliant painter. He has great taste, a great flair for things, for he's a very unusual person.

DELAMATER: He was a designer, himself, wasn't he?

AMES: Yes, he was.

DELAMATER: It always strikes me, too, that there's a great fluidity to his style, to his camera movements. Did that ever present problems? It seems to me that he would require greater sets, for instance.

AMES: We did a picture called *Brigadoon,* and it was a stage play, so we did it as a stage play, except that it had a certain kind of never-never-land look about it. But he was required to shoot three pictures. We had three by four aspect ratio, which was the old-fashioned way of shooting. We had the masked wide screen, which was the latest thing. And then, we had a thing called CinamaScope, which is now called Panavision. And nobody was too sure just how to compose with that, so we were looking at every set-up with two cameras. Consequently, you had to build your sets to all-extreme proportions, and your action for one camera would not satisfy the action for another camera, so we had to recompose it each time. And that proved his patience—he doesn't have patience—but it proved his talents, that he could do this kind of thing. It was very, very difficult. But Minnelli is never away from that camera. He's more of a cameraman than he is a director, because he's composing every frame of his pictures as a composed frame, to the point of exasperation at times, because it becomes terribly difficult when an actor's trying to do something, and he's constantly trying to change his position or his movement or whatever his position is. It's a little distracting, but, nevertheless, when it's all through, it still comes off.

DELAMATER: With shooting *Brigadoon* as they did, that must have presented some problems with Kelly's creating the choreography, too.

AMES: No, nothing fazes Gene.

DELAMATER: Did he have to create different sets of dances or, at least, modify them in some way?

AMES: No, his dance was there.

DELAMATER: I ask because it struck me that there are a couple of dances in there that seemed to be created specifically for the 2.5 to one or whatever aspect ratio, as opposed to three by four.

AMES: In this particular case, and it was a rarity or an actually unique situation where you shot three different pictures, so that Minnelli would compose for that three by four picture. Widescreen, no, because you just crop that. Or he composed for Panavision. I think it's just a question of camera. Maybe, I don't know. I really didn't quite analyze it from that position.

DELAMATER: I was thinking of "I'll Go Home with Bonnie Jean"; they just seem to spread across the whole frame in a nice way.

AMES: This is, again, where he's always composing for his people. I don't know whether that answers your question or not.

DELAMATER: What kind of relationship, let's say other than in *An American in Paris,* did Kelly and Minnelli have? *Brigadoon,* I suppose, specifically. In other words, I'm curious as to how much influence, for instance, Minnelli had on Kelly's choreography, on the camera movement, for instance, during the filming of dance sequences and so forth.

AMES: I would say, offhand, that Gene did his choreography per se and laid it out, and then it was photographed. It was a question of you look at this thing, and you study it, and how far do you go? In other words, how do you cut it? You do segments and be sure that the segments tie in, which was part of Minnelli's talents. But he would never interfere with Gene's choreography, because this is his own particular thing. In fact, it was a thought, at one moment, that Gene should do some of the directing on *An American in Paris.* He felt that Vince had such a keen thinking on his handling of the picture that he relinquished all directorial right to what is ordinarily what he would do on his choreography. There was that rapport. I know they've done other pictures together. I don't think that I've ever done anything with Minnelli and Kelly, other than that picture, truthfully.

DELAMATER: It strikes me, though, that Kelly seems to fit what he's doing in a somewhat different way sometimes with Minnelli as opposed to the ones that he himself directs. The Stanley Donen films have a slightly different look about them, more spare.

AMES: That could be. That's the directorial feeling that you'll get. Meat for one, poison for another. Each man has his own reputation. I've worked a lot with Busby Berkeley. Busby Berkeley will never direct a thing the way Vincente Minnelli would. He's strictly a musical number director, and it's done brilliantly, and he has a style of his own. If Kelly did a thing for Busby Berkeley, it would probably be the same dance, but it would look entirely different.

DELAMATER: What did you do with Berkeley besides *Jumbo*—anything?

AMES: Strangely enough, I did a thing called *Two Weeks with Love.* It was a little thing. It was the first time I ever met a gal by the name of Debbie Reynolds and a fellow by the name of Carleton Carpenter. And they did a little number and a little picture, and they were brilliant. I went off to my friends at Paramount and Twentieth and said, "I've just seen a very, very fantastic gal and you wouldn't believe anything about it." Well, who the hell was I to tell them, so I didn't sell my product very well. She managed to do rather well after that without me. It was that "Abba Dabba Honeymoon" thing, whatever that song was called. It was quite a famous number that she once in a while loves to do. It goes back a long, long ways. That was the first time I worked with this guy. He has a great style with that boom of his. He treats the boom like the baton of a band leader. It's a quite interesting style.

DELAMATER: How was it different working with Charles Walters as opposed to Vincente Minnelli?

AMES: It was night and day, absolutely night and day. Chuck Walters is a very, very sensitive person, and I did a picture with him and Joan Crawford. It was a theatrical show. He was a joy to work with, but you had to be very, very careful that you didn't say the wrong thing and get him all sulky and pouty and upset, because, he wasn't an insecure man, he was just terribly sensitive. Working on *Molly Brown,* I ran into occasions where I suddenly realized I'd said the wrong word. There were sparks. But it was a joy working for the man, because he had great talent, great ability, and he did a magnificent job with *Molly Brown.* It was really a physical thing, tremendously physical, and sometimes a man of that nature isn't quite accustomed to jumping all over the mountains the way I am. He did it, and it was brilliant. You had all that beautiful scenery of Colorado—fantastic.

DELAMATER: What kind of relationship did he, generally, then, have with people who worked as dance directors like Peter Gennaro? Did he work differently with them than, say, Minnelli did with Kelly? Did he allow them as much freedom as Minnelli did with Kelly?

AMES: No, because Kelly is a unique person, again. Gennaro is a choreographer, in the same way as Michael Kidd, he's a choreographer, and they don't have quite the prestige that Gene has. Gene has a very definite place that he's created for himself, and rightly so. I can remember the day that I had lunch with Gene Kelly on a set when he was just doing a bit in a picture. I think it was called *The Cross of Lorraine.* He was sitting down, and he was telling me what he wanted to do. He said, "I want to dance, and I want to direct, and I want to do . . ." this and that and the other thing. He knew exactly what he wanted to do, and he was able to sell himself to people like Arthur Freed and those kinds of people who had respect for what he had to offer.

DELAMATER: I infer from that, then, that Minnelli, generally, did not give quite as much freedom to other choreographers like Michael Kidd.

AMES: No, because he has that upper hand, and it's a very strong hand, and he takes no nonsense from anybody. It's got to be his way. Not that it's the right or wrong way, but it's *his* way. It's his style and his thing. Why not? That's what a director is. And it's a challenge working with this man, because some people require nothing, which is always, to me, a very dull way of working with people. Vincente always felt that you could give him a little bit more, which he appreciated, and you always did try to give him a little bit more.

DELAMATER: A kind of challenge?

AMES: Yes, it was a challenge.

DELAMATER: On *The Band Wagon,* Michael Kidd obviously has choreography credit, but it always has struck me that Astaire had a very strong say, too.

AMES: You had a couple of guys in there, Astaire and the other man with whom he danced, Jack Buchanan, who, after all, was no hay. You get dancers together and there's always a great rapport, a great deal of joking and kidding, very serious business with pleasure and pleasure with business. They get along like you can't believe. It's that. Astaire and all good dancers are great disciplinarians, and they know when somebody says to jump, they jump. Whether or not that's the way they want to jump, that's something else. That's worked out. Somebody's got to be the skipper. It's beautiful to watch. It's fantastic.

DELAMATER: Who was the skipper, then?

AMES: In this particular case, the choreographer.

DELAMATER: Even with Astaire?

AMES: Oh, sure, but togetherness like you can't believe—it was just great.

DELAMATER: Could you discuss the number in the penny arcade—the kind of relationship you had, specifically, as art director on that film?

AMES: Again, there was a gentlemen, in all respect, with whom I'd never worked before; Oliver Smith was hired by Arthur Freed, because he felt that this was, again, a stage play within a stage play. He always wanted the best. He didn't care who you were or what you were. He knew that I could do a certain thing, but he felt that Oliver Smith could do a certain stage thing, perhaps, a little better than I could. No quarrels. But, in this particular case, this was something that was kind of fun to do, because at Santa Monica at that time they had a wonderful carnival going, a real "carny" kind of a look to it. Minnelli and I walked it for hours to see what there was, what happened, what people did, what people around it did, so that he kind of saw this before he ever even saw a stage set. In other words, he realized the potential of the fortune teller and of the gimmick that exploded and the slot machines and all the other stuff that he worked with. He does his homework like you cannot believe. In this case, it was kind of fun, so that your contributions were to find a place, take him and show him, because he's not a naive man, but sometimes there are certain things that you don't know, the "carny" kind of a thing. He was fascinated by it all. That's how that really developed.

DELAMATER: Was it shot at that place?

AMES: Oh, no. We had to create the whole scene with the things that we got from that or we built or designed or whatever it was. It all had to tie in, again, with the choreography. That had to be really laid out, too.

DELAMATER: Did you work at all with Astaire and Kidd on that while you were preparing it?

AMES: Yes, very closely.

DELAMATER: How much did they dictate what changes had to be made?

AMES: It was more, again, with them, what do you do with what you have? What does your toy do for you, and the progression? Should we go from a shoeshine thing to a this to a that or something else? It was a question of letting them out and almost being a property man. It was fun.

DELAMATER: Did the directors of photography, camera operators and so forth get involved in that kind of preparation?

AMES: No, not really. You see, there is preparation and then there is rehearsal, and your rehearsal is on the stage set with everything going, your lights and the works. And then they get very much involved, because they have to see what they have to light, whom they have to light, how they have to handle it, how does the camera move, what are the problems and so on. There they have their moment.

DELAMATER: It comes, actually, during the rehearsal?

AMES: Yes, because your preparation, your pre-rehearsal time could be two, three, four weeks.

DELAMATER: Has it been your experience that directors of photography themselves, then, have some kind of say?

AMES: Not much, no.

DELAMATER: They're told what to do, I suppose.

AMES: Their contribution is good lighting, good photography and, of course, knowing where to put the camera, how to operate, the camera movement or whatever it is. It's a team thing, again, with director and cinematographer. On "Stairway to Paradise," that was a very tricky thing to do with music cues and all kinds of cues that you had to concentrate on and be aware of what the gimmicks were. Kelly did a perfectly wonderful thing in *Living in a Big Way* in which he was involved with the building of a house where he went all over the whole darn framework, the structure, and it was in and out and up and down and all over the place, and it was fabulous. This was very rough on the cameraman.

DELAMATER: I was wondering if you could think of any specific problems that you had in creating the material for any of the films where you worked with Kelly.

AMES: I guess the biggest one was *Brigadoon,* actually, from the point of view of physical design of sets, because the whole thing was a stage set. We never went outdoors once. We had two stage sets on one stage, and, of course, in those days Metro had some pretty fabulous stages. Our stage 27 at Metro was seventy-five feet high, about two hundred and fifty feet long and about one hundred and fifty feet deep, which is a pretty good sized stage. I had a piece of set on one end of the stage, and I had another piece of set on the other end of the stage, and I looked at it one day very, very carefully, and I went back to my boss, Cedric Gibbons (who is the reason that the art department at Metro was what it was, because he created it), and I said, "Mr. Gibbons" (everybody was Mr. in those days), "I have a horrible idea." "What is it?" "I'd like to put those two sets together." And he said, "What did you have in mind?" And I said, "This thing calls for sheep and little running streams and all this other jazz, and I feel I can make it. It's going to cost a little money, but I feel I can make a tremendous thing." So, he said, "Let's take the director down." Minnelli isn't one, ever, to go overboard on appreciation, because he feels that this is part of your job, and he just couldn't believe that all of a sudden out of two things came one tremendous thing. Just to give you an idea of the size of it, there was four hundred and fifty feet long of painted backing for this thing, and forty feet high. It turned out to be very successful, I think. It was fun to do. We had the whole works. It was great. Every show has got some kind of a problem. It doesn't make any difference what it is. We did a thing, which had nothing to do with choreography, but in a way it was choreography. It was a trilogy called *Story of Three Loves*. My third of the picture was called *Equilibrium*. This was with, I think, Kirk Douglas and Pier Angeli. This was a flying act in a circus. The whole thing was based on this one act, like a French circus, a single ring, high stage thing. We spent, I think, three months on the preparation of this number. I designed the number, because I worked with two or three people. One was a catcher, one was a flyer, and one was his wife. It was a team of three, and the producer said, "We would like the most exciting thing you could possibly do." So, I sat down with these three people, and I said, "What can you do?" Everything that I had figured they should be able to do they'd never heard of before. We laid it all out. We sketched it. We practically story-boarded the whole thing, so that you almost had a flip card. The producer was thrilled, and he said, "Can these people do it?" And I said, "If you like it, they'll work on it." And then we started to work on it. It was very exciting. The whole show was this one act. It was for real, and it was great, and it was very exciting, very thrilling. Those are the things that you run into which I call real design, real physical design. That contribution to a picture is a form of writing, which isn't writing, but that's the way we do it. With some people you can work that way. Some people resent it, like I said at the very beginning. I love my work, and I love to be able to work with people. When I can't work with them, then I'm frustrated and end up contributing nothing.

DELAMATER: Stanley Donen, among other people, feels that in certain films shooting in the studio presents a kind of artificiality that he doesn't seem to care for. He said, for instance, that he thought that *Seven Brides* could have been better if it had been shot on location. I was wondering how you felt about that.

AMES: No, I think that's very unfair, particularly for that picture. Let's face it, it was a musical, and it needed the kind of a thing that you could do on a stage, which is controlled lighting, controlled effects, controlled all kinds of things. And, in those days, we spent every nickel that we could scrounge to make the most presentable setting that you could to a point of reality which was unbelievable. It was beautiful, and our boss, Cedric Gibbons, wouldn't have stood for it unless it had been. There is a certain thinking today that no picture should ever be made except outside the walls of the studio. In certain cases, great, I couldn't believe it more. In other instances, it's ridiculous. And, strangely enough, you'll find that a director who insists on going outdoors or going to a location and doing everything for real, suddenly finds that somebody will say to him, "Mr. Director, if we had this on a stage, we'd be able to pull out some of these walls, and you could get some of these shots." All of a sudden they have discovered a studio, and they think that this is pretty great stuff. Why didn't we think of this before? So that the circle has gone around. For Stanley to say that (and I love the man and he's very brilliant and he's very talented), particularly for that picture, is very unfair. Everything has its place and just, arbitrarily, to say, "Off with its head," because it's a studio, it's a dirty word, I just don't believe it. I can understand certain directors going on certain lots and seeing a crumby looking outdoor set that's in a state of complete disrepair and saying, "Good God, do I have to shoot this?" I don't blame them if they don't spend a little bit of money to clean it up. It's the studio's business to keep the sets up. But, if he has to shoot it, then I don't blame him for wanting to go elsewhere. It's ridiculous. It's a funny situation, and I think, strangely enough, we're all coming back to the studio.

Interview with Randall Duell

My interview with art director Randall Duell took place at his office in Santa Monica, California, on 14 November 1973. He was then the president of his own architectural firm, Randall Duell Associates.

DELAMATER: I have a number of questions, relating to the musical in general and to your work, particularly in musicals and, specifically, on *Singin' in the Rain.* Is it customary for art directors, or frequent anyway, to have an architecture background? I know Preston Ames does.
DUELL: In the motion picture industry, about the time I got into it, they began to feel the need of a little more realism in pictures, and the scenic artists and the scenic designers, the set designers, at that time were not architecturally oriented. The architects, then, began to infiltrate the motion picture business because of the demand of more detail and realism. Of course, I didn't know much about the motion picture business at that time.
DELAMATER: How did you actually get into it?

DUELL: I got into it out of sheer need of making a living. It was during the Depression days. The architectural offices I was associated with had been fortunate for several years in having some work, and all of a sudden it ran out. So, in order to keep body and soul together, I was offered a job at the studio; friends of mine were there.

DELAMATER: Was this at MGM?

DUELL: Yes. Really, my first assignment was with Selznick. At the time he was doing *The Garden of Allah* and *Gone with the Wind* and the art director was Lyle Wheeler who was an old friend of mine and needed some help. So, I went out to help him. Then, I went over to MGM. They were doing a picture called *Romeo and Juliet*. *Romeo and Juliet* required a great knowledge of traditional architecture and history and that sort of thing.

DELAMATER: This is the *Romeo and Juliet* with Leslie Howard?

DUELL: And Norma Shearer, yes. That was really my first assignment to work on these sets purely from an architectural point of view, since, as I say, I was not too well acquainted with the motion picture techniques, but you learn pretty fast when you have to.

DELAMATER: How long did you stay?

DUELL: I stayed twenty-five years. I was always at Metro at that time. I figured that, after twenty-five years, I should retire, which I did. I retired and started this business.

DELAMATER: This is not much of a retirement, I wouldn't think.

DUELL: No, it just kind of pyramided. I didn't plan on it this way, but I've been very fortunate at my age to have built up a business as nice as this one is. I'm really proud of it. I've been at this now about sixteen years, I guess. I started about sixteen years ago. I retired at fifty-five, now I'm seventy.

DELAMATER: Cedric Gibbons, generally, has credit, at least primary credit, on most MGM films. What's the story on that?

DUELL: Metro was a little stronger than the other studios in this regard; they had a supervising art director. And it was a necessity, because they were doing so many pictures. Each picture had an assigned art director who was also under Gibbons's supervision, and for many years he got total screen credit. Then, when pressure became a little stronger in the guilds, the art directors got together and said, "Well, look, why don't we get at least a joint credit?" Finally, they got a joint credit with him. Of course, today that's all gone. Supervisors are no longer needed, because they don't have the production. At Metro, at that time, they were doing about fifty-some-odd pictures a year, and we had about fifteen art directors, so there was a need for a head. He was a fine person to work for and work with, and I enjoyed every minute I worked with him. He was a talented man, and he was great to work with—high imagination—and he always stimulated you to think a little deeper than just what you normally may be doing.

DELAMATER: What kind of freedom did you have?

DUELL: Complete freedom. After all, he was looking for ideas too. We would have meetings with the directors and the producers and arrive at a method to proceed with, and then we would take the ball and go from there and prepare the sketches and models and design the things, and then we would have a meeting with all the producers and directors and Mr. Gibbons and so on. From there, we would decide we're going to spend X number of dollars on this set or we're going to do so and so. Once in a while, particularly when we got into musicals, it was more difficult to say we're going to set a budget on this until we had a little better idea of what the whole story was. Take a dramatic story where you had a written script, that's one thing, but, when you take a picture like *Singin' in the Rain* that grew from day to day, it was terribly difficult to put that down in dollars and say, "We're going to spend $60,000 on this number." What is this number? No one knows yet what the number is. We know there's going to be a number. You really grew up with those numbers from the tempo track on.

DELAMATER: I infer from that, then, that you must have worked pretty closely with the directors and so forth during the whole creative process.

DUELL: Yes, we were closer to them than, I guess, almost anyone on that company up to a point. As a matter of fact, we were responsible, actually, for everything that you see on a film other than the actors. Occasionally we got involved with wardrobe; on one show I was actually involved with color wardrobe.

DELAMATER: Could you elaborate on that a bit? A couple of years ago Betty Garrett spoke at Northwestern University and said that she had always felt that the art director was the most underrated creative talent in films.

DUELL: Of course, we like to feel that. We all like to say what we did was the most important thing in the world. If you did your job as an art director and did a good job, you *were* important. We were never out in the limelight and publicity and all that, because, I don't know, we seemed to come from a strain of characters who were more interested in what we were doing than in getting the publicity. But it was terribly important, because not only just the action of the picture, not only just the looks of the picture, but the entire development of action and controlling of the schedule and all that had to be part of our business. For instance, on several shows that I was on and a lot of others, we actually laid out continuity sketches, and they photographed directly from these sketches. For instance, I did one show with a whaling sequence. In that whaling sequence, they photographed it according to the script, but the man who wrote the script wasn't too familiar with how you catch a whale and bring it aboard and render it out. As a result, I had to do a tremendous amount of research on whaling and prepare a new set of sketches, and it was rephotographed. I was on the stage for every scene that was photographed and set them up with the director, and this is, finally, what got into the picture. It's knowing what you can do with the elements that you have, knowing the limitations of your camera and the limitations of your facilities— miniature facilities, for example. You know these things at your finger tips, so, when you make these sketches, you know how you're going to do it. You know how much of it's going to be painting, how much is going to be real, and it gets to the point where the director is almost forced to do it according to the way you've laid it out.

DELAMATER: So, you, actually, have quite a bit more control over the visual style and what the director's doing than one would infer, ordinarily.

DUELL: On technical things, yes, because most art directors are very good technicians. They had to be in order to create some of the things that they wanted to create. It's one thing to have an idea. It's another to know how you're going to produce an idea. It's the same in the architecture business. We have ideas and all, but how are we going to get it built or how are we going to get it fabricated or what are the people going to think? Motion pictures and architecture are pretty much the same when you get right down to it. They're dealing with people and what people do, and your purpose is to entertain them any way you can find to entertain them.

DELAMATER: How closely did you work with Gene Kelly and Stanley Donen on *Singin' in the Rain*?

DUELL: Of course, I had worked with Stanley and Gene before *Singin' in the Rain*. Stanley was sort of an assistant choreographer to Gene, and he came over to work on the dance numbers. Stanley, of course, went on to be a good director, and he's done a fine job. Actually, the best way to explain it, I guess, is to take a specific case, which is pretty typical of how a dance number evolves out of talk and finally gets down to being photographed. It's quite a long process in between. Actually, what usually happens, the director, the producer and Gene would get an idea that they wanted to do a number in this particular section of the script. One of the numbers is the "Singin' in the Rain" number where he paddled down the street and splashed in the puddles of water. That number was started with just the three of us, actually, with Gene and Jeanne Coyne, who was his assistant. And I went out to the back lot. They didn't want to spend a lot of money on building a set on a stage. Gene said, "Maybe we can do it on the street." So, we went out to one of the little streets and finally picked a street where we thought it might work out. Gene, being the very imaginative sort of guy that he is and a delightful person to work with, said, "Let's try to lay it out on this street." They took a piano out on the street with a tempo track, just for the beat of the music, and began to work with that, and Gene began to work out his numbers. For instance, there's a wrought-iron fence there, and he bop-bop-bopped, and that grew out of just the fact that the fence was there and it gave him an idea that you know how kids will take a stick and run it along a picket fence and make a sound. And then, of course, once the dance was developed and we knew that, generally, the area of the street was going to work, they developed the music. Then, with the music track and Gene (and by now the company had grown to a half dozen or so), we went back to the street and laid out every step. For instance, when he would jump off a box or down on the pavement or something, he had to land in a puddle. We would draw a circle where that puddle was to be built. We would rearrange the architecture of the thing to accommodate the exact split second when he was there to test whatever it was. Then we would dish out the street and repave it and make all these puddles so that he hit exactly where he was going to go. When the company went out to shoot it, the street was wet down, and it was raining, and everything was lovely. They ran the number, it was photographed, and the puddles happened just by accident to be in the right place, and no one knew the difference. But we knew the difference, because it was several weeks of working directly with Gene to get them.

DELAMATER: I always get the impression from watching Kelly's dance numbers, in particular, that he must have worked very closely, also, with cameramen, directors and photographers and so forth.

DUELL: Yes, he's a good technician himself, and he's knowledgeable in the field of photography. He knows some of the limitations and some of the things that you can do and some of the things you can't do, and every once in a while he comes up with an idea that they say, "My God, I don't know whether we can do this or not, Gene." It's like dancing with the cartoon figures. He wanted to combine this and dance with the cartoon. We got with the cartoon boys Hanna-Barbera, Bill Hanna and Joe Barbera (they were in charge of the cartoon department at that time at Metro). So, we worked with them, and I had to work with them, because as the cartoons grew, when the cartoon figure did things or Gene did things in the cartoon, for instance, if he jumped off a table or piece of furniture or something in the set, that wasn't a table; that was just a platform at that height for the position he wanted. We had to build all these different levels; although it was cartooned later, the jump-off had to be on to something. So, that's where, again, Gene and the cartoon department and I had to all get together and build this thing so it would work. That cartoon number is kind of interesting for that reason. It was fun to see it grow and get it drawn as well as photographed.

DELAMATER: There's a particular scene in *Singin' in the Rain,* the "Good Morning" number with Debbie Reynolds and Donald O'Connor and Kelly. During one particular take, the camera has moved to the right, they run up the stairs, and then the camera moves back again, and, in the time that the camera has moved back, a coat stand has come into the scene, and, obviously, someone must have run on with that coat stand, because it's all one take. I was wondering if you could tell me something about that.

DUELL: It often happens that something is in the way of the camera, the camera moves over, and then as it gets up to it it's pulled aside or put back in position. You usually try to avoid situations like that, because nine chances of ten, if it is phony, it's going to look phony. It's better to arrange it so that you have a complete continuation of your scene. That's why we try, sometimes very desperately, to make models, to make sketches and rehearse it and make sure that we don't have to have something real phony out of it.

DELAMATER: It's funny, though, while it is a kind of phony thing in a sense, I'd never noticed that it had been added to the set until I ran it through a moviola and realized that it was all one take, and, therefore, it must have been added while they were on another part of the set.

DUELL: This is often the case, that you see a film, and there will be some darned thing wrong with it, but you don't notice it at the first running. But, after you run it two or three times, you say, "My God, why didn't I notice it before?" You didn't, because you had a good story, and you were interested in your story—what was going on. Some of these things are incidental things, that are not right, kind of get by. It's terribly expensive to set up a retake. Often times, a film is better looking in the first viewing than when you see it three or four times.

DELAMATER: There are quite a few special effects numbers in *Singin' in the Rain*. Did you work, also, closely with special effects men and so forth?

DUELL: Oh yes, surely.

DELAMATER: Whose ideas were they, generally?

DUELL: They grow out of conversation and you say, "Well, gee, let's do the honky-tonk bootlegger's joint, the speak-easy." For this, then, you say, "Well, we've got about ten of these things to do. We don't want to build all these sets. You can't afford to do it with a montage of things." So, that's why I came up with the idea of doing the big dance number scenically. The set was mostly just scenic painting, exaggerated, and, obviously, it was what it was. These things are built—on a team effort, I think, is the fairest way to put it.

DELAMATER: You said that Donen had been Kelly's assistant choreographer. Is that true in the breakdown of responsibilities on *Singin' in the Rain,* in particular? They share co-director and co-choreographer credit.

DUELL: Well, Gene ran the show. Stan had some good ideas and worked with Gene, but he was still the "office boy" to Gene, in a sense, although Gene had great respect for him. But they made a good team, because they were very compatible. I wouldn't say that everyone in the world would get along with Gene, because he's highly imaginative and very opinionated, but I found him fun to work with. There's a challenge, because, often times, he didn't have the budget to do some of these numbers that he wanted to do, and he put a lot of faith in me that I would come up with something without a lot of money. For instance, we had a set that we did where he danced up the street, the oriental street. He wanted very desperately to do this, and they said that the set was going to cost somewhere around $100,000. I just put together, one night, a whole bunch of set pieces that I took off the back lot and got a crate and just moved them all in and stacked them up, then took Gene in. We kept low key lighting on it, and I didn't have to worry about patching all the holes. We hung fishnets and downspouts and things to cover the joints. In two or three days, we built a fantastic set, and he loved it, and we did it for a lot less money than they thought it was going to cost. It was because of his cooperation you could do this. You take a real picky guy, and he'll go in there and say, "What's all this stuff?" Well, you're not going to see it, because you're going to keep the lights down. That's why it was fun to work with him.

DELAMATER: You also did *Silk Stockings.*

DUELL: Yes, with Cyd Charisse and Fred Astaire.

DELAMATER: Rouben Mamoulian directed that.

DUELL: That's the old Russian story. I did *Ninotchka,* too, with Greta Garbo. So, it was kind of fun to do the musical version. Fred is a different type of person than Gene. He's like Gene in one way, that he's a perfectionist. He's a hard working guy and almost impossible to satisfy with the texture of the dance floor. He wasn't very pleasant about it. And I said, "Well, Fred, we can make any kind of a floor you want. All you have to do is tell me what you want or show me what you want. I'll prepare an eight by eight sample floor, and you try it out. I'll put it wherever you want it, in the rehearsal hall or on the stage somewhere." And he's a nice guy, so he said, "O.K." So, I put it in the rehearsal hall, and he'd come in, and he'd try this piece of floor. No, it was too slow or it was too fast or too this. After about thirteen or fourteen tries, we finally got a piece of floor, and he said, "That's great." He said, "I know you're not going to be able to keep it that way." I said, "Look, if you like that floor, it's going to be kept that way. It's going to be exactly like that every time you dance on it." He said, "Well, that will be the first time." We managed to satisfy him with the floor, and he was very pleased with it. We pre-fabbed it in the mill and the paint shop and did a very hard coating on it. We put a coating on it, a marbleized pattern that wouldn't show skid marks, because when he slides sometimes they show the marks. That was one of his objections, but, with this marbleizing, it looked like a big marble floor and managed to cover up all these things. We were able to keep it clean after every take and keep the texture of it right. It was all a problem. Cyd was a very sweet gal to work with. She was hard working, very nice.

DELAMATER: There are two choreographer credits on *Silk Stockings,* Hermes Pan and Eugene Loring. I was wondering if you could tell me something about exactly how that worked and how Astaire himself contributed to the choreography.

DUELL: I think they had the two choreographers on, because one was on one number and one was on another. (You take me back a long way with these, you know.) They were on different numbers. Hermes Pan was a different type of choreographer than Loring. Pan knew about the technical things in a motion picture and the problems that you had. Loring was more of a dreamer, I think.

DELAMATER: *Silk Stockings,* if I'm not mistaken, was in CinemaScope, and I was wondering what kinds of problems creating sets for CinemaScope films presents, as opposed to academy aspect ratio.

DUELL: No problem. It was just a matter of knowing where your camera was going to be and designing to the camera. Often times, you'd design a set, particularly if you had very well confined areas which are stages; they often times confined us. We could only do so much on a stage. The size of the stage would limit you as to the heights but mostly on the widths. We had no trouble laying it out. Our trouble was keeping the cameramen and the director in tow so that they didn't get some wild ideas after the thing was all built and want to do something they couldn't do. The sky is not the limit in the technical aspects of making motion pictures.

DELAMATER: Can you think of any special problems that happened during *Singin' in the Rain,* in particular?

DUELL: I think one of the toughest problems we had was the Times Square episode with all the signs and the lights. That took two stages to do. Fortunately, we were able to back up into a stage with a crane. There was a crane right through this. It was a tremendous line-up job. I was days riding the camera and lining up all these signs. First off, we had to lay it out perspectively to know what size to make them. After they were made and hung, we had to adjust them. Of course, most of them were miniature. The farther from the camera that they were would vary the size of the light bulb we could use, so we were a little bit tied up to light bulb sizes at that time, in order to get the right perspectives. The camera started high, going through these things as they came on. Of course, it all had to be done to the beat of music, so we had what we called a piano. We had finally rigged all the signs on a switchboard where they could turn them on and adjust them to flash with the music. To time the lighting with the beat of music and the movement of the camera took several days of, really, just dry rehearsal with all the technicians rearranging; it would take two or three hours to move one sign. Then you had to go back and ride the crane again. Technically, it was very satisfying to finally see it completed.

DELAMATER: I guess that's the nature of the beast, in a sense; it just looks so beautifully simple.

DUELL: We're glad that it did.

DELAMATER: In the number, "You Were Meant for Me," Gene Kelly and Debbie Reynolds dance on the sound stage. How much of that and other areas of the film were actually intended to look like the MGM lot? Were they at all? I assume that must have been done right on a sound stage. How much did you actually set up a sound stage for that number?

DUELL: Very little. Actually, I'm trying to recall what did happen. Gene wanted to pick a spot to do this number, and he said, "We don't want a set. We don't want to build anything. We want to just pick something." So, we walked on to an empty stage, and there were a few lights standing around and the ladder (remember the ladder?) right out in the middle of the stage. We walked over to the ladder, and it was dark in the stage, and he said, "This is great. We'll use the ladder, and we'll bring in these lights. We'll bring them all in. This is all we want, a big empty stage with a few lights and a ladder." That's the way it started, and that's the way it ended up. That was purely Gene's idea.

DELAMATER: How about the sequence in which he and Donald O'Conner are walking past a number of films being shot? There's a scene with a railroad car with rear screen projection and a scene of a native number.

DUELL: We did that with continuity sketches. We would go through it roughly, then we'd make these sketches, and, of course, Gene would approve, and they would use those as their guiding key when they photographed.

DELAMATER: You say there were a number of scenes where you had used lots of things that were already on the lot. What was the breakdown in that regard? How much did you actually newly design for the film?

DUELL: It's hard to say, because, actually, the studio had at that time a fantastic backlog of what we call units, stock units. We would take units from some other picture, possibly, and use some of the basic units and redesign them to fit our set. It saved us a lot of money by being able to use some door units and window units and things of this nature. Or, if there's a big stairway or something where we could just change a rail or something, we could use it. We used things that way. Almost every set we built, if it had anything to do with hard wall, we would use our stock walls as much as possible and then decorate over that and dress over that. Otherwise, you couldn't get them built in time—on *The Swan,* for instance, with Grace Kelly, and the big stair hall we had on the set I needed some big baroque caps, and we didn't have time or money to model them and cast these things. It would cost a fantastic amount of money. So, I got this idea; we had some little porcelain stoves that were made for I've forgotten what picture, but they were little baroque stoves, and I used pieces of these stoves for column caps. I turned them upside down. You're always digging for ideas to use what you have in a little different way, and we still do it in the architecture business. As a matter of fact, we purchased a lot of units from Metro when they were going out of business, some panels from *Marie Antoinette* and a lot of their stock forms and all. In order to protect them, we purchased them. We now own them and use them, and some of our clients have access to them. The day is gone when you can find sculptors and modelers to do this sort of work. It's almost a lost, dying art.

DELAMATER: Did the studios, in general, employ a certain number of people just to create that sort of thing?

DUELL: Oh, yes. A friend of mine who is now semi-retired, except he's doing a lot of work for a museum, is a sculptor and modeler and handled all the stuff at Metro for several years, a very talented man, just fantastic; no one can touch him. He had a way of carving clay that no modeler I ever knew could touch. Rather than just modeling it with his hands, he'd take a knife, and he carved it out crisp and beautiful.

DELAMATER: There's a published script of *Singin' in the Rain.* In the preface to that, Comden and Green wrote an article about how they wrote the script. Then a couple of months later, Stanley Donen in an interview in the magazine *Film Comment,* said that what they said was wrong. I was wondering, are you familiar with that slight controversy? Comden and Green had said that they were called out to the West Coast by Arthur Freed, and then they simply went and wrote the script without much consultation, didn't necessarily have Gene Kelly in mind, and so forth. Donen has said that that's not true.

DUELL: If they did, it wasn't used, let me put it that way. I'm sorry I didn't save my scripts, but I didn't once I left the business; I said, "I guess I've had it." (It would have been a lot of fun, because I had a lot of notes and things in my scripts, but I didn't save them.) But I would say that Stanley was nearer right, because an awful lot of the stuff Gene and Stanley cooked up. They spent night after night after a day of rehearsal. They'd meet in their dressing room and cook up all these ideas. I'd say that they were almost totally responsible.

DELAMATER: You said, earlier in our conversation, that there was quite a bit of "building" during the actual filming itself of musicals per se. Did they pretty much have the dance sequences prepared ahead of time, before the film was shot or did they, in fact, seem to grow as the filming was going on?

DUELL: For instance, in the montage things, they would insert in the script: they would go into a montage of a something. They knew that this block was going to be worked out, and that problem was worked out on down the line. An awful lot of it grew as they went along. They had a basic idea of the story, but the numbers themselves had to grow as the picture developed. They had as many of them roughed in as possible before the picture started, because we had to get sets built and up to a production schedule. They had some fun at the end of the picture. In those days, at the end of a show, the producers and directors always had a big party for the cast and the crew. Usually it was up to us to pick a spot and decorate it, decide what we were going to do, pick some set, and we would have the party on the set. Gene came to us and said he wanted to take one of the sets, and so I came up with the idea (I probably should have gotten fired for it, but I didn't); we picked a set and moved a few walls around and made it so that it was impossible to get into the set except that you go through this one gate, and we had the prop boys out there with umbrellas, and we rained in the whole set. In order to get into the party, you had to go through the rain. So, everybody had an umbrella. Of course, they all loved it.

Interview with Jack Martin Smith

The interview with art director Jack Martin Smith was conducted in conjunction with Paddy Whannel at Mr. Smith's office at the Paramount Studios, Hollywood, California, on 19 November 1973.

SMITH: It's interesting that musicals are still talked about, and they're back to a point now where memories are great things. It's fun to remember General Custer, and it's, likewise, fun to remember *Meet Me in St. Louis* and *On the Town.* The interesting thing to me, right off the bat, about Gene Kelly is the fact that he's still active. A few days ago I was standing in stage 23; the large stage door was open, and the sunlight was coming in on me, and I just paused there a minute to look up and down the street, and right toward me walked Gene Kelly. He had his make-up already on, and he was on his way to the stage with a busy assistant who failed to provide a car for him to take him to the stage. Of course, he said, the minute he looked up, "Jack Smith." I said, "Yeah, how about this floor?" Because we always had a thing with Fred Astaire and Gene Kelly, regardless of what the set was, regardless of what you were doing, you could be sinking the *Titanic,* to them as dancers what the floor is was more important than anything in the world. So, I was running my foot over the shabby floor in the stage, and he said, "It'll never do." He looked great. He's trim and lithe and active and got a sparkling eye. He's just one hell of a guy. His wife died most recently. Her name was Jeanne Coyne, and she was in show business at Metro and was a dancer and was an assistant dance director at times, too, because of her value and her merit. She was very good.

In the great days of Metro, in the time that I was there—I spent seventeen years at Metro and twenty years at Fox and three months here at Paramount—in the great days at Metro, the years during the war and shortly thereafter, the musicals were, for a distinct reason, very popularly received, simply because there was a war, and our guys out in the Mid-East and the European Theater and the South Pacific and so on, they *loved* to see Hollywood pictures, and they loved to see America represented by smash musicals, and they loved to see precision beauty, which is about what the musicals were. Consequently, we had a terrific era then. It was not something that we did all of a sudden.

My training and my early years go back to Ziegfeldian days. Flo Ziegfeld was in show business in New York, and when I came out of college—I graduated from USC College of Architecture, five years—I was ready to graduate, which I did, but three or four months prior to that, I won a little competition, and I got a job at Universal[*sic*]. I was working on a picture, *The Great Ziegfeld,* which, of course, was a musical. I did nothing but dream and get sets together synonomous with that whole era. Then following, I worked on the two shows after that. *The Great Ziegfeld* was the first one, *Ziegfeld Girl* was the second one, in black and white—the first one being black and white, also—and the third one was the *Ziegfeld Follies,* all in color, in which each was a separate musical number. In that series, we photographed quite a few numbers, and they used just a few, the best of the takes, the best of the numbers themselves, when they released the picture. We had a number with Fred Astaire and Gene Kelly in that, which was a lot of fun to work on. It was fun for the lot to see them both together.

Another nice picture, a really nice, elegant, quality picture, was one that Chuck Walters directed, called *Easter Parade.* That was an Arthur Freed picture, and in that Gene Kelly and Judy Garland were cast. We went into rehearsal with the picture, and the picture got quite a ways along (in other words that meant $100,000 or $200,000 had been spent on it already), and Kelly broke his ankle. Fred Astaire stepped up and said, "I will be glad to do it," which wasn't that easy because there were contract difficulties to discuss, but Fred Astaire went into the picture. It was a nice picture. He and Judy did very well together, I thought. Quite a little age difference, but they did beautifully. In that show we had the duplicator machine traveling matte in the final scene, where we panned up on St. Patrick's Cathedral and showed the traffic up and down Fifth Avenue for the actual Easter Parade. I think it was in the 1915 period, roughly. It worked quite well. The only thing that I thought, having planned the shot, and after it was done and we'd spent the money on it, I'd like to have seen the camera go even higher. I just brought it up to a horizontal position and didn't go on up the spire, but in bringing it to a horizontal position, I didn't lose the people and the carriages, because we had eight hundred extras and carriages, and that costs so much a throw.

DELAMATER: How much of the choreography and so forth that had been prepared for that did Fred Astaire retain?

SMITH: Choreography passed over from Gene Kelly to Fred Astaire would be non-existent. Actually, Fred, as most of the world knows, works on his numbers very, very hard. He's a man who in those years drove a little Plymouth coupe, unostentatious, and would arrive at a rehearsal stage, which still exists at Metro, with a white tie knotted around his neck and a cardigan sweater, and he'd go into his rehearsal and work all day, timing his stunts and deciding on what to do. He always made his feats unathletic looking; in other words, he didn't do them the way a pole vaulter or a tumbler or a gymnast or a football player or anybody would do. He always did them like Fred Astaire should do them, which was interesting to me. He was greatly admired by the whole lot and, of course, by me, and he had—a very funny thing in passing— he had a marvelous little stand-in—Joe—I forget what his name was—but Joe was always handy, and he was in show business, and he got Fred his first job or some such story like that, and Fred retained Joe, quite a bit older than he was.

But he always did crotchety steps following Astaire so that the camera could line on just the right position. He'd be behind the wings practicing how high Fred's hand was when he finished a pirouette or something. He was quite a guy.

WHANNEL: But there was no connection between the choreography as it was designed by Kelly and what appeared in the actual film?

SMITH: No, as I remember it, there was not. Fred does separate numbers. And he and Judy, in that show, as I remember it, had quite a montage of numbers in one on the stage. We had a stage called stage 5 and 6 at MGM which had a proscenium arch and an eighty-foot grid and a section for the audience. We could put in different footlights resembling several theaters. In those days, doing musical after musical from Nelson Eddy to Jeanette MacDonald and on down, we had to have different prosceniums to put in. So, we'd take a pair of prosceniums and put a new set in, new boxes for the audience to sit in and new seats and velvet or gold colors on the chairs. We'd transfer them by the day. But they did those numbers, which was a great era of smash numbers, and believe me everyone was competing to get the biggest and best number out; Busby Berkeley had stunned the world in 1933 at Warner Brothers, but we're talking now about 1948. *Meet Me in St. Louis* had been out. Judy had made a success in that with Minnelli, and now we're into *Easter Parade*. She's more mature, and she can dance. She can mimic. She learned mimicry from Mickey Rooney, and she learned it from herself, because they're both masters at it. And she could do any dance or follow pretty near any routine that Kelly or Fred Astaire could do. So, those numbers were interesting, but they weren't lavish numbers. We spent seven hundred dollars per number, which consisted of bringing a stop backing and rolling it down and lighting it with correct curtains to travelers and so on.

Now, I want to explain something about musicals, a thing that really made a big difference to the studio in those years. The subject is called the era of opulence. The era of opulence maintained from Busby Berkeley, or actually from Ziegfeld and before that if you want to go to a hippodrome with the disappearing acts and Annette Kellerman, the swimmer. (We made a picture with Esther Williams, Mervyn LeRoy directed it, based on her life—*Million Dollar Mermaid*.) Anyway, if you want to go back in history and trace down the era of opulence, it maintained and maintained and maintained until finally the audience became glutted. The audience became glutted about 1943, I think, with films like *Ziegfeld Follies*. We over-saturated with whipped cream. Nelson Eddy's numbers, things like *Sweethearts* where they tried to copy the "melody number" which had been so successful in *The Great Ziegfeld;* we had a revolving stage already built-in in stage 6 at MGM. And we could do the up and down effect with the stage, and we could do pretty near anything. We went to bubbles, and we went to water. We went under water. We did almost everything that could possibly be conceived, at great expense, great expense to the picture itself and to the studio for the equipment which was inherent in getting those scenes together. I had Fred Astaire dancing on stage 27, which was one of the biggest volume stages in Hollywood, through bubbles that were ten feet deep, and he put up with it. It was difficult to do choreography there because of those bubbles, which was aerosol with hot water and steam injected into it. We had to make a macadam floor for him to dance on. Choreography naturally depends on the floor, which is the first point I made. With the bubbles on it, the macadam lasted very well. It gave a good bite for it, but he ruined several tuxedos, and the pants were wet, and he had to change them all the time. So Arthur Freed instigated the term, "Let's bring it back to the audience; let's bring it back to earth; let's do away with the era of opulence," and from then on the picture called *Easter Parade* was done, and that de-emphasized the false opulence of all the girls and all the ostrich plumes and everything.

I did a set for *Ziegfeld Follies* which was an all-white merry-go-round set with a beautiful backdrop and all beautiful girls. Lucille Ball was in it, Cyd Charisse danced, and somebody sang. But I had real live white horses on the merry-go-round, and we built a separate merry-go-round on the back lot out of wood, for quite a bit of money, and trained the horses to sit still for the thing moving under their feet. Then when we finally got them onto the stage, the girls got up on top of the horses, and instead of sitting astride they stood on them. The merry-go-round pole was stationary so it didn't upset or rock them, and they had ostrich plumes on, and the whole thing moved around. That was opulence, you see. Those sets in those days cost seventy to a hundred thousand dollars, depending on what it was, and that was about the course. With the age of de-emphasizing opulence, we got into some very interesting numbers. Pictures like *Singin' in the Rain* . . . you couldn't put more charm into a picture. I didn't do it. I wish I had, but it was a lovely thing.

I did a picture called *The Pirate* where we had to adopt a scheme of decoration; we had to adopt a color style for the picture, and we had to invent everything that was in the Caribbean Islands, a mythical Caribbean kingdom, and put it on the screen and also pay for it, and it's a neat trick. The Nicholas Brothers were in that. Gene Kelly was in it. The Nicholas Brothers were great dancers, and I saw Gene Kelly, one day, dance those Nicholas Brothers into the ground. They're like spiders, those guys; they were like monkeys. Their big act was to jump off an eight-foot platform and land in a split then draw it up, and they did that day after day, and Kelly kept after them and after them, and he finally had them tuckered out. I never was so amused in my life, but he really had them tuckered out. Of course, he was in great shape then as he is now. I admired him so much.

WHANNEL: When you mention the art direction in that, it's very striking,

the whole coordination of the color schemes, that would include costuming?
SMITH: Yes, it includes hand-and-glove with the costumer, with the designer. I forget who did the show, now, whether it was Helen Rose or who was on that. You'd have to look that up in the credits. At Metro in those years (Technicolor was fairly new) Mrs. Kalmus used to come out and advise on the initial pictures, and by the time we got up to a picture like *The Pirate* there was more or less a staple way to arrive at what colors we used. We no longer do that very often, because it's a different ball game now. Technicolor in those days was three by four proportion on the small screen like the tube is now. That's why a lot of these pictures are very good on the television tube, although the prints do fade. First of all, when you talk about Caribbean, you're talking about bright blues, azures and then all the warm colors, the oranges, the corals, the reds, the whites. It's not like if you're up in Maine and just showing the grey house and the beautiful knotty tree beside it and a piece of grey-blue water. You're down in the Caribbean, so you want to see really go-to-town colors. We used to lay out for each set a card and paste on there the color samples that the walls were to be painted, and what the floor was going to be, and what Kelly's costume was going to be, what Judy's costume was, and what the dancers were all going to wear. We had three Technicolor guys working in the art department doing nothing but cutting swatches, and we'd paste that on there. I think it was for *The Pirate* that I also made big presentation-type sketches of the pirate cart and Manuela's neighborhood, the whole house and everything and all the sets and the interiors. I made those, and then the Technicolor man would take a sheet and do a collage in flat tones without any shadows or anything showing to see what the presentation was going to be like, if it was going to be suitable. That was a further stimulus to all the people who worked on the film, like the cameraman and the director and the producer and the costumer and the stars. We used to go to that extent in those days to formulate an intelligent color scheme. Nowadays, there have been so many color pictures made that, although we do do presentation-type sketches, we more or less shoot what is there, and the cameraman judges how much light or whatever it should receive.
WHANNEL: In laying out a picture like *The Pirate,* you would work closely with Minnelli, I imagine.
SMITH: Absolutely, oh yes. You see Minnelli's background was from Radio City; he was a designer himself and laid out things himself. I worked on the second picture he made, and by the time he arrived at Metro he had definite tastes and likes and dislikes, and he also had to learn the picture business. A lot of people there, including myself, knew quite a bit more about it than he did at that time, but he was very good because of his stage background. He got along famously and made a marvelous career and brought a lot of enjoyment to the audiences. I consider him one of the best directors.

DELAMATER: How did the kind of contribution you made in working with various directors change from director to director? Say Minnelli as opposed to Donen as opposed to Charles Walters and so forth. Were there some who seemed to prefer a certain kind of style?

SMITH: On anybody that works on a movie lot, the word is passed around so fast that you can hardly leave a room before everybody else in the studio knows what kind of a guy this is. They know me from Adam. I mean, they know me very, very well by the time I do one show. When I came over here to Paramount to work three months ago, the head of construction said, "I just called Ivan over at Fox to see what the hell kind of a guy you were." Your name is on the credits. One of my favorite things in looking at pictures is to look at the screen credits, and "My God, there's so-and-so. I guess he did that." The director, the cameraman and the art director and, go down the list, to see what kind of a shot it was by just looking at the screen credits. Sometimes they fool you, but usually you peg the picture. News travels fast. In changing from a Norman Taurog to a Minnelli or a Pop Leonard [Robert Z. Leonard]—Pop Leonard did some musicals—in changing from Pop Leonard to Chuck Walters you take that in stride just like friends you have to dinner. They're all different, so you give one guy wine, and you don't serve anything to somebody else.

WHANNEL: I can well imagine that Minnelli had quite strong ideas.

SMITH: Very strong. He also was a "clipper." He cut things out of magazines and handed them to you. That's the same system I've always employed. I've always had my personal research in folders, and I cut things out that I like, and when I have a chance to use them, I use them. There are no tricks that I consider tricks in art or movie making. I do paint a lot. I'm a fine painter, a fine artist in every medium, and I don't hesitate to project the initial thing onto a canvas and quickly pencil it in. It's all covered up with oil anyway. I use everything that is possible to use in the art branch, sculpturing or whatever.

WHANNEL: Did Donen and Kelly have the same preoccupation with visual design as Minnelli had, say comparing *On the Town* to *The Pirate*?

SMITH: Everything that I brought to Minnelli he seemed to like well. I did seven pictures altogether with him, and he and I had an understanding. He was very nice to me. The things he didn't like just didn't get built, and the things he did like he was crazy about, and we followed them meticulously, like the little car that pulled the people and that cute little stage. (I threw that sketch away, and I wish I hadn't.) I had the sketch of the stage with the little proscenium, and I built it. I took it from a book of heraldry, where you have the oak leaf clusters, and I painted one side white and the other black so it curved around. I made a nice little Baroque theater out of that. Then we took black and white canvas drapes instead of a tent and just put up side drapes, and there was our show. It looked like it could all be wrapped and put in the wagon. We built those things. I had the sketch, and I got a piece of Kelly's costume and a piece of Judy's costume (Kelly's was red and Judy's was a plaid green), and I put a mat around the picture which was actual pieces of the costume snippings, and I had it for a long time. That was quite a while ago, thirty years ago.

DELAMATER: Could you describe the set in the big "Niña" number that Kelly did?

SMITH: The "Niña" number, oh yes. In those days, I used to go with Kelly and we'd make hand holds and diving boards and foot emplacements and move rocks so that he could jump from place to place and put sandpaper on the roof and fix the vine so he could climb up and all that. He went up and down the drainpipe there, and he was very good at it. He was like a monkey himself. That held over to the "Niña" number. In the "Niña" number, from my personal research, I designed a little pavilion, and he got on that thing and rode it around the center shaft, and the dancing girls were on it. (We had a collection of girls on all of those pictures who were really marvelous dancers, and they'd be used in picture after picture. We had girls like Jean Douglas who was a dancer at Metro and an assistant choreographer, and she was damn good. She's out of show business now, but, boy, she was terrific. Anyway, we had good dancers, and we had beautiful girls.) The center post in that pavilion had a ball-bearing top and bottom and a little foot rest right above there so the person could run in and put his foot on it and sail around and round and round. When they grabbed on that they were secure, and they had the centrifugal force to take them around. The outer six poles—they came in and grabbed those and pirouetted this way and that way and made a figure S on it. That was the basis of the little pavilion. And the set was fixed so that Gene could run up and down it like a cat.

DELAMATER: Did he actually come to you with specific ideas already in mind?

SMITH: He actually came to me, yes. I was a gymnast myself. I used to take great delight in helping him. He'd say, "I need to go over here." On the window you could step here. We'd work it out. He got whatever he wanted. He was a big star then.

The Esther Williams things were choreography, but they were all in the water, and they were a whole separate subject. Those were interesting to do, and she was a nice person to work with. Just in passing, the color concept of all of those things was done by making tests. We'd paint a canvas piece bright orange, then dip it in the water and get out and look at it twenty feet away and ten feet away, and it would pretty near go grey. It was very hard to get intense, brilliant color under the water. We made periscope lights that came down under the water and did every possible thing with bubbles and bright costumes and sparklers—everything to try to get brilliance and opulence in those numbers. We made one really nice picture with her called *Easy to Love,* and we did the water ski bit at Cypress Gardens. We set up a place there (they give four water ski shows a day), and we went down and shot our whole picture there. We did what we called a big ski number, and we had fifty skiers on the water at one time; that was with Busby Berkeley.

DELAMATER: Kelly actually worked on some films in which he doesn't have choreographer credit. He shares credit with Robert Alton on *The Pirate.* I was wondering how he worked with people like Alton.

SMITH: Very well. Kelly could do anything, but Alton was a master at staging. Alton was also a master at holding his troupe together. He always worked with a great number of girl dancers as well as boys or whatever, but when he was on the stage he was just marvelous. A dancer's routine involves athletic prowess, and they have to do it over and over again to playback, having pre-recorded the music, and, say, one dancer's shoelace comes undone, Alton teases the person out of it right away, like that. Then the next time they all get together, he'll say, "Poor Mary she'll just line up, too," and the girls laugh, but they're all in there right away. He was like a football coach or like any person that perceives humanity. He was very good at that, I thought. He could also kick higher than any guy I've ever seen. He'd say, "You want to see," and he'd go boom. He'd hit a chandelier if he wanted to reach it.

WHANNEL: Was his role in *The Pirate* primarily in terms of that kind of staging?

SMITH: Yes, he had groups to stage. He had the show itself, what the performers had to do, and the ballet number was a single number really, but it had other people in it. That was on stage 5 and 6, too, and we pretty near burned down the studio putting it on, but it was a hell of a number, I thought—savage, beautiful, piercing music.

One of the nicest numbers that I ever had the pleasure of working on was "Slaughter on Tenth Avenue" from *Words and Music* with Roger Edens who was Arthur Freed's associate and who was a master musician. (He had an office right beside Freed's in the main building at Metro, and he had a nice grand piano, and he could play and carry on a conversation and direct traffic and everything.) Music was just like writing to him. He came roaring into my office one day. He came skidding to a stop, running through the door, practically. He said, "Jack, Jack, just draw a thing like this." And I said, "What is it?" He said, "It's underneath the subway and he's got to get up to the bedroom and everything." So I started to draw and went like this with a yellow piece of paper, and we built the whole number that way. That's how fast, I made a turntable. I built it on this turntable set which was marvelous. We had to go into the interior in order for the killing to occur, and we introduced the thing on a subway street where the subway goes off into perspective in about forty feet of distance, similar to the *Hello, Dolly!* set which Kelly directed and

I worked on years later. And over here was a building interior, and when the thing turned around, that turned into the grand stairway. The actors entered down the stairway, and the killing was on the stairway, and there was a little room up here which was again the climbing stunt. Kelly got up into this bedroom. There's no careful, surefire, formula method to lay out a set. Roger was a great master of his trade and a great leader of the things that happened at Metro. He took Judy in hand, and he took most people in hand and told them how to act. Remember the interview number in *Ziegfeld Follies* with Judy Garland, one of the best numbers ever, I think, and that was Roger's number. Chuck Walters directed it, but Roger got the thing together. I think Roger invented the title, "Madame Crematon."

DELAMATER: I have some specific questions about some particular sequences. There's a scene in *Royal Wedding* where Fred Astaire walks on the walls and the ceiling. Could you tell me how that was done?

SMITH: You've come to the right office. I invented a squirrel cage. I say I invented; I had an awful time explaining it to people on the lot, because a lot of people could not visualize it. In order for a man to walk up the wall and across the ceiling and down the other side, you'd have to rotate that set. Now, he's on the floor standing there, and you can rotate the set. Now, he steps over here as the set becomes a new base, and he can walk across there and do anything he wants, and then you give it another eighth turn like that, and he can step and go around that way. It's very simple. So, you have to say if it's that long we can't light it. Where do we put the lights? We had to have all four sides. There had to be a ceiling, and the only place to light is where this wall is missing if you're going to shoot this way. We had to build a ring round the set to mount all the lights, so that the light is all front light, and we had a few lamps.

DELAMATER: The lights were just next to the camera, then?

SMITH: Yes, and all the cushions on the chairs had to be sewn to the chairs, and all the books, everything had to be fastened down, which is easy. But the next step is the hard part. The lamps are all out here and the set has to rotate. How do you feed the lamps? So we had a big commutator ring on the back. You know what a commutator is on a motor? Well, it's a collector ring that imparts power to the circuit here and it rides on a central shaft. It's a copper thing that goes in contact and permits the electricity to get through. So, we have a commutator ring. Then, how do we swing all of this? We had to send to steel foundries to get several great big rings. They were about twenty feet in diameter, and we put the house, the set, inside, and here is Fred Astaire in about that proportion. These rings, then, in turn, rode on other glides down here, and the stage door was in here, so that the whole thing would turn. Now, we had a star who was fragile, and we had to get him in it and say, "All right, boys, take it easy." And he'd say, "Yes, O.K., keep it going, keep it going," because you'd lose your balance, so we had a certain kind of a thing to keep up plus the walls had to be dance finish. In those days it was before acrylic paint, and I always used fresh masonite with shellac base paint. I'd put a very thin coat on first to penetrate the masonite a little bit and then put on a finish coat which would carry the color of the set. Beyond that, that's all I cared to photograph, and the result was that the material never got what they call "paint sick" or soapy. The worst thing that can happen to a dancer is to have a soapy texture where he doesn't know where the stop is going to retard his foot. On this other surface, it stops the same way each time; that's the secret of a dance floor. Astaire and Kelly could both dance on glass or diamonds or whatever, but they preferred that kind of a floor, and I used to have to take masonite up and do it over after it would get so worn that it would be impossible. I built a little model, a quarter-scale model to show people how it would work, what would be the effect. Now, the camera also had to ride with that. That's the part I forgot. The camera can't stay out here on the stage floor while this thing is going around. The camera had to go with it. The camera never knows if you're not right side up. Here's Fred Astaire standing on the floor there, and he goes like this, and the camera stays right with him. So, what we did is built an ironing board out front and strapped a cameraman on there with straps with his camera in front of him, and he looked through the finder; he was upside down.

There was also a tilting set in *Royal Wedding* where he did the slides when the ship got in the storm. We had the boat on the high seas, and Fred Astaire in the picture consents to give an exhibition for the people who are on the boat and are crossing the Atlantic. But they get into a storm, and the boat starts to rock. He's got his number worked out and the band has its cues so the boat has to go up like this and he slides and the drum slides across the floor. We had to move the whole set. The lights had to move too because you can't have the lights stationary and the set move or you'll give yourself away. With a set like this—a big ballroom—the lights had to go with the set. We had a huge scaffolding all across the set all braced up. But the basis of the set was the dump tank on the back lot at MGM which was used in all the big ship pictures. It was used in *Captains Courageous*. The principle of a dump tank is that they have a slide with a receptacle on top with about forty bathtubs of water, let's say, that goes on a trip and pours down on deck to simulate a huge wave. Now down below they had a platform that locks with pneumatic jacks on four sides so you could make the deck of a ship simulate a violent rocking motion. We took that machinery, which is already installed, and I put outriggers on it to make it quite a bit bigger so that we could do a huge dance floor and have the audience and see into the other fake rooms like the cocktail room and so on. Then we put them to work and just let 'em slide. We'd tilt her until he would slide, and, yes, he would slide. We had to practice that and rehearse it and then call the extras and shoot the bit. It wasn't as pretentious looking on the screen as it was actually being there. The whole thing had to be tarped in. (It was not sitting on a sound stage; it was outdoors.) We had to tarp it in with black cloth and it was as hot as the dickens.

DELAMATER: How about Astaire's walking-on-air number in *Belle of New York?*

SMITH: The principle involved there (a photographic trick of the blue backing) is an optical process that is still being used. It is called a traveling matte. If you photograph an actor in front of a cobalt-blue painted backing and there's no light on the backing then you separate the film—in those days we had three-strip cameras—then you make a separation print and then you can photograph at a different time and a different place in the world and bring that piece of film and combine it with what you just shot, the actor standing in front of the blue backing. When you combine them, the blue will be canceled out and the background, shot in Afghanistan, say, will be behind the actor. Everywhere you see blue will be canceled out and the other background will come through. It worked better than a rear projection process. Prevalent today is front projection; 3M Co. has invented a process where they coat a screen with little pebbles of glass (they're beads so that you can photograph a screen even at an angle perpendicular) and each bead will reflect the light right back to your camera. For the picture *Tora! Tora! Tora!* we built an eighty footer so that we could have a whole airplane hanging in front of a background which had to be shot in Honolulu with diving planes and so on. It is a very useful trick. In *Belle of New York* we had Fred Astaire dancing on tops of buildings, off of buildings on to other projections and so on. So I painted the whole damn thing blue. I painted the floor blue and I even got trampolines and painted them blue so he could hit a trampoline and go up in the air. They didn't make the best matte for the optical department, but they created the illusion all right. Dangerous number to do. Trampolines are a dangerous rig for a normal person to work on. Fred was good and his ankles were strong so he didn't have any problem.

WHANNEL: The impression that we have when we look at the Minnelli films is that they are more Baroque in style than say the Donen and Kelly films. I don't know whether that is your impression but, particularly, *On the Town* has pared sets. A Minnelli picture seems more full of things. I wonder who made that kind of stylistic decision, how it came about.

SMITH: Baroque in those days was a way of saying that we are really on the in-group here; we're showing you Baroque. It was used at Warners and Metro and Universal. Everybody got on the Baroque kick. Along came Minnelli later on and, while he didn't join the Baroque crowd, his taste was similar. He loved things like the titles in *Father of the Bride.* If you run the titles of that you can see some of his handiwork in shafts of wheat and ribbon, champagne glasses and beautiful lighting. He liked that kind of thing. We did a picture called

Madame Bovary, which was not a dancing picture, but it had Jennifer Jones and Van Heflin in it. He and I got together and collaborated on the decoration in that. But he was way above the bold use of Baroque that had been used in the early thirties.

WHANNEL: In that case, Donen and Kelly were both dancers and that influenced them?

SMITH: We had some different kinds of sets. We were in the city of New York there. I know I built a big set on stage 30 where we had a ten-foot pit, 90 x 90. I built the top of the RCA building in there for that scene. I painted the whole panorama of New York behind that with lights coming through holes of different sizes we cut in the cyclorama. The reason it was in a pit was simply because if you build on a flat stage and put a backing up, you see the foot of the backing. But, if you put the backing down ten feet and shoot off a precipice, you have another ten feet of grace before you run out of room. It was a gorgeous set, just breathless.

The visual style of the "Miss Turnstiles" number was decided for us by what we could afford and by the fact the show took place in New York. Many of the sets like the museum (interesting prop there), and the top of the building, the inside of the subway car—whatever New York had we didn't try to gloss 'em; we just showed. We got off the hook for whatever we had to spend on them. That was the story. And we didn't say they were beautiful. We said this is New York and this is where Miss Turnstiles walks through. Another problem we had was how to build a dinosaur so that it will collapse the second and third times. There was a guy in the special effects property department who always figured out my problems. He devised the method. He took corrugated cardboard and pasted it together and made cubes out of that. He made the vertebrae pieces by running them through the band saw and then took a file that had coarse barbs on it and shaped the bones. He had a ripcord through the center of the vertebrae that we could pull, and he had that on a compound winch device that pulled it very fast.

WHANNEL: My impression is that in the beginning of *On the Town,* there is a lot of subtle cutting between location and studio.

SMITH: We usually try to dovetail location shots with studio ones. In *Summer Stock* we had outside scenes at the farm in Hidden Valley and then on the stage. For the musicals in those days we were often on the stage. George Sidney took a big musical outside with *Annie Get Your Gun* and did a marvelous number with a hundred horses.

But you know here is a lad like myself who goes to architectural college and learns all the things that are supposed to be in good taste. And a few years later I am trying to decide how to draw a dinosaur. And you have to laugh to yourself when you're doing it.

DELAMATER: You saw Kelly working in a couple different eras in his career. What about Kelly's and Kidd's work on *Hello, Dolly!* "

SMITH: That picture was done when I was a supervising art director. John DeCuir was production designer on that and worked with Michael Kidd. I was not too close to the picture. I did have a piece of deciding where to build that street since that was a big budget expenditure. That's a nice set now, but nobody can afford to populate it except in sections. If someone were to want to use it, I would say, "O.K. Do you have $80,000 to put the awnings back up and $100,000 for the wagons and vehicles and if you want the street lights back on?" All of those things add up, and consequently it is there and it is usable, but it is expensive. Those numbers were quite lavish. Kelly was in his heyday with it and I thought he did a good job for what he had to do.

WHANNEL: Do you think location shooting is important?

SMITH: No, it is possible to do anything to begin with. Period generally stops a certain percentage of location shooting; for example, if you go to New York and want to show twenty or thirty years ago, right away the automobile problem is a massive one—to get cars that were built thirty years ago, forty years ago. In the last twenty-five years location shooting has been a very profitable thing to do. People like seeing other places. Audiences like to see locations. They like to see where they have been. They love to talk about it. I call it place dropping instead of name dropping. I just got back from Jamaica. I did three pictures for American Film Theatre. The vogue has been to show real places. We shot *Lost in the Stars* which was shot as if it was Johannesburg, South Africa, and we shot it in Jamaica because there was the railroad there and what most people think looks like South Africa, which was the tropical foliage, but that is not right. South Africa looks like Glendale. It looked like what the audience thinks it is, which is fine. We got up to the railroad sequence and they said there is a train strike now, so we had to move back to Oregon with their little railroad up there. We built a South African station and got seventy black people who posed as Zulus. That picture will benefit from having been shot in Oregon and Jamaica. I'll name some of the pictures I've worked on where locations have meant a great deal. One was *Boy on a Dolphin.* I built sets in Greece and we used the natural exteriors. We shot on the island of Hedra which is about fifty miles south of Piraeus which is the San Pedro of Athens and a charming place to be, and I built Clifton Webb's yacht. I took an already-existing steamship, and I stripped the deck and put in all the beautiful wicker furniture. Lovely upholstered pieces, and I built circular mattresses for Sophia Loren to lie on. I got the head mosaic man in Greece to do two beautiful mosaic pieces for me out of cardboard so that the vibration of the ship wouldn't shake the stones out. Another picture was *Valley of the Kings* with Robert Taylor, done for MGM. On *The Agony and the Ecstasy* John DeCuir was production designer but I made the original survey with the director who was getting together the property. During my tenure on

Cleopatra we visited and traveled in Northern Italy and all the Tuscan country.
DELAMATER: Would you say that it was less important in making the traditional musical if you go on location?
SMITH: Musicals are often stage presentations; or use circuses or carnivals. Often you have night conditions, but if you can't reach them with the light you might as well be on stage.

Interview with Vincente Minnelli

The interview with Vincente Minnelli was conducted at his home in Beverly Hills, California, on 23 November 1973.

DELAMATER: Would you elaborate somewhat on how you first started in motion pictures?
MINNELLI: I had two shows running on Broadway at that time, and everyone said, "Oh, you have to come out to Hollywood." I didn't want to, because I was in love with New York, but Arthur Freed convinced me by saying, "I'd like you to come out for one year, not having any titles or anything, not bringing any of your staff, and just working with me, and working with all producers. Any producer can call you and ask for ideas on a picture, and work in the cutting rooms." Lena Horne came out about the same time I did, and I shot all her numbers, but they were for different pictures. At the end of that year, I directed *Cabin in the Sky;* it was my first musical picture.
DELAMATER: George Balanchine had done *Cabin in the Sky* on the stage, and there must have been much more dancing in the stage production. What kinds of decisions were made about the dancing for the film?
MINNELLI: No, there wasn't much dancing in the film. There was much more on the stage, but for film the story stops when you go into an elaborate number. So we had to scrap a couple of the dance numbers and go into new numbers that Harold Arlen and Yip Harburg wrote like "Life's Full of Consequence," "Cabin in the Sky," and "Happiness Is Just a Thing Called Joe," which helped to tell the story.
DELAMATER: *I Dood It* was your second picture and Bobby Connolly had dance director credit. Would you tell me something about his work and that film?
MINNELLI: Connolly had already shot about two numbers. One was a very elaborate one with a lot of rope spinning and so forth. And the ending, the last number, was taken from Eleanor Powell's film *Born to Dance.* I just did the numbers as they came in. First it's Lena Horne's number, the rehearsal number, the audition number that they did on a bare stage with just a few

props, "Jericho." It wasn't a very good story, so I was disappointed in it after doing *Cabin in the Sky*.

DELAMATER: There isn't much actual dancing in *Meet Me in St. Louis* either, but Charles Walters has dance director credit. What was his contribution to the film?

MINNELLI: The first dance he did was "Skip to My Lou," which he did beautifully. That had to be done according to the limitations of the room and the camera because it had to be done as though it were in the living room of a house, although it started outside. It started through the window. Then there was the "Trolley Song." Originally they went to the site of the St. Louis Exposition when it was half finished. That scene was eventually cut out, as well as a number there. But it had to progress the story, so I had that idea of his not being able to make it and her being so disappointed and singing the "Trolley Song," and suddenly he does make it and runs after the trolley. She's happy, and she ends singing it and is embarrassed. It had a story point. The number that was cut out, at the fairgrounds site, was from when the fair was half finished. You saw mud around and sacks of cement. It was a Rodgers and Hammerstein song called "Boys and Girls" which had been cut out of *Oklahoma!* The picture was long and everyone said, "The only thing that can be cut out entirely is the Halloween number." I was beside myself because that's one of the reasons I wanted to do the picture so badly against the whole studio. We ran the film for Freed and all the people involved, and after the picture was run, Freed stood up and said, "It's not the same picture at all." It became just a boy and girl story whereas *Meet Me in St. Louis* is the story of a family. There were so many things that connected with the Halloween sequence, and it was so unusual.

DELAMATER: In *The Ziegfeld Follies* you directed several of the numbers without directing the whole film.

MINNELLI: The reason for that was that in order to get all of those stars together you had to adjust your time to their time. Often I'd be shooting other things, and somebody else would be shooting another star.

DELAMATER: You directed the Kelly and Astaire number, "The Babbit and the Bromide." Could you tell me something about how they worked together in creating that number?

MINNELLI: It took a long time in rehearsal because they both had such respect for each other that they would Alphonse and Gaston each other all over the place. One would say, "Well, do you think we might at this point do so and so or this kind of step? No, I guess not." "No," the other said, "we'll try it." Well it took *so* long. Astaire was the grand old man of the dance. He was the greatest, the star, and Kelly was younger. That condition conditioned them. They were both so anxious to please each other that it took a long time. We thought we'd never get it on.

DELAMATER: Did you work closely with them in deciding things like camera angles?

MINNELLI: Yes. Gene and I think very much alike about those things. The dance is terribly important to him and also the continuity, keeping the ball in the air. That doesn't mean as much to Fred as long as his dances come off on the screen, are literally beautiful, like those things that RKO worked on with two or three cameras. I usually shot with just one camera but moved it an awful lot.

DELAMATER: Could you outline that use of a fluid camera style in your work? Did you find yourself becoming more aware of it as your career progressed or did you start doing it very early?

MINNELLI: I very seldom would shoot with a still camera, because there was always movement. You either shot with a small boom or an enormous boom, but, by using the impulse of the actors, their moves—or sometimes there's movement for itself—you can achieve movement without drawing attention to itself so that you say, "Where has he cut here?" That's an intuitive thing. That's always done in a different way. Sometimes I use very long takes, as much as a full reel almost and twenty or thirty stops, because you cannot break certain things, and you say, "All right, we do the rest in over-the-shoulders or in close-ups." Each scene would have its own over-shoulders or develop into them more, go into its own close-ups and move back when the actors move back. It's mostly the impulse of the movement of the actors. I've always done that, I guess, because of musical training, because I felt that you should hold the dancer, for instance, in tight close-up but move to the best angle with the dancer. Then I found that in doing scenes in musicals and also in dramatic pictures the same thing applies.

DELAMATER: In a sense, then, there was a close affinity between the dance and the camera; you must have almost "choreographed" your cameras.

MINNELLI: Yes, there are certain times when breaking into a close-up or an over-shoulder shot is jarring. The photography is different so you have to change the lights and so forth. But so many times, nearly always, it can be done with one camera that has several moves to it. That way you can also keep in what you want in the background or the props or the best angle of the actor. Sometimes the camera's high and sometimes it's low. It goes around, and the actor moves into full shot. But the idea of having a full shot and then over-the-shoulders and then . . ., I never liked that. It always jarred me.

DELAMATER: Would it be fair then to say that you "choreographed" your camera even for non-musical films?

MINNELLI: Yes, but intuitively, not consciously, not by any rules.

DELAMATER: Were there particular cameramen that you worked with that you found especially receptive to your desires in that use of camera?

MINNELLI: You generally cast the cameraman as you would cast other people. There were certain cameramen who were such artists—Joseph Ruttenberg, George Folsey—that they could do anything, and you could get such beautiful effects. In the ballet for *An American in Paris,* John Alton, who had written a book called *Painting with Light,* was not like many of his colleagues. They felt that he was very pretentious, but I always got along fine with him, and I had done *Father of the Bride* with him. He was so fascinating. But you needed someone who would be spectacular and daring in his use of lights; there were so many light changes and effects in the ballet movement that I wanted him. It took quite a while to get him, but everyone was very pleased when he finally did it.

DELAMATER: How much camera rehearsal and preparation did you have generally?

MINNELLI: We would do a lot of thinking beforehand. I remember one thing in *Meet Me in St. Louis* where the boy comes in and helps the girl turn off the lights. That took practically a whole reel, because they were in the hallway and moved into the living room, and they had to turn off light after light after light, gas and electricity, and onto the dining room and then back into the hall from a different angle. It was her turning out the lights in exasperation and running up the stairs, but all that was done in one take. So that first day I didn't get a take, but the next morning by noon, I had everything we wanted. The preparation saved about a day and a half of shooting. They were very nervous about the fact that I hadn't gotten a take, but they were used to me by then.

DELAMATER: Everything you have said so far suggests your awareness and desire to achieve a sort of integration between the camera and the film's material. Would you comment further then on your ideas about integrating the dance material into the totality of the film?

MINNELLI: I have always concentrated on that. A musical—if you're going to make it well—has to take just as much time and thought and energy and research as a dramatic film or a comedy (and I have actually done many more of those than I have musicals, though I seem to be known most as a musical director). The dance has to progress the story. You cannot let the story stop and have a number and then go on. Even if it's a backstage musical, you have to progress the story somehow.

DELAMATER: Was that a related reason for almost no dancing in *Gigi?*

MINNELLI: Yes. Alan Lerner started that kind of school of musicals that had very little dancing, and the lyrics are like dialogue. It was the same thing with *Gigi.* It's of the same school. It didn't call for dancing any more than *My Fair Lady* did, but it didn't even have a ballroom number like *My Fair Lady.*

DELAMATER: That seems true of *Bells Are Ringing,* too, though Charles O'Curran has a dance director credit.

MINNELLI: There were just bits and pieces of dance in that. The number on the stairs, "Drop That Name," for instance, but mostly they were character things. There wasn't a lot of dancing per se in that, but he did what he was supposed to do very beautifully. I hadn't worked with O'Curran before and only know him as a charming fellow who is very professional.

DELAMATER: How much were some of the various dance numbers in the films actually written into the scripts? How about the ballet in *The Pirate*?

MINNELLI: That had not been written into the original script. We had shot the whole picture, including Judy's close-ups at the window and the beginning of the realistic part. Then Gene and I went into a huddle and made this thing up. Gene is very athletic, and the great thing in this was the slide up this enormous pole, but you had to show that it was he who actually did it and not a double. As he came down, then, this tiny figure stopped right in front of the camera, so that you saw this was in the same shot. Within the context of the film, of course, that's all imaginary in the eyes of Judy. When she looks out and sees him there, she has just learned very convincingly that he is indeed Macoco. Then she imagines through these dances that he is doing these wild things, burning villages, exploding bombs, that he is a ruthless pirate.

DELAMATER: Had the penny arcade number in *The Band Wagon* been written into the script?

MINNELLI: No. We combed Dietz and Schwartz's music, their songs, to find "Shine on Your Shoes." (In fact, it had been in my first show in New York. Dietz and Schwartz had written the music for it, and Ethel Waters had sung it.) The situation was there in the film because the Astaire character looked down 42nd Street and noticed how it had changed, all full of shooting galleries and so wild. Somebody (I forget who it was) found the black boy, who actually used to do the same thing downtown somewhere, and Fred worked with him. That is the kind of number Fred contributes an awful lot to himself. He and Michael Kidd worked on it, but it had to be surrounded with all that jazz so that it was an entity in itself. You could not just *do* that number.

DELAMATER: You made two feature films with Fred Astaire, *Yolanda and the Thief* and *The Band Wagon;* could you tell me something about Astaire's working method, perhaps how he differs from Gene Kelly in actually preparing things?

MINNELLI: He's a worrier. He worries tremendously. I've always found that he needs so much reassurance. He never thought he was any good, because everything he did fell short of his idea of perfection, what he started out to do. He never looked at rushes, but he'd stay outside in the alley by the cars and question you as you came out. You'd stand there for an hour. He'd say, "What about so and so?" I'd say, "That's marvelous," which all could be eliminated had he gone and looked at the rushes himself. He never saw what he did until he had to see them and put in the taps or dub them, and then only in sections.

DELAMATER: You said earlier that he didn't worry quite so much about the camera the way Kelly did.

MINNELLI: Kelly was much more conscious of the camera. With Fred, he'd put himself completely in your hands. He knew that you knew your business. With Gene you'd have long discussions about it, because Gene loves to discuss; so do I. Some people aren't that way. You approach different stars in different ways.

DELAMATER: How did Astaire work with Eugene Loring who has credit for the dances in *Yolanda* and with Michael Kidd who did them for *The Band Wagon?*

MINNELLI: Fred Astaire is not a ballet dancer. Loring had a background in ballet dancing because he had been a dance teacher himself. He was extra worried about some of the things and a lot of things had to be changed to his style. What Fred would do was use Hermes Pan, who looked like Fred and would do Fred's steps, and then they'd talk about it, so that Fred could watch and change things until he got it to his satisfaction. Some of his dances are so much of a *tour de force.*

DELAMATER: You wrote the narration for the "Girl Hunt" ballet in *The Band Wagon.* How did that come about?

MINNELLI: The trap in *The Band Wagon* is the director, played by Jack Buchanan, based on Orson Welles and other people of that kind who played both in *Oedipus Rex* and other things. He couldn't do just a *bad* show; it had to be funny and in some way entertaining *and* pretentious. The original story for the show they were going to put on was about a man who wrote detective stories on the side under an assumed name. You had to keep that in mind as you went into the show, and Fred Astaire had to do popular things to make the show a success, but it had to refer to that. At that time, *Life* had a spread on Mickey Spillane. It was quite a spread and showed that his books sold more than the Bible. I was going on a vacation then for two weeks. I thought that was a marvelous idea, and I bought all the paperbacks of Spillane I could find. I hadn't read any, and I spent all the time while we were traveling during those two weeks (we went up to Virginia City and San Francisco) reading Mickey Spillane. It wasn't the most wonderful time of my life because my eyes were out on sticks all the time. I must say to satirize his books is improbable, because they all contain the seeds of their own parody. I wouldn't want to alienate the fans of Spillane, one of which I certainly am, but there are certain clichés that occur again and again, and it's those clichés that the "Girl Hunt" number was based on.

DELAMATER: Could you give me some details on your collaboration with other choreographers? Were there some to whom you gave more freedom than others, perhaps allowing them to shoot their own numbers?

MINNELLI: Robert Alton, Charles Walters, and others were all talented people, and we always worked to keep the story going, but I always shot my own dance sequences on every picture except in *An American in Paris.* Gene shot the "I Got Rhythm" number with the little boys. Gene works well with children, and he knew how the number should go. It was his idea so he shot that. But I think that's the only time.

DELAMATER: Would you tell me more about some of Kelly's other work with you? Perhaps the joint work which Kelly and Robert Alton did for *The Pirate;* what was the nature of their collaboration?

MINNELLI: They would both make suggestions. Bob Alton also was from New York and was very resourceful. He could change a whole dance within minutes. He had this faculty, if he didn't like something, of changing all that, a whole section. Gene is much more deliberate. He knows himself so well. He patterned the character on John Barrymore and Douglas Fairbanks . . . which was absolutely right, because it was an actor; he was showy and aimless. In "Niña," for instance, which was all Gene, he was always the center of everything. All three of us worked very hard on that. The set was designed for that because he had to jump up on balconies and stick his head out of windows and go across and slide down and so on. The set was very Spanish. It's very difficult to differentiate who did what because it's completely a matter of collaboration, and we all got along so well.

DELAMATER: Who were Gene Kelly's assistants at that time?

MINNELLI: I don't remember, but later on his assistants were Jeanne Coyne and Carol Haney. Haney had worked with Jack Cole who was a very difficult taskmaster. She was fantastic, a fine assistant. They came from a "jazz" school. Jack Cole had a certain way of moving parts of the body that nobody else has ever moved. They were an enormous help to Gene.

DELAMATER: What is the story about the extra number which didn't get into *The Pirate;* was it a different version of the "Pirate Ballet" as I have read?

MINNELLI: No, it wasn't that. It was originally a number called "Voodoo" which didn't come off; it wasn't exciting enough. And we substituted the one with Judy Garland where she sang under hypnotism, "Mack the Black." "Mack the Black" had already been written but had been used only in the beginning. I had shot all the dramatic points around the number, the hypnotism and the awakening. Then Bob Alton restaged the thing completely for "Mack the Black," and it was much more exciting.

DELAMATER: Did Gene Kelly actually walk the tightrope in that film?

MINNELLI: Yes, he had a wire attached to his back. At one place, if you look very carefully, you can see the wire. It pulls up his shirt. Down below were mattresses and everything in case he did fall. That had been in the show in New York, too.

DELAMATER: In the number later in the film, "Be a Clown," which Gene Kelly does with the Nicholas Brothers, how much did the Nicholas Brothers contribute?

MINNELLI: I think it was mostly Bob Alton and Gene. There are a lot of typical Gene Kelly steps in that, because it was a rabble-rousing number. It was an audience number and quite acrobatic. But it also suited the style of the Nicholas Brothers, the dances they did in their acts; splits and handsprings and turnovers and so forth were incorporated. You use the people to their best advantage. But there are an awful lot of Gene Kelly steps in that, good old standby, flag-waving steps.

DELAMATER: What is the nature of your collaboration with screen-writers?

MINNELLI: I've always been able to work early on with screenwriters, and we've worked very closely. There was only one picture, actually, that was given to me that I thought was absolutely perfect and I didn't change a line. That was *Home from the Hills,* which was a beautiful screenplay. The Ravetches (Irving Ravetch and Harriet Frank) write so dramatically, and they're so right with regional dialogue. It's so simple, and it's almost biblical in its simplicity. It's absolutely beautifully done. I've done about five pictures with Alan Lerner, and he is marvelous about going to any lengths, sitting with you and changing things, because it doesn't matter to him about changing things until he thinks it is right. Betty Comden and Adolph Green were marvelous, simply wonderful, and they also did their own revising. I love them.

DELAMATER: Can you give me a general impression of how much you changed scripts during the actual filming and what the nature of those changes was?

MINNELLI: My feeling has always been that you must prepare. I prepared everything right up to the nth degree. And then that leaves a lot of space for improvisation for the chemicals which are the actors, when they actually play. Some scenes don't play and some do. You have to sense that, find that out, why it doesn't play. Then when you come against those scenes, there has to be improvisation. I both prepare and leave myself open, but I do believe in a great deal of preparation. I believe in a great deal of preparation with the designers and costumers, too, and I always have calls for various extras so as to weed them out and pick them out. Each one has something special, as a group or as individuals, because a party scene, for example, is terribly important; they have to progress the story like everything else. You have to go among the groups and tell them what they're talking about as the camera passes among them. They can't just go, "Walla, walla, walla, walla" and then you cut to a close shot. They have to be characters at a real party.

DELAMATER: You say you prepare with the designers and the costumers, and your films always have an important use of color. How much of that is prepared and really conscious, your choice?

MINNELLI: A lot of it isn't really conscious at all. My theory has always been that the decor and the props used and all that play an important part in showing the characters, because people are not seen in an isolated way. You and I are sitting here, and you're surrounded by so and so, and so am I. That's part of character. Having been a designer, I pay particular attention to design, whether it's elegant or cheap or vulgar or whatever. I think all that helps character. Costume color can be used for emphasis. For instance, in the satirical ballet in *The Band Wagon* when Cyd Charisse is seen dramatically leaning against the bar, she's wearing a green coat. When she takes off that coat, underneath she has a brilliant red costume. That's a very obvious example. Sometimes colors are muted, and sometimes color is used for great emphasis, just to punch something up. They're dramatic tricks, but the musical is a kind of dramatic entity; it must make sense, the farce or the musical. You must believe it. There must be a part of you that goes along with it and does not hold back and say, "I do not believe this."

DELAMATER: In that regard then do you have any general ideas about the use of locations versus studio for shooting musicals?

MINNELLI: That depends on the film. *Gigi*, for instance, had to be done in Paris, and a lot of the interiors were done in Paris. All of the scenes in Maxim's were done in Maxim's. (We had three days in which to do all those. There were about four of them, and a couple involved numbers. They closed it for Saturday, Sunday, and then Monday. All of that had to be done very fast, and we got them all.) For *Brigadoon* the experts all told us that shooting in Scotland was absolutely hazardous, because the weather was so violent, and it was very difficult to dance over the heather on the hill, and that night shooting. . . . So, we used one enormous stage and had many colored pictures of different places in Scotland. We decided that wherever you looked was to be a different aspect of the mountains and the passes and the bridge and the water and forest and so on. And the ruined church had to be put in as a set because that part of the scene was used first as the going to the fair. The people had the fair every year and gathered all the animals and chickens and so forth.

We shot *The Reluctant Debutante* in Paris, though, because Rex Harrison and Kay Kendall couldn't do it in England for tax purposes. In order to find English people in Paris our assistants had to go into schools and hospitals to get them.

DELAMATER: What do you feel about CinemaScope as a means of filming dance?

MINNELLI: I don't care much for CinemaScope. I never did, because I think CinemaScope is such a gyp. Actually, it's not wider; it's just that the top and bottom are cut out, that's all. I much prefer what they call widescreen, which a lot of films are made in nowadays, because you get height there, and in close-up you can still get hands, for example, which I think are so helpful. When *The Band Wagon* was released, it was just at the time that CinemaScope was launched in *The Robe* at Fox. In a lot of theaters they used mattes and cut off part of the head and feet of Astaire, which is a crime. But it couldn't be controlled because every theater would automatically do what they wanted, and they weren't educated to abstain.

DELAMATER: How closely, generally, do you work with your editors, and who, among the various ones you have worked with in the past, were most skilled in getting things that you wanted?

MINNELLI: The one I worked with most was Adrienne Fazan, and she was especially good. She was the best musical cutter there was. She could cut right on the notes. I used to work with her a great deal in preparation, and she was also very good at dramatic pictures. She did a great many dramatic films, and I worked with her a great deal at Metro. But most of the studios had very fine cutters. You sit in a room with a cutter and do a preliminary, and, eventually, you work in the cutting room with the cutter at the moviola and say, "Stop. Go back. Right there," but that's the knitting. That's when you get down to the nitty-gritty.

Interview with Joseph Ruttenberg

My interview with cinematographer Joseph Ruttenberg took place in Beverly Hills, California, on 28 November 1973. Mr. Ruttenberg, who had long since retired from active work in the industry, was one of the most candid people I talked with. He was eighty-seven years old but was remarkably alert. He had obviously thoroughly enjoyed his years making films.

DELAMATER: How much actual preparation did you do with Gene Kelly on the films you photographed with him?

RUTTENBERG: Of course, they did lots of rehearsal—months, weeks ahead of schedule—before the picture actually started. And the crews are not invited to watch over this until later, when they get closer to photographing the picture. Then we have rehearsals with the crew because there is always a lot of movement in dancing. At the time we were photographing *Brigadoon,* we didn't have zoom lenses; therefore, we used tracks and booms to catch all the movement. In *Brigadoon* they were all over the place. We had one big set, four hundred some odd feet long and one hundred some odd feet deep, and we were jumping all over the place. This was all done in the studio; it looks like it was done outside, but it was really done on a stage. The technicians are called in to watch a rehearsal. The director takes the rehearsal himself and the technicians sit back and watch what is going on. The director rehearses with Kelly, who sets the mode of working on the dances because he choreographs the dances himself. Vincente Minnelli likes to rehearse the whole thing himself with everybody away from the set, to rehearse with the dancers, discuss it with them, make changes if they have to, and work out shots that will benefit the dances or favor Gene Kelly who, naturally, since he originated the dances, wants to be the focus of the whole thing.

One day is set for the crews to rehearse with the booms. These booms are quite heavy. Three men sit on the booms: the operator, the director, and the director of photography. And we go through this whole thing for hours, back and forth, back and forth. Sometimes these shots are so difficult that it is impossible to do, and we have to change them around to suit the equipment. Then the cinematographer has to light the set to be able to get all these angles and to photograph them as beautifully as he possibly can under the circumstances. And that is about all that the cinematographer has to do with the dance numbers.

Now, of course, there are all kinds of dance numbers. You've got to be careful that you get the steps on a long shot after you've been in close-up—be sure to get back far enough to get the feet and so on. These are the things that you work out with the technicians, the grips who handle the boom. *Now* it is easier because they have the zoom lens and can take everything from one spot and can zoom the lens back and forth, which I hate to see. The cinematographer doesn't do much more than help by an occasional suggestion that perhaps an angle might be better from a lighting point of view for the dancer. And you discuss this with Gene, and he agrees or disagrees. He is very fussy and will go on for hours or days to get what *he* wants and what *he* thinks is right.

There are different ways of doing dance numbers. Take the dance number in *Gigi:* the little number, "The Night They Invented Champagne." It is a little number in the living room set, and that was rehearsed while we were in Paris shooting exteriors and stuff, and that was directed by Charles Walters. When we returned, Minnelli, of course, took over. It was a short thing, but it required a lot of rehearsal because none of the people were dancers except Leslie Caron, who had been a ballet dancer. It came out very nice, and it didn't take very long to shoot, but it did take them a long time to rehearse, a week or more. The director wasn't there at all, and when we came back, there weren't any changes at all. So the dance director has full control; they leave him alone pretty much; they don't bother him. He is supposed to know his business, and that's what they were hired for, and they are clever most of them, very clever.

Now Busby Berkeley was very clever with the camera. He worked out every detail by himself, weeks before the picture ever started, and he had some very difficult camera angles which he insisted upon. He would build things, contraptions on the set to take the camera up or down or whatever. They were very expensive things in those days, and you couldn't even do them now. But in those days MGM was spending a lot of money on musical numbers, and the expense was no problem. You just went ahead and built them. You built a huge elevator or tracks so that the camera could go up or down or whatever.

[At this point I asked Mr. Ruttenberg to comment about his work on *Broadway Melody of 1940*. He replied that he had done a small part in dramatic sections of the film but couldn't remember what else. Then he said, "I've done seventy-nine pictures for MGM, 118 pictures altogether, and, you know, I just cannot remember everything. Things come back occasionally, but it is hard to remember when the pictures are not fresh."]

DELAMATER: What different approaches did, say, Jack Cole have in working with you from the way Kelly did; how did Minnelli work differently with the two people? Minnelli and Cole did *Kismet,* which you also photographed.

RUTTENBERG: Minnelli was a stage director at the Music Hall in New York. He's quite an artist himself, and he's very particular. He was better able to talk with Cole than with Kelly because Kelly was quite set on his ideas, and he insists upon the things he wants, and quite rightfully, for that's his job. In *Brigadoon* Kelly had his way, but in *Kismet* Minnelli had the most to say. Minnelli has a lot of fine ideas and was very artistic. As a matter of fact, Vincente could probably have choreographed any of the dance numbers as well as anyone else. But Kelly has his mind set on the way he wants the things done. He gives it a lot of time and a lot of rehearsal and feels this is his number; this is the way he wants it done, and so it is done that way. Most directors who work with Gene Kelly give him his way. They will discuss things with him, of course, but after all, the dance is *his* business. Gene Kelly is a nice guy and I like him; I love him, but he is stubborn. This is the way he wants it, and this is the way it has to be: no matter how much it takes, no matter how much it costs. This is what he was being paid for, I suppose.

I think that in most of the numbers in all the great musicals, it was *all* done by the choreographer, throughout. He was in full charge; the directors didn't interfere much at all. Van Johnson was in *Brigadoon* and had to be taught a lot of things to do—acrobatic stunts. So really it was a one-man job as far as dancing was concerned.

It was wonderful in the years of the big musicals at MGM; they never stopped at any expense. In *The Great Ziegfeld* the picture was finished, and they went back and spent another $100,000 or $150,000—"A Pretty Girl Is like a Melody." They took almost a month to prepare for this thing and built the most fantastic sets on the stage with revolving things. You couldn't do that overnight the way they make pictures today. I don't think we'll ever have it again.

DELAMATER: Could you give some specifics about shooting the combined live-action/animation sequence, "Sinbad the Sailor," in *Invitation to the Dance?*

RUTTENBERG: That was a lot of work, a lot of time and a lot of patience. The camerawork is important to the point where everything must be set just so; you can't deviate from it because the cartoonists working on this thing must match movement frame by frame. The camera must be perfectly steady. The camera is chained down to the floor. Kelly would rehearse with an assistant, everything being done on counts, against a neutral background, sometimes blue, sometimes all white, and perfection is the result; it has to be just so, just right. All *I* did was photograph Kelly's part. I had nothing to do with the animation; that was a different department. They take each frame and enlarge it to approximately a five by seven print and put it on a table with glass over the photo and match it in the animation a frame at a time with the dancers. After they photograph the live subject, it takes almost six months before they complete the whole thing. It requires thousands of little separate drawings and movements, and it has to go with the music. The dialogue is recorded before and they must match the mouth movements to the sound.

DELAMATER: What is your general attitude toward wide screen?

RUTTENBERG: Well, in the beginning it was difficult to accept; one director—I think it was George Stevens—said one time that CinemaScope was invented to photograph cathedrals and not succeeding things. You had to adjust yourself to the composition and to the anamorphic lenses. The difficulty was that you had to have two focusing men, one had to focus the anamorphic lens, and the other had to focus the regular lens. To coordinate a thing like that was terrible. And the pictures weren't very good; the regular sets weren't built for CinemaScope. (I was in Paris one time when this was starting, and I went to visit Henri Chrétien at his home, and it was quite interesting.) Panavision has nice lenses, but now it's bad because they use the pictures on television, and it cuts everything off, ruins the whole thing. I don't know why they ever show them.

Brigadoon was shot with two different color processes: Kodak and Ansco, which also required two cameras on the boom, one camera alongside the other. The director had to sit on the boom, and the operators had to sit on the boom, and the counterweight was terrific: and to move these things! They move by electric motor, but they are very heavy. And you have to be careful not to get a jerky move or something, back and forth. Rehearsal took a long time, and then there were the times we'd have to wait and reload or something and that took a long time. (Once Van Johnson got a little peeved. In their contracts they had a clause about when they were supposed to be finished: in at a certain time, finished at a certain time. Usually if an actor has to work an hour or half-hour extra, it doesn't matter, but in this instance Van was a little bit peeved, and we had to reload, and it took a little time. It was close to six o'clock, and just at six, Van took off his wardrobe and walked off the set and that was too bad; it upset the whole company and we lost a whole day as a result, and that was expensive.)

I went to Europe to photograph all the exteriors for *Lust for Life,* and I was on my own. On that picture we had to take two separate takes for the same picture, one with Kodak and one with Ansco so we had already taken one shot with Kodak and then we would replace it with another magazine with the other film. It was a bloody nuisance.

DELAMATER: What kind of working relationship did you have with the various Technicolor consultants?

RUTTENBERG: At the beginning we had a three-color process photographed with filters like a lithograph system. So they always sent their technicians, who sort of stood by, and all the color technique was handled by the people from Technicolor. It was a terribly cumbersome camera. Four men were needed to pick it up and set it on the tripod or the boom. The cinematographer has very little to do with the actual color because the color is already in the film, and all we had to do was worry about composition and the combinations of colors on the sets, but of course that is the art director's job, too. I like black and white. Three of my Oscars are for black and white pictures. But color has done a lot for pictures; musicals and dance numbers are fine in color. And now that we are having so much trouble in this country, if we had musicals, they might pep us up a little bit. I miss them.

Notes

Chapter 1

1. Mr. Edison and the Chicago Exhibition," *London Times,* May 14, 1891, p. 5.

2. *Movement and Metaphor: Four Centuries of Ballet* (New York, 1970), p. 4.

3. The Art of Making Dances, ed. Barbara Pollack (New York, 1959), p. 17.

4. Myron Howard Nadel and Constance Gwen Nadel, *The Dance Experience: Readings in Dance Appreciation* (New York, 1970), p. 1.

5. "Towards a Film Aesthetic," *Cinema Quarterly,* 1 (Autumn 1932), 7-10, 11. Also "The Poet and the Film," *Cinema Quarterly,* 1 (Summer 1933), 202, in *Film: A Montage of Theories,* ed. Richard Dyer MacCann (New York, 1966), pp. 166-67.

6. "Toward True Cinema," *Film Culture,* no. 19 (March 1959), pp. 10-17, in MacCann, pp. 171-179.

7. *Film as Art* (Berkeley, 1971), p. 181.

8. In his book *Film and Theater* (New York, 1936) Allardyce Nicoll contends that there are four kinds of cinematic movement, the fourth being the movement caused by the variations of camera speed. It seems to me, however, that such delineation also requires delination in other areas (e.g., the movement of the dissolve as different from the movement of the straight cut); furthermore, that particular movement seems to fall between two others: strictly speaking, it is a movement of the subject—even though the subject as shot has been altered by a technical aspect of the camera.

9. Maxine Sheets, *The Phenomenology of Dance* (Madison, 1966), p. 115.

10. "Notes on Choreography," *Dance Index,* 4 (February, March 1945), pp. 21-22. Applying theories of the phi phenomenon may even reinforce Balanchine's analogy as well.

11. Noel Burch, *Theory of Film Practice,* trans. Helen R. Lane (New York, 1973), p. 4.

12. Kinesthesia is the actual movement of the body's muscles, tendons, joints, etc., and the sensations experienced from that movement; synesthesia, on the other hand, acts

vicariously: by watching movement one allegedly can experience a sympathetic sensation of movement.

13. "A Filmic Approach to Dance (A Theoretical Exploration)" (M.A. thesis, University of California, Los Angeles, 1967), pp. 3-4. I disagree strongly with many of Ms. Snyder's conclusions; however, the thesis does provide an interesting and valuable exploration into the ways in which film theory can illuminate the aesthetics of dance. Strictly speaking, she is not concerned with the theories as they apply to the filming of dance.

14. *Journal of Aesthetics and Art Criticism*, 21 (Fall 1962), 19-26, reprinted in Nadel and Nadel, p. 5.

15. *Film as Film: Understanding and Judging Movies* (Baltimore, 1972), pp. 154-55.

16. Cohen, p. 9.

17. In Arthur Knight and others, "Cine-Dance," *Dance Perspectives,* no. 30, p. 21.

18. "Three Kinds of Dance Film: A Welcome Clarification," *Dance Magazine*, 39 (September 1965), p. 38.

19. *Dance to the Piper* (Boston, 1952), p. 179.

20. "Film Dance and Things to Come," *Dance Magazine*, 42 (January 1968), p. 37.

21. "Dance on Film," Walter Sorell, ed., *The Dance Has Many Faces*, second ed. (New York, 1966), pp. 164-65.

22. Compton, pp. 35f.

23. Ibid., p. 37.

24. Interviewed by Gretchen Berg, *Film Culture* (Spring 1967), p. 54.

25. Snyder, p. 34.

26. Slavko Vorkapich, "Cine-Dance," *Dance Perspectives,* no. 30, p. 42.

Chapter 2

1. Kevin Brownlow, *The Parade's Gone By* . . . (New York, 1969), p. 2.

2. *The Rise of the American Film: A Critical History* (New York, 1968), p. 11.

3. *The Movies in the Age of Innocence* (New York, 1971), p. 27.

4. *A Million and One Nights: A History of the Motion Picture* (New York, 1964), pp. 117-18.

5. Ibid., p. 339.

6. *Edison Catalogue,* 1901, cited in Jacobs, p. 17.

7. *Film Notes* (New York, 1969), p. 2.

8. Jacobs, p. 17.

9. *Film Notes,* p. 46.

10. Doris Hering, ed., *25 Years of American Dance,* rev. ed. (New York, 1954), p. 137.

11. Quoted in Arthur Todd, "From Chaplin to Kelly: The Dance on Film," *Theatre Arts,* 35 (August 1951), p. 88.

12. Ibid., p. 88.

13. Quoted in Marshall and Jean Stearns, *Jazz Dance: The Story of American Vernacular Dance* (New York, 1968), p. 292.

14. Ibid., p. 13.

15. Ibid., p. 132.

16. Ibid., p. 140.

17. John Russell Taylor and Arthur Jackson, *The Hollywood Musical* (New York, 1971), p. 12.

18. Ibid., p. 10.

19. Richard Collins, "Genre: A Reply to Ed Buscombe," *Screen* (July-October 1970), p. 70.

20. Bosley Crowther, *The Lion's Share: The Story of an Entertainment Empire* (New York, 1957), p. 150.

21. *Film Notes,* p. 77.

22. *The Film Till Now: A Survey of World Cinema* (London, 1967), p. 147.

23. Albert F. McLean, Jr., *American Vaudeville as Ritual* (1965), p. 100.

24. Quoted in John Kobal, *Gotta Sing Gotta Dance: A Pictorial History of Film Musicals* (London, 1972), p. 40.

25. Ibid., p. 42.

26. "25 Years of Sound Films," in Hering, pp. 139-40.

27. *The Lion's Share,* pp. 151-52.

28. Donald Bogle, *Toms, Coons, Mulattoes, Mammies, and Bucks: An Interpretive History of Blacks in American Films* (New York, 1973), p. 26.

29. Ibid., p. 29.

Chapter 3

1. Tony Thomas and Jim Terry with Busby Berkeley, *The Busby Berkeley Book* (Greenwich, Conn., 1973), p. 18.

2. Ibid., p. 21.

3. Bob Pike and Dave Martin, *The Genius of Busby Berkeley* (Reseda, Cal., 1973), p. 27.

4. Ibid., p. 27.

5. Robert Benayoun, "Berkeley le Centupleur," *Positif,* no. 74 (March 1966), p. 34.

6. Alan G. Barbour, "Interview with Busby Berkeley," *Flashback* (June 1972), p. 36.

7. William Murray, "The Return of Busby Berkeley," *The New York Times Magazine* (March 2, 1969), pp. 48f.

8. Thomas and Terry, p. 25.

9. Ibid., p. 25.

10. Pike and Martin, p. 61.

11. Murray, p. 56.

12. Thomas and Terry, p. 26.

13. Pike and Martin, pp. 32-33.

14. Murray, pp. 51f.

15. Interview with Jack Cole, Los Angeles, Cal., November 1973.

16. Pike and Martin, pp. 51f.

17. Ibid., p. 53.

18. Tom Shales, "Warners Musicals—Busby and Beyond," *The American Film Heritage: Impressions from the American Film Institute Archives,* ed. Kathleen Kerr (Washington, 1972), p. 87.

19. Pike and Martin, p. 50.

20. Arthur Knight, "Dancing in Films," *Dance Index,* 6 (1947), p. 184.

21. Nahma Sandrow, *Surrealism: Theater, Arts, Ideas* (New York, 1972), p. 18.

22. Trans. Richard Howard (New York, 1965), p. 12.

23. Sandrow, p. 29.

24.   *Surrealism: The Road to the Absolute,* rev. ed. (New York, 1970), pp. 21-22.

25.   Interview with Jack Cole.

26.   Sandrow, p. 41.

27.   Ibid., p. 39.

28.   *A Concise History of the Cinema,* Vol. II: Since 1940 (London, 1971), p. 25.

29.   Sandrow, p. 95.

30.   Benayoun, pp. 29-30, translated.

31.   Pike and Martin, pp. 71-72.

32.   Barbour, p. 38.

33.   Thomas and Terry, p. 28.

34.   Pike and Martin, p. 84.

35.   Eric H. Rideout, *The American Film* (London, 1937 [?]), p. 97.

36.   Arthur Knight, *The Liveliest Art: A Panoramic History of the Movies* (New York, 1957), pp. 160-161.

37.   *Film Notes,* p. 78.

Chapter 4

1.   *Film Notes,* ed. Eileen Bowser (New York, 1969), p. 102.

2.   *Steps in Time* (New York, 1959), p. 62.

3.   Ibid., p. 89.

4.   Ibid., pp. 238-39.

5.   Marshall and Jean Stearns, *Jazz Dance: The Story of American Vernacular Dance* (New York and London, 1968), p. 114.

6.   Ibid., p. 226.

7.   Astaire, p. 184.

8.   Ibid.

9.   Ibid., p. 196.

10.   Morton Eustis, "Fred Astaire: The Actor-Dancer Attacks His Part," *Theatre Arts,* 21 (May 1937), 378.

11. "The Dancing Screen," *Film Review 1972-73,* ed. F. Maurice Speed (London, 1972), p. 71.

12. Astaire, p. 199.

13. Ibid.

14. Eustis, p. 381.

15. Arlene Croce, *The Fred Astaire and Ginger Rogers Book* (New York, 1972), p. 33.

16. Barbara Berch Jamison, "The Ageless Astaire," *The New York Times Magazine* (August 2, 1953), p. 20

17. Croce, p. 131.

18. Interview with Eugene Loring, Los Angeles, Cal., November 1973.

19. Croce, p. 150.

20. John Russell Taylor and Arthur Jackson, *The Hollywood Musical* (New York, 1971), p. 43.

21. Croce, p. 39.

22. Eustis, p. 381.

23. Astaire, p. 219.

24. Stearns, p. 227.

25. Quoted in Stearns, p. 226.

26. Astaire, p. 227.

27. Ibid., p. 325.

28. Ibid., pp. 6-7.

29. Interview with Eugene Loring.

30. Stearns, p. 167.

31. Quoted in Stearns, p. 223.

32. Ibid., p. 227.

33. Ibid., p. 224.

34. Astaire, p. 42.

35. In Doris Hering, ed., *25 Years of American Dance,* rev. ed. (New York, 1954), pp. 141-42.

36.   Quoted in Stearns, p. 227.

37.   Croce, p. 37.

38.   Stearns, p. 226.

39.   *American Popular Song: The Great Innovators, 1900-1950,* ed. James T. Maher (New York, 1972), p. 40.

40.   Stearns, p. 224; Croce, p. 93.

41.   Wilder, p. 109.

42.   Croce, pp. 90-91.

43.   Cited in John Kobal, *Gotta Sing Gotta Dance: A Pictorial History of Film Musicals* (London, 1972), p. 149.

44.   Eustis, pp. 378-79.

45.   Ibid., p. 380.

46.   Letter from Fred Astaire to Jerome H. Delamater in response to written questions, November, 1973.

47.   Quoted in Croce, p. 127.

48.   Interview with Eugene Loring.

49.   Jamison, p. 20.

50.   Cited in Stearns, pp. 222-23.

51.   Ibid., p. 227.

52.   Ibid., p. 223.

53.   Ibid.

54.   Ibid., p. 228.

55.   "The World and the Theatre," *Theatre Arts,* 20 (June 1936), 409.

56.   "The Seven Ages of the Musical," *International Film Annual,* no. 1, ed. Campbell Dixon (London, 1957), p. 113.

Chapter 5

1.   Arthur Jackson lists seventy-seven musicals from the thirties in *The Hollywood Musical.* Fifty-one of those are ones in which putting on a show provides the major narrative thrust and the impetus for many of the musical numbers. The considerably larger list in Jack

Burton's *The Blue Book of Hollywood Musicals* supports this impression. Titles like *Bright Lights, Broadway Hostess, Song and Dance Man,* and *Star for a Night* suggest the nature of the films. There were many different kinds of shows in these musicals, including a considerable number of films devoted to behind-the-scenes actions of radio (*The Big Broadcast* films, *Twenty Million Sweethearts, Wake up and Live,* for example); nonetheless, the show-business orientation, providing an excuse for the numbers, did seem to prevail. Among the other twenty-six films on Jackson's list (those not necessarily having show-oriented numbers) are the operettas of MacDonald and Eddy, Grace Moore, and others, which in general eschew dancing as a major cinematic element.

2. *Gotta Sing Gotta Dance: A Pictorial History of Film Musicals* (London, 1972), p. 204.

3. Astaire, in answer to my written questions (reply dated November 28, 1973), said, "Eleanor is a great tap dancer and did her own solo choreography. We worked together on our double routines."

4. Astaire, pp. 241-42.

5. Stearns, p. 224.

6. Ibid., p. 232.

7. Ibid., p. 187.

8. Ibid., p. 149.

9. *Toms, Coons, Mulattoes, Mammies, and Bucks: An Interpretive History of Blacks in American Films* (New York, 1973), p. 70.

10. Quoted in Lynne Fauley Emery, *Black Dance in the United States from 1619 to 1970* (Palo Alto, 1972), p. 233.

11. Quoted in Stearns, p. 184.

12. Ibid., p. 188.

13. Emery, p. 233.

14. Peter Noble, *The Negro in Films* (London, 1948), p. 91.

15. Stearns, p. 281.

16. Ibid., p. 282.

17. Ibid., p. 211.

18. Ron Offen, *Cagney* (Chicago, 1972), p. 17.

19. Robert C. Roman, "Yankee Doodle Cagney," *Dance Magazine,* 41 (July 1967), p. 61.

20. Ibid., p. 60.

21. Cohan made the routine popular, but, according to Harland Dixon, quoted in Stearns, p. 53, "Harry Pilser 'ran up the wall and kicked over just like George M. Cohan did later.' "

22. *The Fred Astaire and Ginger Rogers Book* (New York, 1972), p. 120.

23. *Balanchine* (New York, 1963), p. 194.

24. Ibid., pp. 202-3.

25. Ibid., pp. 204-5.

26. Ibid., p. 205.

27. "George Balanchine et le ballet cinématographique," *Cahiers du Cinéma,* 7 (Fevrier 1957), 34, translated.

28. "Dance in the Cinema," *Sequence,* no. 6 (Winter 1948-49), p. 9.

29. Marcorelles, p. 35. translated.

30. Stearns, p. 211.

31. In Doris Hering, ed., *25 Years of American Dance,* rev. ed. (New York, 1954), p. 57.

32. Mervyn Le Roy, *It Takes More than Talent* (New York, 1953), pp. 285-86.

33. Although it can only be inferred that Connolly was responsible for the parade drill as well as the production numbers, the screen credit ("Ensembles directed by Bobby Connolly") as well as the similarities suggests that he did have some say in them.

34. Many of Prinz's films at Warner Brothers were musical biographies of show-business personalities; the numbers, therefore, were often of them or others performing on a stage: *Yankee Doodle Dandy, Rhapsody in Blue* (George Gershwin), *Night and Day* (Cole Porter), *My Wild Irish Rose* (songwriter Chauncey Olcott), *The Eddie Cantor Story, The Helen Morgan Story.*

Chapter 6

1. In the filmography prepared for John Russell Taylor's *The Hollywood Musical* Arthur Jackson lists 143 musicals made between 1940 and 1960. Of those only thirty-nine are ones which seem to have no dance significance at all. Admittedly this is a subjective listing; nonetheless, I feel that thirty-eight (or more than twenty-five percent) are true dance musicals. Sixty-six have a very strong reliance on dance as a major factor in the film. I would call sixty-seven of all those films "integrated" which means that more than fifty percent of the integrated musicals are dance musicals.

2. "Social Values of Entertainment and Show Business," Ph.D. dissertation (Centre for Contemporary Cultural Studies, University of Birmingham, England, 1972), p. 210.

3. Ibid., p. 218.

4.   *Cahiers du Cinéma,* 7 (Avril, 1957), 32-33. "Les Gene Kelly, les Jerome Robbins, les Robert Fosse, ont tous reçu une formation strictement classique, mais ont volontairement choisi l'expérimentation à la scène et à l'écran."

5.   Olga Maynard, "Eugene Loring Talks to Olga Maynard," *Dance Magazine,* 40 (July 1966), 38.

6.   Olga Maynard, "Eugene Loring Talks to Olga Maynard, Part II," *Dance Magazine,* 40 (August 1966), pp. 52-54 ff.

7.   Dyer, p. 221.

8.   Arthur Knight, "Choreography for Camera," *Dance Magazine,* 31 (May 1957), 22.

9.   Dyer, p. 224.

10.   Ibid., p. 223.

11.   In a note in *The New York Times,* June 20, 1976, II, p. 25, Vincent Canby wrote, "Bob Fosse . . . has written to say that one of the reasons the choreography in a scene from 'Kiss Me, Kate' . . . , which I identified as looking like his . . . later choreography, is that he choreographed it, not . . . Hermes Pan."

12.   Interview with John Green. (All interviews will be documented on initial use in Chapters 6, 7, 8, and 9; unless otherwise noted subsequent references to those people's comments will refer to the interviews I did with them and which are included as an appendix to this study.)

13.   Interview with Betty Garrett.

14.   Interview with Gene Kelly.

15.   *The Dance in America,* rev. ed. (New York, 1971), p. 223.

16.   *Jazz Dance: The Story of American Vernacular Dance* (New York, 1968), p. 339.

17.   For an explanation of how these were accomplished technically, see Interview with Jack Martin Smith in the Appendix. Also, an illustration of the rotating room used for *Royal Wedding* can be found in "Astaire in Air," *Life,* March 26, 1951, p. 156.

18.   Quoted in Viola Hegyi Swisher, "A Special for the Special: Fred Astaire and Partner Barrie Chase," *Dance Magazine,* 42 (January 1968), 25.

19.   Interview with Vincente Minnelli.

20.   Interview with Jack Cole.

21.   Dorothy Spence, "Hollywood Dance Group," *Dance Magazine,* 20 (July 1946), 16-19.

22.   Arthur Todd, "From Chaplin to Kelly: The Dance on Film," *Theatre Arts,* 35 (August 1951), 91.

23. Interview with Joseph Ruttenberg.

24. Arthur Knight, "Interview with Jack Cole," *Dance Magazine,* 30 (May 1956), 20.

25. Swisher, p. 25.

26. Knight/Cole interview, p. 21.

27. Ibid.

28. Ibid., p. 20.

29. Ibid.

30. Interview with Eugene Loring.

31. Maynard, Part I, p. 36.

32. *I Remember It Well* (Garden City, 1974), p. 162.

33. "The Camera and the Dance," vol. 2, p. 7.

34. Ibid.

35. Ibid.

36. Ibid.

37. Minnelli, p. 284.

38. Hugh Fordin, *The World of Entertainment!* (Garden City, 1975), p. 435.

39. (New York, 1969), pp. 227-32.

40. "Directing *Dolly,*" *Action,* 4 (March-April 1969), 10.

41. Glenn Loney, "The Many Facets of Bob Fosse," *After Dark,* 5 (June 1972), 24.

42. Joseph F. Hill, unpublished interview with Bob Fosse, September 1974.

43. "Dancing: The End of the Line," *New Yorker,* August 25, 1975, p. 81.

44. Betty Garrett has remarked about Fosse's awareness of music: "Bob has a marvelous feeling about the relationship between music and dance. . . . Bob's very strong musical sense is alot of his talent. 'Hernando's Hideaway' from *Pajama Game* wasn't like that at all when they got it. I think it was a lush tango sort of thing, but that wonderful, rhythmic thing they did with it was all Bob's because of the way he chose to do the dance."

45. Hill/Fosse interview.

46. Ibid.

47.   Loney, p. 24.

48.   Ibid., p. 27.

49.   (London, 1972), p. 299.

50.   Hill/Fosse interview.

51.   Joseph F. Hill, "Bob Fosse's *Sweet Charity* and *Cabaret,*" unpublished paper, Northwestern University, 1973. I am indebted to Mr. Hill for a number of my ideas. Although he writes almost exclusively about *Charity* and *Cabaret,* what he has written, it seems to me, represents a fulfillment within Fosse's work of signs present in his early work. Many of these observations seem applicable to *All That Jazz,* as well, though I have not done an extended analysis of that film.

Chapter 7

1.   Quoted in Jean-Louis Caussou, "Entrez dans la Danse: Eléments pour une histoire du Film Musical," *Cinéma 56* (Mai 1956), p. 34. "Gene Kelly est peut-être le plus grand comédien du monde, parce que le plus complet."

2.   *I Remember It Well* (Garden City, 1974), p. 117. Stanley Donen spoke similarly in an interview in *Movie,* no. 24 (Spring 1977), p. 27: ". . . movies like *On the Town, Singin' in the Rain, Give a Girl a Break* and so on were really a direct continuation from the Astaire-Rogers musicals; they have nothing to do with the Busby Berkeley kind of musical."

3.   Interview with Vincente Minnelli.

4.   Charles Bitsch and Jacques Rivette, "Rencontre avec Gene Kelly," *Cahiers du Cinéma,* no. 85 (July 1958), p. 24. "A mon avis, il n'y avait alors qu'un seul danseur dont le style soit spécialement étudié pour l'écran, c'est Fred Astaire; mais son art était trop personnel pour servir à d'autres qu' à lui-même; quant aux autre chorégraphes, ils ne sortaient pas des numéros avec une armée de danseurs, comme dans les Busby Berkeley."

5.   Interview with Gene Kelly.

6.   Quoted in Albert Johnson, "The Tenth Muse in San Francisco (4)," *Sight and Sound,* 26 (Summer 1956), 46-47.

7.   *Gene Kelly: A Biography* (Chicago, 1975), pp. 119-20.

8.   Quoted in Marc Edmund Houlihan, "An Analysis of Three Examples of the Technicolor Musicals" (M.A. thesis, University of California, Los Angeles, 1953), p. 154.

9.   Ibid., p. 158. Art director Randall Duell noted a similar problem in regard to Kelly's ideas with the animation: ". . . every once in a while he comes up with an idea that they say, 'My God, I don't know whether we can do this or not, Gene.' " Clive Hirschhorn also writes about the difficulties encountered making the split-screen dance in *It's Always Fair Weather,* pp. 242-43.

10.   Richard Griffith, *The Cinema of Gene Kelly* (New York, 1962), p. 4.

11.   "Dancing Master," *Collier's,* May 19, 1945, p. 20.

12.   Griffith, p. 4.

13.   Johnson, p. 46.

14.   Caussou, p. 34.

15.   Douglas Newton, "Poetry in Fast and Musical Motion," *Sight and Sound,* 22 (July-September 1952), 36.

16.   *The Hollywood Musical* (New York, 1971), p. 60.

17.   Quoted in Norma McLain Stoop, "Gene Kelly: An American Dance Innovator Tells It Like it Was—And Is," *Dance Magazine,* 50 (July 1976), 73.

18.   *The Fred Astaire and Ginger Rogers Book* (New York, 1972), p. 82.

19.   Quoted in Stoop, p. 71.

20.   Newton, p. 36.

21.   Ibid.

22.   Hirschhorn, p. 161.

23.   Joel Siegel, "*The Pirate,*" *Film Heritage,* 7 (Fall 1971), 26.

24.   *Anatomy of Criticism: Four Essays* (Princeton, 1971), p. 34.

25.   Paddy Whannel in the interview with Gene Kelly.

26.   "September Calendar: The Museum of Modern Art Presents a Gene Kelly Dance Film Festival," vol. 36 (September 1962), p. 37.

27.   From the interview with Gene Kelly:
      "Delamater: What was the nature of your contribution to the choreography of *Hello, Dolly!?*"
      "Kelly: Not much. Naturally, having worked with Michael before and his being one of the gang at MGM, I talked with him alot about it, but when we got into the real big numbers, it seemed that I was not there as much as I could have been or should have been," "I'd go in and rehearse some of the gang. . . ." "We didn't have as much collaboration as we would have liked."

28.   Quoted in Stephen Harvey, "Stanley Donen," *Film Comment,* 9 (July-August 1973), 5.

29.   Hirschhorn, p. 241.

30.   Quoted by Claire Johnston in Peter Cowie, ed., *A Concise History of the Cinema.* Vol. II: Since 1940 (New York, 1971), p. 27.

31.   Johnson, p. 47.

32.   "How to Get the Most from Screen Dancing," *Dance Magazine,* 22 (June 1948), 34.

33.   Walter Terry, *The Dance in America,* Revised edition (New York, 1971), pp. 228-29.

34.   Griffith, p. 5.

35.   The interview with Jack Cole in the Appendix also gives further comments about Cole's generally negative reactions to working with Kelly.

Chapter 8

1.   Interview with Jack Cole.

2.   "M-G-M Musicals: 1952 Brings a Parade of Brassy Bonanzas," pp. 116-17.

3.   *The World of Entertainment!* (Garden City, 1975), p. 440.

4.   Interview with Betty Garrett.

5.   All from Fordin.

6.   "Bye Bye Musicals," *Films and Filming,* 10 (November 1963), 42.

7.   "The Three Ages of the Musical," *Films and Filming,* 14 (June 1968), 4-7.

8.   Quoted in "Bye Bye Musicals," p. 42.

9.   "The Seven Ages of the Musical," *International Film Annual,* no. 1, ed. Campbell Dixon (London, 1957), p. 114.

10.   John Russell Taylor and Arthur Jackson, *The Hollywood Musical* (New York, 1971), p. 20.

11.   Interview with John Green. Mr. Green commented too of the attempt to work similarly on the film *Oliver!.* ". . . we decided very, very early on to go up an entirely different street from that which obtained in the stage production. The stage show was theatrically impressionistic. We, on the other hand, went, at least design wise, for the total realism of Dickensian London. This was not something that happened as we went along. This was an a priori decision on the part of management, producer . . . , designer, the choreographer, and the music director."

12.   Quoted in Gordon Gow, "Choreography for Camera," *Dancing Times,* 60 (January 1970), 197.

13.   *Jazz Dance: The Story of American Vernacular Dance* (New York, 1968), p. 357.

14.   (New York, 1972), p. 48.

15.   Interview with Vincente Minnelli.

16.   *History of the Dance in Art and Education* (Englewood Cliffs, N.J., 1969), p. 340.

17.   Stearns, pp. 361-62.

Chapter 9

1.   The word *seriousness* is not meant to imply that one form of dance is more serious than another, rather that the film makers began to take all dance seriously. One difference between dance in musical theater and dance in musical films during most of this period seems to have been that innovation in the former usually meant more ballet—greater integration of a high art form—whereas innovation in the latter meant integrating all dance forms and trying to make them popular.

2.   Kelly, of course, was not the only one to be attempting this type of camera-choreography, for many of his contemporaries like Eugene Loring and Jack Cole were also aware of the possibilities of working with the camera as part of the routine itself. By virtue of his being also a performer, however, Kelly became the most popular and, indeed, the most productive of the contributors to integrated forms of dance in the musical.

3.   There were, of course, also many films running simultaneously—notably the musicals of the forties made at Twentieth Century-Fox—which continued to use some form of stage show as the motivation for the numbers.

4.   In contrast certain non-musicals which use dance often violate, so to speak, Bazin's dicta. In Chaplin's *Limelight,* for example, every time Claire Bloom gets ready to perform, a cut provides the opportunity for Melissa Hayden to dance in her stead. Similar cuts plus close-ups of a dancer's feet make a substitution possible for the non-dancing Maj-Britt Nilsson in Bergman's *Illicit Interlude.*

Bibliography

General Film History and Theory

Arnheim, Rudolf. *Film As Art*. Berkeley: University of California Press, 1971.

Baxter, John. *Hollywood in the Sixties*. New York: A.S. Barnes, 1972.

Bazin, André. *What Is Cinema?* Essays selected and transalted by Hugh Gray. Berkeley: University of California Press, 1967.

———. *What Is Cinema?* Vol. II. Essays selected and translated by Hugh Gray. Berkeley: University of California Press, 1971.

Blum, Daniel. *A Pictorial History of the Silent Screen*. New York: G.P. Putnam's Sons, 1953.

Bogle, Donald. *Toms, Coons, Mulattoes, Mammies, and Bucks: An Interpretive History of Blacks in American Films*. New York: Viking Press, 1973.

Brownlow, Kevin. *The Parade's Gone By . . . .* New York: Ballantine Books, 1969.

Burch, Noel. *Theory of Film Practice*. Translated by Helen R. Lane. New York: Praeger, 1973.

Charensol, Georges. *Le Cinéma*. Paris: Librairies Larousse, 1966.

Cowie, Peter, ed. *A Concise History of the Cinema*. Vol. II: Since 1940. New York: A.S. Barnes, 1971.

Dunne, John Gregory. *The Studio*. New York: Farrar, Straus, and Giroux, 1969.

Film Notes. Edited by Eileen Bowser. New York: The Museum of Modern Art, 1969.

Fordin, Hugh. *The World of Entertainment!* Garden City: Doubleday, 1975.

Hendricks, Gordon. *The Edison Motion Picture Myth*. Berkeley: University of California Press, 1961.

Higham, Charles. *The Art of the American Film: 1900-1971*. Garden City: Doubleday, 1973.

Jacobs, Lewis. *The Rise of the American Film: A Critical History with an Essay "Experimental Cinema in America: 1921-1947."* New York: Teachers College Press, 1968.

Kantor, Bernard B., Blacker, Irwin R., and Kramer, Anne. *Directors at Work: Interviews with American Film-Makers*. New York: Funk & Wagnalls, 1970.

Knight, Arthur. *The Liveliest Art: A Panoramic History of the Movies*. New York: New American Library, 1957.

Kracauer, Siegfried. *Theory of Film: The Redemption of Physical Reality*. New York: Oxford University Press, 1965.

Limbacher, James L. *Four Aspects of Film*. New York: Brussel & Brussel, 1968.

Nicoll, Allardyce. *Film and Theatre*. New York: Thomas Y. Crowell, 1936.

Noble, Peter. *The Negro in Films*. London: Skelton Robinson, 1948.

Perkins, V.F. *Film as Film: Understanding and Judging Movies*. Baltimore: Penguin Books, 1972.

Ramsaye, Terry. *A Million and One Nights: A History of the Motion Picture*. New York: Simon and Schuster, 1964.

Rideout, Eric H. *The American Film.* London: n.p. [1937].

Robinson, David. *The History of World Cinema.* New York: Stein and Day, 1973.

Rotha, Paul and Griffith, Richard. *The Film Till Now: A Survey of World Cinema.* London: Spring Books, 1967.

Sennett, Ted. *Warner Brothers Presents.* Castle Books, 1971.

Taylor, Deems, Peterson, Marcelene, and Hale, Bryant. *A Pictorial History of the Movies.* New York: Simon and Schuster, 1943.

Thomas, Lawrence B. *The MGM Years.* New York: Columbia House, 1972.

Wagenknecht, Edward. *The Movies in the Age of Innocence.* New York: Ballantine Books, 1971.

General Dance History and Theory

Emery, Lynne Fauley. *Black Dance in the United States from 1619 to 1970.* Palo Alto: National Press Books, 1972.

Hering, Doris, ed. *25 Years of American Dance,* rev. ed. New York: Dance Magazine, 1954.

Humphrey, Doris. *The Art of Making Dances.* Edited by Barbara Pollack. New York: Grove Press, 1959.

Kirstein, Lincoln. *Movement and Metaphor: Four Centuries of Ballet.* New York: Praeger, 1970.

Kraus, Richard. *History of the Dance in Art and Education.* Englewood Cliffs, N.J.: Prentice-Hall, 1969.

Lloyd, Margaret. *The Borzoi Book of Modern Dance.* New York: Alfred A. Knopf, 1949.

Nadel, Myron Howard and Nadel, Constance Gwen. *The Dance Experience: Readings in Dance Appreciation.* New York: Praeger, 1970.

Sheets, Maxine. *The Phenomenology of Dance.* Madison: University of Wisconsin Press, 1966.

Sorell, Walter, ed. *The Dance Has Many Faces.* First edition. Cleveland: World Publishing, 1951.

———, ed. *The Dance Has Many Faces.* Second edition. New York: Columbia University Press, 1966.

Stearns, Marshall and Jean. *Jazz Dance: The Story of American Vernacular Dance.* New York: Macmillan, 1968.

Terry, Walter. *The Dance in America,* rev. ed. New York: Harper and Row, 1971.

Specific Biographical and Critical Works

Astaire, Fred. *Steps in Time.* New York: Harper and Bros., 1959.

Balakian, Anna. *Surrealism: The Road to the Absolute,* rev. ed. New York: Dutton, 1970.

Breton, André. *Manifestoes of Surrealism.* Translated by Richard Seaver and Helen R. Lane. Ann Arbor: University of Michigan Press, 1972.

Burrows, Michael. *Gene Kelly—Versatility Personified.* St. Austell, Cornwall, England: Primestyle, 1972.

Burton, Jack. *The Blue Book of Hollywood Musicals.* Watkins Glen, N.Y.: Century House, 1953.

Cagney, James. *Cagney by Cagney.* Garden City: Doubleday, 1976.

Cantor, Eddie with Jane Kesner Ardmore. *Take My Life.* Garden City: Doubleday, 1957.

Croce, Arlene. *The Fred Astaire & Ginger Rogers Book.* New York: Outerbridge & Lazard, 1972.

Crowther, Bosley. *Hollywood Rajah: The Life and Times of Louis B. Mayer.* New York: Henry Holt, 1960.

———. *The Lion's Share: The Story of an Entertainment Empire.* New York: Dutton, 1957.

de Mille, Agnes. *Dance to the Piper.* Boston: Little, Brown, 1952.

Ewen, David. *Panorama of American Popular Music.* Englewood Cliffs, N.J.: Prentice-Hall, 1957.

———. *The Story of America's Musical Theater.* Philadelphia: Chilton, 1961.

Frye, Northrop. *Anatomy of Criticism: Four Essays.* Princeton: Princeton University Press, 1971.

Green, Stanley. *The World of Musical Comedy.* New York: Ziff-Davis, 1960.

Griffith, Richard. *The Cinema of Gene Kelly.* New York: The Museum of Modern Art Film Library, 1962.

Hirschhorn, Clive. *Gene Kelly: A Biography.* Chicago: Henry Regnery, 1975.

Knox, Donald. *The Magic Factory: How MGM Made "An American in Paris."* New York: Praeger, 1973.

Kobal, John. *Gotta Sing Gotta Dance: A Pictorial History of Film Musicals.* London: Hamlyn, 1972.

Kyrou, Ado. *Le Surréalisme au Cinéma.* Le Terrain Vague, 1963.

Le Roy, Mervyn as told to Alyce Canfield. *It Takes More than Talent.* New York: Alfred A. Knopf, 1953.

McLean, Albert F., Jr. *American Vaudeville as Ritual.* University of Kentucky Press, 1965.

McVay, Douglas. *The Musical Film.* New York: A.S. Barnes, 1967.

Minnelli, Vincente with Hector Arce. *I Remember It Well.* Garden City: Doubleday, 1974.

Offen, Ron. *Cagney.* Chicago: Henry Regnery, 1972.

Pike, Bob and Martin, Dave. *The Genius of Busby Berkeley.* Reseda, Cal.: n.p., 1973.

Read, Herbert, ed. *Surrealism.* New York: Praeger, 1971.

Sandrow, Nahma. *Surrealism: Theater, Arts, Ideas.* New York: Harper and Row, 1972.

Shattuck, Roger. Introduction to *The History of Surrealism* by Maurice Nadeau. Translated by Richard Howard. New York: Macmillan, 1965.

Smith, Cecil. *Musical Comedy in America.* New York: Theatre Arts Books, 1950.

Springer, John. *All Talking! All Singing! All Dancing! A Pictorial History of the Movie Musical.* Secaucus, N.J.: Citadel, 1966.

Taper, Bernard. *Balanchine.* New York: Harper and Row, 1963.

Taylor, John Russell and Jackson, Arthur. *The Hollywood Musical.* New York: McGraw-Hill, 1971.

Thomas, Bob. *King Cohn: The Life and Times of Harry Cohn.* New York: G.P. Putnam, 1967.

Thomas, Tony and Terry, Jim with Busby Berkeley. *The Busby Berkeley Book.* Greenwich, Conn.: New York Graphic Society, 1973.

Truchaud, Francois. *Vincente Minnelli.* Classiques du Cinéma, no. 23. Paris: Editions Universitaires, 1966.

Waldberg, Patrick. *Surrealism.* New York: McGraw-Hill, 1971.

Wilder, Alec. *American Popular Song: The Great Innovators, 1900-1950.* Edited by James T. Maher. New York: Oxford University Press, 1972.

Unpublished Materials, Theses, and Dissertations

Astaire, Fred. Letter to Jerome H. Delamater, November 28, 1973.

Castelli, Louis. "The Anatomy of a Musical." Unpublished paper, Northwestern University, 1973.

Dyer, Richard. "Social Values of Entertainment and Show Business." Ph.D. dissertation, Centre for Contemporary Cultural Studies, University of Birmingham, England, 1972.

Hill, Joseph F. "Bob Fosse's *Sweet Charity* and *Cabaret.*" Unpublished paper, Northwestern University, 1973.

———. Interview with Bob Fosse. New York, New York, September 1974.

Houlihan, Marc Edmund. "An Analysis of Three Examples of the Technicolor Musicals." M.A. thesis, University of California, Los Angeles, 1953.

Hungerford, Mary Jane. "Dancing in Commercial Motion Pictures." Ph.D. thesis, Teacher's College, Columbia University, New York, 1946.

Snyder, Allegra Fuller. "A Filmic Approach to Dance (A Theoretical Exploration)." M.A. thesis, University of California, Los Angeles, 1967.

Articles from Periodicals, Newspapers, and Books

"Astaire in Air." *Life,* March 26, 1951, pp. 156f.

Balanchine, George. "Notes on Choreography." *Dance Index,* 4 (February, March 1945), pp. 20-31.

Barbour, Alan G. "Interview with Busby Berkeley." *Flashback,* June 1972, pp. 32-46.

Behlmer, Rudy. "Gene Kelly Is One Dancer Who Can Also Act and Direct." *Films in Review,* 15 (January 1964), pp. 6-22.

Benayoun, Robert. "Berkeley le Centupleur." *Positif,* no. 74 (Mars 1966), pp. 29-41.

_____. "Charles Walters, où l'intimisme." *Positif,* nos. 144-145 (Novembre-Décembre 1972), pp. 1-8.

_____. *"42e rue,* quatre heures du matin." *Positif,* no. 43 (Janvier 1962), pp. 1-11.

_____. "Freddie, Old Boy." *Positif,* no. 115 (Avril 1970), pp. 50-55.

_____. "Petits Maitres de la Vision." *Positif,* no. 45 (Mai 1962), pp. 29-31.

Berg, Gretchen. "Interview with Shirley Clarke." *Film Culture* (Spring 1967), pp. 53-55.

Billard, Pierre. "Pour une bulle de savon. . . ." *Cinéma 59,* no. 39 (Août-Septembre 1959), pp. 2-7.

Bitsch, Charles and Rivette, Jacques. "Rencontre avec Gene Kelly." *Cahiers du Cinéma,* no. 85 (Juillet 1958), pp. 24-33.

Bonnet, Marguerite. "L'aube du Surréalisme et le Cinéma: Attente et Rencontres." *Etudes Cinématographiques,* nos. 38-39 (Printemps 1965), pp. 83-101.

Caussou, Jean-Louis. "Entrez dans la Danse: Eléments pour une histoire du Film Musical." *Cinéma 56* (Mai 1956), pp. 27-43.

Chaumeton, Etienne. "L'oeuvre de Vincente Minelli [*sic*]." *Positif,* no. 12 (Novembre-Décembre 1954), pp. 37-46.

Chetwynd, Lionel. "Except for Bob Fosse." *Penthouse,* January 1974, pp. 89-93.

Churchchill, Reba and Bonnie. "Hollywood Diary." *Beverly Hills News Life,* Academy of Motion Picture Arts and Sciences Library Files, n.d.

Ciment, Michel. "Les Aléas de l'alias." *Positif,* nos. 64-65 (1964), pp. 139-41.

Cohen, Selma Jeanne. "A Prologemenon to an Aesthetics of Dance." *Journal of Aesthetics and Art Criticism,* 21 (Fall 1962), 19-26. Reprinted in Myron Howard Nadel and Constance Gwen Nadel. *The Dance Experience: Readings in Dance Appreciation.* New York: Praeger, 1970, pp. 4-14.

Collins, Richard. "Genre: A Reply to Ed Buscombe." *Screen* (July-October 1970), pp. 66-75.

Compton, Gardner. "Film Dance and Things to Come." *Dance Magazine,* 42 (January 1968), 34-35f.

Crichton, Kyle. "Dancing Master." *Collier's,* May 19, 1945, pp. 20f.

Croce, Arlene. "Dancing: The End of the Line." *New Yorker,* August 25, 1975, pp. 78ff.

Cutts, John. "Bye Bye Musicals." *Films and Filming,* 10 (November 1963), pp. 42-45.

_____. "Kelly . . . dancer . . . actor . . . director." *Films and Filming,* 10 (August 1964), 38-42 and (September 1964), pp. 34-37.

Domarchi, Jean. "Evolution du Film Musical." *Cahiers du Cinéma,* no. 54 (Christmas 1955), pp. 34-39.

Elsaesser, Thomas. "The American Musical." *Brighton Film Review,* no. 18, pp. 15-16.

Eustis, Morton. "Fred Astaire: The Actor-Dancer Attacks His Part." *Theatre Arts,* 21 (May 1937), pp. 371-86.

Freed, Arthur. "Making Musicals." *Films and Filming,* 2 (January 1956), 9-12f.

Galling, Dennis Lee. "Vincente Minnelli Is One of the Few Hollywood Directors Who Has an Art Sense." *Films in Review,* 15 (March 1964), pp. 129-40.

Gilson, René. "Les Activités nonaméricaines de la comédie musicale," *Cinéma 59,* no. 39 (Août-Septembre 1959), pp. 110-13.

Gow, Gordon. "Choreography for Cinema." *Dancing Times,* 60 (January 1970), pp. 193-98.

_____. "The Dancing Screen." *Film Review 1972-73*. Edited by F. Maurice Speed. London: W.H. Allen, 1972, pp. 68-75.

Hall, Mordaunt. "Police Hold Throng at 'Show of Shows.' " *New York Times*, November 21, 1929, p. 24.

_____. "The Screen." (Review of *Broadway Melody*.) *New York Times*, February 9, 1929, p. 15.

_____. "The Screen." (Review of *Fox Follies of 1929*.) *New York Times*, May 27, 1929, p. 22.

_____. "The Screen." (Review of *Gold Diggers of Broadway*.) *New York Times*, August 31, 1929, p. 13.

_____. "The Screen." (Review of *Hollywood Revue*.) *New York Times*, August 15, 1929, p. 20.

_____. "The Screen." (Review of *Love Parade*.) *New York Times*, November 20, 1929, p. 32.

Harriton, Maria. "Film and Dance: 'they share the immediacy that mirrors the subconscious.' " *Dance Magazine*, 43 (April 1969), p. 42.

Harvey, Stephen. "Stanley Donen." *Film Comment*, 9 (July-August 1973), pp. 4-9.

Hastings, Baird. "The Denishawn Era (1914-1931)." *Chronicles of the American Dance*. Edited by Paul Magriel. New York: Henry Holt, 1948, pp. 225-37.

Henry, Michel. "L'espace vital de la Comédie Musicale (Quatre films de Charles Walters)." *Positif*, nos. 144-145 (Novembre-Decémbre 1972), pp. 9-15.

Hillier, Jim. "Interview with Stanley Donen." *Movie*, no. 24 (Spring 1977), pp. 26-35.

Hover, Helen. "Popping Questions at Gene Kelly." *Motion Picture Magazine*, October 1944, pp. 41ff.

Hungerford, Mary Jane. "How to Get the Most from Screen Dancing." *Dance Magazine*, 22 (June 1948), pp. 30-37.

Isaacs, Hermine Rich. "Gene Kelly: Portrait of a Dancing Actor." *Theatre Arts*, 30 (March 1946), pp. 149-156.

Jablonski, Edward. "American Songwriter: Harold Arlen." *Stereo Review*, November 1973, pp. 54-65.

_____. "Filmusicals Are a Form of Entertainment that Sometimes Touches Art." *Films in Review*, 6 (February 1955), pp. 56-69.

Jamison, Barbara Berch. "The Ageless Astaire." *The New York Times Magazine*, August 2, 1953, p. 20.

Johnson, Albert. "The Tenth Muse in San Franciso (4)." *Sight and Sound*, 26 (Summer 1956), pp. 46-50.

_____. "Vincente Minnelli." *Cinéma 59*, no. 39 (Août-Septembre 1959), pp. 39-52.

Kelly, Gene. "Directing *Dolly.*" *Action*, 4 (March-April 1969), pp. 8-10.

_____. "Musical Comedy Is Serious Business." *Theatre Arts*, 42 (December 1958), 18-19ff.

Kidd, Michael. "The Camera and the Dance." *Films and Filming*, 2 (January 1956), p. 7.

Knight, Arthur. "Choreography for Camera." *Dance Magazine*, 31 (May 1957), pp. 16-22.

_____. "Dancing in Films." *Dance Index*, 6 (1947), pp. 180-199.

_____. "Interview with Jack Cole in New York." *Dance Magazine*, 30 (May 1956), pp. 20-23.

_____ and others. "Cine-Dance." *Dance Perspectives*, no. 30 (Summer 1967).

Kyrou, Ado. "Histoire de la comédie musicale au cinéma américain." *Cinema 59*, no. 39 (Août-Septembre 1959), pp. 8-15.

_____. "Notes sur L'Erotisme des Films Dansés." *Positif*, no. 12 (Novembre-Decémbre 1954), pp. 33-36.

_____. "Tous en scène." *Cinéma 59*, no. 39 (Août-Septembre 1959), pp. 114-119.

Lockhart, Freda Bruce. "The Seven Ages of the Musical." *International Film Annual*, no. 1. Edited by Campbell Dixon. London: John Calder, 1957, pp. 107-15.

Loney, Glenn. "The Many Face of Bob Fosse." *After Dark*, 5 (June 1972), pp. 22-27.

Lusted, David. "Film as Industrial Product—Teaching a Reflexive Movie." *Screen Education*, no. 16 (Autumn 1975), pp. 26-30.

McCaffrey, Donald W. "Much Ado about Show Biz: The Musical." *The Golden Age of Sound*

Comedy: Comic Films and Comedians of the Thirties. New York: A.S. Barnes, 1973, pp. 54-73.

McGilligan, Patrick. "Just a Dancer Gone Wrong." *Take One*, 4 (May-June 1973), pp. 22-27.

MacPherson, Virginia. "Sinatra Told 'Pick-up' Technique," *Hollywood Citizen News*, July 1, 1944, Academy of Motion Picture Arts and Sciences Library Files, n.p.

Marcorelles, Louis. "George Balanchine et le ballet cinématographique." *Cahiers du Cinéma*, 7 (Fevrier 1957), pp. 32-35.

————. "Prélude à la Danse." *Cahiers du Cinéma*, 7 (Avril 1957), pp. 32-33.

Maynard, Olga. "Eugene Loring Talks to Olga Maynard." *Dance Magazine*, 40 (July 1966), pp. 35-39.

————. "Eugene Loring Talks to Olga Maynard, Part II." *Dance Magazine*, 40 (August 1966), 52-54ff.

"M-G-M Musicals: 1952 Brings a Parade of Brassy Bonanzas." *Life*, April 14, 1952, pp. 116-18.

"Mr. Edison and the Chicago Exhibition." *Times* (London), May 14, 1891, p. 5.

Murray, William. "The Return of Busby Berkeley." *The New York Times Magazine*, March 2, 1969, pp. 26-27ff.

Myrsine, Jean. "Gene Kelly: Auteur de Films et Homme-orchestre." *Cahiers du Cinéma*, no. 14 (Juillet-Août 1952), pp. 34-38.

Newton, Douglas. "Poetry in Fast and Musical Motion." *Sight and Sound*, 22 (July-September 1952), pp. 35-37.

Paul, Dora. " 'Can't act; slightly balding; dances a little.' " *The Seventh Art*, 2 (Summer 1964), 8-9ff.

Perez, Michel. "It's So Good to Have You Back Where You Belong . . . ." *Positif*, no. 115 (Avril 1970), pp. 58-61.

————. "Le Musical avant Busby Berkeley." *Positif*, nos., 144-145 (Novembre-Décembre 1972), pp. 48-52.

————. "Le Musical ou le Cinéma par Excellence." *Image et Son*, no. 201 (Janvier 1967), pp. 22-34.

————. "Sur Trois films de Gene Kelly." *Positif*, no. 12 (Novembre-Decémbre 1954), pp. 47-50.

Pratley, Gerald. "Fred Astaire's Film Career: Began in the Depression and Continues Unabated at the Height of our Prosperity." *Films in Review*, 8 (January 1957), pp. 12-19.

"Quelques réalisateurs trop admirés." *Positif*, no. 11 (Septembre-Octobre 1954), pp. 49-59.

Read, Herbert. "Towards a Film Aesthetic." *Cinema Quarterly*, 1 (Autumn 1932), pp. 7-10, 11. Also "The Poet and the Film." *Cinema Quarterly*, 1 (Summer, 1933), 202. Reprinted in *Film: A Montage of Theories*. Edited by Richard Dyer MacCann. New York: Dutton, 1966, pp. 165-70.

Roman, Robert C. "Busby Berkeley: Retrospect on a Hollywood Dance Film-maker of the 30's." *Dance Magazine*, 42 (February 1968), 34-39ff.

————. "Yankee Doodle Cagney." *Dance Magazine*, 41 (July 1967), 58-61ff.

Rosenheimer, Arthur, Jr. "Towards the Dance Film." *Theatre Arts*, 26 (January 1942), pp 57-63.

Roth, Mark. "Some Warners Musicals and the Spirit of the New Deal.' *Velvet Light Trap*, no. 1 (June 1971), pp. 20-25.

Sauvage, Pierre. "Charles Walters: Vie, Danse, Théâtre et Films." *Positif*, nos. 144-145 (Novembre-Decémbre 1972), pp. 34-47.

————. "Entretien avec Charles Walters." *Positif*, nos. 144-145 (Novembre-Decémbre 1972), pp. 16-33.

Scheuer, Philip K. " 'Brigadoon' Set One of Costliest in Years." *Los Angeles Times*, February 28, 1954, Academy of Motion Picture Arts and Sciences Library Files, n.p.

Scott, John L. "Virginia Comes to Hollywood to Dance with an 'Old Friend.' " *Los Angeles Times*, February 21, 1954, sec. IV, p. 4.

"September Calendar: The Museum of Modern Art Presents a Gene Kelly Dance Film Festival." *Dance Magazine*, 36 (September 1962), pp. 36-37f.

Shales, Tom. *"Broadway."* *The American Film Heritage: Impressions from the American Film Institute Archives.* Edited by Kathleen Karr. Washington: Acropolis Books/An American Film Institute Publication, 1972, pp. 151-53.

———. "Warners Musicals—Busby and Beyond." *The American Film Heritage: Impression from the American Film Institute Archives.* Edited by Kathleen Karr. Washington: Acropolis Books/An American Film Institute Publication, 1972, pp. 80-88.

Sidney, George. "The Three Ages of the Musical." *Films and Filming,* 14 (June 1968), pp. 4-7.

Siegel, Joel. *"The Pirate."* *Film Heritage,* 7 (Fall 1971), pp. 21-32.

Snyder, Allegra Fuller. "3 Kinds of Dance Film: A Welcome Clarification." *Dance Magazine,* 39 (September 1965), pp. 34-39.

Spence, Dorothy. "Hollywood Dance Group." *Dance Magazine,* 20 (July 1946), pp. 16-19.

Stoop, Norma McLain. "Gene Kelly: An American Dance Innovator Tells It Like It Was—and Is." *Dance Magazine,* 50 (July 1976), pp. 71-73.

Swisher, Viola Hegyi. "A Special for the Special: Fred Astaire and Partner Barrie Chase." *Dance Magazine,* 42 (January 1968), pp. 24-26.

Tavernier, Colo and Bertrand. "Talking in the Sun (entretien avec Stanley Donen)." *Positif,* no. 111 (Decémbre 1969), pp. 33-47.

Todd, Arthur. "From Chaplin to Kelly: The Dance on Film." *Theatre Arts,* 35 (August 1951), 50-51ff.

Torok, Jean-Paul and Quincey, Jacques. "Vincente Minnelli où le Peintre de la Vie Rêvée." *Positif,* nos. 50-51-52 (Mars 1963), pp. 56-74.

Vaughan, David. "Dance in the Cinema." *Sequence,* no. 6 (Winter 1948-49), pp. 6-13.

Vorkapich, Slavko. "Toward True Cinema." *Film Culture,* no. 19 (March 1959), pp. 10-17. Reprinted in *Film: A Montage of Theories.* Edited by Richard Dyer MacCann. New York: Dutton, 1966, pp. 171-79.

Warner, Alan. "Thanks for the Memory." *Films and Filming,* 18 (October 1971), pp. 18-33.

Wood, Michael. "When the Music Stopped." *The Columbia Forum,* Spring 1972, pp. 8-15.

"The World and the Theatre." *Theatre Arts,* 20 (June, 1936), p. 409.

Index